The Spaghetti Western

The Spaghetti Western
A Thematic Analysis

BERT FRIDLUND

McFarland & Company, Inc., Publishers
Jefferson, North Carolina, and London

LIBRARY OF CONGRESS CATALOGUING-IN-PUBLICATION DATA

Fridlund, Bert, 1947–
　　The spaghetti Western : a thematic analysis / Bert Fridlund.
　　p.　cm.
　　Includes bibliographical references and index.

　　ISBN-13: 978-0-7864-2507-5
　　(softcover : 50# alkaline paper) ∞

　　1. Western films— Italy— History and criticism.　I. Title.
PN1995.9.W4F75　2006
791.43'62780945 — dc22　　　　　　　　　　　　2006022309

British Library cataloguing data are available

©2006 Bert Fridlund. All rights reserved

No part of this book may be reproduced or transmitted in any form or by any means, electronic or mechanical, including photocopying or recording, or by any information storage and retrieval system, without permission in writing from the publisher.

On the cover: Promotional artwork for *A Fistful of Dollars* (1964) featuring Clint Eastwood (United Artists/Photofest)

Manufactured in the United States of America

McFarland & Company, Inc., Publishers
　Box 611, Jefferson, North Carolina 28640
　　www.mcfarlandpub.com

To Ingrid.
I never get over those blue eyes

Table of Contents

Preface	1
1. The Spaghetti Western Film as an Object of Study	3
2. Enter the Infiltrator	15
3. The Code of Cunning	57
4. Intruding into Gringo Territory	66
5. Stories of the Deprived Hero	93
6. A Partnership of Bounty Killers	122
7. A Partnership Without Tricks	140
8. Stories of Betrayal	204
9. Triumph of Comedy	231
10. Un Minuto per Pregare — Concluding Remarks	256
Appendix A. Top-Grossing Italian Westerns, 1964–1975	263
Appendix B. Films Quoted	266
Chapter Notes	279
Bibliography	287
Index	291

Preface

The inspiration for this project sprang from two sources. The first was the fascinating mixture of familiarity and alterity that I experienced when watching the spaghetti Westerns, as they were shown in Swedish cinemas in the late '60s and early '70s. The second was my long-term interest in the similarities and dissimilarities between the predominantly personal forms of cultural communication in "pre-industrial" social formations and the mass-mediated culture that occupies such a prominent place in the industrial societies.[1]

Consequently, I describe and analyze the content of the Italian Western during the '60s and '70s, using concepts and constructs borrowed from scholars such as Vladimir Propp and Claude Lévi-Strauss studying pre-industrial narratives. Also, my text represents an application of Will Wright's landmark structuralist study of the American Western, *Sixguns and Society*. Through the text I comment on earlier works on the spaghetti Western, especially Christopher Frayling's essential *Spaghetti Westerns*. Chapter 1 delimits my research domain, spaghetti Westerns, and in chapter 2, I introduce my method in discussing the infiltrator constellation/plot and its corresponding set of codes that organize the seminal *Fistful of Dollars* and a wide range of Italowestern films produced in its wake. Central to this plot and its typical character constellation is a cunning hero harboring two conflicting motives, one monetary, and the other non-monetary. Among the codes, this ambiguity is reflected by the modes of the ironic and the pathetic, respectively, with a metacode of excess applying to both.

In the following chapters I continue to extract other variations and constellation/plots that emerge among the spaghetti Westerns, as other successful films such as Sergio Corbucci's *Django* and Leone's *For a Few Dollars More* and *The Good, the Bad and the Ugly* contributed to constellations/plots of avengers, vindicators, prodigal sons, and tragic mercenaries often carrying an internalized double motive, or with double motives embodied in a pair of heroes in sleeping, malignant, tutorship, social bandit/specialists and other unstable partnerships. Eventually, the strain of the ironic mode strengthened, replacing an excess of degrading violence and terror with an excess of violent action in the betrayal and "specialist betrayal" constellation/plots. This development peaked with the last significant success of the genre — the comedy/parody of Enzo Barbone's Trinity films and others in their following.

Because of practical considerations, I have largely confined my analysis to what is generally delimited as "content," as opposed to "expression." While this does include much of what is most exciting in spaghetti Westerns, it leaves out other important qualities, such as the poignant camera work and music that enhance many of the most well-known instances of the genre. Now and again along the way, however, I find it necessary to stray, or can't keep myself from straying, into these aspects of the films studied.

I will consider the present book a success if, after reading it, the reader feels some kind of familiarity when approaching these films—almost like an habitué from the less prestigious cinemas of the city of Uppsala, where I first encountered them.

This book is based on material presented in my doctorial dissertation,[2] which in its critical stages was tutored by Professor Jan Olsson, Department of Cinema Studies, Stockholm University. Among others who supported me, I especially thank Dr. Per-Olov Qvist for his patience in assisting with literature and illustrations. Most of all I thank my wife, Ingrid, who endured it all.

CHAPTER 1

The Spaghetti Western Film as an Object of Study

Rick Altman and the Study of Genre

The spaghetti Western has been described as an inferior imitation of the American Western, a revitalization of the same in terms of visuals and music, or in terms of added realism. It has also been described as a counter-genre expressing criticism of the American Western, or an entirely separate genre with only superficial resemblance to the American one.

Whatever the merits (and demerits) of these conflicting positions, they indicate that when engaging the subject of spaghetti Westerns, I am moving into a disputed generic territory. In an influential article published in 1984, Rick Altman suggested that a number of problems in the critical thinking about genre can be addressed by employing two parallel approaches to genre. One is the *semantic*, defining genre with "a list of common traits, attitudes, characters, shots, locations, set and the like," and resulting in an *inclusive list* of films. The other is the *syntactic*, basing its definition on "certain constitutive relationships between undesignated and variable placeholders," producing an *exclusive list* of films.[1]

An Inclusive Definition of the Spaghetti Western

What films should then be the primary objects of my study of the spaghetti Western, and which ones should not?

As a starting point, I will take Altman's discussion of the "adjective" cycles in the historical development of new genres. He supplies several examples where a new genre starts as a variation on an established one, denoted as an "adjective" to an established genre, such as "Western romance" or "musical comedy." The films so recognized form a "cycle," which might — or might not — establish a genre of its own, like when "Western" or "musical" is promoted from adjective to noun. Then, in its turn, the genre becomes eligible to be the base of newer cycles, such as "urban Western" or "backstage musical."[2] However, note that in the "spaghetti Western" adjective cycle, the "noun" genre name "Western" is referred by content, while the "adjective" cycle name "spaghetti" basically refers to an institutional fact, the predominance of Italians in the production of these films.

"Spaghetti"

"Spaghetti" as an institutional concept signifies that Italians make these Westerns, in the sense of

- Italians financing the production of the films, and/or
- Italians in significant participation "behind the camera" as directors, writers, cinematographers or composers, and/or
- Italians in significant participation "in front of the camera" as lead actors, or at least making up a majority of the actors involved

To further explore what this may mean in practice, consider the following cases.

The Savage Guns/Tierra brutal was shot in Spain in 1962 and co-produced by a Spanish and an American company. The producer and the director were British (Jimmy Sangster and Michael Carreras). It had three American actors as male leads (Don Taylor, Richard Baseheart and Alex Nicol), with Spaniards (Paquita Rico, Fernando Rey, et al.) making up the rest of the cast. The movie is rarely discussed in analyses of spaghetti Westerns but is sometimes mentioned as the first "true" Western produced in Spain.[3]

A Fistful of Dollars (hereafter referred to as *Fistful of Dollars*) was shot in Spain and Italy in 1964 and co-produced by a German, an Italian, and a Spanish company. It was scripted and directed by Italians (Sergio Leone, Duccio Tessari) and with Italians (Gian Maria Volontè), Spaniards (Pepe Calvo), Germans (Marianne Koch, Wolfgang Lukschy), and one American (Clint Eastwood) in the main parts. It is generally regarded as the pathbreaking spaghetti Western that "made" the genre.

Winnetou II was shot in Germany and Yugoslavia in 1964 and co-produced by a German, a French, an Italian, and a Yugoslavian company. It was scripted and directed by Germans (Harald G. Petersson and Harald Reinl) and with the main characters played by Germans (Karin Dor), French

(Pierre Brice), English (Anthony Steele), Italians (Mario Girotti), and one American (Lex Barker). This film is part of a series based on characters created by the German author Karl May, and to my knowledge these films have never been denoted as spaghetti Westerns.

Trinity Is Still My Name was shot in Italy in 1971. It was scripted and directed by an Italian (Enzo Barboni, alias E. B. Clutcher) and starred Italians (Mario Girotti, alias Terence Hill and Carlo Pedersoli, alias Bud Spencer) in the main parts, with an American (Harry Carey Jr.) in a minor part. In terms of box office, this was the most popular of the Italian Westerns. In fact, at least up till 1992, it remained the top-grossing Italian film ever.[4] Still, this film and its (also very successful) predecessor *They Call Me Trinity* (1970) are seldom discussed in analyses of spaghetti Westerns, except as signs of decline.

Evidently, applying the concept of "spaghetti Westerns" to these four films has uncovered several problems. Before proceeding, I will introduce the term *Eurowestern*, which I will use for films, like the four above, that are shot in Europe and produced with European involvement, not only in financing, but also behind and in front of the camera. The term does not comprise Westerns shot in Europe and produced, directed, scripted and composed by Americans, with Americans in all the main parts: for example, *Guns of the Magnificent Seven*. Then again, Spaniards are cast in many of the minor roles even in this film, so the delimitation of Eurowesterns also must involve personal judgment.

Eurowesterns are not necessarily regarded as spaghetti Westerns. My tentative definition as "made by Italians" would exclude *The Savage Guns*. However, Italians do play their part in the production of *Winnetou II*, while Germans and Spaniards participated in the production of the seminal *Fistful of Dollars*. Indeed, most Eurowesterns are co-productions between companies from different countries, so even if Italian companies are represented in a qualified majority of these co-productions, any realistic institutional definition will have to allow for other nationalities on the set.

Especially significant is the role of Spaniards as minor partners. Where an Italian Western was produced in partnership, the partners almost always included a Spanish company. Spanish personnel behind and in front of the camera often played significant roles in the production.

Consequently, I qualify my production criterion for spaghetti Westerns to make "spaghetti" signify that the film is produced with a substantial participation of Italians *or* Spaniards in financing and actual production behind and in front of the camera. Even so, I will sometimes just refer to *Italowesterns* as a synonym for "spaghetti Western."

Western

Altman quotes Jean Mitry to exemplify a semantic, inclusive definition of Westerns—"film whose action, situated in the American West, is consistent with the atmosphere, the values and the conditions of existence in the Far West between 1840 and 1900."[5] For the "Western" part of my definition, I will follow his lead and use "film whose action is situated in the American West or Mexico sometime between 1840 and into the twentieth century," thus taking in account the very frequent use of Mexico and the Mexican–U.S. border as an arena for the action, as well as characters and events of the Mexican revolution between 1910 and 1920.

The "Mexico" element is easily related to the institutional part of the definition, as Spanish and Italian actors and shooting locations favor stories taking place on the Mexican–U.S. border involving confrontation between Anglos and Mexicans, rather than stories of Anglos and Indians fighting on the prairie. However, it is not necessarily dependent on sheer expediency; it could also be explained by preferences of producers, directors, scriptwriters and/or audiences, especially after the success of *Fistful of Dollars*, which is set in such an environment. There are also quite a lot of Italian-produced Westerns without Mexican characters, and some even offer actors and extras appearing as Indians.

I desist from any "atmosphere" or "values" definition requirements, as such considerations are better suited for discussions of the exclusive core of the genre (see below).

My "Western" inclusion criterion excludes Zorro films, as they generally take place in the West, typically California, but in an earlier period, typically during Spanish rule, and feature swordplay rather than gunplay. Films featuring Zorro, or Zorro-like masked heroes were made in Europe, most notably in Spain in 1954 (with a hero called Coyote) and in 1962–63, but also in Italy. The criterion also excludes the Zanna Bianca ("White Fang") cycle of films with dog co-heroes appearing in the snowy slopes of Alaska or Canada. The same goes for Joe D'Amato's successful *Giubbe rosse*.

My composite definition will include most of the Westerns produced in Europe during the era of the spaghetti Westerns. However, the "substantial" criterion will exclude the Karl May cycle of films (and some similarly produced films) because of the dominance of personnel from the Federal Republic of Germany behind the camera, while the participation of Italo-Spanish actors remained minor. It will also exclude a cycle of films produced from 1965 onward in the Democratic Republic of Germany and also some scattered productions in France, England and a few other countries.

Time Period

So, when does the "era of the spaghetti Westerns" begin and when does it end, for this investigation? The European Western has a long history pre–WWII, including the parents of Sergio Leone.[6] During and after the Second World War, there were scattered European uses of Western settings, mostly as environments for comedy or even musical comedy.

In Italy *La Sceriffa* (1959) initiated a cycle of Western comedies, featuring comedians such as Walter Chiari, Ugo Tognazzi, Raimondo Vianello and Fernandel.[7]

In 1962, contemporary with *The Savage Guns*, came the first German Karl May film, *Der Schatz im Silbersee*, and its box office success was most probably the main inspiration for a wave of Spanish-Italian Westerns. They met with mediocre reception with audiences (and critics), until the commercial triumph and artistic distinctiveness of Sergio Leone's *Fistful of Dollars* put real sparkle into the production. In table 1A, the drama of the European Western is told in figures.

The discrepancies between listings depend on differences as to films included, and in some cases different opinions on year of production. These time series situate the heydays of the spaghetti Western in the period 1964–73, with a short revival at the end of the decade (in terms of percentages if not in absolute figures). From 1966 to 1968, the genre had a remarkably strong position with more than 20 percent of the Italian films produced being Westerns.

Since 1980 there have been but a few isolated releases. The most notable have been of a more or less nostalgic "return of..." type, such as *Django 2 — il grande ritorno* (1987) with Franco Nero and *Botte di Natale/The Troublemakers* (1994) with Terence Hill and Bud Spencer.

Spaghetti Western: The Critic's Canon(s)

As hinted in my comments on the four example films, one may deny or question the status of a film as "spaghetti Western" because its content is not compliant enough with some canon, which outlines what should and should not be a "real" spaghetti Western. This would most probably be the case for *Winnetou II*, possibly for *The Savage Guns*, and perhaps for *Trinity Is Still My Name*.

"Spaghetti Western" was originally a derogatory term, and most critics scorned the films for not being "genuine" Westerns, and also for being excessively violent. In the beginning of the '70s this "inferior imitation"

Table 1A.
Production of Eurowesterns, 1960–1980, according to some filmographies

	Eurowesterns			Italian Westerns in AGIS/Bolaffi	
	According to Lhassa (1)	According to Weisser (2)	According to Fridlund (3)	Numbers (4)	% of (total Italian production)
1960	1	–	1	2*	(135)*
1961	5	4	1	*	(152)*
1962	4	2	2	*	(160)*
1963	22	14	14	*	(164)*
1964	39	27	35	13	8.1 (160)
1965	37	42	58	34	18.7 (182)
1966	61	69	68	52	22.9 (227)
1967	56	66	70	66	27.7 (238)
1968	75	83	73	71	29.6 (240)
1969	44	43	33	26	10.8 (241)
1970	30	34	42	35	15.9 (220)
1971	54	54	51	39	18.4 (211)
1972	53	51	44	42	15.5 (277)
1973	25	24	20	18	7.7 (234)
1974	19	19	12	8	3.3 (240)
1975	12	10	13	5	2.5 (201)
1976	6	5	3	2	0.85 (234)
1977	4	4	2	3	2.0 (150)
1978	2	3	3	2	3.5 (56)
1979	0	–	1		
1980	1	1			

Sources: (1) Lhassa (1983) p. 121–127; (2) Weisser; (3) Unpublished filmography, based mainly on notes and reviews in magazines like *Monthly Film Bulletin, Filmecho/Filmwoche, Revue du Cinema/Image et Son, Cineinforme, Bianco e nero*, etc.; (4) AGIS except *= Catalogo Bolaffi.

school of thought was infiltrated by less prejudiced and more analytical essays by younger critics and academics, who treated the Italian Western not as an abject abomination but as an intriguing object of study. If one reads through about 30 attempts to analyze the genre in the years 1967–75 and cull the most frequently recurring features, the following picture emerges:

> The characters in a canonical spaghetti Western are inhabitants of a cruel, anarchist universe, where might is right. The institutions of society are inefficient and/or corrupt. The hero is an alienated expert at weapons and a ragged outsider. He is cool and controlled and cares for his own interests in an environment that does not allow for moral scruples. To achieve his goals he

has to temporarily waive his own personality and integrity. He is an expert in killing and conquers through superior technical skill and tactics. He is also endowed with a mythical aura, is known by strange, mystic names, and presents a distinct style of demeanor and dress. The characters are driven by greed or vengeance, while female characters and love play minor parts. Weapons, coffins, and other occurrences related to death play a large part in the story, as does violence, brutality and torture. There are recurring moments of "black" humor. The typical location of the story is on the U.S.–Mexican border and the hero must manipulate and fight several opposing camps. The story is enigmatic and packed with dramatic events. The characters are defined by their actions, without personal depth. Nature is likewise functional and depicted without lyricism. Formally, both the visual work of the camera and the music are stylistically obtrusive and play an important role in the telling of the story. While the American Western is classicist, the spaghetti Western is romantic.[8]

This critic's canon represents Altman's syntactic approach, and it is indeed based on a few choice films, most of which are made by a few choice directors, the most important one being Sergio Leone, with *Fistful of Dollars* (1964), *For a Few Dollars More* (1965), *The Good, the Bad and the Ugly* (1966), *Once Upon a Time in the West* (1968), *Duck You Sucker* (1971), and (as producer and co-director) *My Name Is Nobody* (1973).

In the second row, one finds the Westerns directed by Sergio Sollima— *La resa dei conti*, *Faccia a faccia* (both 1967) and *Corri, uomo, corri* (1968)— usually discussed under the heading "political Western," together with Sergio Corbucci's *Il mercenario* (1968) and *Vamos a matar, compañeros!* (1970), and also Damiano Damiani's *Quién sabe?* (1966).

Also part of the canon are some of the other Westerns directed by Sergio Corbucci, usually *Django* (1966) and *Il grande silenzio* (1968), Giulio Questi's "extremist" *Django Kill!/Se sei vivo spara* (1970) and Duccio Tessari's two first Westerns, *Una pistola per Ringo* and *Il ritorno di Ringo* (both 1965). Of course, some other films are also occasionally referred to. One should note that apart from some references to Eugenio Martin's *The Bounty Killer* (1966), hardly any films by Spanish directors appear in the critic's canon, and the same goes for actors, apart from some honors for the ubiquitous Fernando Sancho, specialist in big, talkative and flamboyant Mexican bandits.[9]

Notice that while based on an exclusive list, the critic's canon distilled above does not really meet Altman's requirement that the spaghetti Western should "privilege specific syntactic relationships"— like his examples from Jim Kitses (garden vs. desert) and John Cawelti (a border situation and the hero in between outlaws and townspeople).[10] The spaghetti Western canon delimits its exclusive list of spaghetti Westerns by a *core of*

The ubiquitous Fernando Sancho, right, as Ortiz in *Minnesota Clay*. Video sleeve also features perennial henchman José Manuel Martin, middle.

semantic traits rather than by a syntactic linking of elements or placeholders. Altman does admit that the frontier between the syntactic and the semantic is not exactly clear, though.

Spaghetti Western: The Box Office Canon

Altman includes Will Wright's study *Sixguns and Society* in the "exclusive list" approach. However, Wright selects his Westerns from among the list of top-grossing films—using some implicit definition of Western that no doubt is of the semantic kind.[11] Consequently, several "core" Westerns, such as John Ford's *My Darling Clementine* and *The Man Who Shot Liberty Valance*, are not included, as they did not make it to the top-grossing list.

I will refer to such a list as a *box office canon*. An Italowestern box office canon can be delimited by the income figures from the listing of 1965–78 Italian films published by AGIS, supplemented by figures for films issued before 1965 published in Catalogo Bolaffi. Those Italowesterns grossing more than 1 billion lire are listed in appendix A.[12]

Included in this box office canon, one finds most of the films mentioned in the critic's canon, except for *Il grande silenzio* (which earned about 309 million) and *Django Kill!* (about 375 million). However, a majority of these 47 films fall outside, implying that a comprehensive analysis of the Italowestern film will have to venture beyond the critic's canon.

Spaghetti Western: Some Notes on the Audience Canon(s)

In Altman (1999), the author revises his earlier semantic/syntactic approach by adding a third, *pragmatic* form of analysis, concerning how genres are capable of simultaneously benefiting multiple categories of users, for example producers, critics and audiences.[13]

It is tempting to simply equate the box office canon with some "audience" canon, but this should be avoided, first because such a label would tend to cover differences between various user segments among the audience. Second, the box office figures—even should they be totally reliable— do not faithfully reflect the number of viewers.[14] To construct an audience's canon, or several, would require one to find out what constitutes a "real" spaghetti Western in the minds of that audience (or audience segment). However, except for the critics, who document their opinions on paper, information on audience canons takes ingenious research to come by, especially when the films in question are not contemporary.

In a way, there are contemporary audiences, at least in Italy and Germany. Spaghetti Westerns are shown regularly on television there. There is also a fandom audience of collectors of videotapes and other aficionados. Like other "constellated communities" (to use the term from Altman), they exchange newsletters and fanzines that contain filmographies, biographical articles and interviews with actors, directors, composers, etc., who were involved with Italian Westerns, and also articles of personal appreciation about the films. The fandom canon(s) of spaghetti Westerns will largely coincide with the critic/box office one, as witnessed by the "Hall of Fame" of *Westerns All'Italiana*, voted by its readers through the years.[15] Fandom might also enhance the reputation of "cult" spaghettis overlooked by critics and large audiences alike, as with *Blindman*, which features a blind mercenary protecting a cargo of 50 women against a gang of bandits (one of them played by Beatle Ringo Starr). Connoisseurs of violent films might canonize a critic's choice spaghetti Western such as *Django Kill!* (one of the few Westerns that was censored in Italy), but also an item like *Cut-Throats Nine*, which is unheard of in any critic's discourse of the genre.

The Inclusive-Exclusive Overlap

Altman presents as one advantage of his distinction between complementary inclusive and exclusive genre definitions that it explains overlap cases. "Pennsylvania Westerns," such as John Ford's *Drums Along the Mohawk* (1939), do not belong according to the inclusive definition, but still have a "syntactic" resemblance strong enough to be included in the generic definition. The opposite is when a film "belongs" according to the inclusive definition but does not meet the standards of the exclusive one (in an Altman example, *Fun in Acapulco* is not regarded as a "real" musical like *Singin' in the Rain*[16]).

Among spaghetti Westerns answering to the inclusive definition, but unlikely to pass into the semantic core, are the early wave of comedies (see the previous "Time Period" section). In fact, all Italian or Spanish Westerns released up to and including 1964, if mentioned at all, suffer the critical verdict of being bad imitations of American Westerns and without interest compared with later Italowesterns. Also, the Trinity Westerns, and others influenced by their special brand of comedy, also find their status as "real" spaghetti Westerns questioned.

Inversely, there are some predominantly British or French productions that I believe pass the semantic core criteria for spaghetti Westerns.[17] However, productions that are semantically close but made outside Europe — from *Two Mules for Sister Sarah* (1970, Don Siegel, starring Clint Eastwood) to *Dollars for the Dead* (1998, Gene Quintano, produced by former Italowestern director Tony Anthony) — are not included in this study.

The qualifications for time and place in my inclusive definition prompt the exclusion of Hugo Fregonese's Spanish/Argentine/U.S.A. "Pampas Western" *Pampa salvaje* (1966), and also Giovanno Fago's "Brazilian bandit" film *O cangaceiro* (1969). However, for semantically related reasons I will include Mario Camus's political drama *La collera del vento* (1970) that most probably, though not explicitly, takes place in Spain. Also, even though I exclude Zorro films, I include *Il magnifico texano*, with a masked redresser of wrongs as a hero.

Finally, where does this leave us with *The Savage Guns*? I am sorry to say that with its American-British-Spanish production mix, it remains a "quandary" with respect to my inclusive definition. Anyway, its early release and lack of participants related to the later "golden era," leave slim chances of its ever being considered for any critic's pantheon.

Nevertheless, I will return to *The Savage Guns* and other "first-wave" Italowesterns.[18] On the other hand I will find few reasons to discuss the early Western comedies, or their successors, the genre parodies featuring Franco Franchi and Ciccio Ingrassa, even though the latter films bagged a far larger box office intake between 1964 and 1972 than the vast majority of "serious" Italowesterns.

Genre delimitations, whether inclusive or exclusive, are essential in projects intent on making comprehensive lists or genre filmographies. For a project such as mine, there are two purposes:

- By delimiting a genre/subgenre/cycle of films, one is also awarded the opportunity to outline its bottom-line history, which is necessary even if the main objective is not historical description.
- It presents the proper moment to justify why certain films were not deemed suitable to consider in the context, like why I will not discuss films such as *Winnetou I–III*, *Pampa salvaje* or *Two Mules for Sister Sarah*.

"Original Versions" and Titles

As mentioned above, the European Western films were usually produced with companies from different countries involved and released in several national markets with different language versions at roughly the same time. Consequently, I find it questionable to assume that, say, the Italian version or the English one is the "original."

Versions can become an issue when there are differences in meaning, e.g., when two characters in *Uno straniero a Sacramento* are brother and sister in the Italian version and married to each other in the English version. At least in Germany, after the success of the Trinity films new versions of earlier "serious" spaghetti Westerns starring Terence Hill were released with more "comical" dialogue dubbed in!

I will mostly refer to the films discussed by their Italian titles, using English titles only for the films I consider well known enough in the English-speaking countries—the Sergio Leone films, the two Trinity Westerns and some later Westerns also starring Terence Hill or Bud Spencer.

CHAPTER 2

Enter the Infiltrator

A Note on Methodology

My methodological approach is mainly inspired by Lévi-Strauss's studies of American Indian mythology[1] — and especially his employment of the concepts *armature, code* and *message* to describe the relationships between myths, their likeness and differences, as *transformation systems*. Even though these concepts are not explicitly used, Will Wright's *Sixguns and Society* presents such a transformation system analysis for the (commercially most successful) American Westerns.

In his study, Wright distinguishes four periods. Basing his categorizations on a method employed by Vladimir Propp, Wright describes the films of these periods by their *plots* — sets of functions, each one describing a generalized action or an attribute of a character. For the first one, which "revolves around a lone gunfighter hero who saves the town, or the farmers, from the gamblers, or the ranchers,"[2] he sets forth *the classical plot*, consisting of the following functions:

1. The hero enters a social group.
2. The hero is unknown to society.
3. The hero is revealed to have an exceptional ability.
4. The society recognizes a difference between themselves and the hero; the hero is given a special status.
5. The society does not completely accept the hero.
6. There is a conflict of interests between the villains and the society.
7. The villains are stronger than the society; the society is weak.
8. There is a strong friendship or respect between the hero and a villain.
9. The villains threaten the society.
10. The hero avoids involvement in the conflict.
11. The villains endanger a friend of the hero's.

12. The hero fights the villains.
13. The hero defeats the villains.
14. The society is safe.
15. The society accepts the hero.
16. The hero loses or gives up his special status.[3]

Lévi-Strauss defines *armature* as "a combination of properties that remain invariant in two or several myths."[4] Many of the Lévi-Straussian armatures consist of generalizations of story elements, and in this sense each of these plots constitutes an armature for the group of films it subsumes.

Inspired by Lévi-Strauss, Wright uses binary oppositions for the conceptual meaning of the subjects appearing as the plot functions—the hero, the villains and the society. He finds that three basic oppositions—inside (society, villains)/outside (hero), good (society, hero)/bad (villains), strong (hero, villains)/weak (society)[5]—are enough to distinguish the three types of characters. These oppositions I regard as *code dimensions* that in their turn are generalizations of more directly *observable codes*, such as types of clothes, looks, and actions. Wright's societal interpretations of his plots, e.g., "the conceptual conflict in capitalist market society between the values of bourgeois society and the social institution of the market" for the classical plot, can be regarded as descriptions of their *messages*.[6]

For the present study I will use the concept of plot in the same manner as Wright, and I designate as *constellation* its corresponding set of generalized characters with each such type of character—hero, villain, etc.—occupying a *position* in the constellation.

I will largely constrain my reasoning to the story content of the films, corresponding mainly to form and (especially) substance of content in the terminology of Seymour Chapman, and template and prototype schemata by David Bordwell, and only occasionally refer to other aspects of what is revealed on the screen, such as the narrative ordering (*syuzhet*) of the story line (*fabula*), or properties of "visuals and soundtrack."[7]

The Constellation/Plot Armature of the Infiltrator

Leone's *Fistful of Dollars* tells the story of a lone gunfighter entering a village devastated by two rival gangs of smugglers. He joins one gang but deceives both parties and manipulates them for his own purposes. He is disclosed and severely beaten, but he escapes and returns to destroy the surviving gang and then leaves the town in the hands of some old men.

In *Una pistola per Ringo*, which was released the following year and directed by Duccio Tessari, who co-scripted *Fistful of Dollars*, a Mexican gang robs a bank the day before Christmas. They are overtaken by the posse and take the inhabitants of a ranch as hostages. The sheriff enlists a gunfighter to join the gang in order to save the hostages and restore the booty for a percentage. He reveals the plan to the bandits and asks for a higher percentage to save the gang. In the end he honors the original deal, kills the bandits and leaves with his share.

There are several common plot functions that can be constructed from the two films. They are presented below in rough chronological order:

The hero (main protagonist) kills a group of gringos: Joe kills some Baxter men and Ringo kills the Bensons.[8]

The hero sees opportunities to make money on a conflict between a Mexican camp and a gringo camp: Joe's reasoning on the balcony that "money could be made in this town" after getting information from saloon owner/sidekick Silvanito (who discourages him), and Ringo learns about the reward from deputy/sidekick Tim (who, inversely, encourages him).

The Mexicans conquer a great value: The Rojos take the transport of gold; Sancho's band robs the bank.

The hero joins with the Mexicans but manipulates both camps to his own enrichment: Joe joins with the Rojos and arranges the fight over two (dead) "witnesses" to sell the (partly false) information to both parties. Ringo changes sides to the one that will give him the larger percentage of the loot (only this bargaining also turns out to be a ruse, meant to mislead the Mexicans).

A woman is transferred between the camps with assistance from the hero: Joe takes Marisol to the Baxters and later tells her to go back to Ramon after her reunion with her family on the street. Ringo joins the Mexicans to rescue Ruby (and others) and at first pretends to instead make a deal with them (a weaker instance of the function), but later he sends her away to the sheriff.

The hero helps the woman return to her family: Joe liberates Marisol from the Rojo guards and sends her off with her family. Ringo kills the rapist Pedro and later scares off the wagon with Ruby (and the other hostages). He finally returns to her a watch intended for her fiancé, the sheriff.

The hero is exposed and severely beaten by the Mexicans: Joe's raid to liberate Marisol is accidentally discovered and he is beaten to reveal her whereabouts. A ruse by Sancho reveals Ringo's treachery, and he is bound and beaten.

One of the camps destroys the other: The Rojos kill the Baxters while searching for Joe. In *Una pistola per Ringo*, this situation is weaker in a dramatical sense (and ethnically inversed) the posse beleaguers and decimates the bandits.

The hero is considered dead but "revives": Joe leaves in a coffin (metonymical death) and is believed to have perished in the flames of the Baxter's house. When appearing to save Silvanito, he several times falls or staggers from Ramon's apparently deadly rifle shots, only to "revive" and continue advancing. In the final reckoning, Ringo pretends to fall dead from a shot and then surprises and kills the shooter.

The hero destroys the remaining camp using his cunning and weapons skill: Joe survives Ramon's shots thanks to a hidden shield, kills his other adversaries in a straight shootout, and then lets his pistol beat Ramon's rifle in a load-and-shoot special duel. After tricking two bandits, Ringo kills Sancho with a ricochet shot.

A helper saves the hero from an ambush: Silvanito shoots Esteban, who hidden behind a window aims for Joe. Major Clyde throws the unarmed Ringo a dueling pistol to use against Sancho.

The hero leaves a large treasure behind: Joe leaves the gold in San Miguel to be returned to the government. Ringo leaves the loot at the ranch after deducting his agreed 30 percent.

Plot Models

Some of the plot functions extracted above can be further generalized. There are, for example, analogue actions concerning a woman and money/gold as desired objects. This makes for recurrent runs of the same plot functions that are presented for the two films in table 2A. I will use the term *models* for these recurrences of the plot. The table shows six models of the same plot, four from *Fistful of Dollars* and two from *Una pistola per Ringo*.

The Eastwood image from his Leone Westerns: the hat, the poncho, the squint — but missing the cigar.

The models are differentiated in that

- different story characters perform the plot functions and so "fill in" the placeholders given in each function.
- all of the functions in the plot are not necessarily performed in a model of that plot.
- some of the plot functions in a model may be reordered.

Like Lévi-Strauss, I treat not only equivalence and false (pretended) equivalence but also inversion (of plot functions or other properties) as revelation of an armature. The functions are presented in roughly chronological order for *Fistful of Dollars*, while in *Una pistola per Ringo* the two models are chronologically interlaced all through the action.

Constellation Intersection

The most important characters of the two films can be classified into five types:

	Fistful of Dollars	*Una Pistola per Ringo*
Hero	Joe	Ringo
Camp 1	Baxters	Sheriff/townspeople
Camp 2	Rojos	Sancho's gang
Threatened Family	Marisol, Julio, Jesus	Major Clyde, Ruby
Sidekick	Silvanito (Piripero)	Tim (Chico)

The Infiltrator's Constellation/Plot

Fistful of Dollars and *Una pistola per Ringo* have a common plot and constellation, together making up an armature, an *infiltrator constellation/plot* about a protagonist who joins one (or several) camp(s) with the hidden intention of working against their interests (and in the present cases to further his own). Among the 200 Italowesterns that I have studied, this core situation appears in more than 25 films.

Constellation

INFILTRATOR VARIATIONS

The basic constellation *hero/camp 1/camp 2* is evident in many of the infiltrator films, but a frequent variation, as outlined by Colonel Mortimer in *For a Few Dollars More* (below referred to as *Few Dollars More*), is "one from the outside, one from the inside." His fellow bounty hunter Monco

Table 2A. Intersection of Plot Models for *A Fistful of Dollars* and *Una Pistola per Ringo*

Common plot functions:	A Fistful of Dollars				Una Pistola per Ringo	
	Model (1)	Model (2)	Model (3)	Model (4)	Model (1)	Model (2)
	A: Joe B: Rojos C: Baxters D: (State?) O: Money	A: Joe B: Rojos C: Baxters D: Army (State) O: Gold	A: Joe B: Rojos C: Baxters D: Family O: Marisol	A: Joe B: Rojos C: Baxters D: Joe O: Joe	A: Ringo B: Sancho & band C: Bensons/townsfolk D: Townsfolk O: Loot from bank	A: Ringo B: Sancho & band C: Sheriff & posse D: Sheriff O: Ruby
A watches B take O from D	Joe learns from Silvanito about the smuggling	Joe watches the attack on the Mexican troop	The introduction scene at the "small house"		Ringo in the cell sees the bandits rob the bank	Ringo is informed that the Clydes are taken hostage
A gets an egotistical motive	Joe: "Baxters over there, Rojos there, and me right in the middle ... money could be made in this town!"	The transport of gold	Marisol for himself		Ringo negotiates to get reward and perhaps 30% of the loot to save the hostages	

2. Enter the Infiltrator

		A Fistful of Dollars				*Una Pistola per Ringo*	
Common plot functions:	Model (1)	Model (2)	Model (3)	Model (4)		Model (1)	Model (2)
	A: Joe	A: Joe	A: Joe	A: Joe		A: Ringo	A: Ringo
	B: Rojos	B: Rojos	B: Rojos	B: Rojos		B: Sancho & band	B: Sancho & band
	C: Baxters	C: Baxters	C: Baxters	C: Baxters		C: Bensons/townsfolk	C: Sheriff & posse
	D: (State?)	D: Army (State)	D: Family	D: Joe		D: Townsfolk	D: Sheriff
	O: Money	O: Gold	O: Marisol	O: Joe		O: Loot from bank	O: Ruby
A is warned of O	Silvanito warns Joe	Soldiers by wagon threaten Joe	Chico and then Silvanito warn Joe about Marisol			Ringo is hired to infiltrate the bandits (inverse)	Pedro acts threateningly toward Ringo
A fights against C	Joe kills four Baxter men					Ringo kills the Bensons	
A joins with B	Joe is employed by the Rojos	Joe leaves the Rojos' house (inverse)				Ringo is accepted into the ranch by the bandits	

Table 2A. (cont.)

Common plot functions:	A Fistful of Dollars				Una Pistola per Ringo	
	Model (1)	Model (2)	Model (3)	Model (4)	Model (1)	Model (2)
	A: Joe	A: Joe	A: Joe	A: Joe	A: Ringo	A: Ringo
	B: Rojos	B: Rojos	B: Rojos	B: Rojos	B: Sancho & band	B: Sancho & band
	C: Baxters	C: Baxters	C: Baxters	C: Baxters	C: Bensons/townsfolk	C: Sheriff & posse
	D: (State?)	D: Army (State)	D: Family	D: Joe	D: Townsfolk	D: Sheriff
	O: Money	O: Gold	O: Marisol	O: Joe	O: Loot from bank	O: Ruby
A acquires valuable information/object		Joe arranges the bodies of the soldiers	Joe abducts Marisol from the Rojo house	Joe escapes	Ringo presents a plan to escape through the canyon (false)	Ringo presents a plan to escape hidden among the hostages (false)
A sells the information/object to C		Joe tells Mrs. Baxter about the soldier "witnesses" (partly false)	Joe brings Marisol to the Baxters	Joe is believed to have escaped to the Baxters (false)	Ringo demands 30% of the loot from the townspeople	Ringo says he has been promised 50% by the sheriff (false)

Common plot functions:

	A Fistful of Dollars				*Una Pistola per Ringo*	
	Model (1)	Model (2)	Model (3)	Model (4)	Model (1)	Model (2)
	A: Joe B: Rojos C: Baxters D: (State?) O: Money	A: Joe B: Rojos C: Baxters D: Army (State) O: Gold	A: Joe B: Rojos C: Baxters D: Family O: Marisol	A: Joe B: Rojos C: Baxters D: Joe O: Joe	A: Ringo B: Sancho & band C: Bensons/ townsfolk D: Townsfolk O: Loot from bank	A: Ringo B: Sancho & band C: Sheriff & posse D: Sheriff O: Ruby
A sells information/ object to B		Joe tells the Rojos about the soldier "witnesses" (partly false)	Joe tells Marisol to go to Ramon (from her family) at the exchange of hostages	Joe escapes from the Rojos (inverse)	Ringo demands 40% from the bandits (partly false)	Ringo demands 60% from the bandits (partly false)
B and C fight		The fight at the cemetery	The exchange of hostages (weak)	The Rojos destroy the Baxters	The raid on the ranch by the sheriff/ The raid on the mill by the bandits.	The sheriff shoots at the bandits in the canyon

Table 2A. (cont.)

Common plot functions:	A Fistful of Dollars				Una Pistola per Ringo	
	Model (1)	Model (2)	Model (3)	Model (4)	Model (1)	Model (2)
	A: Joe	A: Joe	A: Joe	A: Joe	A: Ringo	A: Ringo
	B: Rojos	B: Rojos	B: Rojos	B: Rojos	B: Sancho & band	B: Sancho & band
	C: Baxters	C: Baxters	C: Baxters	C: Baxters	C: Bensons/ townsfolk	C: Sheriff & posse
	D: (State?)	D: Army (State)	D: Family	D: Joe	D: Townsfolk	D: Sheriff
	O: Money	O: Gold	O: Marisol	O: Joe	O: Loot from bank	O: Ruby
A gets a reward motive		Joe is paid both by the Rojos and the Baxters for the information	Joe is paid by the Baxters for Marisol	Joe gives money to Marisol (inverse)	Ringo leaves with 30% of the loot	
A gets a non-monetary motive			Silvanito informs Joe about Marisol	Piripero tells Joe that Silvanito is tortured	Ringo is also hired to save the hostages	Ruby gives the watch to Ringo (inverse)
A fights B			Joe kills the guards at the small house	Joe kills the Rojos	Ringo kills Sancho and the remaining bandits	Ringo kills Pedro

Common plot functions:

	A Fistful of Dollars				Una Pistola per Ringo	
	Model (1)	Model (2)	Model (3)	Model (4)	Model (1)	Model (2)
	A: Joe	A: Joe	A: Joe	A: Joe	A: Ringo	A: Ringo
	B: Rojos	B: Rojos	B: Rojos	B: Rojos	B: Sancho & band	B: Sancho & band
	C: Baxters	C: Baxters	C: Baxters	C: Baxters	C: Bensons/townsfolk	C: Sheriff & posse
	D: (State?)	D: Army (State)	D: Family	D: Joe	D: Townsfolk	D: Sheriff
	O: Money	O: Gold	O: Marisol	O: Joe	O: Loot from bank	O: Ruby
A helper saves A from an ambush			Marisol warns Joe for the wounded bandit	Silvanito shoots Esteban	Major Clyde gives Ringo a pistol (weak)	Chico gives Pedro's knife to Ringo (weak)
A returns O to D		Joe leaves the gold that will be returned to the government	Joe reunites Marisol with her family		Ringo leaves the loot (minus his share)	Ringo sends the hostages (including Ruby) to the sheriff/ Ringo returns the watch meant for the sheriff

Table 2A. (cont.)

Common plot functions:	A Fistful of Dollars				Una Pistola per Ringo	
	Model (1)	Model (2)	Model (3)	Model (4)	Model (1)	Model (2)
	A: Joe	A: Joe	A: Joe	A: Joe	A: Ringo	A: Ringo
	B: Rojos	B: Rojos	B: Rojos	B: Rojos	B: Sancho & band	B: Sancho & band
	C: Baxters	C: Baxters	C: Baxters	C: Baxters	C: Bensons/ townsfolk	C: Sheriff & posse
	D: (State?)	D: Army (State)	D: Family	D: Joe	D: Townsfolk	D: Sheriff
	O: Money	O: Gold	O: Marisol	O: Joe	O: Loot from bank	O: Ruby
A is disclosed and tortured by B		Joe declines manipulating U.S.A. against Mexico— "too dangerous" (potential)	Joe is tortured by the Rojos		Ringo is tortured by the bandits	
A leaves				Joe rides away from San Miguel	Ringo rides away from the ranch	

infiltrates the Indio gang while having a secret agreement with Mortimer, who eventually also enters into the group. In this case the constellation becomes *insider (infiltrator)/outsider/camp*. Likewise, in *Sette winchester per un massacro* bounty hunters Stuart and Manuela infiltrate Colonel Blake's Southern renegades. In *Jim il primo*, as in *Se t'incontro, t'ammazzo*, an insider and an outsider eventually turn out to be brothers. In *Tempo di massacro*, Mortimer's saying is the battle tactics outlined for Tom by his half brother Jeff when they attack the ranch where Junior (another half brother) and his gang reside.[9] In *Tequila!* there seem to be two camps (the farmers vs. the rancher deKoven) and two heroes, but the latter infiltrate together as a pair (a doubled infiltrator) and not as distinct insider/outsider.

In stories where the constellation from the outset consists of just one infiltrator/one camp, the latter eventually splits up into two or several factions. Sometimes this happens because of the infiltrator's machinations, as in *Prega per il morto e ammazza il vivo*, where the guide/secret avenger, John Webb, makes the gang members kill each other, and *Un dollaro bucato*,

Infiltrator partners in *Sette winchester per un massacro*: bounty hunters "Manuela" (Luisa Barrato) and "Stuart" (Edd Byrnes).

where Gary O'Hara makes the sheriff and his partner McCorey fight. In *Sartana nella valle degli avvoltoi* and *I crudeli*, men in the camp fall out over a woman who, like Marisol, has been forcibly included, and so is an involuntary infiltrator.[10] The men in *Sette winchester per un massacro* at least grumble when Blake makes Manuela his woman instead of sharing her, like other spoils!

Another variant occurs in the seminal insider/outsider film *Few Dollars More* (though *Jim il primo* preceded it). After the insider and outsider have been exposed, they act as a pair, and as such they are manipulated by Indio to fight his men.

In some films where the infiltration makes up a minor part of the story, the division in the infiltrated camp has other causes, as in *Faccia a faccia*, *Quinto: non ammazzare*, and *California*.

THE THREATENED FAMILY

Threats and misdeeds against innocents such as the Marisol family recur in the infiltration films. In *Few Dollars More* Indio recollects how a young woman shot herself while he raped her after killing her loved one. The bandit also has his men execute the wife and child of the man that betrayed him to the authorities before killing him in a duel. Gary in *Un dollaro bucato* defends the Donaldson family and later saves his own wife from that fate worse than death. The Indian girl Tanu in *La vendetta è un piatto che si serve freddo* is threatened by Perkins's men, a blind man and an Indian girl are murdered in *I crudeli*, the outcasts of Puerta de Fuego are massacred by the vigilantes in *Faccia a faccia* and Burton in *Al di là della legge* starts killing off his women and children hostages until the silver is delivered to him.

The young woman in *Few Dollars More* whose death turns out to be a motive for the "outsider" Mortimer is a part of the infiltrator constellation, while the fate of the informer's family serves only to describe the ruthlessness and style of Indio, and thus belongs to the story setting.[11] In *Fistful of Dollars*, Marisol and her kin serve in both functions of this "terrorized victims" motif, first as a setting, and then as a motive when Joe decides to liberate her — though his reasons are left enigmatic. In *California* neither the senseless killing of his new friend Willie Preston nor Whittaker's massacre of former Southern soldiers makes the hero change his survivalist behavior, but the kidnapping of Helen Preston does. *Una ragione per vivere ... una per morire* holds a sinister inversion, a family that murders straying Union and Confederate soldiers for their belongings.

SIDEKICKS

Sidekicks such as Silvanito and Tim influence the story enough to enter into the constellation. The same goes for Doc — a medicine salesman whose cultivated conversation contrasts with his present circumstances in *La vendetta è un piatto che si serve freddo*. The forgotten old man who believes he is a famous outlaw in *Faccia a faccia* rather belongs to the setting, as do various comic elderly undertakers, drivers or salesmen in other films. The bum mistaken for a reputable bounty killer in *Tequila!* is a sidekick turned into a false hero.

Plot

The common plot functions—the plot intersection—of the infiltrator films are presented below, in a slightly modified version compared with the plot extracted from *Fistful of Dollars* and *Una pistola per Ringo* in table 2A.

1. A is independent of society.
2. B takes something valuable from D.
3. A gets a monetary motive.
4. A fights against C.
5. A joins with B.
6. A acquires valuable information/object.
7. A sells information/object to C.
8. A sells information/object to B.
9. B and C fight.
10. A gets a reward.
11. B threatens E.
12. A gets a non-monetary motive.
13. A is disclosed and tortured.
14. A fights B.
15. A is helped by F.
16. A returns the valuable object to D.
17. A leaves society.

In this setup

- A is the main protagonist/infiltrator hero.
- B and C are camps 1 and 2, or factions of one camp.
- D is some type of societal interest that sometimes is represented by a character.
- E is the threatened family/group.
- F is the sidekick (or may be the partner in an insider/outsider situation).

The plot functions may be mapped to the infiltrator stories more easily when grouped into narrative sequences.[12] These might also be relevant for stories not fully conforming to the infiltration plot.

THE INFILTRATION SEQUENCE—FUNCTIONS 1, 3, 5 OR 1, 12, 5

This core sequence might have monetary or non-monetary motives that are reflected in the alternative sequences. In some stories the infiltration is not performed by the hero but a character that is (or becomes) closely related to him. In *Se t'incontro, t'ammazzo* and *Jim il primo* it is his brother. In *Faccia a faccia* the infiltrator Siringo is an adversary to Bennet, but eventually they become allies against the posse, and subsequently against Fletcher.

THE MANIPULATION SEQUENCE—6, 7, 8, 9

This sequence involves making two parties (the *dupes* of the manipulation) fight each other by handing them information that is partly or wholly false. The template case is the clash, arranged by Joe, between the Rojos and the Baxters over two dead bodies at the cemetery. I have already mentioned Gary O'Hara and John Webb. Pembroke in *Una ragione per vivere ... una per morire* uses a nonexistent treasure of gold to convince his reluctant men to attack Ft. Holmes. Ramon performs a metonymic manipulation — his men in U.S. uniforms fight the Mexican soldiers. In *Mannaja* and *El Macho* manipulation is a prerogative of the villains (consequently, "B makes A and C fight").

In *Una pistola per Ringo* the manipulation is just a pretense to destroy one of the parties, while the other one stays in the background. In such situations there might still appear to be discord, but for other reasons— money (*Un dollaro tra i denti*), a woman (*Sartana nella valle degli avvoltoi*), political ambitions (*California*) or moral principles (*Faccia a faccia*).

Manipulation is closely associated with the motif of one party *observing* two other parties fighting. The calm observation of a fight that he (often) has caused himself is an icon for the manipulative nature of the infiltrator hero. In *Fistful of Dollars* we find the hero watching a conflict that he hasn't brought about (the attack on the gold shipment), and causing a conflict that he doesn't watch (the fight at the cemetery), besides the core situation (the exchange of hostages and also when Joe, hidden in a coffin, watches the Rojos annihilate the Baxters supposedly hiding him).

THE REMUNERATION SEQUENCE—INFILTRATION, MANIPULATION, 10

A reward is given or at least offered to the infiltrator in most of the films. The sequence might be missing if the infiltrator's motive is revenge, or if the infiltration is aborted.

THE PUNISHMENT SEQUENCE—INFILTRATION, MANIPULATION, 13

The torture and violent beating of the exposed infiltrator — his pain, the bruises and marks left on his skin —can be seen as a metaphorical inversion, a piercing of the physical and mental covers that he has used earlier to accomplish his infiltration. However, in *La vendetta è un piatto che si serve freddo* Jim is gravely wounded before the infiltration and in *Se t'incontro, t'ammazzo* it is the outsider, not the insider, that is beaten up. Claire in *I crudeli* falls ill, and Calloway in *Sartana nella valle degli avvoltoi* almost perishes in the desert. Pembroke has to eat dirtied beans as a humiliation in *Una ragione per vivere ... una per morire*.

THE AMBIGUITY SEQUENCE—3, 11, 12

Ambiguity describes the hero wavering between a monetary and a non-monetary motive. In *Fistful of Dollars*, and also in *Al di là della legge* and *Faccia a faccia*, the non-monetary motive becomes more important as the story proceeds, while in most other infiltration stories the hero oscillates between the two motives, or at least seems to do so. In *Una pistola per Ringo*, *El Macho* and *Un dollaro tra i denti*, the hero might go for the whole loot, or keep a deal granting him some percentage. Southern patriotism hides bounty hunting in *Sette winchester per un massacro*, but otherwise open egotism seems better fit to cover for a non-monetary motive such as vengeance or justice than the opposite! Both motives are affirmed in *Tequila!* Shoshena buys his way out of a hanging with stolen money, and while the farmers fight over the loot, he retorts to his partner's objection that he is crazy with "They are!" Simultaneously love triumphs as the son of the rancher boss leaves with his father's dead body, accompanied by the farmer leader's daughter.

THE ASSISTANCE SEQUENCE—13, 14, 15

The assistance sequence is most often active in the insider/outsider constellation variant where one of the protagonists saves the other — with most effect in *Few Dollars More*, where the continuing of the melody from the musical watch signals the presence of Monco, which will turn Indio's execution of Mortimer into a real duel. A comic variant is when the clumsy (and terrified) partner "Jaguar" lets loose some barrels, making it possible for Shoshena to escape his tormentors. In *Una ragione per vivere ... una per morire* Pembroke is saved from suspicious townspeople by Eliah, who runs into town and shouts that the civil war is over. Besides Silvantio, the only sidekick savior in the infiltration films is Doc in *La vendetta è un piatto che si serve Freddo*.

THE RESTITUTION SEQUENCE—2, 14, 16

In all the infiltrator stories where there is a large sum of money or a treasure of some type at stake, the heroes follow the lead of Joe and Ringo, who leave it behind to be collected by the rightful owners. In other cases the treasure never existed (*Una ragione per vivere ... una per morire*), turns out to be worthless (*Quinto: non ammazzare, Sette winchester per un massacro*), or is lost (*... dai nemici mi guardo io!, I crudeli*).

THE INDEPENDENCE SEQUENCE—1, 4, 14, 17

The functions 4 and 14 show the characteristic conflicts between the hero and the groupings in the constellation. The functions 1 and 17 concern the relation of the hero to whatever society there is in the infiltrator stories. The mainstream resolution is that the hero leaves society in the company of a woman—one or both may be wanted by the law, and/or the girls are saloon girls, prostitutes, or gamblers, or belong to persecuted minorities. This recalls Wright's transition theme, where the hero leaves (an intolerant) society together with a woman. In some of the inside-outside stories, the partners leave society together, more like Wright's professional plot. Only *Al di là della legge* conforms to the classical plot, where the hero stays to become a member of society.

The Position of the Woman in the Infiltrator Film

The frequent concluding association between the hero and a woman calls into question one often heard generalization about the inferior role of women in the Spaghetti Western. Leone himself has declared that in the Western the true place for the woman is in the background. Now, it is true that Marisol is mostly a plaything for the male characters in *Fistful of Dollars*—Ramon abducts her from her family, Julio allows it to happen, and Joe liberates her. Her only independent action is at the fight at the small house, when she gives a warning to Joe and thus chooses sides. Yet, as an object of desire, she is very important. For her sake Ramon relinquishes the chance to rid himself of the Baxter threat, and because of her Joe foregoes his profitable manipulations for an act of altruism that almost gets him killed.

Still more powerful as an active object is the female "lead" in *Few Dollars More*, who is dead when the film begins and never even identified by name. She appears only in Indio's flashbacks, and as a picture in the lids of the musical watches carried both by him and Mortimer. In the final reckoning between them, a camera shot foregrounds her photo in the watchcase, hovering over the shapes of the two men whose lives she forever changed by the way that she chose to die, and who now stand poised to kill each other.

This dictum of downplaying women becomes still more questionable when looking at other spaghetti Westerns. Among the characters in the infiltrator films discussed so far, one finds the bounty hunter Manuela, who uses both gun and sex to snare her victims, the redhead Helen, who becomes the hero's comrade in arms in *El Macho*, and Claire, whose very ability at the gambling table is used by Ben to trick her, but who shows herself apt at infiltrator double-play. I also adduce that woman-to-woman talk in *Una pistola per Ringo*, where Dolores, gun-toting bandit and new love of Ruby's father, tells her that even though she is an excellent shot, she does not know how to kill because "only someone who knows how to hate can kill, and only a real woman knows how to hate." Such a one is obviously Joselita Rogers in *Mille dollari sul nero*. When she is saved from attackers and learns that the savior is John Liston, she immediately tries to kill him, because he was condemned for murdering her father. When her friend the judge is exposed as an accomplish to the crime and knocks on her door and begs for his life, she refuses to open and lets him get killed. Gary's wife, Judy, in *Un dollaro bucato*, though unarmed, also proves considerably less gullible and easy to handle than McCorey expects. Still I must grant that *The Belle Starr Story* is rare in the genre with its female main protagonist.[13]

Besides these fighters, there are also traditional femme fatales, such as the Southern belle in *Sartana nella valle degli avvoltoi*, who spends a night with the hero and in the morning has her farmhands try to rope him for the reward. Susanna, who betrays Duke (sexually) with El Macho and the latter (economically) with the banker and sheriff, combines both roles.

Infiltration as a Motif or as a Plot

In most of the films quoted in this chapter and others, the infiltration constellation/plot is *central* to the story in the sense that most of what is going on can be interpreted as expressions of some function (and narrative sequence) in a model of the infiltration plot and that the most important characters in the film can be assigned to the constellation positions of that model. In other films the infiltration constellation/plot accounts for only part of the story.

For example, in the first half of *La vendetta è un piatto che si serve freddo* Jim Bridger takes revenge for his family by killing Indians, until his hatred starts to waver before the Indian woman Tanu, and he learns (from Doc) that Perkins is the real person responsible. Then he infiltrates Perkins's organization. However, the whole story can still be described using the infiltrator plot, as Jim fights camp 2 (the Indians) and joins camp 1 (Perkins) to work against its proper interest, and for his own, in this case vengeance. Though Jim (in a weak sense) uses manipulation when he allies with his former enemies to fight their common enemy, it is preceded by a manipulation by the villain, as Perkins's fraud to blame the Indians has caused Jim's vendetta against them.

Un dollaro bucato about 40 percent of the screening time shows how Gary's brother leaves for the West, how Gary reunites with his wife, how he is confronted by anti–Southern feelings when arriving at Yellowstone, how he is hired by McCorey to arrest "Blackie" (his brother) to get an excuse to gun the latter down — another initiating manipulation by the villain. Surviving, he returns to infiltrate the renegade gang to reveal the truth about his brother.

In *California* the first two thirds of the film are about California befriending Willie Preston in the turmoil after the civil war, Preston's death, Whittaker's massacres on Southern ex-soldiers, California's love for Helen Preston and her abduction. Then California embarks on his infiltration campaign. However, the situation can be expressed through the infiltrator plot. Whittaker and his employers are two camps at odds with each other, a woman is abducted by one side (for forced prostitution this time), and the man that loves her joins the abductor's gang under false pretenses and destroys them. As in *Una pistola per Ringo*, the hero does not fight the other camp. Like in *Fistful of Dollars*, both camps are just as bad though.

In *Una ragione per vivere ... una per morire*, the first part is explainable by one infiltrator model — with Pembroke pitting his rather involuntary companions against the Confederates with a false monetary motive to get his vengeance. The second part follows a second infiltrator model — with Eliah entering the fort and piling one false motive on top of another to cover the nature of his infiltration.

In *Al di là della legge* Cudlip fights camp 1 (Burton's gang) and becomes a part of camp 2 (the townspeople, especially the engineer Novak) in order to enrich himself by stealing the payroll. Instead he ends up defending the money, and staying in society, as an inversion to Angel Face, who pretends to want to steal all the gold but leaves with just his cut. The first part of the story, on the other hand, involving caper-style robberies and counter-tricks (when Novak hides the payroll in his clothes and transports an empty bag), is akin to the betrayal plot.[14]

The infiltration by Gringo of El Condor's band in ... *dai nemici mi guardo io!* is quickly foiled by Hondo, an "outsider" with his own agenda. Such acts of infiltration that have little consequence to the main story are inserted motifs of infiltration and not the full constellation/plot–put into the films because of their popularity in other Italowesterns.

This is not be confused with the inept, comical infiltrators in some post–Trinity spaghetti Westerns. Their travails play a substantial part in stories such as *Alleluja e Sartana figli di ... Dio*—where the fake priest and his partner must cure a dying man (with whiskey) because they are ignorant of the last unction and start a fight in church to avoid performing a wedding—and *Buddy Goes West*, where the fake doctor ad-libs to fool his patients.

There is a common motif that is an inverse variation on the infiltration plot. Instead of the hero destroying the group he is infiltrating because he has hidden information, the group refrains from destroying the hero because he has hidden information. For example, Joe is kept alive (and tortured) to reveal the whereabouts of Marisol, Tuco has to save Blondie instead of killing him because he knows (part of) the whereabouts of the gold in Leone's *The Good, the Bad and the Ugly*, and the hero of *Requiescant* is spared from execution (and tortured) to reveal whether he has spread knowledge (of a massacre) that might cause a rebellion.

Codes of the Infiltrator

The code structures in the other infiltrator films largely conform to those in *Fistful of Dollars* and *Una pistola per Ringo*.

Incomplete families are a common element. The hero is without family, or loses it when a vengeance motive is established. Of the few complete families, one is revealed to be murderers (*Una ragione per vivere ... una per morire*), one is largely incidental (*California*), and one falls prey to selfish monetary values (*Tequila!*).

The hero might have a sidekick relation to an old man.

The wits and superior skills of the hero are set against odds that range from bad to impossible. Strong sheriffs and citizen posses are few, even if the exposed boss is killed by enraged crowds in *Un dollaro bucato* and *La vendetta è un piatto che si serve freddo*.

The environment is predominantly urban, with nature (often barren) as an arena of occasional fights and pursuits, exceptions being some longer treks through wilderness. Examples include *Prega per il morto e ammazza il vivo* (pursued toward the border), *I giorni della violenza* (escaping from a posse), *I Crudeli* (through Union territory with the robbery loot in a coffin) and especially *Sartana nella valle degli avvoltoi* with its extended cat-and-mouse game between Calloway and the Craigs.

Socioeconomic focus is on monetary remuneration and robberies, with heroes guided by self-interest interspersed with some non-monetary motive, or vengeance. As a clear-cut and honest spokesman for fairness and the law, the sheriff in *Una pistola per Ringo* remains alone. Closest are Gary O'Hara in *Un dollaro bucato* and White in *La morte non conta i dollari*, who join the bad guys to cover their quest for justice, and the reformed gunfighter Jim Hart in *Jim il primo*, who fights the bad guys masked by a cover of non-violence.

Terror reigns in the form of atrocities committed against defenseless groups or individuals, and severe beatings (usually dealt out to the hero). There are also more refined tortures, such as water drops, standing on stilts in a hangman's noose, leaving someone tied with dynamite on a burning fuse, or letting people go down in quicksand. A psychological kind of terror is Indio's playing the tune on his watch before drawing on an inferior or incapacitated opponent in *Few Dollars More*. There are also pure humiliations, such as the fight on order in *I crudeli*.

The story includes advanced tactics of cunning and manipulation.[15]

In the rhetorical code of *humor*, the infiltrator stories mostly follow the pattern of *Fistful of Dollars*—more or less pointed irony from tight-lipped protagonists on one hand and talkative old men on the other. I cannot refrain from quoting Indio's words to his men before entering Agua Caliente: "It looks just like a morgue. Look out, it could be one so easily!" (Of course, this is exactly what happens later.) Indio then turns to Groggy and says, "They don't like strangers, eh?" and the answer is, "No, they don't like anybody." An example of sarcasm intended by the script, though not the character, is the presentation of the men condemned to death in *Una ragione per vivere... una per morire*. An officer surveys the bunch: a deserter who has killed two sentries; a man who has murdered his commanding officer and raped the wife; a horse-thief; two looters, one who has stolen medicine and thereby caused soldiers to die; and an Indian "bastard" who has killed a white man that sold liquor to the Apaches. The officer finally comes to "the worst of the bunch"—a religious pacifist agitator! Indirect ironic contrasts pervade *Una pistola per Ringo*—upper-class refinement versus uncouth bandits, ceremonies of Christmas versus practice of violence— and have some following in its kindred, *Il ritorno di Ringo* (see below). Cudlip's partner Preacher excels in parodical bible quotations. The infiltrator Guitar in the early *Jim il primo* displays direct, more good-natured humor. Comic heroes to be laughed *at* instead of with are to be found in some late infiltrator films, like the cowardly and bumbling partner "Jaguar" in *Tequila!* (who accidentally slams shut the safe that Shoshena spent most of the night trying to open), and the all-out comical post–Trinity infiltrators.

Unsuccessful infiltrator Gringo (Charles Southwood, right) with malignant partner Hondo (Julian Mateos) in *... dai nemici mi guardo io!*

Several infiltrator stories display a metacode, in the sense of ambiguous concurrence of several codes, involving violence, gold/money and religious objects and practices, such as Christmas in *Una pistola per Ringo*. The loot in *I crudeli* is transported in a coffin, which gets mixed up with one containing a dead bandit. In *Sartana nella valle degli avvoltoi* and *Se t'incontro, t'ammazzo* it is hidden in a grave, and in *Sette winchester per un massacro* the Southern war chest (in worthless Confederate money) is kept in a cave that is an Indian graveyard. In addition, the bandit leader Aguila is dressed in a monk's robe when he mows down the soldiers in *Un dollaro tra i denti*, as is the sidekick character Doc when he steals chicken in *La vendetta è un piatto che si serve freddo*. At the beginning of *Few Dollars More*, the bounty hunter Mortimer is mistaken for a priest as he sits in his black suit and reads the bible. This intertextual mingling of the circumstances of the sacred with those of violent death and of gold is common in spaghetti Westerns.

I referred earlier to another metacode comparing competence in love and in violence that is expressed in *Una pistola per Ringo*. It also exists in *Faccia a faccia*. As long as Fletcher remains a conscientious humanist in contrast with Bennet's outlaw cynicism, the latter blocks Fletcher's relationships with women. Fletcher embarks on his criminal career with a rape and then is always seen together with women who eventually meet a violent death, while Annie, who opposes him, survives.

The Sociocultural Code

The Anglo/Mexican differences in cultural style are important for distinguishing the constellation positions in *Fistful of Dollars* and *Una pistola per Ringo*, as are the social contrasts between upper-class Clydes and lower-lower-class bandits in the latter. Table 2C shows some Italo-westerns featuring infiltrators distributed over ethnically based and socially based distinctions as aspects of a composite code dimension of *sociocultural style*.

A code is *central* when its values are significant for situations and relations that are decisive for the development of a story, and *peripheral* otherwise. A *distinguishing* code shows different values for characters in different constellation positions in the plot(s) important to the story. *Non-distinguishing* codes separate only characters belonging to the same position, or those belonging to the constellation from those that are part of the setting.

Table 2C.
Sociocultural Style in the Infiltrator Films

Social diff.:	Central		Peripheral		Missing
Ethnic diff.:	Distinguishing	Non-distinguishing	Distinguishing	Non-distinguishing	
Central-Distinguishing	Una pistola per Ringo Un dollaro bucato Faccia a faccia La vendetta è un piatto che si serve freddo **Group 1**		Fistful of Dollars Few Dollars More **Group 2**		Un dollaro tra i denti I crudeli ...dai nemici mi guardo io!
Central-Non-distinguishing					
Peripheral-distinguishing	El Macho		I giorni della violenza	California Sette winchester per un massacro	Una ragione per vivere ... una per morire
Peripheral-Non-distinguishing	La morte non conta i dollari Per mille dollari al giorno **Group 4**		Al di là della legge	**Group 3**	Quinto: non ammazzare Prega per il morto e ammazza il vivo The Belle Starr Story
Missing	Un animale chiamato uomo Se t'incontro, t'ammazzo Tequila! Mannaja Jim il primo				Sartana nella valle degli avvoltoi

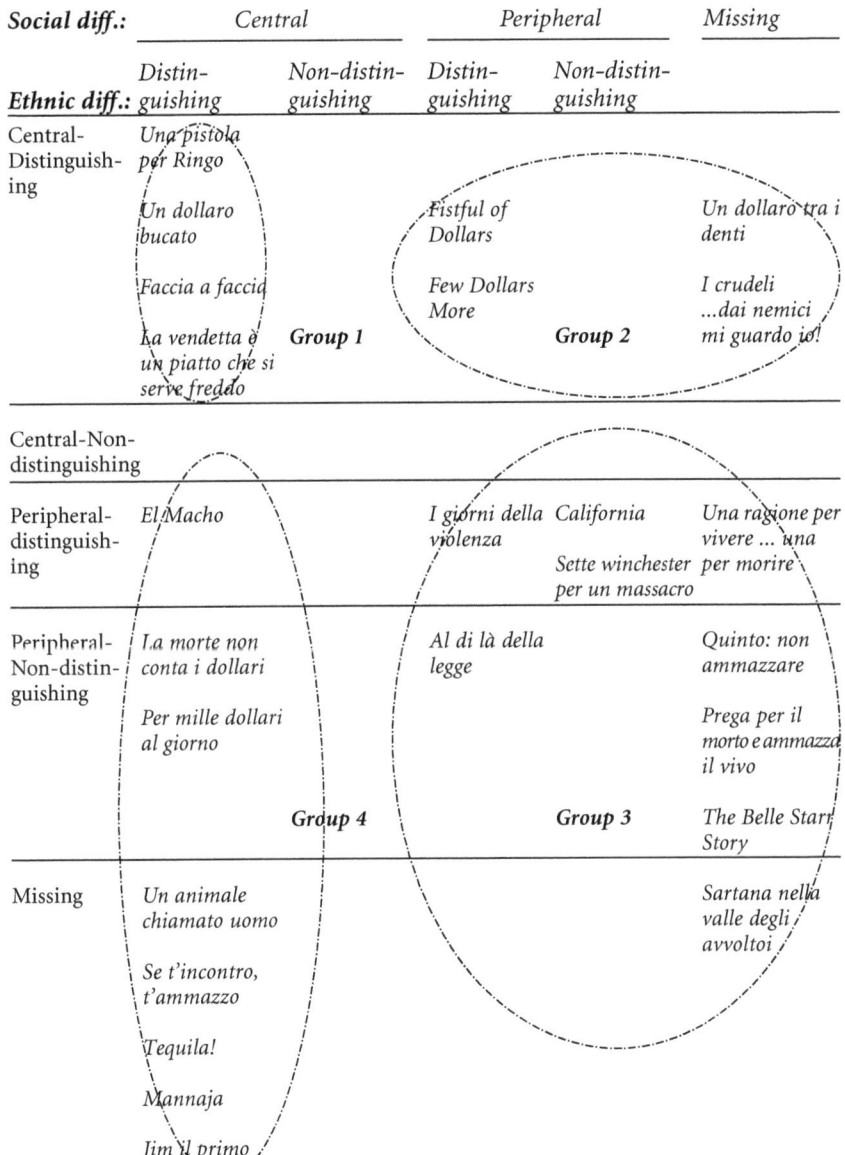

Ethnic differences

The frequent contrasting of Mexican and North American (Anglo, for short) is expressed in secondary codes, such as

- Speech — accent; talkative vs. laconic; heavy laughers vs. grim irony
- Dress — cowboy dress or suits vs. sombreros, embellished vests and large gun belts, or the white dress of peons (carried also by main characters like Indio or Bennet)
- General demeanor — emotionalism vs. rationality, intensity vs. restraint

Furthermore, where the Mexicans appear in bands, they do tend to represent an (illegal) collective against the single infiltrator. Sometimes a caricature traditionalism is associated with the Mexicans — as when the ruthless killer Sancho exhorts his men to "respect tradition" during the Christmas celebrations on the besieged ranch or the metonymic irony when Indio spells out the setup for the attack on the bank of El Paso by way of a fable told from the pulpit of an abandoned church. On the other hand, in the usual proceedings of these stories, the Anglo infiltrator seems to be a representation in the flesh of the possessive individualism referred to by Wright in his interpretation of the message of the classical American Western.[16]

It is also tempting to generalize this contrast between Anglo and Latin to contemporary contrasts between Northern and Southern Europeans (or between Northern and Southern Italians).

Anglo heroes in *Fistful of Dollars*, *Few Dollars More* and *Un dollaro tra i denti* signal a medium (mediating) position by wearing ponchos.

Instances of Confederates, preferably as renegades turned bandits, are usually coded as peripheral/distinguishing as they involve few cultural contrasts beyond the color of the uniform. The exception is *Un dollaro bucato*, where Gary is being discriminated against as a Southerner, and where the Southern preoccupation with "honor" is referred to both by Gary and scornfully by McCorey's men. The evil Southern family in *I crudeli* is not culturally distinct in this respect, but the added ethnic appearance of Indians and Mexican bandits motivate its central coding. In *Sartana nella valle degli avvoltoi* ethnical contrasts are set as "missing" despite the treacherous Southern Belle!

Peripheral/non-distinguishing ethnical codes occur mainly in films where ethnical differences reside only in an ethnically mixed bandit gang. In *El Macho* the proceedings are not significantly influenced by the fact that a Latin hero infiltrates an Anglo band. Incidentally, its second-in-command does wear Mexican clothes but is called Gunnar (or possibly Gunner). Such an easy attitude toward ethnical inconsistencies comes into view throughout the production of spaghetti Westerns. I will refer to it as *casual ethnicity*.

Class Differences

The following class-based types can be distinguished in the infiltrator films:

- **Cultural aristocrats:** Persons of a higher-class upbringing who might exhibit knowledge of fine beverages and literary quotations, and sometimes have manservants and finely laid tables. They are connected to the Old South (Colonel Blake in *Sette winchester per un massacro*, or the DeVinton brother and sister in *Faccia a faccia*), Europe (Duke in *El Macho*) or at least Boston (Brad Fletcher in *Faccia a faccia* and, of course, Major Clyde). The cultural aristocrats are almost invariably shown associating with bandits, their opposites in the class spectrum, often as leaders of gangs. Clyde is a hostage and falls in love with a bandit woman. Fletcher, who is from the East and a man of high learning, goes from hostage to member to leader of a gang where Maximilian DeVinton is a member. Colonel Mortimer in *Few Dollars More*, who was "once ... a gentleman," shows none of these outside cultural trappings, but he is a hunter of bandits and at least pretends to ally with them.
- **Big Bosses:** Embodiments of the classic Western banker villain that let their high social esteem cover the misdeeds committed by their own henchmen and/or some bandit gang in their employ.
- **Citizens:** Farmers and/or townspeople, representatives of Society in the sense of Wright's classical plot. If at all noticeable, they tend to be law-abiding victims of bandits and big bosses.
- **Professionals:** Bounty killers, mercenaries, government agents, Pinkerton agents, Texas rangers, etc. As main protagonists they typically appear alone or in pairs.
- **Bandits:** The ubiquitous band(s) of outlaws, in cahoots with a boss or acting on their own.

Position of the Sidekicks

The saloon owner Silvanito should be a solid citizen, but he is in fact an odd man out in San Miguel, as he does not belong to any of the factions, and the same goes for Piripero, the undertaker. The friends and helpers of the infiltrator heroes occupy marginal positions in society. They might also appear marginalized by running inns in isolated places, as Jeremiah in *Il ritorno di Ringo* does.

Class Coding Categories

The coding for class difference is partly determined by its scope. It's coded as *missing* where the action mainly involves professionals and bandits, even if other social categories might appear marginally, such as the whip-wielding colonel who has killed Belle's parents and who tries first to rape and later to hang her friend Raffico in the flashback part of *The Belle Starr Story*.

In films including big bosses and bandits, the machinations of the bosses are always *central* to the story, and the social differences code is always *distinguishing* in the constellation. I will refer to these Western versions of the mainstay struggle between the hero and a socially powerful villain as *big boss stories*.

In the few stories where the social scope lies between citizens and bandits, I have judged the class code as central in *Jim il primo*, where debates between the citizens over how to deal with the Lindall gang are a prominent part of the story. The social differences among the citizens, Cudlip and Burton in *Al di là della legge* are not, even though they are distinguishing. In fact, the sheriff's daughter's tea party seems to make Cudlip more uneasy than Burton's gang ever manages to do!

The stories bridging aristocrat and bandits are coded as peripheral and non-distinguishing when the aristocrat just leads a bandit gang. *Faccia a faccia* is about the cultural aristocrat Fletcher switching moral position with the bandit Bennet. In *Una pistola per Ringo* the cultural contrasts between the Clydes and the Sancho gang contribute greatly to the enjoyment of the story.

Fistful of Dollars is put as socially peripheral/distinguishing because though the Rojos and especially Baxter — who is a sheriff — technically could be labeled big bosses, as the story is told, they are presented as leaders of rivaling gangs. In *Few Dollars More* the distinguishing social background between Mortimer and Monco is a noticeable but not decisive difference in style, e.g., between shiny boots and dusty ones in their nightly hat-shooting duel in the street.

California, I giorni della violenza and to a certain extent *El Macho* are amalgams of several stories, one involving big bosses (e.g., the general who pays Whittaker to kill unarmed Southerners in *California*) and one involving bandits (California's duping and killing of Whittaker). While social differences are in play in both stories in *El Macho* (the banker and the sheriff who manipulate El Macho and his infiltration of Duke's gang), they are only so in the framing tale of Johs' revenge against the officer, later governor, Clifton, in *I giorni della violenza*, though they are still distinguishing. California (who has a past as a professional gun) is mostly trying to stay out of the big boss story confrontations. The latter come through as part of a description of post-war chaos, like when some vengeful citizens kill California's companion, and thus rather belong to the film's setting. In the bandit story he never fights the big boss camp, just Whittaker, which justifies the coding of non-distinguishing.

Stories According to Sociocultural Type

The infiltrator constellation/plot films are graphically separated into four groups by this double code. Group 4 comprises big boss stories (except for *Jim il primo*) with ethnic differences peripheral or missing. Group 2 contains showdowns between professionals and bandits with significant ethnic differences, while the latter are peripheral (though rarely missing) in group 3. The group 1 films can all be designated special cases. *Un dollaro bucato* and *La vendetta è un piatto che si serve freddo* are big boss stories with ethnical distinctions, but other than Latin/Anglo. In both *Faccia a faccia* and *Una pistola per Ringo* ethnical differences are overlaid with culture aristocrat/bandit contrasts.

The distribution of the infiltrator stories over the sociocultural code suggests a further division into two categories of *theme stories—big boss stories* (largely group 4) where ethnical differences usually are missing or of secondary importance, and *professionals/bandits stories* (largely groups 2 and 3) where ethnical differences are of greater importance.[17] In terms of public reception, the Italian box office hits among these films mostly belong to the second category (and include *Fistful of Dollars*, *Few Dollars More*, *Una pistola per Ringo*, *Faccia a faccia*, *Al di là della legge* and *Una ragione per vivere ... una per morire*).

The Infiltrator Revisited — The Return of Ringo

Il ritorno di Ringo was released six months after my infiltrator reference movie *Una pistola per Ringo*. These two films obviously were shot back to back with the same producer, director (Tessari), scriptwriters (Tessari and Fernando Di Leo), composer (Ennio Morricone), at least partly the

Table 2D. Constellation Set up in the Ringo Films by Duccio Tessari

Actor	Characters — Thematic role(s)	
	Una Pistola per Ringo	*Il Ritorno di Ringo*
Giuliano Gemma	Ringo, alias Angle Face, is a money-oriented, marginalized Anglo hero who killed his first man at the age of seven ("self-defense, naturally"), and has just stood trial for murder. For a money award he infiltrates a predominantly Mexican band of bandits, pretending to be an outlaw.	Montgomery Brown, alias Ringo, has a wife, a large house and a standing in the community, which he returns to from the war. He finds himself deprived of all this by Mexican bandits. He infiltrates the society ruled by them, pretending to be a Mexican.
Lorella De Luca (alias Hally Hammond)	Ruby Clyde, belligerent daughter in a respectable Anglo family; sexually threatened by a Mexican bandit.	Hally Brown, belligerent wife/mother in a respectable Anglo family; mistress of necessity to a Mexican bandit.
Fernando Sancho	Sancho, loud and violent leader of Mexican bandits.	Esteban Fuentes, loud and violent co-leader of Mexican bandits.
Nieves Navarro (alias Susan Scott)	Dolores, armed bandit mistress of Sancho, attracted to major Clyde.	Rosita, unarmed mistress of Esteban, attracted to Ringo.
Pajarito	Tim, elderly comic aide to the sheriff, friendly to the hero.	Morning Glory, elderly comic florist who puts the hero up.
Antonio Casas	Major Clyde, landowner with aristocrat lifestyle and a well-mannered host to the invading bandits. He courts Dolores and is wounded.	Alcoholic, subdued sheriff prompted into action by Ringo, and killed because of an act of Rosita.
Jorge (alias George) Martin	Righteous, sharp-shooting sheriff, engaged to Ruby.	Paco Fuentes, co-leader of Mexican bandits, has taken over Hally, Ringo's wife, and also his mansion.
Child actor (different between the films)	Chico, knowledgeable Mexican boy in the Clyde household, helps Ringo to get a knife.	Elizabeth, knowledgeable Anglo daughter of Ringo, helps him load his gun.

same sets and (as Table 2D shows) roughly the same actors playing a similar set of characters.

The main differences pertain to the characters played by Casas and Martin. Another difference is that Ringo now is a father, and to a blond little doll to boot, but the story steers away from both fatherly authority and

Female master of arms, and in all black to boot — Elsa Martinelli in *The Belle Starr Story*.

sentimentality by having the precocious child help the hero by loading his gun and also by discovering a Fuentes man behind her father's back. She watches undisturbed as Ringo shoots him.

Transformations of Constellation Positions

The Female Aberrant

The female figures encountered in *Fistful of Dollars* and the two Tessari films do not fit easily with the dichotomy of decent woman (schoolmarm/farmer's daughter) and fallen woman (saloon girl) traditionally ascribed to the American Western — not the abducted wife/mother (Marisol, Hally), the matriarch gang leader (Mrs. Baxter), the armed and dangerous female bandit (Dolores), or even the belligerent daughter Ruby, who is ready to shoot it out with Sancho's whole gang.[18]

Even Rosita, the "saloon" woman — who even gets to sing and dance[19] — seems curiously unbound — being attracted but not emotionally tied either to hero Ringo or villain Esteban. Enhanced by the detached, ironic aura of actress Navarro, Rosita retains a position of being an observer and commentator — free of both parties. While the traditional fate of the saloon woman is to die when she helps the hero, Rosita inversely survives her last action in the plot, which is to help the villain escape, and (indirectly) cause the death of the sheriff. Considering the actor constellation, this is also an inversion to *Una pistola per Ringo*, where Navarro's character gets killed because she stands up for the major (Casas) against Sancho (Fernando Sancho), while here it is the sheriff (Casas) who gets killed as a result of her helping Esteban (Fernando Sancho). Anyway, she is absolved by Ringo with one of his catch phrases: "Everyone has a right to make a mistake." In the end Ringo stays to regain his position in society, and it is Rosita who takes over the leaving scene, riding off on a mule wearing Ringo's hat in what might be a conscious reference to the departure of Joe at the end of *Fistful of Dollars*.

The Female as Involuntary Infiltrator

Ruby is a daughter who — according to Dolores — has to kill to become "a real woman," and who is sexually threatened by a bandit. Hally is a wife and a mother, and so already a "real woman," and she has had to go all the way with her bandit. He wants to marry her, thereby definitely taking the place of her husband. Her startling reply to Ringo's plans for their escape

("Then all these years have been for nothing!") reveals Hally as neither an unfaithful wife nor a hapless victim of circumstances. In her home and bed, she is the woman of Paco, but in her mind she has expected that her husband would return and fight the Fuenteses. Spiritually, she is an infiltrator, though an involuntary one.

Behind Hally looms Marisol—another wife associated by force with the leader a Mexican gang. In fact, there is a close armature of their encounters with the hero:

Fistful of Dollars	*Il ritorno di Ringo*
Joe sees Marisol in the small house outside San Miguel.	At the cantina outside Mimbres, Ringo asks Jeremiah Pitt about Hally—without getting any answer.
Joe sees Marisol at a stair in the Rojos' house.	Ringo sees Hally at a stair in the Fuenteses' house (which is really the Brown mansion).
Joe asks Silvanito of Marisol without any real answer.	Pajarito tells Ringo (whom he doesn't recognize) that Hally hasn't been lonely.
Marisol chances upon Joe in the dark storehouse, where he searches for the stolen gold (but is knocked out before she recognizes him).	Hally recognizes Ringo in the dark bedroom (later he pretends to have searched for valuables there).
Marisol's true predicament is revealed to Joe by Silvanito, at his place.	Hally's true predicament is revealed to Ringo by her, at Morning Glory's place.
Marisol is liberated in the small house and leaves with her husband.	Hally is liberated at the church and stays with her husband.

During the exchange of hostages in *Fistful of Dollars*, Marisol's reunion with the Rojos is unexpectedly interrupted by a true reunion with her husband and son in the street, which shows where her heart really is. This puts the guile and gun of Joe on a non-monetary track when he helps Marisol. His spoken motivation for this is vague ("I once knew someone like you and there was no one there to help"), but in terms of thematic roles, we see the voluntary infiltrator liberate someone whom he recognizes as an involuntary infiltrator. Furthermore, similarly to Joe, she presents us with a mystery. We wonder whether Joe will eventually fight the bad guys or just keep on suckering them for money, and we are at first left in the dark about Marisol's true motivation. Does she live with Ramon for passion, for power or just to protect her family? Will she choose Ramon, her family, or perhaps Joe? In terms of this mutuality, the triangle really consists of Joe, her and Ramon.

Likewise, for the hero of *Il ritorno di Ringo*, the story turns on the revelation of his woman as an involuntary infiltrator, as this offers him the possibility of becoming Montgomery Brown again. "Now you have hope, now you fear," Rosita concludes when she sees him the next time. Joe sends Marisol away with her family, while Ringo leaves behind the sheriff and Hally so they can become a family. Montgomery Brown stays, as the family he reunites from separation is his own.

The Male Involuntary Infiltrator

Is there also any involuntary infiltrator in the intervening film *Una pistola per Ringo*? There is a variation on this role in the relation between the gun-toting Dolores—not the leader, but the love of the leader, of a Mexican gang that takes over the Clyde estate—and the major, who is not the female head but the male head of the invaded family. He is not the passive object but the one who actively courts the (female) bandit. And though it is a tactical move at first (like the consent of Marisol and Hally Brown), it turns into real passion, to the dismay of his daughter. The disruption is strongest in *Fistful of Dollars* (wife physically estranged from both husband and small child) and weakest in *Una pistola per Ringo* (father psychically estranged from older daughter).

Thus Major Clyde shoulders not only the thematic role of Silvanito in *Fistful of Dollars* (older character who supports the hero) but also that of Marisol (character mirroring the double-play position of the hero). Similarly to both, he assists the hero in a fight—Marisol warns Joe in the small house, Silvanito shoots Esteban Rojo, who is aiming at Joe from a window, and Clyde supplies Ringo with a dueling pistol.

That Clyde embodies an involuntary infiltrator gives further depth to the affinities in style that exist between him and Ringo, who blends well in the Clyde household, elegantly lightning the cigarette of Dolores in passing, having a razor of finest English steel just like the major, and just like the latter able to sweep his partner off her feet in a Wiener waltz. Also, the absurd contrast between rhetoric and reality in the scene where Major Clyde offers to take the bandit queen to go shopping in Boston—"Everything that a woman could wish for"—is fully comparable to the one in the scene where Ringo, tied and brutally beaten, demands his share raised to 60 percent to help his tormentors escape. Generally, Clyde, the generous host offering the amenities of the house to the band of cutthroats that is killing off the members of his household, walks the fine line between display and reality with almost the same detachment as Ringo does—though the major's attachment to Dolores becomes more dangerously serious than Ringo's flirting with

Ruby. Consequently, Clyde is the only character that Ringo ever expresses any admiration for. This analogy between *Fistful of Dollars* and *Una pistola per Ringo* is so well hidden under a layer of inversions that it takes the related case of *Il ritorno di Ringo* to uncover it.

Involuntary Infiltrators in Other Spaghetti Westerns

Christine in *I giorni della violenza* and Claire in *I crudeli* are respectively abducted or tricked into a group (and thus involuntary infiltrators). They are at some time saved by a hero who loves them and who belongs to the "infiltrated" group, thus illustrating both the assistance sequence and the pattern of non-hero infiltrators.

In neither film is their "infiltration" central to the story. However, the machinations when Christine is to leave behind markings signifying their direction and leaves the wrong mark to protect Johs, but he discovers it and, refusing to believe her, takes the other road, so that the pursuers are led right, make an accomplished narrative sequence of manipulation. It is surpassed as such by the short speech of Claire, as she stands among the killers that have pressed her into their service, *and* their deadly, but unaware, enemies, the U.S. military, in an attempt to free herself of her enforced mission without endangering the life of the man that she loves. That the speech is enhanced in emotional force by music and cinematography makes its impact all the more disturbingly ironic.

In *Al di là della legge*, Cudlip is an involuntary infiltrator, as the offer to become sheriff comes as a surprise (and as it turns out works like a manipulation by Novak).

Debra McGowan in *Mannaja* is taken hostage and so could be called an involuntary infiltrator, though as lover of the instigator she is a party to the act and supports the band against the hero, which would make her a *false involuntary infiltrator*.

An Inverted Infiltrator ...

The first part of *Arizona Colt* — another Giuliano Gemma feature — is very much concerned with infiltration, though in the form of its refusal. Gordo Watch (again Fernando Sancho as a flamboyant Mexican bandit) raids a prison to recruit members to his gang. Double Whisky is left behind, but is saved by one of the former prisoners, Arizona Colt (Gemma), and brings him to Gordo's camp. Gordo ensures the loyalty of his recruits by marking them with a special tattoo that will bring them to the gallows if they are caught. Arizona's response to the offer is "I'll think about it" (the all-purpose catch phrase in this film, as "It's a matter of principle" is in *Una pistola per Ringo*). He breaks out of the camp and Gordo's attempts to bring him into the fold again result only in bandit casualties. Arizona leaves his final decision with some bandit corpses arranged as a "no."

These happenings constitute an almost perfect inversion of Monco's infiltration of Indio's gang in *Few Dollars More*:

For a Few Dollars More	*Arizona Colt*
Monco intentionally springs Sancho Perez (only) from prison.	Gordo's gang unintentionally springs Arizona from prison (together with a lot of others).
Sancho Perez takes Monco to Indio.	Double Whisky takes Arizona to Gordo (this takes place after the action below).
Indio welcomes Sancho Perez.	Gordo leaves Double Whisky behind.
Indio and his men are suspicious about Monco and ask him why he has come.	Gordo suggests that Arizona joins his gang.
Monco gains entrance by telling the truth masked as a joke.	Arizona refuses entrance, masked as a postponement.
Monco kills some bandits that voluntarily bring him away from the gang (for a raid).	Arizona kills several bandits that want to bring him involuntarily into the gang.

Arizona's refusal might also be seen in the light that the tattoo procedure will make joining the band irreversible, and thus is the opposite of the double play and easy crossover between opposing partners typical of an infiltrator.

Double Whisky also repeats the role of Silvanito, as he takes up arms against Gordo (at the end) and then is supported by Arizona.

... and a Female Hero Double

In *Arizona Colt* Jane is in many ways an equal of the hero. She is the only other character allowed to use his "I'll think about it" catch phrase. When bullets start flying during a robbery, they are the only two in the saloon to keep their cool. When he and Double Whisky stay in the church, she is the only one to find out where they are. Jane and Arizona Colt are different in motivation though, as he is a mercenary and she is a vengeance hero, out to avenge her sister. Arizona demands $5,000 to bring in the killer of her sister, but accepts the $500 available if it includes a night with her.

Jane otherwise represents "good" social values, but she is willing to trade honor for revenge (somewhat similarly to Hally Brown). She becomes Arizona's employer, because just like the sheriff in *Una pistola per Ringo*—though for different reasons—she is unable to take care of things herself.

Female Equivalents

The female characters discussed in this section in one way or another take equivalent positions to the hero as regards some plot functions and narrative sequences. This is contrary to the classical American Western, where according to Wright (and others), women are fully inscribed into society, another part of the constellation, and thus are differently coded from the heroes along the central dimensions of meaning—except for the important convergence that they are both good and nice.

Transformations of Plots

Il ritorno di Ringo Armatures

Il ritorno di Ringo also shares with *Una pistola per Ringo* the ethnic and spatial code of an Anglo town "led" by a sheriff and a Mexican gang that (sooner or later) is besieged in a ranch outside. Anglo society is weaker though. There is no strong sheriff to stamp a posse out of the ground to attack the bandit ranch. The Barnes sons, young look-alikes of the *Una pistola per Ringo* sheriff, are eliminated early in the story by the Fuenteses. Instead society is shattered and dominated by the bandits, and the forming of a posse is something the hero must work hard for.

On the other hand, *Fistful of Dollars* and *Il ritorno di Ringo* share an infrastructure of situations that is not present in the *Fistful of Dollars/Una pistola per Ringo* armature:

- The hero enters the town riding on a mule in Mexican garb, and he immediately sees a corpse/a killing (of Judge Barnes in the Tessari film).
- With Morning Glory, the familiar figure of the comical gravedigger Piripero reappears in *Il ritorno di Ringo*.
- Like Joe, the hero lodges in an intermediate place in town, by Morning Glory, or outside of town to recover (by Jeremiah Pitt).
- Joe has his hand trampled during the torture. Ringo has his stabbed by Paco, and later he pays back by shooting him several times in

the arms. (This damaging of the extremities would escalate still further in *Django*.)
- Both films feature the "mystic" reappearance of the hero, like a ghost returning from the dead at a place where his enemies are gathered: In *Fistful of Dollars*, Joe appears in his poncho at the backdrop of the smoke and thunder of explosions. In *Il ritorno di Ringo* at the church, Ringo is dressed in his army uniform, at the backdrop of windblown sand.

Also, like Angel Face and (still more obviously) Joe, Montgomery appears as a mediator, but unlike other Mexicans in Mimbres, he doesn't wear a gun and doesn't join the Fuenteses.

Like in *Una pistola per Ringo*, the hero deals with the situations with methods of deviousness and guile. In the beginning he disguises himself, taking on the role of Mexican to protect his identity. For the same reason he later takes on the role of a thief (in his own house) to be able to explain away his presence (in the quarters of his own wife) and submits to punishment. He is also an observer, at the confrontation between the Fuenteses and the Barnes brothers. Later he shows detachment even to the extent of not using his own concealed gun when Sancho aims to kill him.

Il ritorno di Ringo Non-Armature

Though the hero's disguise as a Mexican is an act of infiltration, the ensuing development of *Il ritorno di Ringo* does not adhere to the functions in the infiltrator plot. For example, Montgomery Brown does not hire himself out as a pistolero to the Fuenteses (or as a deputy to the sheriff) in order to use both sides as means to his own ends. Also, he never shifts loyalties— or plays at shifting them — like Joe and Angel Face. His disguises, stratagems, and irony are always directed against the Mexicans.

Unlike Ringo/Angel Face, Ringo/Montgomery Brown is not a money-oriented character. The invasion of the Fuenteses has deprived him of everything — his father, his home and his wife. Paco Fuentes proceeds to literally bury him (using another corpse) and then presses to marry his wife, and so totally annihilate his social identity. The disguise that he takes on, as a nobody of unsure ethnic identity ("Gringo, Indian, Mexican, or perhaps your mother doesn't know," as Esteban chides him), is in fact all that is left for him, and it threatens to be permanent. It is significant that when the coffin with the false Ringo arrives in town, the true Ringo awakes in another coffin (at Morning Glory's). Rosita says that in a way he does not even exist, with no future and consequently no fear. She also adds, "I don't think I like bravery like that."

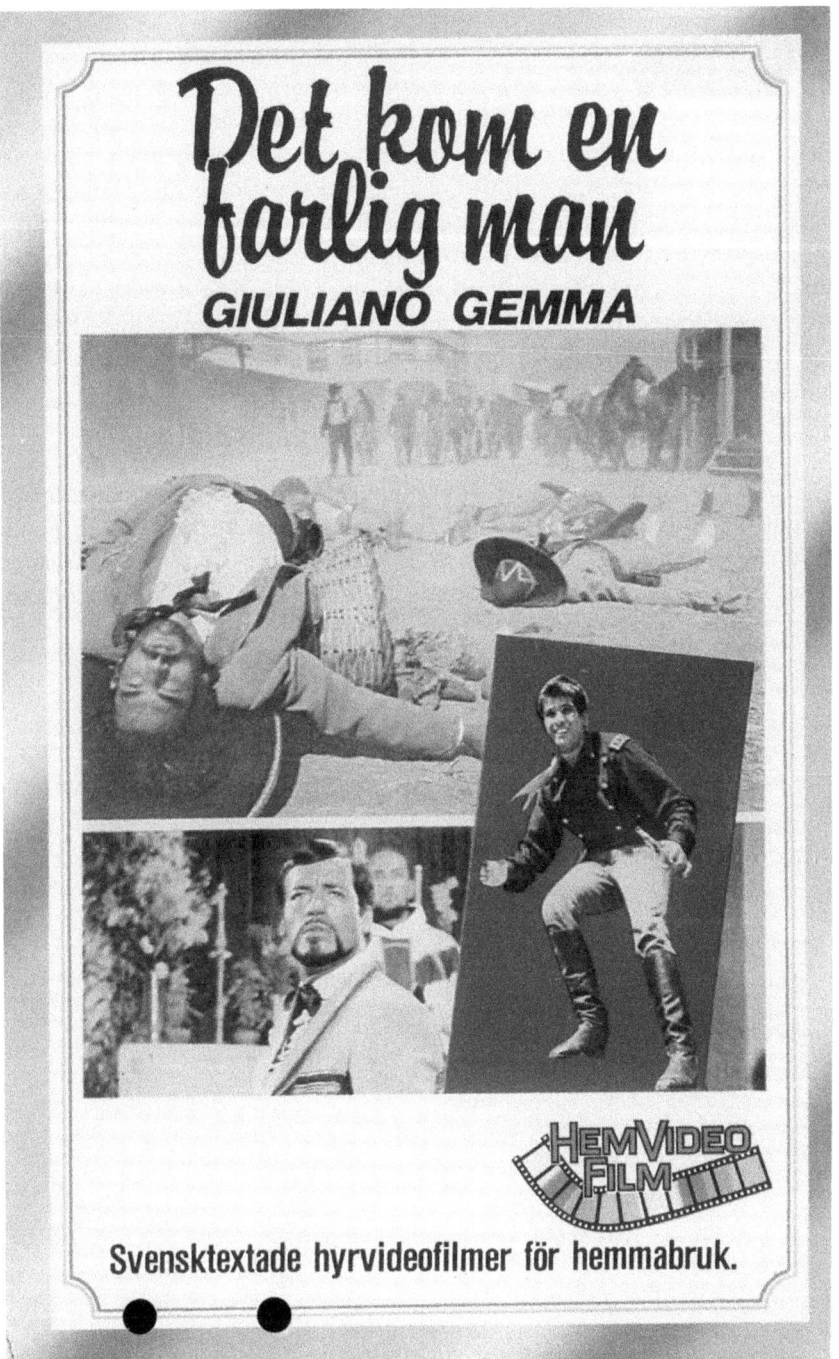

Il ritorno di Ringo: video sleeve featuring George Martin as Paco Fuentes, bottom left, and Giuliano Gemma as Ringo, bottom right.

Montgomery Brown is thus a victimized hero in a much more urgent way than Angel Face, whose concern is to earn the money and stay alive — that, under the circumstances, is no mean feat! Still, his whole identity is not on the line. One sign of the urgency of the situation is that while Angel Face never loses his cool in the complicated and deadly game that he is playing, Brown does—when he is drinking after seeing his daughter for the first time, and spurns Rosita, thus provoking a fight. The stories of Joe and Angle Face do also include restoration — Marisol to her family and Hally to her fiancé the sheriff—*by* the hero but not *of* himself.

Transformation System of *Il ritorno di Ringo*

The preceding discussion shows that *Il ritorno di Ringo* cannot easily be positioned on any linear transformation between *Fistful of Dollars* and *Una pistola per Ringo*, because two different aspects of *Fistful of Dollars* dominate each of the two Ringo films— the maneuvers of the infiltrator and the tragedy of a disrupted family.

Table 2E. Main motifs in the Ringo films compared to *A Fistful of Dollars*

A Fistful of Dollars	*Una pistola per Ringo*	*Il ritorno di Ringo*
Money orientation of hero	Somewhat stronger (the haggling with percentages recurs through the entire story).	None.
Infiltrator maneuvering two sides against each other	Somewhat weaker version (only pretended, as he stays committed to one side).	None.
Disrupted family (mother separated by villain from son and father who is not the hero)	Weaker (fiancée separated by villain from fiancé, who is not the hero).	Stronger (mother/child separated by villain from husband/father who is the hero).

I would say that this relative prevalence in *Il ritorno di Ringo* of the more "serious" theme of family disruption over the core infiltrator themes, mainly concerning irony and cunning, is emphasized by some scenes with mirrors, closures and dark spaces, such as the ones captain Brown must traverse before at last meeting his love in the dark of the bedroom that is now the realm of another man. Later, his change of heart after his talk with Hally is illustrated by framing his walk with openings and colored windows.

Earlier, he viewed himself in a mirror in the ceiling in the room of Rosita. These scenes are more visually emphasized than comparable scenes that might be sifted out from *Fistful of Dollars*—when Joe searches the warehouse in the dark looking for a (money) secret, encountering Marisol—or from *Una pistola per Ringo*—when Ruby flees from Pedro in the fields at night, encountering Ringo.

Moments of the Pathetic and Moments of the Ironic

There are certain moments in Leone's *Fistful of Dollars* when visuals and the soundtrack further enhance emotionally engaging content in a very elaborate way, expressing the mode of the *pathetic*, in its sense of emotionally touching, impassioned and suffering. The moments of the pathetic in *Fistful of Dollars* occur in the following contexts:

- The exchange of hostages, which exposes the situation of the disrupted family.
- The excessive beating and torture of the hero by the villains.
- The appearance of the hero, believed to be dead.

Though *Una pistola per Ringo* is not without displays of visuals and music, none of its scenes really expresses the mode of the pathetic. On the other hand, the pathetic commands a large space in *Il ritorno di Ringo*, where the hero is a part of the disrupted family.

Coexisting with the pathetic mode in *Fistful of Dollars* is the mode of the *ironic*, the play of pretense, the contrast of the cloak and what it hides. This mode dominates the proceedings in *Una pistola per Ringo* and also has great significance in *Il ritorno di Ringo*, especially relating to the demeanor of the hero, his recurring sayings, etc. The hero flaunts similar traits in *Arizona Colt*, particularly in a scene where Gordo's men empty their guns into a doll made of his clothes, and then are all shot except Kay, because he has the best clothes to replace Arizona's own perforated ones!

The Return from the Dead

Two of the central moments of the pathetic in *Fistful of Dollars* were to become standard motifs in subsequent spaghetti Westerns—the torture of the hero, usually after his double play has been revealed, and his "return from the dead." In effect, the "awakening" of the dead hero can be seen as model two of the same plot (or narrative sequence) as his exposure, the main difference being that the second time it is the hero who calls the shots:

Exposure of the hero	*Return of the "dead" hero*
The hero has a secret.	The hero is believed to be dead.
The hero is exposed/surprised by the villain.	The hero reveals himself to/surprises the villain.
The hero is punished/beaten or maimed.	The villain is punished/killed.

Normally, these two models are consecutive in time. However, just like observation can take place without manipulation, the presumed death sequence can take place on its own, as in *Wanted*, where the hero pretends to be dead to escape an ambush in the beginning of the film. The same logic of this exposing/punishment/return cycle works behind that memorable scene of absurd humor in *Una pistola per Ringo*, where Ringo, bound and beaten after his double play has been exposed by Sancho's change of signal from the mill (the hero is exposed/surprised by the villain), offers to take advantage of his alleged deal with the sheriff to help the bandits escape if he gets a bigger cut of the loot (the hero reveals himself to/surprises the villain). Sancho almost throws a fit before the audacious bargaining of his fettered and bruised prisoner, before giving in (the villain is punished).

CHAPTER 3

The Code of Cunning

The use of cunning and deceit, as a metacode negotiating the difference between surface and substance, is highly significant for the stories of most spaghetti Westerns. In table 3A I summarize its main forms, ordered according to the following criteria:

1. Whether they are *tactics* used in fights, or long-term *strategies*. *Trap* might belong to either perspective, and *caper* comprises both.

2. Whether they typically are executed by the villain, always from a position of power (from above), or by the hero, who will be outnumbered or otherwise disadvantaged (from below), with those equally employed by both in the middle.

Infiltration and *manipulation* have been described above as narrative sequences in the infiltration plot. They are especially elaborate cases of *double cross*, the breaking of an agreement.

Plays of Identity

Angel Face at first pretends to be an escaped horse thief, Montgomery Brown appears as a Mexican, Siringo and Gary O'Hara as outlaws, and Stuart in *Sette winchester per un massacro* as a former Southern officer. Infiltrators often employ such a relatively long-term usage of *false identity*. I distinguish it from short term, tactical *disguise*, as when Fletcher and his outlaw woman Maria dress up as bourgeois customers to rob a bank.

I have already touched on the inclination of the Italowestern hero to become *presumed dead*—either as a moment in his own scheme or when he is left for dead but survives to come back for retribution. Joe is smuggled out of town in a coffin (a metonymical death). The false deaths of the hero in *Bandidos*—reportedly killed by himself!—of Bennet at the end of

Table 3A. The Use of Cunning in Spaghetti Westerns

	Strategic	*Tactical*
From "below"	Infiltration	Surprising tricks
(Hero)	Presumed death	Supervised duel
	Enigmatic	Make-believe duel
	Unpredictable	Sneak fight
	Observer	Special duel
	False identity	Temporary disguise
	Manipulation	
	Double cross	
	Unequal battle	Trap
		Caper
		Hidden weapon
		Ambush
		"Stacked-deck" duel
From "above"	Conspiracy	Provocation
(Villain)	Usurpation	False quarter

Faccia a faccia, and of California (Gambler: "Oh, by the way, California, I heard you fought in the war"; California: "Yes, and I died"), respectively, provide them an opportunity to start a new life. However, in *Il ritorno di Ringo* it is the villains who present a coffin presumably containing the dead hero. Clyde Hamilton in *Quella sporca storia nel west* claims that his brother has stolen government money and then been murdered by the bandit Santana, whom Clyde in his turn has killed. In reality, Santana is in hiding, and Clyde is the real murderer.[1] His nephew Johnny (called Hamlet in the alternate film title) accuses him, saying that for $300.000 dollars he has buried the living and slandered the dead!

Enigma is underlined by the personal style of many heroes. The primal example is Joe in *Fistful of Dollars* (and his follow-up Monco in *Few Dollars More*). He uses a covering poncho and hat as an outer analogy to his hidden intentions. Likewise, his reluctance to show his mind to the world is pantomimed by the wait his interlocutor must abide while he lights, or at least inhales and exhales smoke from his cigar, before producing an answer. This coverage is not only a question of style. It has a decisive tactical value when the poncho covers the iron shield over his heart toward which he directs the fire from Ramon's rifle, with his hoarse voice taunting, "The heart,

Ramon, don't forget the heart. Aim for the heart Ramon, or you'll never stop me." On the other hand, the hero of *Una pistola per Ringo* manages to be enigmatic without any outer trappings. In spite of his easygoing demeanor, Ringo's actions are indirect and devious, bewildering Ruby, Sancho *and* the spectator, who can never be sure of what he really is up to. His contrast is the sheriff, whose actions always mirror his intentions.

Unpredictability is another attribute that keep opponents (and audiences) on their toes. Again Joe is the role model. He almost consistently acts against all advice and directives that he is given. He does *not* leave San Miguel as Silvanito suggests, he does *not* forget about Marisol as Chico and Silvanito warn him, and he does *not* live with the Rojos as Miguel says. This continues all the way to the ending, where he does not attempt to manipulate the American and Mexican government as Silvanito hints. Also, in the concluding duel it is precisely Ramon's predictability (always shooting at the heart) that defeats him.

The Italowestern hero often is satisfied with an *observing stance* in situations where a red-blooded American Western hero would immediately intervene to strike a blow for what is good and right.[2] Generally, observation has a strategic rationale (to gather information for future action), as well as a stylistic one (underlining the detachment and unpredictability of the hero). Most annoying to the spectator's expectations is probably the hero of *Django*, who watches how the Mexicans tie up Maria and whip her and then watches how they are killed by Jackson men, who start to prepare for her burning before he finally intervenes.

A Plethora of Duels

In *Few Dollars More* we encounter a *supervised duel* as a special case of observation. Mortimer faces Indio at an impossible disadvantage as his revolver is lying on the ground, making it an example of a "stacked-deck" duel (see the third paragraph in this section). However, when the chimes from Indio's watch fade to signal the time to draw, the tune is picked up again from another watch held by Monco, who suddenly stands there with rifle in hand. Instead of disarming or shooting Indio, Monco hands his gun to Mortimer and then sits down and starts the tune again to observe them draw against each other on equal terms. This is not a case of true manipulation, as he sets up the two men to fight each other of their own will and not for his personal gain. In the three-way reckoning in the next Leone film, *The Good, the Bad and the Ugly*, Blondie *is* a manipulator as well as a combatant, with information that gives him an advantage. Only he knows that one of the others has an empty gun. Furthermore, they duel over a gem of information, a stone where Blondie supposedly has carved the name on the cross over a grave containing the gold — but it would be useless to the others as the cross in question actually carries no name.

The supervised duel appears in several other films. In *Il mercenario* Kowalski supervises a duel in a bull-fighting arena between his enemy Curly (dressed in black suit with a white carnation) and his partner cum adversary, Paco (dressed as a clown). An outrageous example is *Scalps!* where Matt is wounded and terribly weakened after being dragged by horse with hooks fastened to his chest.[3] His Indian partner/lover, Jarrin, "equalizes" the duel by shooting two arrows straight into the chest of his opponent Connors, and then watches as they try to find the strength to raise their guns against each other!

The *stacked-deck duel* is a tactical distillate of *provocation*, denoting a weaker party enticed to a confrontation that he cannot win.[4] It is often employed by mentally unbalanced characters such as Indio (against a man that betrayed him to the authorities), big boss Cobb in *Vendetta* (against two runaway slaves), and Adam Saxon in *Il grande duello* (against an old sidekick type). In *W Django!* gang leader O'Connor kills the husband of his mistress in a duel after giving him an empty gun. The founding instance of the *special duel* is the final reckoning in *Fistful of Dollars*, where Joe and Ramon stand with empty revolver and rifle, each with one bullet on the ground, and must be the first to load and shoot. Joe deliberately shoots his last bullet in the air to create the precondition for the duel. In *La resa dei conti* and *Corri, uomo, corri* Cuchillo duels with a throwing knife against a revolver. In the former film follows a confrontation between Corbett, with a gun tucked in his trousers, and the dueling specialist von Schulinberg, who has a specially designed holster for quick draw (this also qualifies as an unequal battle). In *Sartana* there is another loading duel between Sartana and Lasky where both parties "stack the deck" by having bullets left in their weapons.

A remarkable instance is the protracted duel in *El Desperado* between Steve and Asher that takes place in the same deserted town where Asher and his men earlier committed the murder and rape that Steve is out to avenge. Steve takes Asher's empty revolver and puts in one bullet. Then the bandit is handed Steve's gun. When Steve walks away Asher pulls the trigger twice, and the gun clicks. Then Steve strikes him down on the street and kicks mud in his face. He walks around Asher and ducks while the blinded malefactor tries to shoot him with his remaining, real, bullets until Steve kills him with his only shot. In *Fistful of Dollars*, Joe's walk-down, which precedes the seminal special duel, is also a variant of it, with Ramon's superior rifle range against the hero's hidden armor (an inverted weapon).

In a *make-believe duel* two parties are poised to draw, but then suddenly turn to gun down some third party, (usually) hiding to kill them both. This happens in the early *All'ombra di una colt*— otherwise a traditional "gunfighter story" with no cunning tricks. Steve Blain is confronted by Buchanan, Blain's former tutor of gunplay and now brought by town bosses to kill him. Their old friendship prevails and together they turn their guns on the bosses and their men hiding in ambush to better Buchanan's odds. This became a common practice, and after executing the second one in *Testa t'ammazzo ... croce sei morto ... mi chiamano Allelujah!*, the hero self-consciously reflects: "A bad habit, these make-believe shootouts." In *Un dollaro bucato* the infiltrator Gary is supposed to shoot it out with a traitor who has betrayed the gang, but as the two are in cahoots, they both turn their weapons against the watching gang. However, their weapons turn out to be empty, because the duel is a trap. The ill-matched brothers Ted and Monty in *Vivi, o preferibilimente morti* are about to shoot it out over who is to marry the beautiful (but overbearing) Scarlett. In this parodical inversion Scarlett is the "villain" causing them to fight, but instead of attacking her together, they run off and thus escape her together!

The following table of transformations relates different kinds of duels described in this chapter. A and B represent combatants of a duel and C a third party; "+" and "-" represent "hero" and "opponent," respectively.

Category of cunning	A	B	C
Standard duel	+	-	None
Supervised duel	+	-	+
Make-believe duel	+	+	-
Observation	-/+	-	+

Cunning Tactics

Traps are set both by heroes and villains. The double play of Joe is exposed by coincidence, but Angel Face is disclosed when the men of the posse send the signal that the bandits are supposed to send from the mill, because, unknown to Ringo, Sancho had changed it.

Ambush can be used by the hero, as in the canyon when Ted Barnett uses a rifle at long range to destroy the men sent by Gomez in *Vendetta*, or when Sabata picks off the Virginian brothers with a long-range rifle after the bank heist in *Ehi amico ... c'è Sabata, hai chiuso!*. However, usually they are set up against the hero and so have scant success, such as when the surviving outlaws aim for Joe and Monco, respectively, in the concluding scenes of the two Leone films, or when the bounty killer waits among the cliffs for Burt Sullivan in *Texas addio*.

False quarter applies to a situation where someone is given a chance to escape, only to be killed anyway by a sadistically inclined villain. The nucleus occurs at the ambush of the soldiers in *Fistful of Dollars*, when Ramon takes his time aiming before dropping a survivor at long range. Major Jackson in *Django* uses running peons for target practice and shows his prowess by letting one Mexican almost reach safety before he shoots him down. The Austrian colonel Skimmer closely repeats this scene in *Indio Black, sai che ti dico ... sei un gran figlio di....* In *El Desperado* and *Arizona Colt* captives are turned loose and shot from behind.

Hidden weapons are produced by heroes and villains alike. Mortimer breaks every Southern code of chivalry when he kills the hunchback Wild with a derringer hidden up his sleeve. Concealed weapons appear in abundance with Mortimer's successors Sabata and Sartana.[5] In *Ehi amico ... c'è Sabata, hai chiuso!* an assassin disguised as a priest has a derringer wrapped in his handkerchief ready for Sabata, but the latter gets the first shot with a gun hidden in a bag and fired by a string. Similarly, the alleged lawyer in *Black Killer* fires guns hidden in books by this method. In *Tequila!* Shoshena produces a gun hidden in a fried chicken when deKoven's strong-arm men come to crash the farmer's party.

There are other *surprising tricks*. In *Preparati la bara!* the hero is to give up his gun but swings it on his finger to shoot the receiving man. Often recurring—as in Monco's introductory episode in *Few Dollars More*—is when a protagonist about to be shot in the back shoots the assassin without turning his head, guided by a reflection in a mirror, or by some unexplained instinct. A guard in *Un dollaro bucato* has his cigarette lit by a suddenly appearing hand, says, "Thanks amigo," and is struck down by a revolver butt. Still bolder, a guard in Corbucci's *Vamos a matar, compañeros* approaches a hand waving to him from an opening. Then the hand becomes a fist and strikes him down.

Spaghetti Westerns contain many *unequal battles*—usually the hero facing opponents superior in numbers and/or weaponry and often using cunning to come out on top. Joe is outnumbered first against the Baxter men and later at the small house, and in the end faces the crack rifleman Ramon Rojo and five others. Ringo goes against Sancho and two other bandits with only one bullet left. In *Django* the hero kills five Jackson men by the bridge, five more in the saloon, extinguishes most of the remaining 48 with a machine gun produced from a coffin, and finally, with his hands crushed, confronts Jackson and five men—also a prime example of a special duel.

Sneak fight denotes that adversaries use facilities of the locale for cover to get an advantage, hiding oneself and/or trapping the enemy and tricking him into exposing himself, rather than facing it off in the open. A choice example is the fight at Agua Caliente in *Few Dollars More*:

1. Monco and Mortimer load their guns and see groups of men running over the "street" far away at both sides.
2. The bounty hunters advance on each side of the street but are frozen by a cat crossing the street and making a loud noise.
3. The bounty hunters advance as before, and a camera shot from longer range show two bandits standing behind them at a distance. They turn simultaneously and shoot the bandits down.
4. A man behind a curtain of sticks in a shed is shooting at Mortimer, who skulks behind a wall. Then Mortimer runs past a wagon and takes cover again. There are two men in the shed, and one climbs up to the second floor. Mortimer shoots off a rope holding the wagon, and it rolls down and crashes into the shed. The man upstairs falls down on the floor. Mortimer bursts in through a door and shoots the other two.
5. Two bandits are advancing on Monco. He goes inside a house. When they approach, a sound is heard from the door. They position themselves on both sides of the door and slide it open carefully. The back of Monco with the poncho and hat is seen. They smile, rush in and shoot. Joe, sitting in a chair with the back to them, swivels around and shoots them. He then puts on the hat and poncho that he had arranged as a dummy.

Narrow streets and building complexes are typical scenes of sneak fights. Other typical settings are large houses (the country houses in *Una pistola per Ringo* and *Il ritorno di Ringo*, or Scott's ranch in *Tempo di massacro*), barns and stables (where Django kills men of Rod Murdoch and is nearly hung by his brother Luke in *Django il bastardo*) and cliff formations (where Burt Sullivan outsmarts the ambushing bounty killer in *Texas addio*). An undertaker's shed with empty coffins is used in *Arizona Colt* and *Sartana*. These are all environments with limited visibility that offer many possibilities for surprises, traps and flanking maneuvers. Barns and stables also offer easy access to alternate weaponry such as hatchets, pitch forks, axes, whips and even buckets and harnesses. Probably due to the urban predominance, forests are seldom exploited for sneak fights—the most notable exceptions being the green wood where the escaped interns from the asylum kill the pursuing bounty hunters in *Ciak Mull*, and the gloomy place were Bill Kiowa and his hired companions gradually annihilate the band of Elfego Baca in *Oggi a me ... domani a te*.

A pitched variation on this motif is when a hero with afflicted eyesight overcomes his enemies in a dark space, such as the nightly fight between the blind Clay and Fox's men in *Minnesota Clay*, or when the temporarily blinded hero of *Mannaja* kills his pursuers in the tunnels of a mine.

Monetero (Gilbert Roland) and Clayton (Edd Byrnes) in sneak-fight environment in *Vado, l'ammazzo e torno*.

Villains' Versions

Conspiracy is usually administered by a villain against a hero, as when mayor Gold in *Wanted* arranges a murder and a false testimony to implicate the new sheriff Gary Ryan to stop his investigations about Gold's rustling ring. *Usurpation* is a common feature in films answering to the "prodigal son" constellation/plot.[6]

Capers

This means some action against an almost inaccessible target that requires exact coordination between several cooperating parties. Many Italowesterns transplant the caper from its usual modern, high-tech environments— such as the manipulation of Drake's crooked roulette in the concluding episode of *I quattro dell'Ave Maria*. The attacks on a heavily guarded train in *Un esercito di cinque uomini* and on the union fort in *Amazzali tutti e torna solo* require the bringing together of diverse kinds of expertise. In *Ehi amico ... c'è Sabata, hai chiuso!* a troupe of acrobats, the Virginian brothers, is employed to enter the second floor of a bank guarded by the military. In *La più grande rapina del west* the gang starts a fire as a diversion, while they rob the bank and put the loot into a hollow statue of a saint, after conveniently finding a "parking lot" just outside the bank window! Spaghetti Westerns where the caper encompasses the main story usually conclude with a falling out over the loot, for example *Le due facce del dollaro* and *El más fabuloso golpe del far west*. However, in *Un genio, due compari, un pollo*, such a falling out is just another ruse in an extremely complicated (and tongue-in-cheek) con game.

CHAPTER 4

Intruding into Gringo Territory

Before the Beginning? The Pre-Leone Spaghetti Westerns

A *Fistful of Dollars* is generally regarded as the starting point of Italian innovations to the U.S. Western genre. To test this conventional wisdom, let us consider the story content (and in some instances also elements of form) of some European Westerns produced in the '60s before *Fistful of Dollars*. The titles discussed below account for about 60 percent of the films in question.

U.S.–Spanish Classical Plots

I have already mentioned *The Savage Guns* (1962) as the first non-comedy Western made in Europe after 1960. The story, with a gunfighter helping out a farmer family against a rapacious landlord, is very close to Will Wright's classical plot for the American Western (*Shane*, for example). This is also the case with the American-Spanish coproduction *Gunfighters of Casa Grande*, which had its Spanish release in April 1964, several months before *Fistful of Dollars*. Here, an unknown gunfighter, Wanderer, saves the local society twice, first when fighting, together with the villain Joe Daylight, against the bandit gang of El Rojo, and again later when killing Daylight, who plans to steal the locals' most important property, the cattle.

THE PSYCHOPATH VILLAIN

In these two films, the actor Alex Nicol embodies a remarkable bond with earlier developments in the American Western film, with re-enactments of his psychopath performance in Anthony Mann's *The Man from Laramie* (1955). Referring to the scene where Nicol's character shoots at the hand of the defenseless hero, Dave Kehr comments, "There is something in the extremity of this scene, in its sheer cruelty and arbitrariness, that points its way completely out of the classical Western tradition" and "the next stop is the chaos and absurdity" in the Westerns of Sam Peckinpah and Sergio Leone.[1]

In *The Savage Guns* Nicol plays Danny, top henchman to the landowner Ortega. He runs away after a scrape with the hero Fallon, but returns to murder Ortega and take his place, and to take out his revenge on Fallon — whose hands have been rendered useless! Broken hands would later appear in the genre centerpiece *Django*, with a final confrontation taken still further into "chaos and absurdity," as the hero, with both hands crushed, alone faces six armed enemies in a graveyard.

While Danny is portrayed as a delightfully opportunistic coward, Joe Daylight in *Gunfighters of Casa Grande* is no coward, and his opportunism is of a more strategic kind. He hides the loot that his gang is waiting to divide and instead claims that he has used it to buy a hacienda (actually won at cards), offering each a share. That way he keeps them available for his next scheme. He also tricks the hidalgo ranch owners into gathering all their cattle in one place to protect them from the bandit El Rojo but also in order to steal them himself. At the same time he strikes a bargain with El Rojo, and then, expecting El Rojo to be equally deceitful (which he is), prepares an ambush for the bandits when they attack.

Both the Nicol characters are unpredictable psychopaths, and one can never be sure whether they will react to a situation with benevolence or violence. This trait is also salient with spaghetti Western villains like the ones played by Gian Maria Volontè in Leone's first two Westerns. Consider for example Ramon's orgiastic laughter when he mows down the soldiers with the machine gun, his verbal outbursts after Joe's escape, and the merciless slaughter of the surrendering Baxters. Other examples are Fernando Sancho's sudden changes between joviality and mercilessness as Sancho in *Una pistola per Ringo*, and Tomas Milian's bravura performance as the outlaw José Gomez in *The Bounty Killer*.[2] Also non–Latin actors such as William Berger and especially Klaus Kinski enriched the genre with a brood of mentally unstable blond beasts. These performances might often overshadow those of Nicol, but then they also have a strong support in music and visuals in bringing over their evil characters. Also, there is usually a host of henchmen who also laugh hysterically as they beat, maim and kill their victims. Nicol, on the other hand, is all on his own trying to convey insane evil in a predominantly classical Western environment with standard, restrained visuals. Only at the end of *Gunfighters of Casa Grande*, when the Mexican gang is annihilated in a grand set-piece battle with ambush and explosives, does the visual rendering of the story attain some level of excitement.

In these U.S.–Spanish stories, some faint *Fistful of Dollars* ambiance is also glimpsed behind the classical plot machinations when "good" characters exterminate villains without an equal chance at the draw: for example, when the farmer Summers kills Danny (to save Fallon).

THE ETHNIC CODE

Both stories take place in Mexico, and the Mexican/Latin ethnic element is very much present, though compared with *Fistful of Dollars* and *Una pistola per Ringo*, life south of the border in *Gunfighters of Casa Grande* has a more exotic slant: for example, the frequent appearance of the Mexican hacienda owners, hidalgos, in their gray embroidered jackets. In fact, there are more hidalgos on screen in *Gunfighters of Casa Grande* than in all other European Westerns I have seen put together!

On the other hand, the Mexican thugs look and act just like the henchmen of Ramon and Sancho in *Fistful of Dollars* and *Una pistola per Ringo*, respectively. Especially the appearances of El Rojo and his captain Cabajal are cut and dried for a future line of grisly *bandoleros*. The former is played by Aldo Sanbrell, who was to feature in this type of role in more than 30 Italowesterns.

Spanish Vengeance Variations

In 1963 there were two Westerns released under the direction of the prolific Joaquin L Romero Marchent. The second one, *I tre spietati*, was the most successful Mediterranean Western at the Italian box-office before *Fistful of Dollars*.[3] Another indication that these films were commercially successful is that the Italian distributors used the Italian title of the first one, *I tre implacabile* (*Tres hombres buenos* in Spanish) as a template for the Italian titles of several other Westerns. For one, *I tre spietati* was called *El sabor de venganza* in Spain, and in the following years came a lot of films by Spanish directors, or with a strong Spanish participation, where the Italian titles (quite unlike the Spanish ones) had similar linguistic structures: *I due violenti* (1964, Spanish title *Los rurales de Texas*), *I sette del Texas* (1964 *Carmino del sur/Antes llega la muerte*), *I quattro inesorabili* (1965, *Los cuatro implacables*), *I tre del Colorado* (1965, *Rebeldes del Canada*). Some titles did not use the "tre" signal but picked up other "catch words," for example, *La sfida degli implacabile* (1965, *Pistoleros en Golden Hill/Oeste Nevada Joe*) and *I ranch degli spietati* (1965, *Oklahoma John*). This series of titles in fact constitutes the first "name pattern" used in the Italian Western, soon to be superseded by title templates spawned by later (and bigger) successes such as *Fistful of Dollars* (keyword "dollari") and *Django*.

Plotwise, both *I tre implacabile* and *I tre spietati* concord with Wright's vengeance variation, where the heroes at first are inside society. A wrong is committed, and they must go outside it — even becoming outlaws — to measure out retribution. The culprits are respectable men inside society, a fact that confirms the inability of society to enforce the law.

The brothers Jeff and Chris Clark in *I tre spietati* nicely illustrate Wright's reasoning about the double message concerning revenge in the vengeance variation — that the hero must give up his revenge to rejoin society, but that he at the same time fulfils it by defeating the villains. Chris pursues it (and dies an outlaw), while Jeff gives it up for legal methods (and in all probability will stay inside society, as sheriff). On the other hand, in *I tre implacabile* the avenger Guzman gets his revenge on the men that killed his wife, and he does not rejoin society but leaves it together with two friends.

Il Vendicatore di Kansas City (directed by Augustin Navarro) constitutes a variation on the situation in *I tre spietati*. The sister of gunfighter Frank Dalton is killed in connection with a murder trial, and he arrives in town to find the one who framed her. Dalton at first gives up his revenge by holding back and letting the sheriff conduct an investigation, and later also gets to kill the villain in a duel. This is a whodunit in Western gear, as focus is on the labors of the sheriff in finding the identity of the villain.

These films do have much in common in the coding. For example, guile is the prerogative of the villain, not the hero, and nature is mainly depicted as green, rather than barren. There are instances of *narrative weakness*, leaving the spectator with a sense of unfinished development of the potentials of an introduced plot, motif or character. There are doublings of plot and characters that tend to run on parallel tracks, and even crowd each other. The avenger Guzman is assisted by Silveira, who also investigates another murder instigated by another bad boss. Furthermore, the two unrelated villains on separate occasions employ the same gunfighter (McCoy) for separate attempts to kill Guzman. In the other Marchent film, Jeff and Chris are not allowed any climaxing confrontation. In many instances one gets the feeling that the story is just going through the paces of familiar American Western story elements, marking their presence more than actually investing any effort in development. On the other hand it is hard to find any weakness in the tightly knit stories of *Fistful of Dollars* and *Una pistola per Ringo*. Indeed I have shown how each plot appears in several models to form the totality of the story.[4]

Spanish Ethnics

In *The Savage Guns* and *Gunfighters of Casa Grande*, U.S./British producers and directors tried to paint a Latin environment, even if the main characters (including Wanderer) kept an Anglo appearance regardless of nationality. In the films made by predominantly Spanish personnel, there appears an *inverse exotism*— whether the protagonists are named Clark, Guzman, Silveira or Dalton, they have the looks, dress and argot of Anglos. The same goes for most of the villains and for the representatives of society — in towns named Vientes Cedras and Vera Cruz! Later, I will return to the sole Latin flies in this Gringo soup, the Abrilez/Ramirez characters. Besides, there are several cases of casual ethnicity: Latinos with Anglo looks, and vice versa. Among early, Spanish-directed Westerns, there are two films where ethnic difference effectively influences the course of the story.

Just like in the Marchent stories, society in *Gringo* cannot punish the murderer of the hero's (foster) father — as the culprit, in fact, is the sheriff! The antagonistic brothers in *I tre spietati* are here transformed into Gringo (played by the same actor who plays Jeff, Richard Harrison), who wants to take the case to the law, and his foster sister Lisa, who argues that they will have to find their own justice. This time, developments confirm her point of view.

Racial prejudice against Mexicans is an issue in the story, but it is relegated to some side characters, while the villainous sheriff is interested in the family gold mine. Gringo is raised in a Mexican family, and he returns from fighting in the Mexican revolution, but in dress, speech and demeanor he is squarely Anglo, without any mediating traits. Even with racial prejudice as a theme, the cultural environment in this Spanish Western is predominantly Anglo.

Ethnically based conflict appears as a theme also in the 1965 release *I tre del Colorado*, where French-speaking partisans fight British rule, and especially the powerful Hudson Bay Company. However, the Hudson Bay minions and the rebels act and look pretty much the same, except that the latter have French names and some of them wear long topknot hoods as an alternative to fur caps.

Except for their halfheartedly executed racial themes, *Gringo* and *I tre del Colorado* share most of the other less exciting characteristics of early Spanish-produced Westerns spelled out previously. This concerns especially the latter film with its several examples of weakness in the story, and not least the sight of Ann, daughter of the Hudson Bay boss and future love interest of the hero, being taken by him through the wilderness with immaculate makeup, unruffled coiffure and her long, beautiful dress without a scratch!

Revisiting the Fernando Sancho Character — The Balcazar Version

The only real exceptions to the suppression of Latin ethnicity in the early Spanish Westerns reviewed so far are characters embodied by the actor Fernando Sancho. His Abrilez in *I tre implacabile* is a folkloristic Mexican. He is comic in being superstitious and an energetic womanizer, but he is also a deadly gun, the equal of co-hero Silveira and the one who eliminates the dangerous McCoy. Ramirez in *I tre spietati* is similar in style, but less prominent. Both characters are thoroughly Latin in dress, argot and demeanor and contrast with everyone else in these films.

I have already referred to Sancho as one of the mainstays of the spaghetti Western, appearing typically in parts such as the evil Mexican bandit leader Sancho in *Una pistola per Ringo* (released May 1965). The difference between these threatening figures and the basically "good" characters in his first Westerns for Marchent is spanned in two films that were directed by Alfonso Balcazar, *5000 dollari sull'asso* (released in 1964, two months after *Fistful of Dollars*) and *L'uomo che viene de Canyon City* (released in 1965, five months after *Una pistola per Ringo* but before *Few Dollars More*).

Enter Carrancho — *5000 dollari sull'asso*

The story of *5000 dollari sull'asso* moves along swiftly in a string of confrontation scenes, but beneath this smooth surface two different plots coexist. One is a classical plot, where the gambler Jeff Clayton wins half a ranch and helps the other owners — Helen and her brother David — against the crooked lawyer Dundee and his tame gunfighter Rossen. The other plot concerns Jeff's relations with the Mexican outlaw Carrancho. They save each other's lives, but Carrancho also rides off on Jeff's horse, leaving Jeff with the ranch deed as his only asset. As Jeff gets a non-monetary motivation, saving David from a false accusation, he needs a testimony from the Mexican, and forces his reluctant cooperation for the concluding part of the story. Carrancho, on the other hand, remains firmly money-oriented, and unreliable, but in the final confrontation it is he who saves Helen from Dundee with an expert knife throw, after Jeff has killed Rossen. Before riding off, he presents Jeff with a watch that he has just swiped from the judge.

The Carrancho episodes are in fact models of a plot and constellation quite different from the classical plot, with a couple of "heroes" that sometimes cooperate, albeit with conflicting motivations, against one or several villains, but also often deceive and work against each other.[5] Wright argues that for some films in his study, the existence of classical subplots "in the midst of a vengeance story reveals the essential compatibility of these two narrative structures."[6] However, the two plots in *5000 dollari sull'asso* appear rather incompatible. Instead I would describe them as *interleaved* with each other within the bounds of a single story.

CARRANCHO'S RETURN—*L'UOMO CHE VIENE DE CANYON CITY*

In *L'uomo che viene de Canyon City* Fernando Sancho again reappears as Carrancho—with exactly the same garrulous, cunning, greedy and deadly personality, and similarly coupled with a straight-shooting Anglo partner, this time called Red. The film was released a year after *Fistful of Dollars*, and, following its lead, both "heroes" are motivated by money and also perform infiltrations. There are also more elaborated expressions of violence, such as when Red is mercilessly beaten, or when Carrancho has an enemy spy tied between four horses and promises just to shoot him instead if he'll talk. Carrancho keeps his promise!

As in *5000 dollari sull'asso* the relation of this couple sometimes is *disjunctive* (pulling them apart) and sometimes *conjunctive* (drawing them together). At first, the iron chain holding the two together as they escape prison is an incontestable conjunction that overrides their disjunctive disagreements over their next course of action. When the physical chain is severed, a large sum of money belonging to the mine owner Morgan becomes a golden chain that still keeps them in close contact, first in a hotel room where they fight over a bag that turns out to be empty, then in Morgan's house when they unexpectedly meet at night at his safe. But their conjunctive greed is also disjunctive, as each one wants the loot for himself, and consequently they both lose it, when Red unwittingly gives away the books where Carrancho has concealed the money. However, they joined forces in the preceding fights, and they are still together at the end (conjunction).

In both Balcazar films it is Carrancho who sets the pace for the contending relation—by stealing the horse of his savior in the first film and by the trick of the fake coin to decide the route of the chained couple in the second. In *5000 dollari sull'asso* Carrancho is only part of the story when in Jeff's company. In *L'uomo che viene de Canyon City* his independent story thread is even more important to the final outcome than Red's, partly because the story takes place in a Mexico that—unlike the other Spanish Westerns discussed so far—is really populated by Mexicans, with a clear differentiation in dress and demeanor compared with the Anglos. As the bad guys are all Anglos (except for a Mexican stoolie), the ethnical code is also more central to the story than in the Spanish-American *Savage Guns* and *Gunfighters of Casa Grande*. Furthermore, there is a Mexican revolution subplot—Carrancho appears among forced mine laborers as a general

Italowestern ethnics: The O'Hara brothers Gary (Giuliano Gemma, left) and Philip (Pierre Cressoy), display their shooting skills as Confederate POWs in the introductory scene of *Un dollaro bucato*.

collecting funds that are supposed to be "for the revolution"(!), but, just like Joe, he gets a non-monetary motivation when he sees them killed and brutalized by the boss's men, and very competently starts a rebellion for real, with assistance from Red.

Otherwise, Carrancho is totally immoral and selfish, apart from his not very obligating fondness for his (respective) Gringo companion. He is the character in early spaghetti Westerns who has most in common with Ringo and Joe. Like them — and unlike Abrilez/Ramirez — he is money-oriented and especially in the second film also shows himself to be a master of cunning. He is also unpredictable with an inkling of the grotesque, like the totally unexpected fight in the kitchen where he subdues the Gringo henchman Grieves by using different foodstuffs as weapons, or when he pretends to be blind to rob the gun store, "suddenly" regaining his eyesight and telling the manager that he looks like a pig! And there is always a hearty laugh every time he hits, shoots or cuts someone! Only a few more steps into viciousness, and he would become the deadly Sancho of *Una pistola per Ringo*.

The Early Italians

Massacro al Grande Canyon

The story of Sergio Corbucci's 1963 Western mainly obeys the Wright classical plot, and also conforms to all the less exciting features of the Spanish vengeance variation—for example an all–Anglo environment and an overwhelmingly traditional, "decent" female lead. However, the film at times attempts a less transient visualization of the story. In this respect it points toward the more flamboyant and obtrusive delivery of visuals and also music in the Italowestern films from *Fistful of Dollars* onward.

The most ostentatious example is the ride of the Whitmore host, where the rustle and movement of the riders are efficiently contrasted with the silent rocks and close-ups of the faces of the men waiting in ambush at the pass.

This sequence conveys a different ambience than the typical Leone confrontation scene, even though he also uses close-ups. A post–Leone Corbucci sequence of similar content, the ride of Duncan's gang in the title sequence of *Navajo Joe* from 1966, might serve to highlight the difference. The Whitmore posse advancing at full gallop is shot with a backtracking camera at close (waist) range. The effect is one emphasizing speed and force. The *Navajo Joe* gang is shot most of the time with a backtracking camera, but from a longer range, taking in the whole front of the gang, alternating with shots from straight above, both kinds of shots emphasizing elaborate, calculated and deliberate power. Aside from camera position, several other facts contribute to impress this on the viewer:

- The diversity — the group displays a virtual anthology of different kinds of dress, as opposed to the uniform cowboy dress of the Whitmores.
- An impressive main theme of the film — by Morricone — plays during this sequence (music is absent in the *Massacro al Grande Canyon* episode).
- The complexity of context: In *Massacro al Grande Canyon* Whitmore has been cued to the audience as being more "good" than his adversaries, the Dancer family. In *Navajo Joe* we have just seen this colorful and powerful bunch raid and massacre defenseless women and children, and the scalps that they are carrying remind us.

The deliberate pacing of the *Navajo Joe* sequence recalls the narrative methods of Leone, such as the slow advance of Joe against Ramon's expert rifle fire in the final shootout scene in *Fistful of Dollars*. *Massacro al Grande Canyon* comes closer to the Leone style in the scene where Clay Dancer is to be hung because his family has broken the truce for which he is a hostage. For a moment, the action is frozen, and we are shown several shots of the people who motionlessly watch the proceedings. There is a correspondence here to one of the stylistic high points in *Fistful of Dollars*, the scene when Marisol is exchanged for the young Baxter. The latter scene leaves a far stronger impression because it is more protracted, with several actions embedded, and also is supported by highly emotional music, while the Corbucci episode is cut short by the arrival of the hero.

However, both scenes carry a sense of moral ambiguity. Clay is good, and the ones who take part in his hanging, Ollie and the townspeople, are also basically good. Consequently, one good party is about to lynch another. In *Fistful of Dollars*, inversely, both parties in the exchange are bad, and the hero stands aside watching, though we know that he is the one who has orchestrated the whole thing. Ambiguity shows when the Baxter son is hugged by his mother and then immediately slapped — probably because he has allowed himself to be caught! Inversely, the bandit mistress Marisol is suddenly exposed as loving mother and wife, as her child runs to her in the street and her husband follows.

Le pistole non discutono

With an impressive disregard for the biographies of famous Western personalities, this story has the brothers Billy and George Clanton rob the town bank during the wedding of Sheriff Pat Garret. They skip back to their Mexican base, where they are surprised and subdued by Pat, who decides to bring back his prisoners through the desert to avoid the Mexican authorities. During the trek Billy escapes but is killed by the gang of Santiero, who stalks the party for the sake of the loot. They seek refuge with the young ranch owner Agnes north of the border. George escapes but returns with cavalry, and the bandits are routed. Pat tells the army officer that both Clantons have perished in the desert, and George stays with Agnes. As far as this is the story of George, it reads like a classic plot variation of a young outsider integrating into society under the tutorship of an older hero. It should be noted that this gradual conjunction starts with a habitation similar to the one of Joe—in a posada in Mexico—and concludes in the safe haven of a U.S. family home.

However, just as in *5000 dollari sull'asso* there are functions of another plot interleaved in this story, describing a battle of wits over the possession of money among Pat, Billy and Santiero. All three are cunning strategists like Joe, Ramon and Ringo. The main difference is that — using the terms of Wright — Pat is good (in the sense of commitment to social values) as well as nice, rather than money-oriented and sarcastic, like the later heroes.

Also, I cannot desist from remarking that the actor José Manuel Martin, in between getting killed as the captain of Ortega in *The Savage Guns* and getting killed as Sancho's rapist second man Pedro in *Una pistola per Ringo*, also plays the captain of Santiero in *Le pistole non discutono* — and guess what happens to him!

Early Warnings?

CONSTELLATION/PLOT

Fistful of Dollars introduces the distinct infiltrator constellation/plot, while the earlier films can be ranged into traditional Wrightian plots, mostly classic ones (the Spanish-American) or vengeance variations (most of the Spanish dominated). *Le pistole non discutono* comes closest to the *Fistful of Dollars* plot with the three-way scheming that directs the middle part of the film, but its story still contains a hero committed to values of law and order rather than personal gain. The money-motivated contending couple in *L'uomo che viene de Canyon City* did not appear until after Leone's mercenary protagonist in *Fistful of Dollars*. Furthermore, it was not until *Fistful of Dollars* that difference along the ethnic code was made central, in the sense of differentiating the main poles of the constellation, and also by making the hero a mediator in this code. Partly, the Carrancho films and *Le pistole non discutono* show that these innovations were somewhat "in the air," though.

VISUALS AND SOUNDTRACK

As for visuals and soundtrack, notice that among the pre–*Fistful of Dollars* films discussed in this chapter, it is the two with Italian directors that come closest to *Fistful of Dollars*—*Massacro al Grande Canyon* in attempts at less transparent visual delivery and *Le pistole non discutono* in the area of music.

In fact, it was not in *Fistful of Dollars* but with the incidental music of *Le pistole non discutono* that Ennio Morricone introduced the innovative musical style that was to be one of the most characteristic parts of the typical Spaghetti Western.[7] However, in the preceding year the composer employed a different style, as exemplified by the theme song for *Gringo*— using a driving rhythm and an aggressive male tenor voice with overassertive lyrics: "Be the first one to fire/Every man is a liar," and so on. There is a similar theme song in *Massacro al Grande Canyon*. Both these songs are different both from the later "Morricone" style and, for that matter, from the folkloristic style that we recognize from American Western music (or the folkloristic Mexican music appearing in *Il vendicatore di Kansas City*). They do represent attempts in the direction of force and assertiveness that are largely congruent with the visual delivery in the *Massacro al Grande Canyon* sequence discussed earlier, obeying aesthetic principles other than the deliberate, ironic and ambiguous ambience that Leone and Morricone established as the ruling stylistic paradigm with *Fistful of Dollars*.[8]

MOTIFS BEFORE TIME

Earlier films contained several motifs that at the outset of my investigation I regarded as innovations by Leone (at least with respect to the spaghetti Western):

The musical watch, used as a dramatic token in *Few Dollars More* and ad nauseum in later spaghetti Westerns (See chapter 6), does appear in similar, though less powerful and elaborate, roles already in *Il vendicatore di Kansas City* and (as a music box) in *L'uomo che viene de Canyon City*, as well as in the somewhat lame-brained vengeance story *Le maledette pistole di Dallas*—where the bad guys shoot up the town and then burst into song—released in December 1964.

In the same Leone film there is an episode when future allies Joe and Mortimer shoot at each other's hats. Similar *ersatz duels* appear twice in *I tre implacabile* (between Abrilez and McCoy and, immediately afterwards, a friendlier one with Abrilez and Silveira). In *5000 dollari sull'asso* Rossen uses a whip to shove Jeff's hat down the street. Again Leone's version comes off as more impressive, described with a series of different angles and frames, and with relativizing comments from Mexican street urchins watching.

- The motif of the trek through a merciless desert that is the fate of Blondie in *The Good, the Bad and the Ugly* is no Leone innovation in the Italowestern context. In *The Savage Guns* Fallon exhausts himself wandering through the desert. Chris Clark gets his mortal wound there, as does Billy Clanton.
- In the succession of eccentric undertakers in spaghetti Westerns, Piripero in *Fistful of Dollars* is predated by the part-time undertaker who also sells clothes from the other half of his office in *I tre implacabile*.
- The relations between Mexican and Anglo heroes in the Carrancho films are analogue to some of the "unstable partnership" constellation/plots treated in chapters 6 and 7 and were in fact released before the template partnership story *Few Dollars More*.
- *5000 dollari sull'asso* presents sneak fight situations (both on the rocky slope of a cliff and in a barn) the year before the Agua Caliente sequence of *Few Dollars More*.

- The Mexican rebellion in *L'uomo che viene de Canyon City* appeared one year before Damiano Damiani's *Quién sabé?* presented another Mexican/Gringo couple in a similar situation but answering to a different coding (money-oriented Gringo versus Mexican guerrillero-bandit).[9]

MEN IN BLACK

Regarding the style of the characters, there are a remarkable number not only of villains but also heroes dressed in black. *I tre implacabile* sets the tone with no fewer than *three*—Guzman, Silveira and McCoy. Other black-clad characters include

- Fallon in *The Savage Guns*
- Chris in *I tre spietati*
- Wanderer in *Gunfighters of Casa Grande*
- Billy in *Le pistole non discutono*
- Rossen, who even goes under the name "Jimmy the Black" in *5000 dollari sull'asso*
- Red (hero) and Grieves (villain) in *L'uomo che viene de Canyon City*

Villain Mendez (Henry Silva), dressed in all black, fights it out with Horner's men in *Un fiume di dollari*.

In the otherwise humble *Tre dollari di piombo* (released in December 1964), there is an impressive outfit of bad guys almost uniformly dressed in black and all bearded or unshaven. Conversely the villain Danny is mostly dressed in white in *The Savage Guns*.

All-black dress is a very powerful visual sign, often ominous in the American Western tradition. The coldhearted professional gunfighter Wilson in *Shane* is dressed in black. McCoy and Billy might be of the same breed, but this is not the case with the avenger Guzman and his friend Silveira, and certainly not Wanderer, while Chris is a hero/avenger gone bad. Either as a way to portray the hero as not traditionally good or simply as flashing a significant style, I suggest that all-black dress expresses an aspiration in the pre–*Fistful of Dollars* films to somewhat diverge from a traditional American Western hero style.

Also in this area *Fistful of Dollars* presented a whole new paradigm when Joe burst into San Miguel sitting on a donkey with his unshaven look and squinting eyes, wearing a poncho and hat, with a leather vest lined with fur. He condensed the uneasiness of traditional cowboy garb into a fresh and potent style with many possible variations.

The Big Mexican Bandit

The most lasting contribution to the Italowestern genre from the pre–*Fistful of Dollars* days I would say is the big Mexican bandit typically played by Fernando Sancho, but even he needed an injection from the colorful evil of Gian Maria Volontè's Ramon to attain his final form as Sancho in *Una pistola per Ringo*. Santiero in *Le pistole non discutono* is evil and cunning enough but is lacking the loud talk and deceptive joviality.

The Place of the Women

In *The Savage Guns*, the rancher Summer's Mexican wife Franchesa is the one advocating the use of force to stop the villain in spite of her husband's pacifism, and there is an analogue inversion of traditional gender attitudes between the hero and his foster sister in *Gringo*. However, their activities, as well as those of other fighting females in *Gunfighters of Casa Grande*, *I tre del Colorado* and *L'uomo che viene de Canyon City*, are largely secondary to the story resolution, and the same goes for their meeker sisters in the pre–Leone Italowesterns, performing the more conventional tasks of the respectable fiancée of the classic Western hero, which is to complicate his life by misunderstanding his actions, and by being taken hostage by the villain. One exception is the mother in *I tre spietati*, though she is the instigator of a revenge that the story attempts to prove futile. Most congruent to the ambience of the Italowesterns in the wake of Leone is Virginia, the wife of mining boss Morgan in *L'uomo che viene de Canyon City*.

After learning that her husband has murdered her father, she does not immediately confront him, but practices with a gun and then shoots the bastard. Then she tells her father's portrait that he is avenged. Short on screen time, actress Loredana Nusciak gives an eerie quality to this character — almost retarded innocence suddenly awakened to grim reality.

Conclusions

In table 4A I compare important traits of the classical American Western, as analyzed by Wright, with those of the Italowesterns in the wake of *Fistful of Dollars*.

The "early warnings" indicated in the text above notwithstanding, the pre–*Fistful of Dollars* European Westerns discussed in this chapter largely correspond to the left-hand "classical" column. Also, at least compared with the Leone film, they show many instances of weakness in the carrying out of their story. The stories of the pre–Leone Italowesterns reviewed here fit well within the plots used by Wright to explain the most popular U.S. Western films. Thus, conventional wisdom largely holds sway — the innovations divulged with the sudden success of *Fistful of Dollars* did indeed shape the Italowestern.

Looking over the Shoulder — Compromise Strategies

Anti-Armature of *Una pistola per Ringo* and *A Fistful of Dollars*

I have used the common properties, the armature, between the stories of *Una pistola per Ringo* and *Fistful of Dollars* as a starting point to describe the infiltrator constellation/plot. What about the differences between these films?

SADISTIC PLAY

Compared with *Fistful of Dollars,* the Tessari film shows some "additions" that recur in several later spaghetti Westerns. Most remarkable is the "roulette" when a revolver is dropped to randomly kill a hostage, with the bandits making side bets. This kind of sadistic play with defenseless victims would recur, for example in *Django*, where running Mexican peons are used for target practice by Major Jackson, or *Tempo di massacro*, where Junior and his upper-class friends hunt a human "fox" with dogs.

THE WAVERING CONSTELLATION

The most salient difference, however, is to be found between the two constellations, and it moves *Una pistola per Ringo* closer toward the

Table 4A. Significant Properties Discriminating Classical Westerns and Italowesterns

Exemplary Classical Western	*Exemplary Italowestern (e.g., A Fistful of Dollars)*
Classical plot or vengeance variation.	Infiltrator constellation/plot.
Constellation is good/weak society and strong/bad villain with a threatened family closely associated with society.	Two equally bad and (almost) equally strong camps with an independent family threatened by at least one of the camps.
Society is functioning.	Society is desolate and inoperative — there are "only widows and gunfighters ... nobody works any more," Silvanito say.
Hero who believes in the ideals of civilized society, and acts according to them.	Hero who is cynical about the ideals of civilized society and acts (most of the time) to further his own money-oriented interests.
Hero who has an Anglo appearance and an open and direct style, using his strength in a straight and honest way to accomplish his aims.	Hero who has a mixed Anglo-Latin appearance and an ironic and indirect style, using guile and deceit to accomplish his aims.
Society might be led by a strong, good leader, who can be identical with the ideal-directed hero.	One of the camps is led by a bad, corrupt sheriff.
The hero has a special relation to a young man or boy belonging to the family (and society).	The hero has a special relation to an old man who is marginalized in relation to the camps.
Women are marginal to the story, at most as assistants to the men, and fall into the conventional categories of respectable woman or saloon girl.	One or several women are important to the story, do not fully conform to conventional categories and appear as independent agents.
The ethnic environment is predominantly Anglo-Saxon, with Indians being the other important culture, if any.	Anglo-Saxon and Mexican (Latin) are more or less equally important cultural environments.
Folkloristic Western music.	"Morricone"-style music.
Traditional, transparent visuals.	Elaborated, obtrusive visuals.

American Western patterns of Wright's classical plot. Just like in *Fistful of Dollars*, camp 1 is a Mexican band led by a charismatic leader, camp 2 consists of Anglos led by a sheriff, there is a threatened family (the Clydes) and there is a hero maneuvering between the other parties. However, in the *Fistful of Dollars* constellation, both, camp 1 and camp 2 are strong and bad and pose a threat to the family. In *Una pistola per Ringo* both are strong (while the bandits best the townspeople in gunplay during the robbery, they fall for the sheriff's fire, and the posse organized by the sheriff is stronger than the bandits), but camp 2 (the townspeople) is mainly good and an instance of society in the sense of Wright's analysis. The town in *Una pistola per Ringo* has stores, a bank, a sheriff's office, people moving in the streets and also Christmas celebrations. In the village of San Miguel in *Fistful of Dollars*, the deserted streets come to life only when used for negotiations, exchanges of prisoners or gunfights. Society has ceased to exist — "nobody works anymore."

Compared with *Fistful of Dollars* the family is closer to one of the camps (the townspeople) — for example, the sheriff is to marry Holly — but it is far from being the pillar of it. The Clydes differ with respect to their aristocratic lifestyle. Also, the well-mannered cynicism of the major is indeed very far away from the classical plot and its commitments to schools, churches and other "good" values of society that in this story are echoed by the sheriff. Furthermore, the Clyde family is actually brought in danger not only by the bandits, but also by selfish money values of the colonel, who sends for troops to storm their ranch.

As for the hero position, it is in words only that Ringo is equally detached from both camps. Unlike Joe he stays committed to his original deal with the sheriff.

The Devious Hero and the Straight Sheriff (Retake): *Johnny Oro*

There are many similarities between *Una pistola per Ringo* and *Johnny Oro*, directed by Sergio Corbucci and released one year later.

In the first scene of this film, the circumstances of Marisol are invoked as the bandit Perez blackmails a woman to marry him. The bounty killer Ringo arrives and kills the bandit and his brother, which is symmetric to the introductory gunfights in *Una pistola per Ringo* and *Fistful of Dollars* — though inversed in the cultural code, as Mexicans are killed instead of Anglos, and by a Mexican hero.

The scenes in Coldstone City, when Ringo is jailed for five days after killing the next Perez brother and his men, represent a weaker version compared with *Una pistola per Ringo*, where Ringo/Angel Face is jailed on suspicion of murder for killing four Anglos.

When Juanito Perez allies with the Indians and threatens the town unless Ringo is handed over, it is equivalent to the siege in *Una pistola per Ringo*, with a negation of terms, as the bad guys lay siege to the good guys, still with Ringo inside. The relation of Ringo to the inside camp — he is physically separated from them by prison bars, by their choosing — is similar but inverted compared with Angel Face, who is secretly planning to double-cross the bandits and so is mentally separated, by his choosing.

Ringo's nocturnal outing to prepare the water tower with his enemy Gilmore's own explosives is symmetrical to the windmill episode in *Una pistola per Ringo*, where Ringo kills the bandits who have ventured out with him, places dynamite in the canyon and then returns. It is partly an inversion though, because the bad guys are instead venturing into the jail, and it is weaker because he merely imprisons them for a while. Also, Ringo's secret is not exposed like in *Una pistola per Ringo*.

With the exodus of the citizens, Coldstone is turned into another San Miguel, with the town deserted except for the two camps and a saloon owner in between. But this time the saloon owner is bad and not allied with the hero, and consequently he is killed by the Mexican/Indian camp. As in *Fistful of Dollars* the Mexicans besiege the sheriff's (Baxter's) house, only the hero is there too, and while the Rojos triumph with fire and explosives, this time explosives are set off when the hero destroys their counterparts. Moreover, parts of the town are destroyed with them in a pyrotechnical frenzy that trumps not only *Fistful of Dollars*, but also most subsequent spaghetti Westerns. Also it turns out that Johnny — like Joe — is after a hidden booty. Again, like in *Fistful of Dollars*, at the end he leaves it behind (after it has been accidentally exposed).

THE HERO

Johnny Oro has the alternative title *Ringo dalla pistole d'oro*, and its hero is consistently called Ringo both in the English and German versions. For clarity, I will refer to him as Johnny when I compare him to the protagonist of *Una pistola per Ringo*.

Johnny, a half-breed with dark complexion and a thin moustache living among Gringos, is a mediator between Anglo and Latin culture, like the blond and blue-eyed Ringo, who (inversely) is an Anglo living among the Mexicans.

Ringo will not agree to an assignment unless he gets at least 30 percent of the money involved, and Johnny is a bounty killer who won't take on a villain unless there is a reward out for him.

Like Ringo, Johnny uses mirror effects, observing the Perez brothers in a saddle buckle, and using reflections from a cigarette holder to blind Juanito in the final reckoning.

Ringo always pays lip service to the law by killing "in self-defense," and Johnny readily accepts his prison sentence, as the law gives him business.

Like Ringo during the bank robbery, Johnny acts as an observer behind bars. He also proves himself to be a master of guile as he, during the turmoil of the Mexican/Apache assault on the town, coldly sets out to obtain, in a legal way, the cannon where he alone suspects that booty from an earlier robbery is hidden. Also, he foresees Gilmore's attempt to abduct him, and uses it to his own advantage.

Compared with the pungent and laconic Joe, both characters use an open and amiable parlance, carrying sarcastic witticisms (most frequently Ringo, the best one of Johnny being when he explains that his guns are made of gold because his father had told him that gold must be put to work).

THE SHERIFF'S STORY

In *Johnny Oro* the actions of the sheriff command a more substantial part of the story than in the Tessari film. Both lawmen voice harsh criticisms of the hero's money-oriented style, but while attempts at fairness and lawfulness tend to be brushed aside by the developments in *Una pistola per Ringo*—like in the speedy acquittal of Ringo from the murder charge—Bill Norton in Coldstone insists on the matter of principle that Johnny shall serve his five-day sentence, even if it puts the whole town in jeopardy. Another important story element echoing Wright's classical plot, with society at risk and saved from its own weakness by a strong hero, is the appearance of Indians, traditionally seen in Western films as a menace to civilization per se rather than (like the Mexicans) as a variation of it. The fact that the citizens abandon town out of fear of the Indians clearly points out that—like in the classical plot—the existence of society is at stake. Another set of events, that the citizens leave the sheriff behind to fight together with his wife (who previously wanted them to leave for the East), recalls more of Wright's transition theme (e.g., *High Noon*).

THE OLD AND THE YOUNG

Dan, the son of the sheriff, admires Johnny, who shows him his skills with the knife, while earlier the sheriff has declined to teach Dan to shoot until his schoolwork had improved. Later Johnny saves the boy's life, after his father has been wounded. Their relation recalls the friendship between the hero and the farmer's son Joey in the exemplary classical Western *Shane*.

In *Johnny Oro* there is also an old-timer named Matt, who sees to it that he is regularly thrown into jail to get food and lodging. His words set Johnny on the trail of the missing booty, and he also suggests that they become outlaws together. This character recalls Silvanito and Piripero, the old men surrounding Joe in *Fistful of Dollars*. The transformations of the age code between these films follow a certain pattern:

- Shane gives Joey shooting lessons, and in the final confrontation Joey warns Shane of a back-shooter. Shane has no special relation to any old man.
- Johnny shows Dan knife tricks and saves him and his father. Johnny's protection of Matt is in the ironic vein: When he locks Gilmore and his men into his cell, they are warned not to wake up Matt— whom Johnny himself has just knocked unconscious! Matt unwittingly gives important information to Johnny (about the whereabouts of a booty).
- Ringo is shown playing with Mexican children, and later he (inversely) *gets* help from Chico, a young Mexican boy in the Clyde household. Ringo saves the life of Tim, and Tim gives Ringo important information knowingly (about the reward for recovering the money).
- In *Fistful of Dollars*, the hero has no direct relation at all to the boy Jesus, or to his father. Marisol is the only member of the family that he shows any interest in. In the final confrontation, Joe saves Silvanito, and the old man saves Joe from a back-shooter. Before, the gravedigger Piripero saved Joe by smuggling him out in a coffin. Silvanito gives Joe important information knowingly.

The comparison above implies that the American classical plot hero typically is associated with/protects a young man or boy who admires him and learns from him, while the spaghetti Western hero Joe typically is associated with/protects an older man who (grudgingly) admires him and supplies sarcastic world-wise comments. This tendency corresponds to other significant differences between the constellation/plots.

Wright describes society in the classical plot as typically consisting of women and older men. In *Fistful of Dollars* Silvanito and Piripero are outside both the warring factions that have replaced society. In the other two films, Tim and Matt, by way of personal style and/or social position, are marginalized characters in society rather than typical of it.

Furthermore, the verbal comments of these old men, as well as their whole lifestyle, cast a sarcastic light on the ways of their societies (especially in the case of Matt, who breaks the law to receive food and lodging in jail), and in this respect they resemble the hero. It might also be significant that when the hero helps and relates to older men, this will enhance his youthfulness, especially compared with situations where he takes on the role of father figure for a young boy.

The motif of the hero protecting and educating a boy or a young man seems a fitting contribution to a situation where the existence and development of society according to good social values are defended, like in Wright's classical plot. Inversely, if hypocritical self-interest and greed are penetrating society, and this is exploited by a hero for his own self-interest, his association with a disillusioned and marginalized old man seems equally fitting.

The Straight Hero and the Devious Outlaw:
Uno Straniero a Sacramento

Both *Una pistola per Ringo* and *Johnny Oro* display the coexistence between a money-oriented and crafty hero (Ringo/Johnny) and a defender of the law (the sheriff), associated with traditional (screen) Western society—with a greater scope for the latter in *Johnny Oro*. Sergio Bergonzelli's *Uno straniero a Sacramento* shows the same duality but with the "straight" justice-oriented hero in the lead.

During a cattle drive Mike Jordan finds his father and brothers murdered and their herd stolen. He is met with suspicion by the local sheriff and population. Eventually, Mike is able to expose the rancher Barnett as the perpetrator. He is assisted by Liza, Barnett's former sister-in-law, and Chris, a wanted horse thief.

Obviously, Mike is not an infiltrator playing out two culturally different but morally equivalent camps against each other for his personal gain. Instead he tries to find those who murdered his father and brothers, recuperate their cattle and be cleared of murder charges. The story rather conforms to Wright's "vengeance variation" of the classical plot, as Mike has to go outside society to find justice. The two camps that he has to deal with (led by the sheriff and Barnett) are not culturally different. On the contrary, both the sheriff and Barnett sport suits and moustaches, while the other characters—all Anglos—constitute a veritable ocean of clean-shaven Mediterranean extras dressed in cowboy clothes.

THE STRAIGHT HERO

Fitting for the hero in a traditional (U.S.) Western plot, Mike Jordan wears the traditional cowboy outfit, with shirt (sometimes even checkered), jeans and bandanna. Likewise, his demeanor has nothing of the waiting games and deviousness of Joe, Ringo and Johnny. More like the sheriffs in *Una pistola per Ringo* and *Johnny Oro*, his style is direct. In fact, it rather comes out as reckless—like when he invades Barnett's ranch by himself and has to shoot his way out, or when he at gunpoint brings out (what seems to be) the total male population of the town to show his innocence, a plan that backfires and almost costs him his life. Sometimes it crosses over into unintended parody, when Mike grabs people, shakes them and yells questions and shouts, "Talk to me!" or "Answer me!" On the other hand, when talking nicely to Liza, his smile and intonation signal insipid sweetness. Mike, who is able to cry out, "There must be justice!" is indeed far from the cynicism and sarcasm of the infiltrator heroes, even though he occasionally is capable of both irony (when telling a hanging party that he has hung their look-out) and guile.

Mixed with Mike's directness is a dose of ruthlessness. For example, his decision to kidnap Barnett's innocent daughter Rona, or when he buries a man up to the head and waits for thirst to make him talk—actions certainly out of character for Shane or Sheriff Norton!

THE DEVIOUS HELPER

Chris, on the other hand, acts more consistently in the vein of Ringo, et al. At their first meeting Mike saves him from a flogging and subsequent hanging ("He stole the sheriff's horse"). When Mike gets into a fight with three of the hanging party, Chris calmly watches and then takes a horse and gun and rides off. Chris—who is another one of those characters dressed in black—later agrees to help Mike if he gets paid, after a substitute duel when they shoot cigars out of each other's mouths! He twice materializes to save Mike, both times shooting the villains from behind. To spring Mike out of prison, he does not burst in waving a gun like Mike would have done. Instead he steals a doctor's bag and uses his rifle as a blowpipe to shoot a chloroformed piece of cloth close to the nose of the sleeping deputy and then fishes for his keys with a rod. Just like Johnny in Coldstone, Chris stands out as an implant from the Leone/Tessari types of stories in an otherwise predominantly traditional Western.

Coexistence Without Doubling: *Minnesota Clay*

In *Minnesota Clay*, also directed by Sergio Corbucci and released the same year as *Fistful of Dollars*, the hero, Clay—who suffers from an illness that threatens to make him blind—breaks out of prison and returns to his hometown. There, his friend Jonathan has raised his daughter Nancy, who doesn't know that Clay is her father. Clay also recognizes the town sheriff

Fox, a former outlaw, whose men "protect" the town from the bandit Ortiz, but also use their position to exploit the citizens.

The situation in *Minnesota Clay* is close to *Fistful of Dollars*, as the hero enters a conflict between a Mexican and American camp, with an American (Fox) holding the badge, and with both camps just as bad, and threatening society. However, like in *Una pistola per Ringo* and *Johnny Oro*, the town also contains gainfully employed citizens, though they are wavering under contributions. There is also a "family"—Jonathan, Nancy and her young admirer Andy—threatened by both camps. Compared with the Leone film, the Anglo position carries a greater weight. Clay stays with an Anglo, and in the final reckoning he faces Anglos, not Mexicans.

However, Clay never attempts any infiltration, though both sides try to recruit him. The infiltrator motif instead is carried by Estella, the wife of Ortiz and also the lover of Fox. She manages to turn Ortiz and Clay against each other, thereby exposing both. Her motive isn't money but love, and thus more conventionally female. She is independent enough to quickly turn her allegiance to Clay when Fox lets her down, though.

Nancy, the Anglo daughter, is the conventional "respectable schoolmarm," with the typical knack of this character to come bumbling into the scene just in time for the villain to catch her and use her for a shield (an aptitude she shares with Liza in *Uno straniero a Sacramento*).

The circumstances when Clay finally loses his eyesight among the flames of a beleaguered house are largely analogical to the punishment meted out to Joe in *Fistful of Dollars*, and subsequently to a long line of tortured and bruised Italowestern heroes. Also, his plan—to let his daughter fetch the military, and thus cash in Clay's own reward money, and at the same time also stop the fighting and force Fox to witness to his innocence—is cunning enough, though it never materializes. Instead he dies, after killing Fox. Furthermore, Clay does live up to the *Fistful of Dollars* ideal of harsh irony in the scene where he, standing in the middle of grumbling Mexicans, calmly remarks to Ortiz, "I can understand why you are afraid of Fox, general. You are surrounded by a bunch of morons!"[10]

Clay, like Johnny, in the final showdown saves a younger character, a pseudo-son and unknowing daughter (a doubly inversed relation) respectively, while Joe saves an older man who is not a relative. The walk-down in *Johnny Oro* leaves a strong impression, with Johnny advancing against a certain death to save the boy that admires him, but emotion soars still higher when Nancy advances against her blinded father, who is supposed to shoot her, according to Fox's plan. It is the latter who is the real master of schemes in this story, though his last one goes awry. He is also an observer, holding his men back until the time is right to move against Clay.

Unlike the Joe/Johnny/Ringo heroes, Clay isn't money-oriented. He is out to be cleared from a false accusation, even though he is cynical about the law ("*Me*, getting a new hearing!"). He shows no Latin infusions in looks and dress and in several scenes his actions are far from indirect or ironic. He shows unselfish heroics by saving a man he just had a fight with, and male friendship is displayed in the scenes with the prison doctor. His final words to his daughter are sentimental, without any irony.

Clay is mostly a classic Western hero, while the environment he finds himself in is closer to the infiltrator situation of *Fistful of Dollars* than to *Johnny Oro*.

Interleaved *Fistful of Dollars*: *Ringo del Nebraska*

Superficially, the situation in *Ringo del Nebraska* recalls Wright's classical plot (e.g., *Shane*). The rancher Marty Hillman is under attack from the powerful Carter and his partner Felton. The drunken sheriff is unable to help. The stranger Jim, who is good with a gun, appears and agrees to work for Hillman—and arouses the interest of his beautiful wife, Kay. Hillman appears as a typical specimen of society under threat. He looks older than his enemies, and his farmhands offer meager support—one gets killed at the start of the story, another runs away and the third fails to bring the doctor in time to save his life.

However, this classical setup is soon called into question. Even at the outset, we see Hillman beat Kay when she tries to leave him. As the story unfolds, it is revealed that Hillman, Carter, Felton and the father of Kay once belonged to a band of outlaws, and that the conflict really is about hidden loot. The constellation of *Fistful of Dollars,* with several evil camps fighting each other, thus so to speak imposes itself upon a classical plot constellation. The role of the infiltrator never infects the main character, though. Jim from Nebraska does not show any of Joe's unpredictability or virtuoso art of deceit. He faithfully stands by the side of his employer as long as the latter is alive. It is the villain Carter who is the master of deceit. He prepares a trap and manages to get Jim wrongfully accused—even being foul enough to kill Jim's horse in the process! Jim, however, also uses cunning and is, at least metonymically, "presumed dead" when he lies under the shroud of Hillman and eavesdrops on the others. He also leaves without taking the loot, just like Joe does.

Kay, in a way, "transcends" the traditional Western dichotomy of decent girl/saloon girl. In her red hair and generous décolletage she has all the looks of a saloon girl who has been abruptly lifted into the place of a farmer's wife. She does contribute a thick layer of sensuality to life on the range, but the poor fit between style and social role flouts the traditional dichotomy rather than transcending it.

The Frills of *Fistful of Dollars*: *Uccidi o Muori*

This is the story of a notorious gunfighter (in fact called Ringo) who hides from his reputation under another name. He takes work at a farm owned by a beautiful damsel in distress who is threatened by a local boss and his mean sons. In the end he rids the area of these fiends and can live happily with his love, as the sheriff will let it be known that Ringo has been killed. This is a common American Western gunfighter story, though it is filled with some details recognizable from the infiltrator Italowesterns discussed above.

The hero wears a poncho, though only in the first scenes, where he performs as a violin player(!). Later he sports a shirt and vest, and a buckskin jacket in the final scene. Robert Marks as Ringo also goes for the unshaven look of Eastwood's Joe, but he looks too good-natured to really convince. Admittedly, on one occasion he is severely beaten and left buried up to the neck to die. He also prefers cunning tricks to traditional walkdowns—in one case he disappears from the sight of his opponents when a horse-driven haywagon passes, and he then suddenly appears behind them. There is also a special duel, when Ringo puts a bullet each in his and the opponent's guns, then holsters his iron, and draws and shoots when the opponent cocks his gun.

The most significant scene of the film is the opening, though, where the villains pepper the coffin of the heroine's father and she alone stands by it while the other mourners duck for cover. Otherwise the story is more conforming to the American Western in that the sheriff is honest and resourceful and that there is a scene where the hero gives shooting instructions to a young man. Furthermore, the villain is the master of cunning.

Classic Western and Italowestern–Compromise Strategies

In the first part of this chapter I singled out some story features that typically discriminate classical U.S. Westerns, as described by Wright, and the infiltrator constellation/plot present in *Fistful of Dollars* and many other spaghetti Westerns. In the second part, I have discussed some films that in their juxtaposition of characters, motifs and plots represent compromises-dilutions of the new story pattern into the old one.

In *Una Pistola per Ringo*, *Johnny Oro* and *Uno straniero a Sacramento*,

Video sleeve for the English version of *Pochi dollari per Django*, where the hero is in fact called Regan!

an infiltrator-type character is placed in a classic environment and paired with a classical-type hero. The larger role for the classic hero in *Johnny Oro* than in *Una pistola per Ringo* translates to a limited elbow room for typical infiltration story elements, while in *Uno straniero a Sacramento*, where the classical type is the main hero and the Italowestern type is his second, few other traces of *Fistful of Dollars* remain.

Minnesota Clay and *Ringo del Nebraska* use the inverse method of placing a single (more or less) classical hero in an infiltrator environment. *Uccidi o muori* has a classic environment and a hero showing only some very weak infiltrator behavior.

I remarked previously about instances of narrative weakness in the pre–Leone Italo-Spanish Westerns, and they are also to be found in the "compromise" stories. Especially in *Uno straniero a Sacramento*, several issues that influence the story are hinted at but never explained to the spectator, mostly concerning the dark family affairs of the villain Barnett.

Even those two films made by Corbucci, who was to evolve into one of the core directors of the spaghetti Western, are not untouched. There are some minor threads left dangling from the story of *Johnny Oro*. For one, is Johnny's arrival at the scene of the wedding just a coincidence or requested by the unwilling "bride" (who later is killed on this suspicion)? Furthermore, all the characters surrounding the hero—the sheriff, the villain, the "decent" wife, and the "indecent" saloon girl (who gets to sing a song)—pale beside their counterparts in the movie's predecessor *Una pistola per Ringo*. Some spirit resides with the short-lived bride, who throws the wedding ring on the ground and spits on it after the sudden demise of her "bridegroom." This film, as well as *Minnesota Clay*, also features some long riding sections that are weak in the sense of being dramatically unnecessary.

CHAPTER 5

Stories of the Deprived Hero

"Djangoism"

Django— The Movie

The frequent use of the name "Django" in Spaghetti Western titles testifies to the profound influence exercised by Sergio Corbucci's film from 1966.

Django— similarly to Joe — arrives to a desolate town, whose population mainly resides in Nathaniel's brothel, which serves two armed bands that dominate the neighborhood. Major Jackson, who exploits the peons, leads renegade confederates often carrying red hoods and burning crosses, while the band of General Hugo is composed of former revolutionaries escaped from Mexico. The hero, who is dressed partly in Union uniform and dragging a coffin behind him, saves a prostitute — Maria —from being burned at the stake by Jackson men (after she has been whipped by the Mexicans). He proceeds to mow down Jackson's force with a machine gun (kept in the coffin). Using the prostitutes as a cover, Django and Hugo's gang rob Jackson's gold from a Mexican army fort. When Hugo starts a celebration instead of splitting the gold, Django steals it. However, he finds Maria waiting with a rifle, demanding that he take her with him. By accident, the coffin now containing the gold is submerged in quicksand, and Django is saved from the same fate by Maria. She is wounded by the arriving Mexicans, who have horses crush Django's hands for punishment. Hugo and his men are killed in an ambush by the Mexican army and Jackson. Django, who cannot pull the trigger, manages to remove the guard on his revolver, and just when Jackson and his five men arrive, he leans it against the cross on a grave (belonging to a woman who has been killed by Jackson) and thus manages to shoot them.

Django Transformations

Django and the Infiltrator Hero

Django is not a complete infiltrator story, as the hero allies only with Hugo (and it is left open whether his subsequent betrayal is triggered by the latter's unwillingness to share the money or was planned from the outset). In a way, he does manipulate Jackson when he lets him escape so that his money will be made available.

Like Joe, Django has two motives. He eventually sees through his vengeance against Jackson, but for a time he is ready to leave the major alive and start a new life with the latter's money. He uses enigmatic trappings similar to Joe, with covering clothes, and his coffin hides the machine gun as effectively as Joe's poncho conceals his iron shield. Django is also unpredictable, when he at first refrains from helping Maria during the whipping, and then helps her against Jackson's men. He surprisingly "gives her back" to Hugo without fuss, and later unexpectedly chooses a Mexican prostitute instead of her (as part of his plan to steal the money).

The Serious

Django voices opinions that are democratic ("Jackson has no right to consider anyone inferior") and generally humanist ("A woman shouldn't be treated that way"—a reasonable contention as Maria is about to be tied to a cross and burned!). This is different from Joe and Ringo, who both might support the defenseless in action, but verbally keep to sarcasm (like when Joe expresses admiration for Ramon's ingenuity in holding Marisol hostage under threat to kill her child, or Ringo extols the expediency of shooting people in the back). Likewise, Maria says that Django's protection makes her feel like "a real woman." This use of worn-out phrases, since long ridiculous clichés— whether attributable to weak scriptwriting, translation or sophisticated reuse of shopworn phrases for surrealistic effect—contributes to a sense of greater seriousness compared with the preceding Leone films.

If these clichés seem embarrassing for those who want to regard spaghetti Westerns such as *Django* as fresh compared with American conventionalism, they can console themselves that its hero otherwise does not adhere to any "code of the cowboy." He draws and shoots the Jackson men threatening him without warning, and he is ready to disappear with the gold and leave Maria behind. He also retains the harsh manners of Joe, hiding his eyes behind the hat brim, dismissing Nathaniel's questions with "It's none of your business" and those of Jackson's priestly spy by spitting a cork in his face!

The Spectacular

Compared with *Fistful of Dollars* there is a strengthening and overbidding in the realm of the spectacular:

- Where *Fistful of Dollars* shows one massacre on a large scale (the killing of the army troops at the river), *Django* has two: the massacre of Jackson's "army" by Django, and of Hugo and his men by Jackson and the Mexican army. The former is a fight where the hero faces impossible odds, like Joe's showdown with the Rojos, but *Django* supplies a second one, the final showdown at the graveyard.
- The barren nature in *Fistful of Dollars* is still more barren in *Django* with dangerous quicksand and wet mud that leave more manifest and degrading marks on the characters.
- Compared with *Fistful of Dollars*, society in *Django* is even more devastated, and the threatened family is matched by one prostitute, Maria.
- The sadistic streak of the laughing torturers in *Fistful of Dollars*, returning with the roulette of death in *Una pistola per Ringo*, is doubled in *Django*, with a distinction in style of execution between Jackson's aristocratically planned shooting at human targets and burnings on one hand and Hugo's physical cutting of ears and crushing of hands on the other. Furthermore, Jackson is described as insane, and the mentally retarded look of his man Ringo is showcased still more than the similar physiognomy (of the same unbilled actor) as the wanted man killed by Mortimer in *Few Dollars More*.

Furthermore, to underline the enigmatic aspect of a hero by making him drag a coffin is tangible close to the unpractical. To make him bring the coffin while breaking into a room through the ceiling would reasonably bring this "gimmick" over the brink of parody. However, if this is comedy or parody, it is absolutely deadpan, and there is only one situation that directly invites the spectator to laugh—the grotesque fight between the prostitutes in the muddy street. Irony is also thick in the intimate depiction of bordello life, when Nathaniel plays a languishing tune on the violin for his girls, while one drinks, one has a consumptive cough and two peacefully sit winding up wool. However, none of this reflects on the serious and even tragic aura of Django himself. It might be the dead seriousness in conveying impossibly exaggerated actions that gives this movie its strange ambience.

THE TRIUMPH OF THE PATHETIC

Besides their common dismissiveness in dress and argot, Django also resembles Joe in that he is unshaven and dusty, and that the violence he is submitted to leaves terrible marks. Again, *Django* takes it to more extreme forms: Joe is dusty, Django is in contact with mud and all but drowned in quicksand; Joe has his hands trampled on, Django has them crushed. In the concluding confrontation at the graveyard, Django's life is on the line as he grunts and uses his teeth to release the trigger guard to be able to fire his gun. He drops it several times and has to try to take it up between his palms while Jackson and his men are approaching. Joe hints to Marisol about some earlier somber experience, but Django has returned to the grave of a woman to take revenge, and his wavering almost kills his new woman. Moreover, he is always seen dragging and carrying things: the coffin (which he once explains contains someone named Django) and later the wounded Maria. Add to this his seriousness toward Maria and his lack of sarcasm (compared with Joe). Django appears as a much more suffering, *deprived* hero than Joe (or Ringo). This is also underlined by the title song, which is both more serious and more conventional ("Django, have you always been alone?") than Morricone's quirky, ironic music for *Fistful of Dollars*.

There is also guilt involved, as Django's turn from non-monetary (vengeance) motive to a monetary one results in Maria's getting wounded (though she might survive). When Joe turns from a monetary to a non-monetary motive (liberate Marisol), he is caught and beaten, but she escapes unharmed.

The added emphasis on suffering, seriousness and guilt concurs to an amplification of the mode of the pathetic in this story compared with *Fistful of Dollars*, where the mode of the ironic plays a larger part.

THE FEMALE DOUBLE

The two episodes at the bridge over the muddy streak called a river present a significant, and neat, inversion.

First sequence at the bridge	*Second sequence at the bridge*
Assault (Maria is whipped by the Mexicans).	Django wants to cross the bridge but is halted by Maria, who offers her love.
Intervention by false rescuers (Mexicans are killed by the Southerners).	Almost submerging into quicksand (Django).
Intervention by true rescuer (Django kills the Southerners).	Intervention by true rescuer (Maria seizes Django's hand).

First sequence at the bridge	*Second sequence at the bridge*
Submerging into quicksand (dead Southerner).	Intervention by false rescuers (Maria is wounded by the Mexicans).
Maria wants to cross the bridge but is stopped by Django, who offers his escort.	Assault (Django has his hand crushed by the Mexicans).

These chronological inversions epitomize the battering and humiliation of the hero, but also tell of Maria's rise to comparable status with him — an ascendance of the female hero compared with Marisol. In fact, Maria can be regarded as a doubling of Django. She is more of an infiltrator than he is — she has left the brothel for Hugo, and then left him also. Possibly she has earlier been with Jackson; in any case he has sent his men to burn her at the cross. When she faces Hugo again, she insists, "I am not your property"— just like Django later says no to the offer to join Hugo's force. Maria is also the only other character whom the spectator is invited to share a view with (in one scene). She alone understands what Django is up to and anticipates his plan to steal the gold. Just like Django, she is subjected to brutalization and shows the marks of suffering — whippings, bruises, mud and a bullet wound. The countenance of suffering and tragedy that the actor Franco Nero conveys to Django is comparable to the one given to Maria by Loredana Nusciak.

Joe is a mediator, a Gringo dressed in a poncho who stays with a Mexican. Django might follow Joe in being more acquainted with the Mexican side (Hugo), but in dress (Union uniform) he is unlike both the Mexicans and the Gringos/Southerners. Maria is a half-breed — "Yankee and Mexican. You got the worst blood of both of them in you" says Hugo — thus she is of both, while Django is of neither, so they mirror each other.

Django as a Trans-Story Hero

Among scholars commenting on the spaghetti Western, it is Christopher Frayling who has reached out to discuss films outside the ghetto of the critic's canon. With the ambition to review all the films in the series, "not just the most successful," he discusses 17 films that recycle the Django formula.

He encounters a bewildering variety — the hero might be a bounty hunter or an avenger, he might reach his goal in a number of different ways, the stories might be serious or parodies — with some common significant features, as a "continuous series of connotations" for the Django character — "the growth of beard, the shabby clothes ... the coffin, the penchant for firing a machine-gun from the hip" and "recurring noteworthy moments, like Django's prowess with an assortment of guns, his manipulations of one party against another," etc.[1]

Frayling refers to Umberto Eco's analysis of the Superman comics, where such a "continuous series of connotations" is put forth as a solution to the contradiction between the mythical status of this hero that should be unchanged over time ("inconsumable") on one hand, and the alleged expectations of the readership that he should exist in a realistic environment and take on tasks that have a beginning and an end.[2]

Now, while I agree that — at least for some mass-mediated fictional characters — such "distractions" might be more important for spectator pleasure than the actual story line, his explanation is simply not valid for a hero like Django. Audiences will expect Superman to be a persistent character between strips, *biographically bonded*, like Wyatt Earp appearing in different Westerns. However, I very much doubt that the Spaghetti Western audiences expected the row of Django characters to have the same kind of identity as Superman — that the original Django played by Franco Nero is the same person as the married transport guard dressed similarly but played by Terence Hill in *Preparati la bara!* and that they both are the same as the Confederate survivor (or possibly ghost) out for vengeance in *Django il bastardo*.

Django appears in several stories under the same name but without being biographically bonded. I will label this kind of popular-culture hero a *trans-story hero*. In spaghetti Westerns Django was followed by Sartana, Sabata and Trinity. Similarly, in the Italian "sword and sandal" films, a hero like Maciste appears with the Mogul Great Khan, the Russian tsar, sheikhs, men from the moon and even Zorro (in Spain!) when he is not, so to speak, on his original turf in Rome, as a gladiator.[3] Italo-Spanish Zorro movies likewise tend to stray much further from the original Don Diego de la Vega story line than their American counterparts. This cavalier disregard for biographical aspects in the Mediterranean popular film also permits the title character in *Uccidete Johnny Ringo* to be a Texas ranger working undercover on a case of counterfeit money, far removed from his real-life namesake.[4]

Trans-story heroes are neither story characters (like the hero in *Django il bastardo*) nor thematic roles (like the fat, boisterous Mexican bandit). They are more comparable to name brands but, unlike "Superman," are unprotected ones and so frequently abused. In fact, they are notoriously easy to "tag" on to a different character, for example by simply putting the name in the film title or using it for the character in another language version. In fact, there are at least 47 German film titles that include "Django,"

Terence Hill as trans-story Django in *Preparati la bara!*

while the corresponding Italian films sport only 14, and the French 15. On the other hand there are at least 11 French Djangos where I find no German counterpart (and for 5 of these no Italian either).

Frayling tries to avoid retitled Django films in his own list. However, he includes the "Trojan horses" *Django the Condemned* and *Django Does Not Forgive,* both all–Spanish productions (*El proscrito del Rio Colorado* and *Django non perdona/Mestizio,* respectively) that have been renamed for export. They are most probably examples of distributors pulling a "fast one" on the Italian audiences by offering Django pics that didn't have any of the familiar stories and (most probably) none of the familiar connotations either.[5]

However, I would not argue that all cases of retitling would leave an audience of Django aficionados feeling tricked. The same year as *Django,* Franco Nero starred in *Texas addio* as Burt Sullivan, who carries a long coat and has a similarly dismissive attitude. Together with his younger brother, he goes south of the border to bring in Delgado, the man who has killed his father. Delgado is a big landowner who upholds a regime of terror with land grabbing and white slavery, while the local authorities look the other way. Complications arise when Delgado turns out to be the natural father of the younger Sullivan, revealed at the same time as some locals ask Burt for help to fight the landowner.

In *Tempo di massacro,* also 1966, Franco Nero is the gold prospector Tom, who is called back to his hometown, but not by his brother Jeff, who instead is anxious for him to leave again. Their home has been taken over by the big landowner Scott and his son Junior, who is a sadistic psychopath. It turns out that Scott has killed their father but is the natural father of Tom. In the end Junior kills Scott, and then Tom and Jeff destroy him and his men. Tom does not wear any covering coat (only a fur-lined skin vest similar to what Joe wears under his poncho), but he has the same unshaven countenance as Django, eventually also marked by a whipping.

That the German versions of these films—*Django der Rächer* and *Django— sein Gesangbuch war der Colt—*add a Django association seems far from unreasonable, considering the fate and the connotations of the Franco Nero characters.

The Deprived Hero

John (Gianni) Garko plays the bounty killer Django in *Diecimila dollari per un massacro.* He is asked by the landowner Mendoza to liberate his daughter from the bandit Manuel Cortez (Claudio Camasco). Django, however, finds the sum offered too small, and instead cooperates with Cortez in a stagecoach holdup, in which Django's beloved Myanou is killed. Django then liberates the girl (who turns out to be in love with Cortez) and kills the bandit. The same actor appeared the same year in *Per centomila dollari t'ammazzo*, where he plays the bounty hunter John, who captures his wanted half brother Clint (again Claudio Camasco), who has earlier killed their father and blamed John for it. When the bounty is not paid due to the dissolving of the Confederate administration, he instead joins Clint to share a hidden treasure of gold, and that leads to the killing of John's woman Annie.

In *El Desperado* Steve — who isn't called Django even in the German version — tries to swindle his partner Asher for their common loot, and that results in the rape of the girl that he has come to love and the death of a blind old man (who believes that Steve is his son returned from the war).

Thus we find heroes not named Django abiding the same circumstances and fates as heroes with that name. These heroes have in common an unshaven, dusty countenance, worn and dusty clothes, and a dismissive style. They also share certain conditions — they have lost, or eventually lose, someone precious to them. Often such a loss is at least indirectly the result of their own courses of action. This description fits Django, but it does not at all fit Angel Face, and — components of personal style apart — it does not fit Joe very well either.

Notice that though some of these pseudo-Django heroes originally are bounty hunters, they are stricken by an experience of deprivation, similar to the murder of kin (or comrades) creating the avenger. Just like Django, they are heroes of the pathetic because of a deeply felt personal loss. I will call such heroes *deprived heroes*. They come in different categories — *the prodigal son, the avenger, the vindicative hero* and *the tragic mercenary* — with different types of constellation/plots associated with them.

The Prodigal Hero

The stories of *Tempo di massacro* and *Texas addio* both contain murdered fathers, murdering natural fathers, and brothers disclosed as half brothers. Among the spaghetti Westerns studied, there are similar stories. As they all are about a returning son who finds himself bereft of his rightful place in the family, I will refer to films following this characteristic constellation/plot as *prodigal son stories*.

The Prodigal Son Constellation/Plot

GOOD/EVIL AUTHORITY

The hero usually finds his father murdered by a villain who also has taken over the father's corresponding social position. Thus a *good authority* has been replaced by an *evil authority*. In several stories there are doublings or fusions of these positions. In *Tempo di massacro* and *Texas addio* the evil authority turns out to be a natural (and welcoming) father of the hero or his half brother, respectively. In *Ciak Mull, l'uomo della vendetta*, where the hero Chuck is an amnesiac gunfighter escaped from an asylum, his father, inversely, is falsely presented as an evil authority by the true evil authority — his enemy Udall.

POSITIVE/NEGATIVE EQUIVALENT

With these Janus-headed father figures follow ambiguous relations between brothers. The half brothers in *Tempo di massacro*, *Ciak Mull, l'uomo della vendetta* and *Keoma* all embody threats to the hero, and they have taken the position of the prodigal son vis-à-vis his father. Similarly, the sheriff in *Gringo*, Douglas (also sheriff) in *Vendetta* and Paco Fuentes in *Il ritorno di Ringo* have taken over the relation of the hero toward the girl he once left behind. As they usurp the very place of the hero in his family (and/or sexual) relations, they are *negative equivalents* in the constellation.

There might also be *positive equivalents* — half brothers who offer assistance more (*Texas addio*) or less (*Tempo di massacro*) willingly, friends such as Rafael in *Il pistolero dell'Ave Maria* and the companion from the asylum in *Ciak Mull, l'uomo della vendetta*.

CONTESTED/EQUIVALENT WOMEN

A *contested woman* in these stories belongs to a villain, but is a former girlfriend of the hero, and turns her loyalties back toward him. She might be an accessory to the murder of the good authority, such as Maria in *Gringo*, or Anna Carrasco in *Il pistolero dell'Ave Maria*. The latter is not the girlfriend but the (supposed) mother of the hero. The mother in *Dans la poussière du soleil* — who is forcibly married to her husband's brother and murderer (wearing black at the wedding) with an ensuing nuptial rape — is bridging both roles, as the spectator is cued to an incestuous attraction.

Lisa, the tomboy foster sister of the hero of *Gringo*, instead is a clear-cut positive equivalent who becomes a girlfriend, as she is differentiated along the gender code. She appears armed at his side in the final battle, together with her (biological) brother, another positive equivalent! Unarmed but belligerent are Isabella, the sister in *Il pistolero dell'Ave Maria*, and Hally, the wife in *Il ritorno di Ringo* (who might be a contested woman in body, though not in spirit).

The mother in *Mille dollari sul nero* is a female matriarch among all this patriarchy. She does transcend the dichotomy by going from evil authority (supporting the evil brother Sartana) to good (supporting the hero Johnny). She still dies though.

THE PRODIGAL SON PLOT

1. The hero returns to his home.
2. An evil authority kills/has killed the father of the hero.
3. The evil authority is very powerful.
4. The evil authority terrorizes the society.
5. A negative equivalent usurps the family position of the hero.
6. The hero is falsely accused of a crime.
7. The hero seeks the truth.
8. A positive equivalent helps the hero.
9. The hero defeats his opponents.
10. The hero is cleared of charges.
11. The hero regains his family position.

This plot plays out so to speak on two different levels, using two sets of circumstances, that of family position, and that of social position. Some of the functions, and the corresponding narrative sequences, are relevant only for one set.

MODELS

Some stories play out several models of this plot. In *Tempo di massacro* it is revealed to Tom that Scott Sr. has killed his father (2). Later he learns that Scott is his biological father, who wants to acknowledge him (because his other son Junior is mad). Scott is killed by Junior, another

Table 5A. Narrative Sequences of the Prodigal Son Plot
(Plot functions in parentheses).

Family position only	Common to both	Social position only
	Return (1)	
Usurpation (2, 5)		Terror (3, 4)
		Conspiracy (6)
	Help (7, 8)	
	Fight (Usurpation, Conspiracy, 9)	
Confirmation (2, 5, 11)	Cleared (6, Help, 10)	

instance of 2, but also of 5 and so a complete usurpation sequence. Scott Sr., who is the evil authority in the first model, is in fact the good one in the second model. Besides, Jeff at first acts as a negative equivalent, when he insists on Tom's leaving, before he becomes a positive one.

In *Texas addio* the evil authority similarly welcomes John, the brother/positive equivalent of the hero, while Delgado's foreman fights John and thus performs as a negative equivalent to John and also eventually kills him (by accident, as Burt is the intended target).

There are further complications in *Ciak Mull, l'uomo della vendetta*, where the Udalls are introduced as false quasi-father and quasi-brother. In the *first model* Chuck believes that he is a Udall who must fight the evil authority Caldwell, who has killed his brother (weak 2) and terrorizes the area with cattle rustling. In the *second model* Udall is the evil authority who is behind robberies and thefts and who almost succeeded in making Chuck deprive himself of his father. After the Udalls have been killed, in the *third model*, his brother Alan is disclosed as a negative equivalent who has deposed Chuck from his family position (by a murder attempt that causes his amnesia) and who deprives him of his father by disclosing that he is not Caldwell's natural son.[6]

Codes of the Prodigal Son Films

Motifs and thematic roles associated with the mode of the pathetic are very significant in these stories. As for the disrupted family, the prodigal hero is in fact part of it. Furthermore, the "happy ending" hinted by the *confirmation* sequence may exist only as a negation — Chuck leaves his home rejecting reinstatement and the hero of *Keoma* has no family left when he leaves, just like Burt Sullivan, who returns to Texas with the bodies of John and Delgado.

Terror

The *terror* sequence subsumes extreme atrocities and abuses. For example, Scott Junior in *Tempo di massacro* entertains his young friends with a "fox" hunt where a man is the quarry of the hounds, and later they cheer when he whips Tom. In one scene, Scott Sr. tries to convince the head of a family who leaves because the pay is too low by saying that he has buried his dead there. When the man replies, "None of my dead are buried here," Junior shoots his son and says, "One will be now."

Cobb in *Vendetta* kills two runaway slaves in a "stacked-deck" duel and later beats down Dolly without mercy. We see him entertaining with a special kind of arm-wrestling where the loser gets his hand pierced by a knife. In *Texas addio* Delgado, in another convincing case of grizzled brutality, sells young Mexican women into prostitution. He executes the sons of another landowner, and then attacks him with a clawed glove. Caldwell in *Keoma* bases his power on the raging epidemic and tries to block all outside assistance.

CONSPIRACY AND MYSTERY

Contrary to the typical infiltrator story, strategic cunning is the game of the villain rather than the hero, who finds himself at the losing end in *usurpation* and *conspiracy*. He might display shrewd tactics though, such as the sneak fights of *Tempo di massacro* and *Ciak Mull, l'uomo della vendetta*, or the ambush Burt helps the revolutionaries prepare in *Texas addio*.

False accusations befall Gringo and Keoma, as well as Ted Barnett in *Vendetta*, while other heroes encounter hidden truths about their parentage, such as Chuck Moll. Sebastian in *Il pistolero dell'Ave Maria* is twice deceived regarding his mother. Even when unaware of the existence of this secret, the prodigal heroes are on a quest of discovery. Tom asks around for Scott's ranch, and Burt and John Sullivan seek Delgado, and they all run up against silence, as well as armed men, who seem curiously reluctant to take their lives (as one of them is the son of their boss).

The punishment for stealing meted out to Montgomery Brown, though unjust, has the opposite meaning story-wise, because he initiated it himself to hide his true identity.

RHETORICAL CODES

It is only in *Il ritorno di Ringo* and *Vendetta* that a prodigal hero exercises long-term cunning and manipulation to overcome the power of the Fuentes and convince the judge of his innocence, respectively. Significantly, they also feature the rhetorical code of *humor* as the heroes' game.

There is one remarkable inter-code connection in *Tempo di massacro*. During the literal manhunt organized by Junior that sets the tone for the story, the human quarry dies under the attack of the hounds in the river, and the camera follows his blood diluted in the flowing water during the introductory credits until it halts at Tom finding a gold nugget in that same river. In the spirit of the coffin/machine gun/gold merging in *Django*, this establishes a metonymic link between terror/violence and gold, and also between Tom and the manhunt, immediately confirmed by the message delivered to him.[7]

On the Sociocultural dimension expressed in table 2C, the "prodigal son" films typically belong to group 4, as the villainous authorities/equivalents typically are big bosses, and ethnical differences are mostly peripheral. *Keoma* is an exception to both, with its theme of racism (against

Tempo di massacro: Distinguished guests contemplate evil equivalent Junior (Nino Castelnuovo) whipping prodigal hero Tom (Franco Nero).

Indians and African Americans), and thus is a group 2 film. Mexican ethnicity is significant in group 1 stories *Gringo, Il ritorno di Ringo* and *Texas addio* — with its two gringos in the middle of a strange and mysterious Mexico. *Tempo di massacro* contains a few Mexicans plus a Chinese sidekick undertaker/pianist/blacksmith delivering Confucius quotations of dubious authenticity. The gringo Jeff is something of an ethnic mediator in this film, as he drinks tequila and dislikes whisky!

"Prodigal Son" Variants

STORIES HYBRIDIZED OR INTERLEAVED

In *Tre colpi di winchester per Ringo* a blow has blinded Ringo Carson. When the men of big boss Daniels kill his mother, another blow restores his sight. He keeps this a secret until he has exacted his revenge, which involves facing Frank, an old friend and also rival for Ringo's girl Jane. At the showdown Frank cheats in a special (gun-loading) duel, but is shot by Jane. He then kills Daniels after taking a bullet meant for Ringo and dies.

In this story a good (female) authority is killed, and Frank is a tentative negative equivalent, as he also wants Jane. However, he never wins her, and Daniels's deed doesn't really dislodge Ringo from his social position. The film remains mainly an avenger story.

Per centomila dollari t'ammazzo shows in flashbacks Clint driving his brother John off, crying that he is illegitimate, and when their father runs after John, he is shot by Clint, who proceeds to denounce John for the deed — i.e., prodigal plot functions about loss of family position due to a negative equivalent, and the loss of a good authority followed by a conspiracy. John becomes a bounty hunter, and his dealings with Clint follow what I describe later as the *tragic mercenary* plot.[8] In the final reckoning, they go down and die in each other's arms. The concluding shot (flashback or metaphoric vision) of the brothers riding away together on a beach represents a symbolic version of the hero regaining family position.

The story of *Per centomila dollari t'ammazzo* mixes two different plots by *interleaving*, the same way *5000 dollari sull'asso* did, discussed in chapter 4. *Tre colpi di winchester per Ringo*, on the other hand, is an example of mixing by *hybridization* — in the sense that actions and characters answer to plot functions and constellation positions even though a coherent model of the corresponding constellation/plot cannot readily be constructed from the story. In *Massacro al Grande Canyon* (see chapter 4), Telly Dancer is an evil equivalent insofar as he has taken Wes's girl, while the sheriff, who before was Wes's deputy, is a good equivalent. The father of Telly is an evil patriarch who is ready to sacrifice his other, good son. Furthermore, the father of Wes has been killed — though the vengeance takes place at the beginning of the film. The Dancers are unrelated to the death of Wes's father and so are not usurping his family position, making these dispersed parts of the prodigal son constellation/plot hybrid elements that never tie together. The Dancer family affairs do amount to a subplot about an evil patriarch and his good and bad sons, similar to the main plot in *I crudeli*.

PRODIGAL SONS—PRETENDED OR REAL

I have earlier used the properties of *false* and *involuntary* to qualify relations and constellation positions such as "infiltrator." These determinations pertain to a metacode of pretense and reality[9]:

		Real	
		Is really	*Is not really*
Pretended	Pretends to be	Proper	False
	Pretends not to be	Hidden	Involuntary

We have already encountered *involuntary infiltrators*—characters abducted or blackmailed to join a camp but still generating discord and dysfunction, just like a proper infiltrator. Montgomery Brown — the returning husband pretending to be a larcenous Mexican — is a *hidden* prodigal son in this respect. Steve Blasco in *El Desperado* qualifies as a *false* prodigal son. The old man gets killed when he interferes for his "son" (function 2), and the rape of Cathy is a contested woman variant. After avenging himself, Steve might later return to Cathy (function 11).

In *I morti non si contano* the wife of big boss Rogers has once helped him to assassinate her former husband. When the bounty killers Fred and Johnny upset Rogers's illegal activities, Johnny's gun is recognized as belonging to Mrs. Rogers's son from the former marriage whom she had put up for adoption. She is struck by guilt and eventually shoots Rogers in order to save Johnny, asks his forgiveness and walks away. However, Johnny has simply found the gun somewhere, and so has his life saved by being an *involuntary* prodigal hero, by misunderstanding.

Furthermore, notice that an infiltrator proper *does* hide his true intentions!

THE PRODIGAL DAUGHTER

In *Scalps!* from 1985 one at last finds a female hero in a prodigal constellation/plot dominating a whole story.[10] The Confederate Colonel Connor offers the Comanches guns in exchange for the chief's daughter Jarrin. When the chief refuses, the soldiers massacre the village. Jarrin is captured and humiliated, but manages to escape. Eventually she receives reluctant assistance from Matt, whose wife, Dolores (the daughter of Connor), supposedly was killed by Indians. Matt is captured, but Jarrin gradually annihilates Connor's troop using Indian weapons and traps. In the final confrontation Matt learns that Connor himself was behind the killing of Dolores. In a grotesque duel[11] he kills and scalps Connor — earlier both the soldiers and Jarrin have done their bit to make the film deserve its name.[12]

As the story progresses, the spectator is cued to understanding that Connor had an incestuous relation with his daughter, that he killed her because she left him for Matt, and that he persists in sending his men after Jarrin because he desires her to take Dolores's place. So Jarrin sees her good father killed by the men of the evil, incestuous authority Connor. Her tribal ("family") position is also threatened by Black Fox, who does not recognize her rights as daughter of a chief. This makes him a negative equivalent, who is killed by Matt, the positive equivalent. As with Gringo and Lisa in *Gringo*, a difference in gender brings with it a love relation between hero and positive equivalent. Correspondingly, as the prodigal hero is female, the threat from the evil male authority also takes on a sexual aspect.

The story of *Scalps!* starts with the troop going from the fort to the Indian village, and then the pursuit to the mountain, where Matt kills Black Fox and Jarrin meets the spirit of her father, followed by Matt's torturous march back with Jarrin's concurrent pursuit, through the remnants of the village to the final confrontation with Connor at the fort. Thus Jarrin returns home "after the fact," and this circular trek matches the search/travel toward the lair of the evil authority found in several of the earlier "prodigal son" films.

The Avenger Constellation/Plot

A basic plot of vengeance situations—in Italowesterns as well as ancient tales or crime thrillers—can be outlined like this:

1. A and B are close.
2. C commits an evil act against B.
3. A seeks out C.
4. A defeats C.

The constellation contains A as the hero, B as the victim, and C as the malefactor.

To compare with the "prodigal son" plot discussed in the preceding chapter, the avenger function 2 corresponds to the prodigal functions 2–6, and the avenger function 3 to the prodigal functions 7–8. The conclusion—corresponding to the prodigal functions 10 and 11—is varying. The avenger might stay/leave with a woman/some comrades-in-arms, or, most commonly, leave alone. The prodigal constellation likewise contains a doubling of both the malefactor (evil authority and negative equivalent) and the hero (with a positive equivalent).

The constellation/plot of the prodigal son thus could be regarded as a more complicated elaboration of the one of the avenger. An avenger plot might also be nested within a "prodigal son" story, as when Chuck Moll fights the killer of his father at night in a graveyard (and at the last moment learns that the opponent instead *is* his father), or when Montgomery Brown lays aim at his unfaithful wife (and discovers that she has born him a daughter).

The Circumstances of the Avenger Constellation/Plot

Among the great number of variations in the circumstances of how the Django stories developed listed by Frayling, he noted that the hero might see the vengeance through, give it up, or find the wrongdoer killed by somebody else. Here I will summarize such variations in a wider range of Spaghetti Western vengeance stories.

VARIANTS OF THE MOTIVATION

The motivation of an Italowestern avenger hero is often complex. In *Django* he wavers between killing Jackson, who has killed a woman from Django's past, or escaping with his money. The spectator is left uncertain as to what he originally had in mind and at what moment he changes his plans. Django is a hero with an *internal second motive*— already encountered in the infiltrator plot with functions 3, "A gets a monetary motive," and 12, "A gets a non-monetary motive."

In the case of *Few Dollars More* the two heroes initially are presented as bounty killers with a monetary motive, but in the end it turns out that one of them all the time was out to avenge himself on the villain. This is a case of an *external second motive*. In the stories where there is a pair of heroes or a group of heroes, an external second (or double) motive might in fact strengthen their cooperation (conjunctive), but it might also threaten or destroy it (disjunctive).

In *Few Dollars More* the double motive works generally conjunctively (in fact Monco neighs in the partnership because he thinks that Mortimer also wants the bounty money). A disjunction might also be a ruse to trick the malefactor — such as in *Se t'incontro, t'ammazzo* (where the avenger and the gunfighter hired to stop him are brothers) and *Lo chiamavano King* (the government agent Collins has the avenger King arrested as a stratagem to catch a smuggling boss, who also is the malefactor).

In the introduction to *Bandidos*, a train is attacked and the passengers massacred by the bands of Bill Kane and Vigonza. On the train is Martin, Kane's former partner and tutor of gunplay. Kane outdraws Martin and destroys his hands permanently. Later we find Martin managing a sharpshooting show. He tutors a stranger to be his performer ("Ricky Shot") and then sends him to join with Vigonza to kill Kane, who has been sold out by some of his men. But "Ricky" has his own agenda, as he is an escaped prisoner wrongly convicted for the train robbery, so instead he helps Kane and is rewarded with one of Kane's traitors as a witness to his innocence. Martin now tries to kill Kane himself but fails and is shot after he has surrendered. Consequently, "Ricky" kills Kane after a sneak fight in a barn. Here, a first model of the avenger plot (Martin/"Ricky" versus Kane) with a disjunctive external double motive is followed by a second model with one avenger ("Ricky" versus Kane).

The deserter John Warner in *Quei disperati che puzzano di sudore e di morte* has a motive to avenge the death of his baby, and the main malefactor is its grandfather, the landowner Sandoval. One of the men in his gang eventually tries to sell him out for the reward. In this case the two motives (revenge and money) are disjunctive. After completing his vengeance, Warner and the remaining gang — two fellow deserters, and one runaway lay brother — die a spectacular (and conjunctive) death in a shootout in a bullfighting arena.

Django in *Preparati la bara!* becomes a hangman who spares the lives of the condemned victims of David Barry's conspiracies as part of a plan to disclose Barry. However, when the "hanged" intercept an attack on a gold transport by capturing Barry's men, they choose to take the gold for themselves. Garcia initiates this betrayal, and he kills the others in the group. He has earlier saved Django's life. This is in fact a story of a hero pair (Django and Garcia) with Garcia carrying an external second (monetary) motive. Garcia later regrets his action and dies assisting Django against Barry. A disjunctive second motive is here first played out and then abandoned, and as Django leaves a sack of gold to Garcia's wife "for you and the children," the two motives in a way become conjunctive.

The internal double motive is usually disjunctive, as for Django, who decides to take Jackson's money rather than his life, with unfortunate consequences. It might also be *false* — the avengers in *Per mille dollari al giorno* and *Prega per il morto e ammazza il vivo* accept money to help the malefactor as a way to destroy him, and for the same reason Mulligan intercepts the robbery loot of the malefactor in *Mi chiamavano Requiescat ... ma avevo sbagliato*. When the hero in *Navajo Joe* (aka *Un dollaro a testa*) avenges himself on the outlaws that have massacred his village for one dollar a scalp and offers to protect the town for "a dollar a head from every man in this town for each bandit I kill," it is rather a symbolic vengeance ritual, and in fact he never receives any money. In *Sella d'argento* a Barret is responsible for the killing of Roy's father, but he reluctantly protects a boy of the malefactor family instead of killing him. This disjunctive internal second motive becomes conjunctive as another villainous Barret conspires to kill the child.

When the wrathful Kakopoulous in *I quattro dell'Ave Maria* kills his deceitful former partner before finding out where the robbery loot is hidden, the internal disjunctive double motive also is external — because his new partners Cat and Hutch expect reimbursement for money that he has pinched from them.

VARIANTS IN PLOT FUNCTIONS

One variant is the *flashback*. In many spaghetti Westerns, function 2, "C commits an evil act against B," is described in a flashback because it takes place before the on-screen action begins and/or as a signification of the avenger's motivation. The flashback was introduced in *Few Dollars More* with the recollections of Indio about a murder/suicide where he is the malefactor, and eventually it is revealed that Mortimer is an avenger for this deed.

Another variant is the *vengeance ceremonial*. Aside from the usual tactical dispositions (e.g., sneak fights, ambushes, traps), function 4, "A defeats C," in a Spaghetti Western vengeance plot may include a vengeance ceremonial. These are of two kinds. First, when the avenger recognizes the malefactor by his looks or some cue, it may be emphasized by some expressional device, such as a musical figure or *leitmotif* and/or a cinematographic cut or a zoom. This is the typical employment of the flashback mentioned above. For example, in *Da uomo a uomo* Bill has a visual memory of a detail for each of the malefactors involved in the destruction of his family, and when he sees it, a flashback from the deed is triggered. Alternatively, the avenger might confront the malefactor with something reminding him of the deed (which might also cause a flashback) to terrorize him, or he might use a method of execution corresponding to the deed:

- The avengers may simply display some gismo from the scene of the crime to make the malefactors recall their deed at the moment of retribution, as in *Il giorno del giudizio* (a toy drummer that triggers flashbacks) and *La vendetta è il mio perdono* (musical watch unwisely left behind by malefactor).
- More elaborate is the use of the harmonica played by the stranger in *Once Upon a Time in the West*. In his last dying breaths, the malefactor Frank has it put in his mouth, and finally recalls putting the same harmonica in the mouth of a young boy, who has an older man (father?) standing on his shoulders in a noose, doomed to eventually stumble and die.
- After the baby in *Quei disperati che puzzano di sudore e di morte* has perished for lack of nutrition, Jack Warner drowns a man in milk for earlier refusing to give milk!
- Django employs the cumbersome vengeance ceremonial of gravestones in front of the houses of the malefactors in *Django il bastardo* but on the other hand he is most probably a ghost.
- A similar unnerving tactic is used by Scott in *Per mille dollari al giorno*. He sends first an undertaker with hearse and coffin and later paid mourners to the malefactors while they still are alive.
- In *Django*, the hero-avenger uses the cross of the victim to pull the trigger against the malefactor.

It is noteworthy that the most important inspiration for these vengeance ceremonials, the musical watch in *Few Dollars More* (see chapter 6), is in fact a tool of the malefactor, Indio, who utilizes this cueing object as a pace setter in duels of the "stacked-deck" category. In the films that followed, the device was "normalized" into being a means of the avenger.

Sociocultural Codes of the Avenger

Compared with the "prodigal sons," the avenger films are more evenly distributed over the groupings of the sociocultural dimension, as presented in table 2C. It is noteworthy that stories with internal double motives fall into groups 2 and 3 — stories with bandits and mercenaries. The films featuring a group of avengers are generally highly placed in the ethnic code, while the lone avenger stories rate low. "Plain" avengers, without double motives, usually fall into group 4, big boss stories where ethnical differentiation is low or absent.

A Vengeance Variation?

Among the films studied, *Il figlio di Django* is the only clear-cut example of Wright's *vengeance variation* on the classical plot, where a hero leaves society to exact retribution but is persuaded to give it up and return (though he usually gets to wipe out some or all malefactors anyway).[13] In *Per mille dollari al giorno* Betty, the sister of the sheriff, constantly questions the vengeance mission of Scott, but is proved wrong, as her brother in the end lends him a hand in killing the remaining malefactor, who has been acquitted. Joanne in *La vendetta è il mio perdono*, another "representative of society" persuading the hero to give up his revenge, in fact is one of the malefactors! Anyhow, Italowestern avengers seldom return to society.

The Vindicative Hero

The position "A" might be identical to "B" in the avenger constellation so that the hero avenges a deed committed directly against him. However, in such cases the vengeance is a subplot, or one of several models—as in *Bandidos* (see page 110). The hero usually becomes the target of severe brutality during the course of the story, but it is usually not this battering and torture that set his actions in motion; it is some preceding act committed against others. In *Oggi a me ... domani a te*, Bill Kiowa seeks vengeance not only for being wrongly convicted, but also for the rape and murder of his beloved. Jeff Madison is tortured, humiliated and maimed in *Mi chiamavano Requiescat ... ma avevo sbagliato,* but in the same scene captured Union soldiers are massacred, and later when he faces the Southern renegades, his Indian girl Swana fights beside him because rebels had killed her parents. The irate avenger Kakopoulous in *I quattro dell'Ave Maria* has another internal motive, shared by his companions, and is partly comic to boot.

Giuliano Gemma stars in a series of films where a hero (in three out of five cases named "Gary") seeks to redress a wrong committed against him. Their common plot functions amount to a story of accusation/vindication:

1. The hero is falsely accused/convicted of a crime.
2. The hero seeks proofs to clear himself.
3. The hero finds proof that implicates the villain(s).
4. The hero defeats the villain(s).
5. A legal authority clears the hero.

The hero usually returns to society (with a woman) at the end of the story — except for *Un dollaro bucato,* where Gary and his wife walk away from the scene where the citizens gun down McCorey.

As the hero is falsely accused or convicted of a crime and seeks to clear himself and implicate the villain, his immediate goal is not vengeance but justice — even if this entails fighting and sometimes killing the latter (*Per pochi dollari ancora, Vendetta*). For this reason I designate this the *vindicative constellation/plot.*

The villains in these films form a three-headed configuration: an influential and respected but law-breaking *bad boss,* a *bad sheriff* (sometimes accompanied by bad deputies) and an *outlaw gang.* The key man is the boss, who is the connection between the other parties.

These situations represent intermediate positions between extremes represented by *Fistful of Dollars*— a bad sheriff and gang in town fight bad Mexican gang in town — and the Ringo films, where a good (strong or weak) sheriff and citizens in town (less or more reluctantly) fight bad Mexican gang in a country house.

The third pillar in the "Gary constellation" is the legal authority to which the hero appeals to counter the charges and be reinstated to his position. In *Vendetta* and *Wanted* the authority is a judge. In *Adios gringo* he is the sheriff, who has to decide what to do with the wanted Brent Landres, but eventually he must bring in a "city judge " just in time to stop the posse from lynching Brent. In *Un dollaro bucato*— where Gary is seeking evidence to clear his dead brother, not himself — the town judge has a weaker presence and is nowhere to be seen when the enraged citizens of Yellowstone finally finish off boss McCorey in the street.

These plot functions and constellation also are present in the military environment of *Per pochi dollari ancora*, where Gary Hammond tries to stop his Confederate comrades-in-arms from a suicide attack orchestrated by three villains—a respected, but bad, C.S. major, and a bad U.S. captain, both in cahoots with the outlaw gang of Riggs. Captain McDonald commands good but deceived troopers (instead of deputies) to pursue and capture Gary (function 1). Also, the Confederates threaten to shoot Gary as a traitor unless he can prove that their commander, Major Sanders, has betrayed them (functions 1, 3 and 5).

Female Equivalents

Similarly to *Fistful of Dollars* and the Ringo films, some of the vindicator stories feature female leads whose situation is structurally like that of the hero.

In *Adios gringo* Lucy is a rape victim, which makes her an (innocent) outcast—like Brent, who is a wanted man, though innocent. Like Marisol, she utters her first words in the film to the hero as a warning. At the end she saves Brent's life by shooting the main villain, Dawson.

In *Vendetta* Ted Barnett's former fiancée, Dolly, has a practical approach to her situation—"I would have sunk down to street level if it hadn't been for Joe (Douglas)," she says. Her actions mirror those of Ted when she plays him out against Douglas. The death of the latter gives her power based on information—Douglas's records. Cobb's unmitigated violence denies her this freedom to maneuver, but his terror does not subdue her, and she goes to the judge. When she thus has committed herself (and saved Ted), she is shot by Cobb. The other woman in *Vendetta* is the belligerent Dulcy, who throws herself into the gunfight at Ted's side. She is caught and thus also becomes a damsel in distress, arranged in a hangman's noose as bait for Ted, holding herself up by the rope.

Other leading ladies in the Gary films, while more conventionally "decent," and occasionally taken as hostages, might still be able to down one villain and hold the other at gunpoint (Evelyn in *Wanted*) or save the hero's eyesight and fulfill his mission (the performer Connie in *Per pochi dollari ancora*). They lack the traditional Western female commitment to nonviolence and law. Only Evelyn tells Gary Ryan to give up his revenge (and gets the appropriate vindicative hero answer that it is "not revenge, justice"). More typical is when Lucy O'Hara threatens boss McCorey that her husband will kill him!

The Pathetic Vindicator

Pathetic themes such as disrupted families, torture, and dramatic returns from the dead occur also in some of the vindicator stories. In *Un dollaro bucato* the O'Hara brothers discover that they are firing at each other, and then Blackie is shot several times by McCorey's men while trying to get to his downed brother. Gary is also later beaten and tied up with salt put in his mouth after he has been exposed. The "return from the dead" motif is expressed in two passes. First, the life of Gary — similarly to Joe — is saved by a "shield," in the shape of a dollar, connected to his brother from an earlier scene. Second, in the final confrontation Gary, again like Joe, advances mysteriously untouched by the repeated gunfire from McCorey. This time the trick is reversed — the poncho of Joe hides a protection while the darkness of night conceals from McCorey the fact that he wields a pistol with a sawed-off barrel that makes its aim useless. Then McCorey is

Moment of the pathetic in *Un dollaro bucato*: Philip/Blackie O'Hara (Pierre Cressoy) is gunned down by McCorey's men after accidentally shooting his brother Gary (Giuliano Gemma).

subjected to the shock of recognizing his "dead" foe — who holds a lamp at his face, with shadows appearing where the beard was in their first encounter.

In *Adios gringo* Lucy is raped and left naked to perish in the sun. This hideous deed also means a disruption of family, as her father will reject her. In *Per pochi dollari ancora* Gary Hammond is buried to his neck and blinded. The frightening "return" here is when the bad guys realize that he can see — and has a gun!

The Ironic Vindicator

Of the vindicator films proper, it is *Vendetta* that presents the most examples of the ironic mode, which informs the personal style of the hero. Ted starts off as a bearded ragamuffin when escaping from jail, but after he has been shaved and barbered by one of his enemies, Dolly finds him trying out his old suits in what is now the house of another enemy. On the morning of his hanging, he declines a drink — "Never in the morning, bad for the health"— but insists on an elegant suite, incidentally containing the sharpened sheriff star that soon will do away with Cobb. Furthermore, he uses the telegraph to announce his impending arrival. When Douglas wakes up hearing the whistle of a (contraband) train returning too early, Dolly comments, "It's the sort of thing Barnett would do."

Other episodes in *Vendetta* that play on the difference in surface/reality in a significant way are

- The introductory escape with its caper-style exactness among the rough surroundings
- The long-range massacre of the men of Gomez at the pass with its unusual visual presentation
- The reckoning with Gomez, a shaving scene that at the same time is a sneak fight
- The humorous acrobatics of the brawl against the men accosting Dulcy
- The two scenes with the surprise appearance of the train, first when it comes backing into the station carrying Douglas's dead guards, and again at the rendezvous with Cobb and his customer, when it carries Douglas's dead body, but not the expected contraband
- Dolly's surprise treachery at the confrontation with Douglas, and Ted's surprise trick with a revolver in a string that fires when he raises his hands
- The sneak fight in the saloon with displays of cunning involving locks and closets

The Gemma Icon

In terms of box office success, the Giuliano Gemma vindicator films grossed more than a billion lire in the Italian market, as did his two Ringo films. In fact, he figures in 11 percent of the top commercial Italowesterns.

Compared with the unshaven, dismissive look, hoarse voice, cynical argot and harsh, curt demeanor of the Clint Eastwood characters continued in many of the performances by Franco Nero (e.g., in *Django*), Anthony Steffen and a host of other second-level stars in the genre, the Gemma icon is distinguished by an open look. On the screen, his blue eyes and blond hair are seldom shielded by broad-brimmed hats, two-day shade or tobacco smoke. In this respect he is not very different from a classical Western hero such as Shane. Also, his demeanor is generally polite. However, the smooth manners and relaxed conversation style of the Gemma hero might contain a money-oriented cynicism comparable to Joe's, as in the cases of Angel Face and Arizona Colt. Even where he is a vindicator forced to go outside society to prove his innocence, he still is prone to infiltrating, tricking and killing his adversaries without giving them any fair chance, quite unlike Shane. The Gemma style commanded few followers, the most prolific being Mark Damon, who plays the lead in *Johnny Oro* and other films.[14]

Other Vindicators

Django in *Preparati la bara!* has his wife killed when the gold transport he guards is attacked by the men of his "friend" David Barry. Django "buries" himself and organizes his band of "hanged" men to bring Barry to justice (see the "Variants of the Motivation" section earlier in this chapter). After his plan has failed (because of Garcia's disjunctive motive), Django kills Barry and his gang in a confrontation at a graveyard (where Django digs up his own coffin, which — believe it or not — contains a machine gun). Django thus starts out as a vindicative hero but becomes an avenger when his initial plan fails. His two motives are *consecutive*, not disjunctive.

The heroes of *Texas addio*, *Gringo* and *La morte non conta i dollari* (Mark Damon in the last film) likewise harbor vindicative ambitions, as they at least start out trying to bring the villains to justice.

Avengers, Vindicators and Prodigal Sons

Motivation and Cunning

In my earlier discussions of *Il ritorno di Ringo* and of *Django*, I found a retreat from the heavily money-oriented position of *Una pistola per Ringo/*

Fistful of Dollars (and also, to name another Gemma feature, *Arizona Colt*), expressed as a story transformation where the disruption of an vital (personal) relation becomes more important than money as a motivation for the hero, who is moved closer to or becomes a part of this relation. This is true for the stories of deprived avengers, vindicators and prodigal sons discussed previously in this chapter. Money is the motivation for villains, not for heroes. Typically, when Gary O'Hara takes an assignment for money, it leads him into disaster, while Brent Landres and Gary Ryan have prices put on their heads. However, these stories retain the money-oriented stories' prominent place for the code of guile and often also the narrative sequences of manipulations and infiltration, or at least themes and situations associated with them.

In several stories the hero combines the thematical roles of avenger and infiltrator. The vindicator Gary O'Hara in *Un dollaro bucato* employs the full range of tactics used by Joe. He *infiltrates* the bandit gang to get proof of his brother's innocence and McCorey's guilt, i.e. a non-monetary motivation. He also treads in the footsteps of Joe regarding *manipulation* when he turns McCorey and his partner in crime, the sheriff, against each other. Earlier in the story Gary sends information to the sheriff about their plans, a typical betrayal of the infiltrated organization, but he is exposed and made the victim of *punishment*.

Gary Hammond in *Per pochi dollari ancora* is a different kind of infiltrator. Still regarded as an enemy by Riggs's outlaw gang, he is allowed free movement because of his alleged blindness (caused by Riggs's torture to make him talk). Consequently, one of the gang is "accidentally" killed by his own knife when the "blind" Gary bumps into him. The next body is found among the horses "kicked" to death — by Gary with a horseshoe fastened to a stick. Then a third bandit is found drowned with his gun missing, and the revelation about the truth of the "blindness" dawns on the remaining men, as the sound of Gary's harmonica spells their doom. His piecemeal destruction of the gang is interleaved with episodes where they submit their "blind" prey to cruel taunting and "pranks," such as giving him heated plates and throwing stones against him — amounting to *punishment* before the revelation.

Brent Landres does not attempt any infiltration/manipulation but is still punished, without disclosure. Inversely, in *Vendetta*, when Barnett, badly beaten by the Mexicans, is "forced" to reveal the hiding place of the guns, he is in fact a manipulator carrying out his plan of making them fight Cobb in front of the judge. Gary Ryan in *Wanted* also "gives in"— "I know when I'm beat"— to mislead his tormentors. In these two cases the punishment constitutes a ruse rather than being the result of a failed one. Both these plans fail — thus completing the inversion from failed manipulation/punishment to punishment/failed manipulation.

In both the Ringo films, as in *Fistful of Dollars*, it is the guile of the hero that keeps the action rolling, and it is his secret that is at the center of the story. In the vindicator stories the hero must uncover the secret link between the respectable town boss (and perhaps also the sheriff) and an outlaw gang, in order to regain his honor and position. This recalls the prodigal hero, who might become the victim of a false accusation and/or at least has a mystery to solve, and also the avenger seeking out the malefactor. It is the bosses that are the masters of cunning, and it is their vile conspiracies that initiate the action. The cunning of the deprived hero is a countermeasure.

Still, the key to success for the deprived hero is all about handling of information. So, in every respect as much as *Fistful of Dollars* and *Una pistola per Ringo*, the world of these heroes is a place where "your life can depend on one mere scrap of information," to quote Miguel Rojo in the former film.

Deprived-Hero Constellations

The vindicator stories, like the ones of prodigal sons, might be described as elaborate versions of the avenger constellation/plot. Conversely, the prodigal son and the vindicator appear alone, so there are no complicating external disjunctive motives. Unlike the prodigal son plot, the vindicator story solely concerns social position, and the threatened families — whose destruction becomes the motivation for avengers and prodigals — disappear from the vindicator constellation (though in some stories they appear as part of the setting).

The story of *Wanted* easily lends itself to an interpretation according to the prodigal constellation/plot. Gary the sheriff (son) is deprived of his position with the good authority (the judge who is forced to set a bounty), due to a conspiracy orchestrated by an evil authority (the mayor Gold) and a negative equivalent, who takes over as sheriff (Lloyd). In addition, Gary gets help to redeem himself from positive equivalents — the gambler Heywood, and the pistol-packing father Carrisco. The tale of Gary Ryan equals a "prodigal son" constellation/plot expressed in professional relations (sheriff/judge/mayor) instead of family ones. One might call him a "secular" prodigal son.

By the same line of reasoning, Ted Barnett in *Vendetta* becomes a semi-secular prodigal son. He is falsely accused of murdering his father, but the mystery of the father is solved in the second confrontation, leaving the problem of restoring his position in society as the central one. Correspondingly, there are no natural or foster brothers to appear as good equivalents. The positions of evil authority (Cobb), ditto equivalent (Douglas), and contested woman (Dolly) are taken though. The good authority—Judge Kincaid—belongs to the vindication constellation. The way the vindication and prodigal constellation/plots shadow each other in *Vendetta* elucidates both their similarities and differences. The main difference is that in the vindication story there exists the judge, a good authority to turn to, whereas in the prodigal story the good authority is dead. Thus the evil of the violent tyrant has no limit, which invites the instances of insanity often exposed in these films. This also brings them closer to the situation and circumstances in the infiltrator story of *Fistful of Dollars.*

The Spaces of Trouble

Spatially, *Fistful of Dollars* plays out in the streets of San Miguel, with the "small house" where Marisol is guarded and other countryside places as additional battlefields. In the two Ringo films, "big houses" outside town, occupied by bandit intruders, play important parts in the stories.

In the deprived hero movies there is a similar topography of conflict. Beside the violent confrontations in town, there is often a countryside ranch or cabin, where avengers, prodigal sons or vindicators fight the villains, are tortured by them, or search for clues. The cabins, and especially the big houses with their many rooms and passageways, become arenas for sneak fights. Prime examples are *Il ritorno di Ringo* and *Tempo di massacro.* In *Per pochi dollari ancora* it takes place in the surroundings of an abandoned mine—another isolated place.

In *Shane*—my U.S. Western reference story per se—there is a home on the range, and the villains reside in the town, but among the films discussed in this chapter, this model is followed only by the early *Gringo*. They also differ from *Fistful of Dollars*, where both gangs have their main site in town, and Joe searches and is brutalized in an urban storehouse. Placing the main body (and in many cases also the leadership) of bad guys in a house far away from town represents to some extent a marginalization of lawlessness.

CHAPTER 6

A Partnership of Bounty Killers

For a Few Dollars More

After *A Fistful of Dollars*, Leone released the still more successful *For a Few Dollars More* (1965) — in this study called *Few Dollars More*.[1] A remarkably large number of features introduced in this film would be objects for repeating, recycling and variation in Italowesterns for years to come. I have already discussed the use of flashbacks in vengeance stories,[2] and also the sneak fight and the supervised duel as instances of cunning.[3]

The Constellation

Instead of one hero between two opposing camps, *Few Dollars More* puts forward two bounty killers (Monco and Mortimer) in an unstable alliance against the gang of Indio, thus introducing a *doubled* hero as the protagonist.

Each corner of this triad has an introductory episode of his own. Indio is sprung from prison by his gang and avenges himself on the man who put him there. Mortimer makes an unlisted train stop at Tucumcari, where he finds a wanted man at the hotel and kills him using superior weaponry. Monco bursts into a saloon, confronts a wanted man, and kills him and his intervening companions in a gunfight. He then denounces the sheriff who alerted the others.

El Indio

Gian Mari Volontè, Ramon Rojo in *Fistful of Dollars*, again portrays a charismatic Mexican leader of an ethnically mixed but mostly Latin gang. Indio also shares with Ramon an apparent unpredictability that every time turns out to have been deliberate, like when Ramon hails peace and Indio kills his cellmate. Like Ramon, he engages in strategies of guile and subterfuge, this time also employed against his own gang (which isn't family-based). He also surpasses the *Fistful of Dollars* character in obsession. Ramon might sacrifice all his plans to regain Marisol, but Indio is obsessed with a woman that isn't flesh and blood anymore. She (Mortimer's sister) shot herself while he raped her. Indio regularly resorts to narcotics to relive these moments, especially after he has killed.

Monco

The name "Joe" in *Fistful of Dollars* (used by Piripero, the gravedigger) might just be an ethnic alias for "North American," but the Eastwood character is even more a "man with no name" in *Few Dollars More*. In a couple of scenes, he is referred to (by others) as "Monco" (or possibly "Manco"). Though going against the grain of the story presentation, I will use this name for convenience.

Monco wears the same poncho as Joe but rides a horse, and there is nothing in the story to confirm any biographical bonding between the characters.[4] He enters the saloon where his prey is playing cards, challenges him to a card game "for his life" then beats and grabs him using one hand (to have the other one free to draw against his companions when they appear). By contrast, Mortimer scares his victim by shoving a wanted poster under his hotel door and then kills him from a distance using special weapons, expounding a deliberate, distant style. Monco also shows "magical" prowess with the gun when shooting a man threatening him from the back, and verbal arrogance at close range when dealing with the corrupt sheriff, or later when personally evicting the unfortunate occupant of the only hotel room with a view of the street. Again, Mortimer's brand of arrogance is based on distance, e.g., when he quietly stares down the train conductor and the ticket salesman. Also he bests Monco in the mock duel with weapon superiority at long range.

Even so, Monco, like Joe, is also a master of cunning — most evidently when he calms the suspicions of the Indio gang by simply telling the truth, that he is after their bounty. This "joke" convinces them that he is a friend (all except Indio, but being another master of cunning he hides this knowledge for later use).

Mortimer

This leaves Mortimer at the Baxter corner of the triangle. Like Baxter he is an Anglo and wears a suit, though in both cases the respectability it symbolizes is flawed. He might be Colonel Mortimer from Carolina (not Virginia, as supposed by a bank manager), with all the connotations of gentleman and the Old South, but, as the old-timer interrogated by Monco says, "Now he's reduced to being a bounty killer just like you." Far from the Doc

Holliday archetype of John Ford's *My Darling Clementine*, Mortimer shows no hints of poems or tuberculosis and a very limited sense of fair play—as witnessed by the gun with extended stock used against the first outlaw and against Monco (in the hat-shooting duel), and even more by the hidden derringer used against Wild, the hunchback. We are here closer to the sinister figure of the back-shooting gambler Hatfield in *Stagecoach*.

In *Un dollaro bucato*—released the same year and where Southern cultural traits are explicitly referred to—the character of Gary O'Hara displays no upper-class aristocratic arrogance, even though his mansion comes with at least one African American servant. It is following *Few Dollars More* that disreputable aristocrats infest the spaghetti Western, whether they are Southerners, such as Jackson in *Django*, DeVinton in *Faccia a faccia*, and the bounty killer Tageo living in a big Southern mansion complete with an African American servant in *Sono Sartana, il vostro becchino*, or Teutonic Europeans, such as the sadistic Austrian Skimmer in *Indio Black, sai che ti dico ... sei un gran figlio di ...* and the arrogant piano-playing duelist von Schulinberg in *La resa dei conti*.

Similarly, the opening scene where the Bible-reading Mortimer is mistaken for a priest initiated a string of gun-toting clergymen in other films, for example the former gunslingers-turned-priests in *Reverendo Colt* and *Il figlio di Django* (both played by Guy Madison) and pseudo-priests such as the Bible-reading bounty killer Preacher in *Una lunga fila di croci*.

The Family Pathetic Motive and the Woman

While the destruction of the family of the man who turned in Indio takes place off-screen, the raped woman indeed forms the core of the pathetic in *Few Dollars More*. Live women are extremely marginal in this film, but the dead sister of Mortimer is a chief driving force, with equal motivating strength as the money theme of bounty hunting.

Just like Marisol in *Fistful of Dollars*—for whom Ramon gives away the chance for an easy take-over of San Miguel by exchanging her for the Baxter son, and Joe ceases his successful manipulation for an unselfish act of charity that costs him dearly—Mortimer's sister (the *woman* with no name!) serves as a "categorical imperative" for the men. As with the involuntary infiltrator Marisol, she also is an inverse of the male protagonists. Her act of using the gun on herself instead of on her rapist recurs in Indio's narcotic dream and is diametrically opposed to the ways of both the bandits and the bounty killers in the story.

Leone's first two Westerns load lots of narrative energy into their main female characters, even if neither gets to kiss the hero! It is rather *The Good, the Bad and the Ugly* and *Duck You Sucker* that merit Leone the nomination as a maker of Westerns without women.[5]

The burlesque landlady who likes tall men and has a dwarf for a husband can be seen as a parodic version of Mrs. Baxter in *Fistful of Dollars*, though far removed from the dark force and tragic fate of the latter.

The Double Hero

In the area of cunning, Monco's infiltration and Mortimer's stance of distance and surveillance both owe a lot to Joe's game. However, compared with the enigmatic, doubly motivated hero of *Fistful of Dollars*, Monco is straightforwardly money-oriented. The enigma reappears in the character of Mortimer, who eventually discloses a revenge motive and even forfeits the bounty money to his partner, thus externalizing the difference between the two motives. Not until then, in retrospect, do we learn that the action has been driven by a mystery (hinted at by the musical watches).

In *Few Dollars More* the relation between the two hero protagonists develops like this:

1. Monco and Mortimer enter El Paso independently to try to catch the Indio gang. They both discover that the other is staying in town keeping things under observation, each by seeing the other with binoculars in his own binoculars.

2. Both make investigations about the identity of the other. True to the difference in their general approach, Mortimer looks in newspapers, and Monco asks an old-timer.

3. Monco tries to run Mortimer out of town. They face off in a symbolic gunfight shooting at each other's hats. Mortimer wins by using his special gun with an extra stock.

4. They decide to work together, Monco infiltrating the gang and Mortimer working from the outside.

5. When their trap for Indio fails (because they didn't know the extent of his plan), Monco wants to end the partnership. Mortimer shoots to give Monco a superficial wound in the neck, as a backup to his cover story. They decide to continue the inside/outside strategy. Monco is to convince Indio to go north.

6. Monco suggests going south to Indio, who decides to go west, to Agua Caliente. There they find Mortimer, who had foreseen this development!

7. Mortimer makes a deal with Indio (for $5,000) to open the safe without destroying its content. Indio locks the money away for one month.

8. Mortimer and Monco independently break into the hiding place the same night. When leaving, they are surprised by the gang. Monco hides the money on the way down, and Mortimer has smeared the lock so the chest seems unopened. Indio tells his men that he will leave the two dead with stolen money to throw the posse off the track.

9. Indio arranges for their escape and sends his men after them. He intends to run off with the gold during the fight but is joined by Groggy, who saw through his designs. However, they find only Indio's wanted poster in the chest.

10. Mortimer shoots Groggy, but Indio gets the drop on him. Then Monco intervenes, making it an even duel. Indio is killed.

11. Mortimer lets Monco have all the bodies for bounty and rides off. Monco asks about the partnership and Mortimer replies, "Maybe another time!"

The main properties of this relation are *cooperation* against strong opponents; *competition* as both parties want the same object (bounty money); *confrontation* in one or more "mock" duels (the duel of hats in the street, Mortimer's shot to scar Monco, and first Monco's and then Mortimer's shooting down apples from a tree to scare off the gunmen of Agua Caliente); and *future of the partnership* in the form of Monco's question at the end and Mortimer's vague decline.

Now, a partnership resting upon mutual greed and the need to fight a common enemy always risks breaking apart and even turning into internecine struggle. These issues are spelled out in the conversation between the two men after the "hat fight." Mortimer suggests an equal partnership, because " there are fourteen of them," adding, "you could make it fifteen to one. Don't forget I wanna play in this game too. As you're aware, when two hunters go after the same prey they usually end up shooting each other in the back, and we don't want to shoot each other in the back." Finally, the two men drink to their partnership, "with no tricks of course" — a toast soon to be abused!

After Mortimer has presented his "inside/outside" plan, the theme from his musical watch bridges over to the narcotic dream of Indio, suggesting a tie between hunter and hunted — a tie later revealed to be based on matters other than money.

As a whole, this "partnership" conversation, with its suggestions and retorts, assertions of power and expertise, veiled threats and innuendoes, expresses the same cat-and-mouse game that was practiced by Joe and Ramon. It is in fact employed already in the presentation scenes of *Few Dollars More*, by Mortimer (the poster under the door, and the deliberate shooting of the escapee's horse at a distance disadvantaging him), by Monco (the card game), and by Indio (the dueling ceremonial with the musical watch).

Plots

THE INFILTRATION PLOT

The infiltration plot, where Monco sets up the inside/outside strategy by springing a friend of Indio's from prison to gain acceptance into the gang, provides models for only a limited part of the story's actions — first when Monco sabotages the infiltrated organization by killing the men sent with him to create a diversion, and secondly at the break-in where he and Mortimer are exposed.

THE MANIPULATION SEQUENCE

I have already discussed Indio's manipulation in the context of the insider/outsider/camp constellation.[6] He also acts as a manipulator when he sends Monco alone into Agua Caliente, pitting him against the gunmen of the village.

A supreme form of manipulation is "the strategy of the quarters" — the maneuvering of the escape routes when Mortimer foresees that the others will end up in Agua Caliente because of his advice to Monco. It is also implied that Mortimer predicts Indio's attack on the bank of El Paso because only "a complete madman" would attempt it.[7]

THE UNSTABLE PARTNERSHIP PLOT

To fully capture what is going on in *Few Dollars More*, the plot functions of infiltration and manipulation need to be supplemented by a plot focusing on the Monco-Mortimer relationship. Like the infiltration plot in *Fistful of Dollars*, it is played out in several models during the story. These models have a common constellation: A — Monco, B — Mortimer, C — Indio.

NARRATIVE SEQUENCES

The functions 4, 5 and 6 in table 6A describe the establishment of the partnership, and also its precariousness. They can be summarized in a narrative sequence that I call the *unstable partnership*. A narrative sequence spanning the total course of the relation, the *partnership*, then encompasses the unstable partnership, 9 and 10 (*a* or *b*). I consider the events described by the unstable partnership sequence as a most distinguishing feature of this story, and I will use this term to designate this constellation/plot and the stories and parts of stories that obey it.

Another key sequence in the partnership plot is that a second motive is established/revealed for one of the partners. If the initial state of motivation

Table 6A. Models of the Unstable Partnership Plot in *For a Few Dollars More*

Functions	Model 1	Model 2	Model 3	Model 4	Model 5
1. *A wants an object*	Mortimer is a bounty killer				
2. *B wants an object*	Monco is a bounty killer				
3. *C controls the object*	Indio has a bounty on his head				
4. *A and B have a fight*	The shooting of hats	Mortimer "wounds" Monco	The shooting of apples		
5. *A and B form a partnership*	The conversation	"The partnership is still on"	Mortimer and Monco re-united		
6. *A tricks B/B tricks A*		"The strategy of quarters"		Mortimer and Monco find each other breaking in.	(Monco takes the musical watch)
7. *A and/or B fight C*	Monco kills Indio's diversionary force	(Indio sends Monco against men of Agua Caliente)	Mortimer kills the Hunchback	Indio's men are killed in the sneak fight	Mortimer kills Indio
8. *B has a second motive*					Mortimer's sister is dead because of Indio
9. *A and B get the object*					Monco collects the bodies
10a. *A and B leave together*					"What about the partnership?"
10b. *A and B separate*					"Maybe some other time"

described by functions 1, 2 and 3 is summarized as a *conflict of objects*, then the *second motive* sequence will be conflict of objects, 8 and 9.

Codings and Motifs

Expertise

In the "partnership" conversation, when disputing the amount of bounty money offered for the members of Indio's gang, the two bounty killers try to outdo each other in the specialist knowledge of their trade. The master of these refined "scraps of information" (to again quote Miguel Rojo) is Mortimer, who has a notebook with sums of bounty. In the realm of specialized weaponry, expertise is highlighted when Mortimer, seeing his prey riding off down the street, calmly releases a roll on his saddle containing a veritable armory of rifles, revolvers and accessories.[8] He again proves himself a master of specialist gadgets when he opens the bank safe using drills and acid. Before that, he has killed the hunchback in a duel expertly, if not fairly, by having a derringer appear in his hand from up his sleeve.

Age

At another moment, in their conversation after the "hat" fight, Mortimer replies to Monco's skeptic comment about his specialized weaponry ("How can somebody in my business walk around with a contraption like this?") with a reference to their difference in age ("Boy, I have reached almost 50 years of age with my system. Not many men last long in these parts. How long do you expect to last?")

At the closing of the story, in the confrontation with Indio, the younger man gets the opportunity to return the taunt, saying, "Very careless of you, old man," as he hands Mortimer *his* gun with belt instead of the "contraption" that Indio has shot out of Mortimer's hand. Then he restarts the watch tune, and the dueling ceremonial. Up to then Mortimer's tactics of guile and reserve have won out over Monco's directness. Monco's "supervised duel" in effect shows that he has learned the game of cunning enough to turn the tables on the older man.

The Musical Watch

The musical watch is used to great effect in *Few Dollars More*, first as a framing ceremonial when Indio draws his gun, then immediately as a backdrop to his dreaming recall of the suicide of the young woman, and then the melody is used to suggest a connection to Mortimer. Finally, in the duel between the two men, the significance of the watch and its tune is further enhanced by the photo seen in its open lid of the woman whose fate connects the two duelists.[9]

The three protagonists of *For a Few Dollars More*, from left, Monco (Clint Eastwood), Mortimer (Lee Van Cleef) and the corpse of Indio (Gian Mari Volontè). The fourth is also present as Monco holds the watch with the photograph of Mortimer's sister!

In fact this gadget might be the most pervasive of the narrative inventions in Leone's second Western, used in dozens of Italowesterns. Sometimes it's a music box instead, and sometimes it has a function other than being part of a vengeance ceremonial.

Archaeology of the Partnership Pair

Compared with the intensive interaction of Mortimer and Manco — oscillating between co-operation and con game — protagonists like Joe, "in the middle" between the Rojos and the Baxters; Django fighting Jackson and robbing Hugo; and Ringo, "on the inside" among enemies with a skeptical sheriff on the outside, might appear to be standing completely alone. At critical moments even their survival requires the assistance of sidekicks or equivalents, though. Joe is taken out of San Miguel by Piripero and later saved by Silvanito from the ambush of Esteban Rojo. Ringo is supplied with weapons first by Chico and later by the major, and Maria saves Django from being engulfed by the quicksand.

Furthermore, certain forms of partnerlike relationships appeared even before *Few Dollars More*. The Karl May–inspired German Westerns that made commercial headway for the spaghetti Westerns in Germany and Italy featured the Anglo (well, originally German) Old Shatterhand (Lex Barker) in a stable pair with the Apache Winnetou (Pierre Brice).[10] In chapter 4 I discussed several hero pairs in the early spaghetti Westerns, some of them markedly unstable, especially Carrancho and his Gringo partners in *5000 dollari sull'asso* and *L'uomo che viene da Canyon City*. The relation prodigal hero and positive equivalent might sometimes border on an unstable partnership, especially for the half brothers Tom and Jeff in *Tempo di massacro*. On the other hand, the avenger/money-oriented hero doubles discussed in chapter 5 are offspring of the *Few Dollars More* relation rather than precursors to it.

Enter the Bounty Killer

It was *Few Dollars More* that introduced bounty hunting into the Italowestern film genre, and its story is framed by this motif. At the beginning there is a line: "Where life had no value, death, sometimes, had its price. That is why the bounty killers appeared" And at the end, Monco is seen calculating the total bounty value of the heap of bodies loaded on his wagon, and being alerted to the fact that Groggy is still alive (and aiming at him) by the fact that the sum is short, thus highlighting the reduction of human flesh and blood to its monetary equivalent.

Monco and Mortimer show their expertise as bounty hunters in their handling of "trade" information about wanted men, and in weaponry and related techniques. Frayling touches on both these aspects when he writes that the Django films according to the bounty hunter schema "show which assignments he is prepared to accept, and the methods he uses."[11] Accordingly, there are two kinds of situations that usually occur for the bounty hunter hero, one where he shows his prowess in getting his quarry (the methods he uses), and one where he considers whether a certain quarry is worth going after (which assignments he is prepared to accept).

The Bounty Hunter Gets His Men

Following the cue from the introductory episodes with Monco and Mortimer in *Few Dollars More*, this is laid out in an independent episode at the start of films with bounty killer heroes.

Per centomila dollari t'ammazzo starts with the Mexican bandit Goncalvez and his three men looking for John Forester in a church. The men are killed by John rising from inside a coffin. Goncalvez empties his gun at it, but still he is killed, because the box was iron plated on the inside.

The beginning of *The Bounty Killer* sets the gritty tone for the story to come. Two riders in a steep, barren, sand-yellow, labyrinthine canyon are stalked by a man out of gun range high up on the cliffs. When one of the horses breaks his leg the man tries to get up behind the other rider, who brushes him off and rides. The man left behind shoots at the stalker, who is riding down. The man makes a dash for the rifle in the saddle of the horse but is shot dead. For the first time we get a look at the bounty killer, Luke Chillson, dressed in a black shirt and vest.

The beginning of *Vado, l'ammazzo e torno* sets the parodic tone of that story when a bounty hunter called Stranger — trailing behind a wagon carrying three coffins — encounters three men who in dress and looks, if not in names, are similar to Joe/Monco, Mortimer and Django. He shows them their wanted posters lying in the coffins before he shoots them.

The Bounty Killer Considers a Mission

The bounty killer might refuse a mission or a bounty because the sum offered is too low to bother with. He might even socialize with such a low-priced criminal.

In the beginning of *Diecimila dollari per un massacro*, the bounty hunter Django meets the wanted Manuel Cortez on the road without reacting, and later he is seen playing cards with Cortez. This is because Django will go after a man only if the bounty is at least $10,000 (as in the film title). At first he refuses to help the landowner Mendoza retrieve his daughter Dolores, who has been abducted by Manuel, because the payment offered is too small. The same rule of thumb goes for Minnesota in *I senza Dio*. He will pursue a partnership with El Santo as long as the bounty of the latter is lower than $10,000. Correspondingly, when Stranger in *Vado, l'ammazzo e torno* has the wanted bandit Monetero in his gun sight during a train robbery, he holds his fire because he expects the bounty to go up.

This particular elaboration of the bounty hunter's trade was introduced in *Arizona Colt* (1966), where the hero, after his initial scrape with the gang of Gordo Watch, still does not disclose Gordo's "Lieutenant" Kay when he encounters him reconnoitering a bank robbery.[12] Later we understand why, when he tells Jane about his tactics as a bounty hunter: He expected a coming attack of the band to create a demand for his services! He also tells Gordo that he won't go after him until the price is right. Owen, the professional gun hired by the town bosses to kill Talby in *I giorni dell'ira*, even warns his intended victim of an assassination attempt to protect his own source of income. An unfortunate decision, as he loses the special duel on horseback with front-loading rifles that he challenges Talby to!

That the hero refrains from fighting criminals unless he gets paid well enough represents an obvious repudiation of good society values—an extreme form of "selfish money values," to use the concept of Wright. It's not surprising then that the bounty killer often partners with the criminal to earn a larger sum of money. Django joins with Manuel to rob a transport of gold. When John Forester cannot get the bounty for his brother paid out, he instead opts to share loot from a robbery with him. Minnesota offers El Santo a share of gold. Acquasanta Joe joins with the wanted Donovan to a share a sum of robbery money. In the first two cases the outcome of this apogee of the monetary motive is tragic (see "The Tragic Mercenary" in the next section). Minnesota turns out to be a government agent who retrieves the gold, but El Santo gets the opportunity to avenge the murder of his father. Neither Donovan nor Acquasanta Joe gets the money because the bounty hunter was only bluffing to make a getaway. However, Stranger has no qualms with sharing the money from the train robbery with Monetero.[13]

The Tragic Mercenary

A great number of the bounty killer films followed the cue of *Few Dollars More* and contained double motives, internal and/or external, disjunctive and conjunctive. Some of them have been discussed previously as avenger films. In some stories with a bounty killer or otherwise money-oriented hero, such as *Per centomila dollari t'ammazzo, Diecimila dollari per un massacro, Django Kill!* and *El Desperado*, a monetary motive (directly or indirectly) entails the killing or wounding of someone close to the hero, who then sets out on a vengeance mission.

This development can be summarized in the following plot:

1. A and B become partners because of a monetary motive.
2. A and C are close.
3. B commits a misdeed against C.
4. A searches and finds B.
5. A kills B.

I will call this the "tragic mercenary" plot. The functions 2 through 5 make up an avenger hero plot while the first brings in the monetary motives.

In both *Per centomila dollari t'ammazzo* and *Diecimila dollari per un massacro*, function 1 is precluded by this narrative sequence:

a. A is a bounty hunter.
b. A accepts a mission to capture B.
c. A and B fight.

In *Mannaja*, the bounty hunter hero Blade gives up his revenge on mining big boss McGowan, who has killed his father — because McGowen "is not worth it" — and instead elects to deliver the ransom for the mine owner's daughter. This mission fails because the daughter is a false involuntary infiltrator.[14] Mark that the same situation appears in *Diecimila dollari per un massacro*, when Django is to liberate the kidnapped daughter of Mendoza from Manuel. Anyway, Blade's economic arrangement with the man he should have killed sets off a course of action leading to his being tortured and to the death of the showgirl Annie, who loves him. The malefactor is McGowen's treacherous foreman Voller, so in this case there is a doubling of malefactors, consecutive in time.

The hero in *Django Kill!* also starts by pursuing vengeance. After killing Oates, who has massacred Django's gang for the sake of a booty, he stays around to find that gold, which in fact is in the hands of the bosses Alderman and Templar. In two models of the same set of functions, Django encounters a town boss and befriends another character, who subsequently is destroyed. Evan, the son of Templar, is taken hostage for the gold by the rancher Zorro.

Django's attempts to help Evan fail, and the young man commits suicide after being gang-raped by Zorro's "muchachos." Then there's Elizabeth, the wife that Alderman uses as bait for Django. While she and Django fall into each other's arms, her husband steals Django's gun and uses it to kill Templar. Django is blamed (he is the only one who use gold bullets!), and Alderman is left with the treasure. However, Elizabeth sets fire to the house and perishes, and Alderman is killed by melted gold. The story of *Django Kill!* leaves a bewildering impression, but lends itself to an interpretation by the "tragic mercenary" constellation/plot. What makes the story seem confusing is that neither Evan nor Elizabeth dies directly because of any wrong choice by the hero, who is relegated to be one puppet of fate among the others. Still, as their demise is related to Django's decision to stay and look for the gold (instead of following advice to "go while the going is good"), he is stigmatized by the guilt of the "tragic mercenary."

This plot is discernible already in Corbucci's *Django*. Django allies with Hugo to get to Jackson's gold (function 1). Earlier he fights not Hugo, but Jackson, but he also has a vicious fight with Hugo's "Lieutenant" Ricardo (function c). After running away with the money, he suffers the same destiny as the tragic mercenaries: His lover is shot (wounded, not killed), and he is badly beaten. Maria's appeal at the river to leave the gold because "it will only bring heartache" (in the typical, threadbare dialogue kept between the two) is analogous to unheeded advice from loved ones in other stories, such as Myanou in *Diecimila dollari per un massacro*. The "tragic mercenary" constellation position "B" is doubled, as Hugo administers the misdeeds, but the ensuing vengeance is directed against Jackson, another malefactor, who in the meantime has killed Hugo. Consequently, the "tragic mercenary" constellation/plot can be seen as a simplified offspring of *Django*.

The hero in this constellation/plot is of the deprived kind, and not only because someone close to him is badly hurt or killed. What's more, the catastrophe is directly or indirectly brought about by his decision to pursue a monetary motive — that is, by a disjunctive, internal second motive. He also undergoes harsh physical punishment — in *Django* his hands are crushed, in *Diecimila dollari per un massacro* and *Mannaja* he is buried up to his neck and left at the mercy of the sun, in *Per centomila dollari t'ammazzo* he is shot and crucified upside down, in *Django Kill!* he is crucified and attacked by reptiles and bats, and in *El Desperado* he is severely beaten and left for dead. In *Lo chiamavano King* and *I lunghi giorni dell'odio*, where the hero pursues malefactors for monetary reasons, their misdeeds against his kin are not dependent on any decision on his part, so the internal double motive instead becomes conjunctive. The fact that these heroes are less physically devastated suggests a co-variation between disjunctive internal motives and punishment.

Inversely, in *Fistful of Dollars* it is Joe's rescue of Marisol, his choice to pursue a non-monetary motive, that leads up to his being disclosed and tortured, while the threatened family escapes unharmed. The ironic twist that a selfish line of action is successful but an altruistic act leads to disaster is indeed more unconventional and even scandalous in modern popular culture compared with how the internal second motive is elaborated in *Django* and in the "tragic mercenary" plot. The non-monetary motives in the intervening *Few Dollars More* are conjunctive both internally (both lead Mortimer toward Indio) and externally — Monco does not mind being left with all the bounty money! The most important influence on the genre from *Django* might be this swing in the relation between the two internal motives: making the pursuit of the monetary motive, not the non-monetary one, disastrous, and not only for the hero (as victim of punishment), but also for someone close to him who becomes the victim of a misdeed, which turns the money-oriented hero into a deprived one — and an avenger.

The Bounty Killer Adversary

In *I quattro inesorabile*, a mainly U.S.–style film from 1966, bounty killers frame the righteous ranger hero for murder, and to further improve business, their leader secretly supports his escape and then (unsuccessfully) tries to cash in on the reward that is posted. In the opening scene of *Texas addio*, a bounty hunter turned away by the sheriff, Burt Sullivan, makes the fatal decision to ambush Burt outside of town. Equally unfortunate are the bounty killers that pursue the escaped interns into the woods in *Ciak Mull*. In *Tequila!* Shoshena manipulates several bounty killers to finish each other off by posting a reward for his own (supposedly) dead body. Sartana is pursued for his bounty by several professional acquaintances in *Sono Sartana, il vostro becchino*, and even if he kills most of them, their relation is mutually respectful. In contrast, the grotesque bounty killers sent by the slave smuggler Spencer against the Chinese hero in *Il mio nome è Shanghai Joe* deserve little respect—a half-naked cannibal with a lecherous one-eyed companion, a sadist, a treacherous gambler and a knife-wielding scalper. In *Wanted*, Gary Ryan's pursuers are ordinary citizens, not professional bounty hunters.

Two films where the conflicts stand between bounty killers and wanted men, including the hero or those protected by him, are the most uncompromisingly pessimistic stories in the spaghetti Western. The wanted Clay McCord in *Un minuto per pregare, un istante per morire* is presented as an inversion of a bounty killer hero. In an introductory scene Clay and his friend Fred outsmart and defeat some bounty killers—instead of the other way around. Instead of considering the amount of a bounty, Clay ponders whether the governor's offer of amnesty and $50 is good enough, and tries to up the price. He is involved in a classic three-part constellation involving the sheriff Colby, who tries to stop outlaws from reaching town to claim the amnesty and also blockades their hideout in Escondido, where their leader Kraut also is opposed to the amnesty, as it threatens his position. These two camps threaten the outlaws and their families—Fred, who is killed by bounty hunters after Clay decides that they should split up; some outlaws who decline Clay's company and are killed by Colby's deputies; father Santana, who is killed when bounty killers set a trap for Clay; and finally Laurinda, who nurses him in Escondido and is killed trying to protect him from Kraut's men. All these killings of innocents thus involve Clay.

He is also a deprived hero because of an affliction that now and again makes his gun arm unusable and that he believes is inherited from his father—a flashback suggests that Clay first became a killer when he avenged him. If Clay's father is an involuntary bringer of evil, there is also a good authority in the governor Carter, unexpectedly proficient in supporting his amnesty policy with fists and guns. He stops the blockade against Escondido and brings Clay to a doctor who takes out the forgotten bullet that has been the real reason for his attacks. Kraut and Colby are killed in a fight. As a cured and free man, Clay leaves town but is gunned down by two bounty killers, who are dismayed to find the amnesty papers on his corpse and conclude that if this amnesty lasts, they will have to go back to buffalo hunting.

In Corbucci's *Il grande silenzio* the mute hero, called Silence, avenges his father by shooting off the thumbs of bounty killers to make them harmless. He enters a highland town during winter. Outlaws hide in the mountains from bounty hunters — the most ruthless being Loco, who eliminates the sheriff by shooting the ice under his feet so he drowns and who has the outlaws captured. When Silence arrives, one of the bounty killers, whose brother Silence has killed, shoots off *his* thumb. Then the hero is killed by Loco and the outlaws are massacred, including Silence's woman Pauline. Rather than a "tragic mercenary" story this is a vengeance story, that turns on itself.

Deprived hero with an affliction — Clay McCord (Alex Cord) in *Un minuto per pregare, un istante per morire.*

Both films present the most outrageous type of ending imaginable in an American/European popular-culture genre, that of the hero being killed by a surviving villain. The victims are not settler families but wanted outlaws. The luring out and massacring of the outlaws in the latter film reappear in a similar way in the director's later *Che c'entriamo noi con la rivoluzione?* where it befalls political opponents of an oppressive regime. Another hapless group of outlaws, including women and children, is massacred in the politically informed *Faccia a faccia*. Still, these latter stories, and others directly touching on political issues, end in defeats for the villains (see "Enter the Revolution" in chapter 7). Not so in *Un minuto per pregare, un istante per morire* and especially *Il grande silenzio*, where the message is, "No mercy for the wretched." I believe that the narrative logic of the deprived-hero stories reaches a limit here.

The Positive Bounty Killer

In *Per il gusto di uccidere* the bounty hunter Lanky Fellow first annihilates the bandit gang of Sanchez and returns its booty. Then he agrees to double his reward by guarding the money from the gang of Kennebeck until an army troop arrives to collect it. Lanky is paid and leaves. On the road he observes the transport being ambushed by another gang of bandits, and grins.

The hero gets the full presentation of a bounty killer. His annihilation of the Sanchez gang serves as an unusually long introductory episode showing the bounty killer's competence. The bounty killer's habit of not interfering until a business situation has evolved is shown at first when he observes their ambush, and later when he kills a vindictive outlaw after concluding that the man will never bring a higher price.

However, what is different from the bounty killer stories discussed so far is that in *Per il gusto di uccidere* the hero is always in control. The developments never put him at the mercy of any villain, so he is never subject to torture. He does not go out of his way to pursue a second motive, and his choices do not put any loved ones of his in danger. Still, these situations and corresponding thematic roles pop up in the story, though related to characters other than the hero. There is a Marisol figure in the form of Isabelle, though in love with the bandit Kennebeck—whose indisputably Mexican countenance and dress are a bona fide case of casual ethnicity! He is her husband and the father of her son, and she mourns when he is killed by the hero. Lanky once has her tied and gagged while waiting for Kennebeck, similarly to Joe's use of Marisol as a pawn in his manipulation game, before he decides to help her.

As a further family complication, Kennebeck's brother John is on the right side of the law, and they take each other's children as hostages. Also, John's daughter runs off with a young (Anglo) bandit set to guard her (in a romantic story compressed into fewer than five minutes' screening time). If the hero is spared torture, it instead falls upon John (by Gus), and also on Kennebeck's man Machete, who is beaten around and severely bruised by John and the sheriff until he talks.

It seems that the featuring of Lanky's methods and tactics — his marksmanship and mastery of observation, his tactics in devising traps with explosives and hiding the gold (as the new stairs of the bank!) — is not expected to bring enough complication and interest to the story. Cleansing the hero of a second motivation and the connected elements of pathos instead make these elements appear in other, less common contexts in the story. *Per il gusto di uccidere* implies that they in fact belong to the "continuous series of connotations" for the (non-comedy) Spaghetti Western.[15]

A second motive of vengeance is in fact ascribed to Lanky, because Kennebeck had killed his brother. As a second motivation it is conjunctive to protecting the gold, and has no actual influence on the story. For example, in the final confrontation it is the Mexican who comes looking for the hero, not the other way around.

In the seminal case of Mortimer, the money and vengeance motives are also conjunctive, but to that story is added the quality of *mystery*, as the misdeed relating Mortimer and Indio, though hinted at, is not revealed until the end. Added are also the elements of uncertainty and guile, both between the partners in their unstable relationship and in the moments of infiltration and manipulations between them and the villain.

The bounty killer hero of *Acquasanta Joe* has no non-monetary second motive. However, he does get involved with the woman of the bandit leader Donovan. Also, most of the story revolves around his unstable relationship with and betrayal of Donovan.

In a similar vein, Italowestern narratives such as *Uccidete Johnny Ringo* or *La colt era il suo Dio*, where the hero is an organizational man on a mission — an officer or an agent for the government, the rangers, an insurance agency, etc.— are fleshed out with emotionally invested side stories, mysteries to be solved and/or unstable partnerships.

CHAPTER 7

A Partnership Without Tricks

The "unstable partnership" constellation/plot introduced in *Few Dollars More* was further developed and modified in other spaghetti Westerns.

The "Sleeping Partner"

The stories of *Un fiume di dollari* and *Cjamango* both present variations on the *Fistful of Dollars* setup. In the first movie, Segal is an Anglo big boss villain while his henchman Mendez — all dressed in black — is a Latin psychopath (cf. Ramon), who is doing the fighting against the city-dressed Horner (cf. Rojos vs. Baxter). The hero Jerry is not money-oriented but an avenger, who infiltrates by joining Mendez and using his inside information to help Horner. After killing Mendez, he infiltrates (in a tactical sense) the house of Segal dressed as Mendez and kills him. There also is a threatened woman (the sister of Segal) and a boy (Jerry's son).

Cjamango is even closer to the seminal example with an Anglo camp (led by Tiger) and a Mexican one (Don Pablo's), and the threatened Mexican woman Pearl, with a boy. Cjamango has a money motive: to regain gold robbed from him after he has won it at cards. He strikes an alliance (rather than an infiltration in the strict sense) with the Mexican side and, exactly like Joe, he orchestrates a fight between them to be able to search for the gold.

Yet, overlaid with the *Fistful of Dollars*–like sequences in these films are the relationships between the hero and another protagonist, the army officer Getz and the ranger Clinton, respectively. They are profiting from the actions of the hero to regain money taken from the government. I call them "sleeping partners," for these government agents take the back seat to the infiltrator hero, who is the one who manipulates the villains and destroys most of them. Thus they adopt a manipulative position vis-à-vis their dupes, the hero and the villain. The partnerships are not explicit. Getz supervises a duel by giving Jerry a gun with two bullets against two opponents and then convinces Segal that Jerry is dead and becomes one of Segal's men. He uses this infiltration to help Jerry, and together they destroy Mendez's gang in a sneak fight. Clinton supports Cjamango in one gunfight, and later informs Tiger when Don Pablo has caught Cjamango. They also escape together during a big shootout.

In neither film is there any conflict between hero and agent about money. Jerry is an avenger who is left united with his son. Though Cjamango's original motive was the gold, he leaves it with Clinton, and departs with Pearl's son.

The theme of an agent manipulating a hero with another motive recurs in *La grande notte di Ringo*, where the gunfighter Jack Ballman is arrested for a series of stage coach holdups. Acting on information from a cellmate that three leading men in Tombstone are among the real culprits, he breaks out, has it out with them, secures and hides the booty, and returns to the cell before morning. Then it turns out that the cellmate is a federal officer, and thanks to Ballman's actions, the ringleader is arrested (the others having been killed during the night). After a fight over the booty, which has disappeared (being apprehended by the judge who arrested Ballman in the first place), the gunfighter leaves with the lawman, in what might become a crime-fighting partnership.

Apart from the partnership, *La grande notte di Ringo* has few similarities to *Few Dollars More*. The characters wear traditional cowboy or city dress, the story relies mostly on dialogues in closed spaces, and violence is direct and unreflecting, lacking spectacularly staged walk-downs with tension-building pauses, as well as big massacres or vicious beatings. The character coming closest to a "spaghetti Western" style also provides the only Latin appearance among straight-faced gringos. José, the hired gun, is dressed in Mexican hat and embroidered jacket. When the stable owner Black Norton (one of those characters dressed in all black)[1] enters his house, he hangs upside down, as he says, to test himself. He then shoots the catch off the door and later the ropes around his boots to get down. After haggling about the price, José and his men (who do not respond to Norton's firing his gun, but rise to José's whistling) agree to kill Ballman, but when José gets the drop on Ballman, the Mexican instead asks, "What will you pay me for not killing you?" After having a fight, and haggling over percentages, they form a partnership to get the hidden loot. Ballman gives back José's gun, and the Mexican says, "That's the sign of real friendship."

"Sleeping Partner" Variations

To have been released as late as 1971, *Anda muchacho spara!* is a surprisingly faithful rendering of *Fistful of Dollars*'s ambience, its production year showing mostly in the amount of exposure of female nudity.[2] The hero Roy (whose real name is mentioned only once in the film) infiltrates and destroys the criminal organization of the banker Redfield, because his prison mate Emiliano had told him about their gold. In the end Roy returns the gold to the Mexican miners that it originally belonged to, and leaves with Emiliano's daughter Jessica — who had earlier been an object of contention and enforced sexual attention among Redfield's men. Redfield is a manipulator who uses Roy to destroy his partners Lorentzon and Newman. The fight between them is indeed supervised both by Roy and Redfield. However, the triumphing manipulator is Emiliano, whose promises of gold and other information to Roy makes the latter his instrument of revenge and thus an *involuntary* avenger, while Emiliano is not simply a "sleeping" partner but a dead one when the film starts!

In *I senza Dio* the "sleeping partner" relation consorts with a bounty killer story instead of an infiltrator one. The government agent Minnesota poses as a bounty killer — with all the trappings.[3] He haggles with the bankers about the bounty, he allies with the outlaw El Santo whose bounty is below his limit, and he collects and cashes in dead bodies. Still he conforms to the "sleeping" pattern and only assists El Santo, who gets to kill both the bandit leader and the bad sheriff. Again there is no conflict about the gold, as Santo turns out to be an avenger who already knows that Minnesota is an agent.

Sleeping Partners and the "Unstable Partnership" Story

I designate the manipulator, who has a hidden motive, as "B," and "A" as the hero/dupe. This does not rule out "A" acting as a master of cunning toward the villains. Jerry and Cjamango manipulate the two camps, Roy fakes a telegram to force Redfield to expose the gold, and Santo uses a gold bar "stolen" from Minnesota to smoke out the conspirators, Jane Barret and the sheriff.

In *La grande notte di Ringo* and *I senza Dio* "B" explicitly aspires to the same monetary object as "A," and they make an agreement about it. In *Un fiume di dollari* and *Cjamango*, the initial ambitions of "B" are different ("a job," "sell whisky"). In *Anda muchacho spara!* the dead Emiliano cannot aspire to anything, technically speaking, but his legacy to Roy, the story about the gold, implies that this is his own motive. Anyway, the other, real motive of "B" turns out to be restoring an object, usually also wanted by "A," to some rightful owners. In the end, "A" will not contest this, as he himself obtains a second motive too—usually a woman and/or a child. It is "A" who fights "C" with some assistance from "B," and so it is "A" who brings out the money object into the open for "B" to restore to its owners.

Generally the partnership is weak and implicit. Only in *La grande notte di Ringo* and *I senza Dio* are there explicit partnerships, and these partners also have fights—in the latter film only a confrontation, while the real enough fight in *La grande notte di Ringo* is the beginning of a second partnership after the first one has run out. Otherwise there will be hardly any fights. "A" will not trick "B," and "B" will trick "A" only insofar as hiding his real motive. The peculiarities of the "sleeping partner" variant are summarized below:

"Unstable partnership" plot	"Sleeping partner" variant
1. A wants an object.	Gold/revenge.
2. B wants an object.	Often gold.
3. C controls the object(s).	Has the gold/is the malefactor.
4. A and B have a fight.	Weak or nonexistent.
5. A and B form a partnership.	Often only implicit.
6. A/B tricks B/A.	B withholds his motive.
7. A and/or B fight C.	A fights C, with varying degrees of assistance from B.
8. B has a second motive.	B is an agent out to restore the gold. A also gets an emotional motive.
9. A and B get their object(s).	B restores gold/A gets woman.
10a. A and B leave together.	*La grande notte di Ringo*.
10b. A and B separate.	The other stories.

Sleeping Partnerships Together with Other Plots

The setup of *Django spara per primo*, in which the hero arrives with the corpse of his father to a town where his father's former partner, Cluster, rules, could very well be the outset of a "prodigal son" story or an avenger story. However, Glenn mostly covets his economic inheritance, and so is best labeled an "economically vindicative" hero.[4] It is true that when given the opportunity, he chooses to fight Cluster, the man responsible for the death of his father, rather than take a third of the robbery loot, but then again, he had earlier accepted an equal partnership with the same malefactor. Additionally, when Glenn claims the bounty for his father, he shows an unsentimental expedience foreign to the remorseless ceremonial of the avenger. The relationship between Glenn and Doc, the two strangers in town, has an obvious resemblance to the sleeping partnerships described above. Doc assists Glenn's quest to regain his heritage but stays in the background. On the other hand, Doc is not a government agent intending to confiscate any property of Cluster's (or Glenn's). Besides, Glenn, who is the hero in the "A" position, is neither from the outset an avenger (like Jerry) nor out to gain or regain stolen money (like Cjamango, Roy and El Santo).

The second motivation revealed for the "B" hero Doc is his bigamist wife, Jessica Cluster. As with the case of Glenn, the plot pattern is fuzzy. That he frees her from the cell should be an attempt at vindication (to get her back) rather than vindiction (to destroy her), and his cunning act of carrying an empty gun is an ultimate test of her allegiance to him. She fails this test when she points it at him, and when she uses it against Cluster, it becomes a deadly trap for her.

In a sense, all the sleeping partners above are vindicative, as they restore some kind of valuable property to its rightful owners. In *Django spara per primo*, where both partners are vindicative, conflict is avoided not because Glenn gives up his motive, but because the motive is different. Additionally, Glenn Saxon in his performance as Glenn recalls the ironic touch and blond gusto of vindicative hero archetype Giuliano Gemma. Most of the actors rather emulating the Clint Eastwood style and demeanor would have had a hard time carrying the scene where Glenn, after a stunt in bed with Jessica, appears in female dressing gown and gun belt!

The robbery loot is first taken by Cluster from his own bank, then snatched by Jessica, then retaken by Cluster, conquered by Glenn and finally seized by Lucy. She does not try to keep it for herself, but uses it to "seize" Glenn, thus ending this chain of acquisition. These relations seem better accounted for by the betrayal plot discussed in chapter 8, as are a number of plot models concerning the entire property:

- Cluster has Glenn's father framed, posts a reward and has him killed, and takes control of the whole town.
- Jessica tries to have Glenn kill Cluster, obviously to inherit her husband's money.
- Glenn makes Cluster disappear and posts a reward, taking control of the town with Lucy and Gordon.
- Cluster's son appears to claim his share — the implication that this will restart the story.

Django Spara per Primo is thus a "sleeping partner" variant with double vindicative heroes, interleaved with a betrayal plot.

Destined for violent deaths, from left, henchman Mendez (Henry Silva), Marisol woman Mary Segal (Nicoletta Machiavelli) and ranch boss/former robber Ken Segal (Nando Gazzolo) in *Un fiume di dollari.*

The Malignant Partner

The story of *W Django!* begins when the wife of bounty killer Django is assaulted and killed when she goes for a gun. Django, who believes that Carranza has an alibi for the killing, saves him from a hanging and demands information. Carranza cooperates with Django to kill the malefactors, and in return he is promised their money and a shipment of contraband. However, these different motivations turn incompatible and reveal an act of manipulation, when Carranza discloses that he is the fourth malefactor and has used Django to get rid of his competitors for the money.

In *W Django!* most of the energy is put into displaying the tactical cunning and effects displayed by the hero in the confrontations with the malefactors — as is common for an avenger film. In *El Cisco* — where the main plot line concerns the hero's finding the real culprits behind the bank robbery pinned on him — the rendering is somewhat threadbare (and leaves several loose ends), but plotwise it includes several manipulation models. For example, the sheriff and the bandit Cascaron manipulate the posse to rob the bank, but the hero gets there first. Cisco later attempts to create discord between the two by means of another robbery loot. He also disguises himself as a Mexican and gets to play out the favorite gambit of pretending to be dead, even as far as a funeral. On the other hand, Cisco is manipulated by Cascaron, who greets him as a friend and, just like Carranza in *W Django!*, assists the hero by fingering the man that he is looking for and who conveniently enough is Cascaron's own enemy, while the Mexican hides his own culpability. The Cisco character is an inconsistent mixture of avenger and vindicator, making the story a weak version of both kinds of story.

In *... dai nemici mi guardo io!* Gringo and the bandit El Condor both hunt a Confederate treasure, with three coins providing the keys to its location. Gringo and Hondo escape together from jail (hidden in coffins), but it is not until Hondo has saved the other after an infiltration attempt (betrayed by Hondo himself) that he attains an equal partnership. When they have killed El Condor and found his coin, Hondo reveals that he has the third one and shoots Gringo. However, the bullet is stopped by Gringo's coin, and the information is destroyed. Hondo is thus a malignant partner who loses both partnership and riches. Gringo, however, has a second motive and leaves with a Mexican woman.

These three stories feature unstable partnership relations where one secret opponent of the hero forms a partnership to use him against the other opponents. This is disclosed at the end of the story and causes a confrontation. The malignant partner is Mexican, while the hero is a gringo. Also, the deadly ending still suggests an emotional bond between the two partners. In the closing scene in *W Django!*, Django, after grabbing the gun, holds for a moment and says, "Adios" to Carranza, who replies, "Adios, gringo" before he is shot. Cascaron, after being stabbed with his own knife, in a way excuses Cisco by saying that he sooner or later would have to pay, before falling from a cliff. In *... dai nemici mi guardo! io* it is less explicitly expressed, but Hondo gives Gringo a sad look when he leaves.

In *Lo credevano uno stinco di Santo* the feared outlaw Trash Benson forcibly brings Dan Carver and his cellmate Paco on a journey to find the loot that Carver once stashed away. Carver dies, but Paco and Benson form a partnership, and besides one unsuccessful betrayal attempt from Paco and Carver (described by Benson as "a sorry sight when two idiots work together"), they keep together — except when they are subjected to a tug of war, where one has to reach water to put out a burning fuse tied to dynamite! However, when Paco finds the money (in a statue of a saint in a

Mexican village), there is an immediate betrayal followed by a pursuit. Paco becomes a malignant partner *by opportunity*.

Partnership in the "Malignant Partner" Films

In these stories the character in the "B" position (manipulative hero) is always secretly part of "C," either as one of the objects of revenge of the (duped) "A" hero (*W Django!*), of the reasons for his outcast situation (*El Cisco*), or because he controls part of the desired object (*... dai nemici mi guardo io!*). "B" allies with "A" to fight the other "C" characters, who control monetary objects. In *Lo credevano uno stinco di Santo*, where no one from the outset controls the (monetary) object, "C" can be interpreted as the several other parties also out for the gold. "B" (Paco) shows himself as belonging to "C" when he tries to take the loot all for himself.

The revelation that "B" belongs to "C" — and thus shares that motive — is the second motive in function 8 of the "unstable partnership" plot. The ensuing fight constitutes another model of function 7, in this case "A fights B." I call this variation of the "unstable partnership" plot the "malignant partner" plot. Contrary to the "sleeping partner" story, "A" usually gets his objective. The exceptions occur when his motive is a monetary one.

The partnership is explicit, though usually not preceded by a fight. Django kills Carranza's gang, while inversely Gringo and Hondo cooperate in a brawl and a jailbreak. As for tricks it is usually "B" who tricks "A" (except for *El Cisco*), though sometimes before the partnership proper — Hondo exposes Gringo's infiltration, Carranza kills Thompson to keep his cover, and Benson and Paco trick each other by not disclosing that neither can read Carver's note, in a show of unsophisticated stupidity.[5] "B" is usually active in fighting (a succession of) "C"—together with "A." After the disclosure there is a fight between the partners where "B" usually perishes, thus making for a definite separation between the partners. The exception is *Lo credevano uno stinco di Santo*, where the pursuit ending in fact is a (weak) form of leaving together.

"Unstable partnership" plot	"Malignant partner" variant
1. A wants an object.	Monetary or non-monetary (revenge, vindication).
2. B wants an object.	Monetary.
3. C controls the object(s).	Money or malefactor.
4. A and B have a fight.	Weak or none.
5. A and B form a partnership.	Explicit.
6. A/B tricks B/A.	B tricks A.

"Unstable partnership" plot
7. A and/or B fight C.
8. B has a second motive.
9. A and B get their object(s).
10a. A and B leave together.
10b. A and B separate.

"Malignant partner" variant
A and B fight C, then A fights B.
B is part of C.
A gets his objective and/or a woman.

B is (usually) killed by A.

Malignant Partnerships Together with Other Plots

The story of *Se vuoi vivere ... spara!* interleaves the two main themestories in the Italowestern sociocultural dimension.[6] It contains a *big boss story* involving Murdoch and his henchman Slim employing the outlaw Mexican gang of Alvarez to force the rancher MacDougal to sign over his ranch. Their plans are thwarted by Johnny Doc, acting as a classical plot hero. There is also a *professionals/bandits story* involving Stack, who is a manipulator villain, bounty killer Donovan and Johnny, whose objective in this context is monetary (actually, to keep his own money). It is the latter story that can be interpreted as a "malignant partner" variant proper, while the former one involves Donovan only as a helper to Johnny. The two stories are interleaved, as they play out at different times and locales. They share the characters of Johnny and Donovan (who is brought into the big boss story by circumstances from the professionals/bandits story) and also the accidental involvement of Stack in the showdown with Alvarez and Murdoch.

Donovan becomes Johnny's partner, formally as his manager in a boxing venture, and more importantly when they eliminate Alvarez and Murdoch (in the big boss story). He turns out to be a malignant partner, holding back that he wants to collect Johnny's bounty (in the professionals/bandits story). When he learns that the bounty is a bluff from Stack, he becomes an observer, organizing a special duel between the two.

Stack is a manipulator, as his wanted posters set Donovan on the trail of Johnny in the professionals/bandits story. However, it is Donovan who is the master of manipulation and cunning. He at one point fakes the death of Johnny; suggests the partnership and then tricks Johnny; supervises the special duel between Stack and Johnny; manipulates Alvarez's and Murdoch's men against each other; and appears once disguised as a Mexican.

Il suo nome gridava vendetta is partly a "prodigal son" story. The (bounty killer) hero Davy returns to find his wife, Lisa, remarried to the gunfighter Hackett (negative equivalent), and reuniting with her becomes his most important objective. However, the Kellogg character does not fit neatly into this constellation/plot. As a judge, he could aspire to the status of good or bad authority, but he is of the same age as Davy and there is no usurpation of any father figure. He claims to be helpful and a friend of the hero yet double-crosses him several times, and in the end he turns out to be the real villain who has committed the crimes Davy is wanted for. In other words, the "prodigal son" story, with a diminished gallery of characters, is supplemented by a malignant partnership relation. This is a case of hybridization rather than two interleaved plots, because some of the functions in the "malignant partner" plot appear in an irregular manner. The "malignant partner" function 5 is inversed, as "B" (Kellogg) involuntarily must join with "A" (Davy) and for that same reason does not assist in fighting "C" (Hackett and his gang) in function 7. Instead, Hackett at the end is killed by Lisa—replacing the first part, "A and B fight C"—after which Davy eliminates Kellogg, true to the second part—"then A fights B."

Phony Sheriff and Bounty Killer

In *L'uomo dalla pistola d'oro* the wanted gambler Doc is pursued by a bounty hunter and assumes the identity of the sheriff, Larry Kitchener, who has been murdered by Reyes's bandits on the orders of the mayor. In *Pochi dollari per Django* the bounty hunter Regan, looking for the wanted Jim Norton, assumes the identity of a sheriff who has been murdered on the orders of cattle baron Bainsbury. Recall also the involuntary infiltrator Cudlip in *Al di là della legge*, an outlaw appointed sheriff who fights first the ruthless gang leader Burton and then his own former partners.

Inversely to the "sleeping partner" variant, these films feature an outlaw who hides his true identity from a professional—bounty killer or company official, respectively. Doc, Norton and Cudlip function as "B," the protagonists with the hidden agendas while agents Regan, Novak and the unnamed bounty killer take the "A" position. In *Pochi dollari per Django* it is "A" who is the phony sheriff and so has a hidden agenda too. In *L'uomo dalla pistola d'oro* and *Pochi dollari per Django* you have "B" = "C," as in the "malignant partner" tales. Also in *Al di là della legge* Cudlip is one of the robbers that Novak tries to stop from robbing the mining company. Together "A" and "B" fight (another) "C," Reyes, Bainsbury and Burton, respectively. Contrary to the "malignant partner" variant, the other motive of "B" this time is not that he shares the motive of (the other) "C." Instead he becomes opposed to those values. Bainsbury resorts to murder to oust the farmers, Reyes eventually falls out with his city boss partner and attacks the whole town, and Burton executes women and children. These villains threaten orderly society, and when fighting them, the "B" hero comes to show commitment to good social values— to bring peace, save women and children, and restore stolen property. At the end he stays in society. Thus at least in message, these stories are concordant with the classical plot in the American Western, according to Wright and to the similar reasoning by Cawelti (1971).

Partnership in the "Phony Sheriff" Stories

In this variant too, "A" and "B" rarely have a fight. Instead Doc saves the bounty killer from an assassination, and Regan helps Norton's daughter, while Cudlip and Novak help each other in tight situations.

The bounty killers in *L'uomo dalla pistola d'oro* and *Pochi dollari per Django* follow the "sleeping partner" agent in letting their partner bear the brunt of the fighting against (the other) "C." In *Al di là della legge* "A" and "B" rather fight the villain together, as in the "malignant partner" plot, but in those terms, where Cudlip already has been described as an involuntary infiltrator (because he does not expect to be appointed sheriff), he could for the same reason be described as an involuntary malignant partner (who fights Burton because the latter is after the same loot as he is), up to the point where he turns against his own gang.

"Unstable partnership" plot	*"Phony sheriff" variant*
1. A wants an object.	To earn bounty/stop robbery.
2. B wants an object.	B belongs to C.
3. C controls the object(s).	Has bounty/intended robbery.
4. A and B have a fight.	Inversed, B helps A.
5. A and B form a partnership.	Implicit.
6. A/B tricks B/A.	Few instances or none.
7. A and/or B fight C.	B fights C with varying assistance from A.
8. B has a second motive.	B adopts good social values.
9. A and B get their object(s).	B stays in society/A does not get bounty.
10a. A and B leave together.	A and B stay together in *Pochi dollari per Django* and *Al di là della legge* (within society).
10b. A and B separate.	A leaves in *L'uomo dalla pistola d'oro*.

Congruous Partners

There are also Spaghetti Western partners that do not enter into the relation manipulator/dupe or otherwise deceive one another. Then again, even in these *congruous partners* variants of the "unstable partnership" plot, instability — apparent or real — is introduced, often using the narrative distinction between the syuzhet, the narrative ordering, and the fabula, the story line.

Conjunctive Partners After the Syuzhet

In the infiltrator stories *La morte non conta i dollari* and *Sette winchester per un massacro*, the partners initially seem to have different objectives. As it turns out, both have hidden motives that are identical, and in effect, a partnership was established before the syuzhet takes off.

In the former story, Boyd is not a gunfighter recruited to be Lester's tame sheriff; he is really the son of the man Lester has killed, while the man pretending to be that son is a friendly lawyer — both intending to nail Lester. The fake White, the "federal lawyer from Washington," lets Boyd (the real White) do the fighting — as we have seen other government agents do! However they both have the same motive, which separates the story from the "sleeping partner" variants.

In *Sette winchester per un massacro* Stuart is not a former Confederate officer, and Manuela is not a patriotic Southern belle. They are both cooperating to collect bounty on Blake and his men, with a gender-based difference in method. (He outlines a campaign to find a treasure of money; she becomes the mistress of Blake.)[7]

The partnerships between Fred/Johnny in *I morti non si contano* and Deaf Smith/Johnny Ears in *Los amigos* are already established at the start of the syuzhet, and initially "instability" takes the mild form of bickering. Both films are basically professional stories about pairs of bounty killers or agents, though the former also harbors an involuntary "prodigal son" plot.[8] The narration in both syuzhets concentrates on the methods of the heroes to reach their goals. In the case of Fred and Johnny, it is mostly their teamwork in fights, and their running gag of referring to earlier situations ("like in Yuma?") when deciding tactics. For Deaf Smith it is the special conditions created by his impairment, such as when a forgotten bell garter in his pocket almost betrays him when he sneaks up on a guard, or when he at the decisive moment knows how to operate a machine gun because earlier he read an instructor's lips at a distance.

In both relations the stability is jeopardized when one of the partners

Deaf Smith (Anthony Quinn) demonstrates the virtues of lip-reading in *Los amigos*.

gets a second motive. Johnny gets interested in a farmer's daughter who is eventually killed, and he stays in the partnership. Johnny Ears eventually forms a pair with the prostitute Susie Q, and the partnership with Deaf Smith is dissolved—by the latter, which makes Johnny upset.

As they appear in the syuzhet, the partnerships in *La morte non conta i dollari* and *Sette winchester per un massacro* seem conjunctive, as they start out unknown to the spectator. However, just like in *I morti non si contano* and *Los amigos*, they were indeed established before the fabula starts. They are steady with regard to the fabula, but (falsely) conjunctive with regard to the syuzhet. In *Los amigos* the partnership is dissolved, rejoined and in the final scene dissolved again. The partnership of Fred/Johnny is only potentially threatened by dissolution but remains in fact steady to the end. The one of Boyd/White is steady during the syuzhet, but they separate at the end. Manuela and Stuart separate, but only to play a similar game on another wanted outlaw.

Conjunctive Partners After the Fabula

Tequila! features a partnership in the comical mode, an alliance between a gunfighting bank robber and a cowardly bum pretending to be the feared bounty killer "Jaguar." The latter is not a cunning "B" partner, though, as the false identity is cast upon him, after he has taken a watch—a musical one, of course—from the corpse of the real Jaguar, through what seems to be a mistake of Shoshena. In fact, it is intentional, to capitalize on Jaguar's reputation—opponents become intimidated by the melody of his watch, for example when Shoshena asks his partner what time it is! Consequently, Shoshena, who seems to be the dupe, is in fact the manipulator of the relationship. Any real second motive is hard to discern here, though at one time Shoshena opts to give up "Jaguar" to a bandit (with a vengeance motive against the real Jaguar) in exchange for money, but it is only a ruse, and they leave together.

Che botte, ragazzi! includes a government agent (Shanghai Joe, of Chinese extraction) holding back on his identity as part of a partnership. However, otherwise its story does not conform well to the "sleeping partner" plot, because Joe is as active in fighting the villain as his partner Cannon, and they stay together at the end. It is consequently a converging "congruous partners" variant.

The story of *Campa Carogna ... la taglia cresce* has the Muslim(!) bounty killer Coran cooperating/competing with soldiers for the wanted bandit Angelo, who has stolen army weapons and abducted a woman. For once, neither bounty killer nor government agents take the "B" position and tries to trick the other, though they haggle about sharing the bounty money (a measly $1,000). Eventually they converge in a formal partnership and leave together (Coran tags along with the others to Washington DC to cash in the bounty).

Plot Functions of the "Congruous Partners" Variant

"Unstable partnership" plot   *Congruous partners*

1. A wants an object. — Money/complete a mission.
2. B wants an object. — Same as A.
3. C controls the object(s).
4. A and B have a fight. — Weak: bickering.
5. A and B form a partnership. — Sometimes already existing.
6. A/B tricks B/A. — None.
7. A and/or B fight C. — A and B together.
8. B has a second motive. — Weak or none/woman.
9. A and B get their object(s). — Varying.
10a. A and B leave together. — All, except for *Los Amigos*
10b. A and B separate. — *Los amigos*

In films with congruous partners, the absence of internecine ruse and manipulation, which is reflected in the weakness of the functions 6 and 8 of the variant, is compensated for by an attention to the methods of conjunction of the partnerships. They might be concealed from the spectator by the syuzhet, or they might threaten to be (or indeed become) dissolved. *I morti non si contano*, where this threat is weak and aborted, has the "unstable partnership" constellation/plot supplemented by a hybrid from another constellation/plot. In the analogous case of *Campa Carogna ... la taglia cresce*, there are several hybrid functions, though all weakly implemented—for example, Dr. Adams's classic act of manipulation and cunning, when, dressed as a Mexican, he delivers Angelo from prison to exchange him for his abducted daughter, though he is immediately disposed of. Likewise, the mutually exhausting fight between Coran and Angelo does not lead to any (unfortunate) partnership, and the abducted daughter herself is unceremoniously killed in the concluding mêlée.

Congruous Partnerships Together with Other Plots

Congruous partnerships are inserted as minor "partners" into other constellation/plots. Steve Blasco in *El Desperado,* previously discussed as a false prodigal son (chapter 5) and as a tragic mercenary (chapter 6), is initially saved from a lynching for horse theft by Jonathan, who is dressed as a priest and offers Steve solace in the form of a revolver hidden in his bible. Later, during Steve's quest for revenge, they chance upon each other again, and give mutual assistance. In their first meeting a partnership between two tricksters is offered, but Jonathan is called away to perform some "priestly" duties. In their second meeting Steve gets to return the favor from the first, but the partnership is never fully consummated, making this a hybridization of a "congruous partners" variant (as well as an infiltrator plot) and a dominating "tragic mercenary" plot.

The main story of *El Rojo* is a well-staged vengeance plot featuring a ceremonial — as the four malefactors are warned beforehand of the order of their execution — and with the attention of the syuzhet on the ingenuity and cunning of the hero in executing his retribution. Nevertheless, there is also a complete partnership plot between the hero, Donald Sorenson ("A"), and the gunfighter, "Black" ("B"), whose scarred face is concealed by a mask.

"Unstable partnership" plot	*El Rojo*
1. A wants an object.	Donald wants revenge.
2. B wants an object.	"Black" is a hired gun.
3. C controls the object(s).	Ortega is a malefactor.
4. A and B have a fight.	
5. A and B form a partnership.	Donald pays "Black" for his mask.
6. A/B tricks B/A.	"Black" surprises Donald (when appearing at the end).
7. A and/or B fight C.	Donald uses the mask of "Black" to kill Ortega.
8. B has a second motive.	"Black" wants part of the Sorenson legacy.
9. A and B get their object(s).	Donald gets revenge, and "Black" demands his part.
10a. A and B leave together.	They stay together (implied).
10b. A and B separate.	

Comprising an extremely small amount of screening time, this partnership leaves a strong impression, as it suddenly is declared at the closing of the syuzhet, leaving the spectator with the question of what might happen between the two "partners" in the future.

Double Manipulators

In *All'ultimo sangue* army captain Norton helps Ted Hunter escape from a hanging so the latter can lead him to Hunter's brother Billy Gun, who has hijacked a shipment of gold. Eventually they ally with the bandit El Cordero to attack Billy. Ted tries to kill Billy and get away with the gold for himself, but instead Billy and Cordero (who have teamed up) capture the two. The army attacks, and the bandits are killed. It is implied that Hunter will be pardoned.

In *I corvi ti scaveranno la fossa* Jeff Sullivan joins a Wells Fargo police force set up to stop robbers such as Glenn Kovacs, because Kovacs has raped and killed his wife. He bribes a warden to get Kovacs' half brother Dan Barker out of a labor camp. There follows a series of confrontations, captures and escapes involving Jeff, Dan, the ruthless Wells Fargo policeman Carranza, and Susan, whom Dan and Jeff save from Carranza's men. Eventually Kovacs' and Carranza's gangs shoot it out during a bank robbery. Jeff kills both men and delivers the wounded Dan to Susan.

In both films an agent — an army officer or appointed corporate lawman — uses an outlaw to gain what he is after. Compared with the typical "sleeping partner" variant, there are two differences:

- The agent is just as involved in the action as the outlaw.
- During at least part of the story, the outlaw resists the relationship and attempts to trick the agent. Hence, both use cunning against each other.[9]

In *All'ultimo sangue* Ted and Norton have a fight before they ally. The two have a fight with Cordero before all three parties ally. Then Ted tricks his partners and allies with Billy, whom he tricks, and they have a fight. Then Billy and Cordero ally (they had their fight earlier) against Ted and Norton. Ted's earlier "escape" sequences also feature manipulations and counter-manipulations. Similarly, Norton seems to have foreseen Ted's betrayal as he leaves while Cordero fights for the (empty) mine. There is also a compressed "tragic mercenary" plot when Ted attempts to get both the gold and his revenge, which leads to the death of his loved one Pepita.

In *I corvi ti scaveranno la fossa* Jeff enforces an alliance on Dan, who

7. A Partnership Without Tricks

Campa Carogna: video sleeve.

first pretends to betray him for Carranza, and then really does turn on him. Jeff and Carranza also have a brief partnership after their fight. The bourgeois Donovan betrays his earlier (criminal) partnership with Dan. Jeff inverses the sleeping partner motivation by starting as an agent, and later coming out as an avenger. Carranza is also a manipulator when he lets Jeff off so that he'll track Kovacs. Dan gets a second motive also, in the form of Susan, even though at first he seems to manipulate her just to get a chance to escape Jeff (who foresees this). Later she stops him from killing Jeff (who interferes when Ted tries to regain his money from Carranza), thus enforcing a non-monetary (social values) motive.

Sergio Garrone's *Una lunga fila di croci* delivers a story involving two bounty killers tricking and allying with each other, like in *Few Dollars More* — only this time the relation ends in deadly confrontation. It involves the bounty killers Brandon and Preacher and the banker Fargo, who uses wanted men to smuggle Mexicans across the border as laborers, not minding killing them in case of inconveniences. The fourth main character is Maya, who helps the Mexicans, and whom Fargo wants to marry.

Just like *All'ultimo sangue* and *I corvi ti scaveranno la fossa*, this is a complex story because the "partners" also ally with (and then betray) their original opponent. In *Una lunga fila di croci* it is therefore hard to differentiate between the "A" and "B" positions. However, Brandon does act on a second (non-monetary) motive when he dupes Preacher and takes Fargo's payoff money to Maya (to help the Mexicans), and Preacher strikes a secret alliance with Fargo. Brandon betrays his partner for a non-monetary reason, while Fargo betrays his own men for a monetary reason. He does have a non-monetary motive in Maya, though. The fight in plot function 4 appears with its basic meaning in the two former films, but is inversed in *Una lunga fila di croci*, where Brandon helps Preacher out against some outlaws before suggesting the partnership.

Larry in *... e per tetto un cielo di stelle* is a gullible gold miner who gets involved with Billy, a con man and womanizer who also turns out to be a famous gunfighter. He is pursued by Pratt, whose brothers he has killed. Pratt is a psycho who needlessly massacres everybody on a stagecoach (where he expected to find Billy), and later cuts a waitress with a bowie knife — for slow service. In this case it is the villain in the "C" position who is an avenger with a non-monetary motive.

The "double manipulators" relationship is here in the comic mode, meaning that most of the manipulations fail or backfire.:

- At first Larry helps Billy bury the stage coach passengers. Then Billy helps Larry at a poker game, but they fail to get back any money.

- Billy tricks Larry for his savings, but Larry finds him and breaks the mermaid basin(!) that he has invested the money in. After a fight they form a partnership to return the money to Larry.
- After failing with a fake telegraph scam (because Pratt arrives), Billy tricks Larry because he gets a second motive (to bed a widow on her funeral night), but Larry eventually discovers this and starts a fight, sending the widow screaming.
- When Billy devises a plan to rob Wells Fargo, Larry tricks Billy by making another partnership. However, it fails because of the mental instability of the new partner, and Billy saves his life.
- When attempting to solve the problem with honest work, it fails because of incompetence (i.e., rabbit farming) and the attack by the Pratts, which is in a way an involuntary trick by Billy, because he is the target.

So neither partner gets his objective(s), but they leave together, forming a conjunctive partnership.

Mixed-Partnership Variants

In *Un poker di pistole* the hero Lucas—who infiltrates casino owner Master's gang for monetary reasons—is in the unenviable situation of having two manipulating partners. George is a malignant partner who plays him out against Masters because he wants to take over the latter's counterfeiting organization. Lazar is the typical sleeping partner, a (Mexican) government agent who takes the back seat and lets the hero smoke out George and Masters.

The town in *Black Killer* is terrorized by the brothers O'Hara — so conspicuously Latin in looks, dress and demeanor that they must represent a high point in Italowestern casual ethnicity. Here arrives first the lawyer James Webb, who starts putting embarrassing questions to the town judge Wilson, and then Bud Collins, whose brother Peter is married to the Indian Sarah. On the suggestion of Webb, Bud becomes sheriff. The O'Haras kill Peter but fail to see the job through with Bud and Sarah, and the two start a vengeance campaign.

This film displays many properties of a low-end Italowestern production. There are blatantly unmotivated exhibitions of female skin and conspicuous gaps in the syuzhet.[10] However, by chance or by design, the story line does offer an interesting play on several variants of the "unstable partnership" plot: It starts out like a "sleeping partner" variant, where James

Webb could be a government agent who observes and lends some help to Bud, the active hero with a vengeance motive. It is congruous to such a relation that Webb in the end restores the unlawfully acquired deeds to the citizens. Then again, he pockets all the money found in Wilson's safe. After the malefactors have been killed, Bud arrests Webb and discloses him as a money-oriented criminal and thus a false "sleeping partner." Outside town Bud lets Webb loose and so turns out to be another money-oriented hero, a false dupe, who has turned on his (secret) partner and arrested him for the purpose of sharing the money. Thus it is Bud who gets a second motive and has the "B" position, not Webb as the story line leads the spectator to believe.

Female Constellation Positions

A Mixed-Gender Pair

In *The Belle Starr Story* the relationship between the gamblers/gunfighters Belle Starr and Larry Blackie conforms to the "unstable partnership" plot. In this partnership of mixed gender, the plot functions are played out on a code of sexual attraction (by kisses, intercourse — and slapping), alternating another code of money-motivated pursuits (by gunplay).

This interchanging is established in the first sequences. She throws down her good cards (money relation) to get him into bed (sexual relation), thus tricking him. He reveals knowing about her card hand, thus trumping her at cunning (and disclosing himself as a cheater as well). She reacts by shooting at him (money/violence), and he jumps her, and their wrestling crosses back into the sexual, to intercourse. In the morning he retracts into the money/violence code, saying that she is just another one-night whore to him, and warning her not to gamble in his territory again. She reacts using the same code, when she comes looking for him and kills his men. When they face each other next time, their armed confrontation (including hat shooting) transforms into (implied) intercourse. Later she attempts to trick him at the money/violence code by beating him to a robbery, and he counters by having his men infiltrate her gang. In the end, she gives the booty back to save him from torture, still acting on the same code. They separate with an intermingling of the two codes, kiss and gunplay, and her parting words ("See you at the next poker game!") imply that their oscillating partnership will continue the same way.

A Note on the "Love Interest"

The "unstable partnership" plot "A" position hero often becomes involved with a woman — so frequently that a function 8b ("A gets a love interest") could be added. In *Se vuoi vivere ... spara!* this is (parodically) reversed for "B" hero Donovan, who leaves pursued by his former mistress Paquita.

Sally, in the same movie, embodies an important distinction. She is a love interest to the "A" partner Johnny in the partnership plot, but also part of his second motivation (to help her family) in the big boss story. Marisol in *Fistful of Dollars* and Mortimer's sister in *Few Dollars More* are providers of motivation, but in neither case are they love interests of a hero (though the possibility is provided as a cue for the spectator in the first film). On the contrary, Juana in *... dai nemici mi guardo io!*, who hides Gringo and Hondo (in her bed) from El Condor's men and after Hondo's final betrayal leaves with Gringo, is a love interest, but not a second motive. Gringo's feelings toward her never made him stray from his primary motive (the hidden treasure). Susie Q in *Los amigos* exemplifies female love interest that also become a second motive in the (same) plot.

The distinction might serve to reconcile Leone's anathema against the role of the women in American Westerns with his use of women as powerful motivators for the heroes in his first two Westerns.[11] It might be interpreted as a critique of the appearance of the woman as just a love interest — at best loosely connected to the main story — and not as a denial of her importance as a motivation. In his *Once Upon a Time in the West*, the character of Jill remains in the concluding scene, when Harmonica (the avenger) rides away and Frank (the villain) and Cheyenne (the bandit partner) are dead. Plotwise, she embodies most of all the monetary motivation, as she owns the land deed that a large part of the action revolves around. Still, Frayling points out that she reacts only to the plans, threats and orders from the men.[12] Here is a difference compared with someone like Maria in *Django*, who transcends the motivating function and rather becomes a doubling of the hero.

The Marisol Woman

A recurring character in Italowestern stories, from *Fistful of Dollars* onward, is a young Latin or Latin-looking woman, often a mother deprived of her husband (and sometimes also of her child). She is also close to, coveted by and/or threatened by a villain. Where she appears, she is usually the main female protagonist. This thematic role does not fit easily in the traditional U.S. Western dichotomy between respectable and fallen woman. Neither is she readily recognizable in the stories used as examples by Cawelti (1971) or Wright. I will refer to such a character as a *Marisol woman*.

In *Anda muchacho spara!* Jessica strikes back at her tormentors by using both her sexuality and her knife to help Roy. She becomes his love interest but does not in any indisputable way change the hero's motivations, (at first) to get the gold and (later) to restore it to the miners.

In *Cjamango* Pearl has her husband killed by Don Pablo, who desires her. Inversely to Maria in *Django*, she goes to the Anglo villain Tiger. This time the woman is killed, after saving the hero's life. It is rather her son who becomes his second motivation, as the hero discloses where he has hidden the gold to save the boy. The two leave together, with her dead body.

Inversely, in *Un fiume di dollari*–the villain Segal's sister (who has Latin looks) is coveted by his Mexican foreman, and there is a boy who is the abducted son of the hero. This Marisol woman is only a love interest. She dies, while the hero is reunited with his son at the end.

Maya in *Una lunga fila di croci* is wanted by Fargo and is something of a mother figure to the poor Mexicans that are victimized by his smuggling activities. She (or that which she represents) becomes the second motive of Brandon, though not an explicit love interest.

In *Campa Carogna ... la taglia cresce* there is a satirical twist to the Marisol woman character, in the scene where one of the heroes tries to get a Mexican to talk by threatening to rape his wife, and she immediately throws herself at him and promises him her body if he takes her away from that wretched place.

The love interest Juana in *... dai nemici mi guardo io!* signifies a weak version of the Marisol woman, as Garcia, who is stabbed to death with a kitchen knife when he tries to rape her, is an accidental character and not a major villain.

Other Female Thematic Roles

Paquita from *Se vuoi vivere ... spara!* and Sorita from *I senza Dio* are examples of bandit women in spaghetti Westerns who easily switch their allegiance to the hero. Another is Chiquita in *El Cisco*, who unties the captured hero for another of the sexually explicit scenes of this story, and so makes possible his later settling of accounts with Cascaron. This recalls the contested woman in the Italowestern "prodigal son" constellation/plot (and the traditional saloon girl associated with the villain in the American Western). They usually pay with their lives, but Chiquita, with her calm stance watching at a distance the desperate fight between her two lovers, rather suggests an observer and perhaps also a manipulator.

Marisol woman under threat — Laurinda (Nicoletta Machiavelli) in *Un minuto per pregare, un istante per morire*.

Unlike Dolores in *Una pistola per Ringo*, these bandit women are unarmed. Except for Belle Starr and some guerrilleras in the "social bandit" films (see below), the female master of arms is a sparse occurrence. Sarah, who avenges her husband's death with her traditional Indian weapons in *Black Killer*, comes through as a doubling of the hero in the avenger plot part of the fabula and is neither a second motive nor any explicit love interest for him, though true to the ambiance of the film, she is naked when he tends her wound!

The woman living with a city boss villain will typically bed one of the heroes, but only to betray him to further her own ends. This goes for Jane Barret in *I senza Dio* and Jessica Cluster in *Django spara per primo*. The first one has her accomplice, the sheriff, murder her husband, implicating El Santo. The bigamist Jessica wants the hero to make her a widow, and later makes a run with Cluster's money before being killed by him. Ingrid deKoven in *Tequila!* is unfaithful to her husband but has no mercenary ambitions and leaves before her husband is killed. Still, she conforms to type by betraying the hero, though inadvertently, when a note from her destroys his alibi.

Of course, the "unstable partnership" films also host a fair share of traditionally "respectable" or "fallen" women. Among the farmer's daughter types, the least conventional might be Sally in *Se vuoi vivere ... spara!*. That she gives in and signs over the deed to Murdoch to save Johnny, against his warning that they will both be killed, might be in the mainstream farmer's daughter vein, but that the nubile Sally later — being properly groomed by Paquita — appears with the dress and the looks of a full-grown woman to catch her Johnny is definitely not.

On the opposite side of the chasm, among women frequenting saloons, Lucy in *Django spara per primo* (who is not a mother but does have a little brother) turns herself into both love interest *and* partner to the monetary motive when Glenn finds the gold in his saddlebags exchanged for her written message! As a saloon singer married to a villain, and the former sweetheart of the hero, Consuela in *El Rojo* pushes the stereotype to the extreme by being killed for helping him. However, she is unconventionally forthright in admitting to marrying for money: "Love doesn't mean anything." Donald answers that there is more than one way to betray a man, thus urging her to disclose the hideout of her husband.

A Note on Dress Code

I have already referred to the triadic code of cowboy dress, all-black dress and Mexican dress in the pre–*Fistful of Dollars* Westerns (chapter 4) and the Mexican cross-dress poncho for the hero in *Fistful of Dollars* (chapter 2). While retaining the latter style (for Monco), *Few Dollars More* introduced another characteristic outfit for the protagonist. Mortimer is dressed in a black three-piece suit with tie, and an overcoat in some scenes. Django wears a similar one over the Union army trousers that triggers the unfortunate hostility of Jackson's men. Subsequent trans-story Djangos wear the same type of overcoat (as in *Preparati la bara!*) or settle for just a coat and a covering hat (as in *W Django!*).

In the "unstable partnership" films discussed earlier, the "B" partner is often elegantly dressed like Colonel Mortimer, though often more outlandishly so. In *Cjamango* Clinton wears a modishly escalated variant of the Mortimer black three-piece suit with patterned vest, shirt with frills, and black cape. In *Un poker di pistole* Lucas is unshaven and wears a fur-lined coat and a yellow hat. George wears elegant city dress, and Lazar is dressed in a dark suit.

The "A" position hero usually is unshaven and wears an outfit or at least some piece of clothing that is out of the ordinary. Cjamango has a yellow leather vest and ditto overcoat with shoulder collar and an embroidered white shirt. In *All'ultimo sangue* Ted is called "El Chaleco" because of the pattern of his Mexican vest. When Cordero's gang captures the partners, he is stripped of it, and when they later ally with the bandits, Ted regains his vest from a man after knocking him out. Norton at first carries a brown coat with fur lapel.

These items of dress might have mediating connotations, as for Joe/Monco (both Anglo and Mexican) and Django (neither Confederate nor Mexican). Anyway, they carry an implicit message of disbelonging, and of flaunting individual style.[13] This *odd dress* is also to be found outside the "unstable partnership" stories. For example, Burt Sullivan in *Texas addio* wears a long sand-colored "duster" overcoat while roaming Mexico and Tom in *Tempo di massacro*—another "prodigal son" played by Franco Nero—sports a skin vest with fur lining. Where the ingenuity of scriptwriter (or props master) would fail, the last straw for odd dress seems to be the leather jacket, worn among others by Minnesota Joe in *I senza Dio*, the hero in *Anda muchacho spara!*, Norton and the villain Billy Gun in *All'ultimo sangue*, and Brandon in *Una lunga fila di croci* (where Preacher has a black Mortimer-style suit).

This odd style of dressing also has a collective version, where (most often) an outlaw gang will encompass very diverse and odd styles of clothing, such as the Duncan gang in *Navajo Joe*.[14] Another fine example is the "force" of the villain in *Gentleman Jo ... uccidi!* as it is presented in a traveling shot exposing all kinds of jackets, capes and headwear.

Significantly, in *Pochi dollari per Django* the one appearance of odd dress—the bounty killer introductory sequence where Regan arrives riding on a donkey wearing covering hat and poncho to kill some outlaws—is connected with the film's only excursion into *Fistful of Dollars*'s cinematic style. Two of the villain's henchmen have Mexican and Confederate outfits, though.

Tutorship Partners

The age difference as a significant coding between the partners in *Few Dollars More* reappears with a still greater importance in two other spaghetti Westerns, where Lee Van Cleef again plays the "old man" against younger actors (and characters)—Giuliano Gemma in *I giorni dell'ira*, and John Phillip Law in *Da uomo a uomo*.[15]

Bill in *Da uomo a uomo* has had his whole family killed by outlaws when he was a boy and follows the stranger Ryan as he seems to lead to the malefactors that Bill wants to avenge himself on. Scott in *I giorni dell'ira* is a poor and despised orphan who teams up with the gunfighter Talby. Bill later realizes that Ryan was part of the malefactor gang, though not to the misdeed, and he refrains from killing him. Scott eventually kills Talby when the latter allies with the town bosses and kills an old friend of Scott's.

In both cases, "B"—the one holding a secret—is the older partner. Unlike *Few Dollars More* the older party is money-oriented while the younger has a different motivation. In *Da uomo a uomo* Bill seeks revenge for his family on the same "C" (Cavanagh, Walcott and their accomplices) that Ryan wants to get money from. The disclosure that Ryan was present at the misdeed, and thus is part of "C," makes the story similar to a malignant partnership. The difference is that Ryan did not take part in the atrocity. A malignant partner would also have used Bill to further his monetary interests, but the activities of the latter in fact obstruct Ryan's original plan to obtain money from the ones who betrayed him.

Not unlike the vindicative heroes also played by Giuliano Gemma,[16] the social outcast Scott Mary in *I giorni dell'ira* aspires to social acceptance and follows Talby as he wants to become like him. It is significant that the gunfighter gives Scott a family name (after his mother's first name, Mary). The society that condemns Scott to a position at the bottom is ruled by precisely those men that, because of their unlawful activities, become the target of his mentor Talby (and him). In the beginning of the *Da uomo a uomo* fabula, Ryan is one of the men in the "C" position. Then he must fight them to get monetary compensation for their treachery. Talby goes in the reverse direction: He fights the city bosses to get a share of their operation, and later on joins their ranks. However, what makes him a malefactor and Scott Mary an avenger is the killing of Murph, who is partly a doubling of Talby, a benign tutor wising up the hero to the tricks of the (potentially) malignant one. Murph straddles different thematic roles—both the famous gunfighter fallen to the lowest level of society who bucks up to save it from evil (from American adult Westerns) and the socially marginalized old man friendly to the hero (from spaghetti Westerns and more humble American Westerns). Murph's stint as reformed sheriff is short and unsuccessful, and in fact he is not seen protecting any honest citizens, only the corrupted city fathers. As the Italowestern sidekick he is unusual because he does not survive. On the other hand, at the end of *I giorni dell'ira*, Scott walks away from society together with another such marginalized character, a "blind" beggar.

The partners have a fight, involving tricks, before forming a partnership.

Talby answers Scott Mary's aspiration to be a fast gunfighter like him with lesson one: "Never beg another man." Then he agrees to bring Scott with him, asks him for his eight dollars and knocks him down with lesson two: "Never trust another."

Undaunted ("must hear lesson three"), Scott continues and catches up with Talby at a cantina, where the gunfighter meets Wild Jack — and lesson three is, "Never stand between a gun and its target."

When Scott follows Talby in not drinking with Wild, he is knocked down and thus is taught lesson four, spelled out by Talby as, "Punches are like bullets, if you don't make the first ones, Scotty, you might just be finished."

Later Talby kills Wild, who had drawn on him — and gives lesson five: "Wound a man, kill him. He might come after you." He then leaves on his own to be later captured by Wild's men and rescued by Scott, who throws him his own gun. Talby then gives lesson six, "The right bullet the right time, well aimed," and points the gun at Scott with lesson seven: "If you untie a man, take his gun before that." The latter retorts with "lesson eight"—"Don't give a man any more bullets than he's got use for!"

The development of this tutorship with the concluding triumph of the pupil forebodes the development of the partnership, with Scott at the end pronouncing the lessons one by one as he kills Talby's men and finally outdraws and wounds the tutor himself, answering Talby's promise to leave town by quoting lesson five before killing him.

The tutorship scenes in *Da uomo a uomo* are less outspoken but follow the same pattern, with the same concluding reversal, when Bill, after springing Ryan from the arrest, leaves *him* behind without a horse.

These relations, with the one meting out the knowledge making it hard for the one receiving it, certainly differ from the basically benevolent fostering relationships in some American Westerns.[17] Such a relationship is typically epitomized in the shooting lessons missing in these two films. Bill is shown practicing *by himself* to become an expert shot. Likewise, Scott Mary has secretly practiced to become a gunfighter even before meeting Talby. An older partner giving shooting lessons to a younger one is featured in *Bandidos*, but this does not signify a traditional paternalistic (or a tutorship) relation, but an unstable partnership where both partners have hidden agendas.[18]

In both films the tutorship ends with a separation. Bill obtains his vengeance, while the dollar bills coveted by Ryan are seen blowing away in the wind. Scott kills Talby and leaves, scorning the social acceptance that he initially sought.

Tutorship Variations

IL GRANDE DUELLO

Less successful at the box office was *Il grande duello*, where a character played by Van Cleef again confronts a younger man. Phillip Vermeer has escaped from a prison sentence for the murder of Saxon, the patriarch of Saxon City, who in turn is believed to be behind the murder of Vermeer's father. The syuzhet opens with the Van Cleef character, Clayton, helping Vermeer escape a swarm of bounty killers, only to immediately capture him. Eventually, they end up in Saxon City, where Phillip seeks the truth about the death of his father. When Phillip is to be hanged, Clayton confesses to have killed the old man Saxon, saying that justice could only be done this way. Clayton kills the three Saxon sons in a walkdown, with some assistance from Phillip.

Clayton and Vermeer form a tutorship couple. They are differentiated by age, and as in *Da uomo a uomo* and *I giorni dell'ira* the older is party to a misdeed against the younger — this time by letting him take the rap for a murder. Their cat-and-mouse game on the road to Saxon City comprises almost half of the total screening time of the film. The play of disjunction/conjunction is inverted, as it is the older protagonist who hooks on to the younger, who tries to leave him behind. The actual "tutoring" is also considerably diluted compared with the advice of Ryan and the numbered lessons of Talby.

The rest of the story adjoins a hybrid "prodigal son" plot. David Saxon is a big boss who considers a political future using the income from the Vermeer silver mine. His brother Adam is a stylish psychopath dressed in white who is seen in a "stacked-deck" duel against an old man, and later ambushes and massacres Vermeer's followers when they leave the city. The third brother, Eli, seeks confirmation that Vermeer really assassinated their father, something that David couldn't care less about. He even knows the truth, as Clayton points out. In fact, up until Clayton's confession, the spectator is cued to believe that it is David who is the guilty party!

Had this been the case, and the old man Saxon had been a good authority, Eli could have filled the position of prodigal son to his brothers' evil authority and negative equivalent, respectively. As the story goes, it is Vermeer who qualifies for a "prodigal son" constellation slot, as his father has been murdered and David, an evil authority and the son of the responsible, now controls his heritage. Vermeer in the end leaves for Mexico with a woman that initially is engaged to the evil equivalent Adam, and thus a contested woman (though not an old flame of the hero this time). Like Ted Barnett in *Vendetta*, Vermeer has escaped from an unjust sentence for killing a father, though not his own! Unlike Barnett, however, his main concern is not to convince the judge (who was "bought and paid for" in Clayton's words). He seeks to regain his position in what concerns his followers and the silver, and he seeks the truth about who killed his father. In this respect he is like Bill, and Clayton—like Ryan—is the one who leads him to the knowledge.

Clayton, the other unwanted visitor to Saxon City, is repeatedly accused of being after Vermeer's reward. However, unlike Ryan and Talby, and rather like Mortimer in *Few Dollars More*, his money motive is false. Instead he is on a mission of vindication to have Vermeer declared innocent. When disclosing himself, he becomes in fact an inverse vindicator.

My Name Is Nobody

My Name Is Nobody was the second most successful Spaghetti Western ever in the Italian market and has inspired more comments than most spaghetti Westerns, mainly because of the heavy involvement of Sergio Leone himself as writer, producer, supervisor and even occasional director.[19] Frayling (1998) discusses at some length its relation to the overall concerns of Leone.[20]

In constellation/plot, the story follows the "infrastructure" of the tutorship variant.[21] The introductory sequence (where the older protagonist, Jack Beauregard, kills three men who have set a trap for him at a barber's shop) is concluded by a question from a boy to his father whether anybody is faster than Beauregard, and the answer is, "Faster than him? Nobody!" This is directly followed by a screen shot of the younger protagonist overwritten by the film title. By way of the sensibility of the spectator, Nobody is given his name by Beauregard, somewhat like Scott "Mary" is named by Talby. This is also a comic inversion, as "Nobody" is an anti-name.

True to the tutorship variant, it is the younger hero who approaches an unwilling older one. Again, the motive for the older is monetary, though markedly modest—ticket fare to leave for Europe. While typically it is the older that serves lessons, though in a harsh and ironic form, here the relation is reversed, as the younger sermonizes that his hero should perform an epic deed to enhance his very myth, by facing the might of the Wild Bunch. Consequently, it is Nobody who manipulates Beauregard against the Wild Bunch, similar to a malignant partner, but not to any material advantage.[22]

There are also inversions in detail compared with key tutorship episodes, especially from *Da uomo a uomo*, where Bill (younger) encounters Ryan (older) at a graveyard with the graves of the family of the younger, who (as we already understand) intends to avenge them. In *My Name Is*

Nobody Beauregard (older) encounters Nobody (younger) at a graveyard with the grave of the Nevada Kid, brother of the older, and (as it turns out) he does not intend to avenge him. Similarly, in *Da uomo a uomo* Bill helps an African American, which involves him in a saloon shoot-out, where his prowess induces a villain to hire him to kill Ryan. Instead he warns Ryan, confronts the villain, and is helped by Ryan. At the fair Nobody helps an African American (who is the target at an amusement stand, but the hero throws the pie at the announcer), then shows his prowess at a saloon shootout (in a contest of emptying glasses of liquor and shooting them in the air). He is then hired by a villain to kill Beauregard (in fact, for the second time). Instead he warns the latter, and helps him kill the men of the villain. As in the preceding episodes, this confrontation is partly in the comical mode. The crowded saloon with its staircases and the door where Ryan suddenly appears are replaced with the mirrors and scary dolls of a funny house.

In the end, just like in the original tutorship films, the two protagonists face each other for a concluding showdown (in a city street in front of a cameraman). It is neither carried through (*I giorni dell'ira*) nor aborted (*Da uomo a uomo*), but faked, making Beauregard a presumed dead character.

IL TEMPO DEGLI AVVOLTOI

In *Il tempo degli avvoltoi* Kitosch escapes from his boss, Don Jaime, after being whipped and branded for consorting with the foreman's wife and approaching the one of Jaime himself. He joins with the gunfighter Black Tracy, who sets out to avenge himself on his wife, Traps, and his former friend Big John (for turning him in). Eventually, Kitosch is repelled by Tracy's violent methods and suggests that they share the loot that they have come across and then split. Tracy considers killing Kitosch (both before and after the loot is lost in a shootout caused by Tracy), but instead he suggests that they should rob Don Jaime. They take Jaime's wife as a hostage, and after they have fought off his men, Jaime delivers the ransom. Tracy now declares he will shoot Jaime and leave with his wife, but Kitosch tricks and kills him, though he gets wounded in the process. He declines the ransom and leaves.

From a psychoanalytic perspective, this dark and twisted tale should offer enough parental figures, symbolic castrations and displaced desires. However, it also emerges as a tutorship story. Kitosch seeks a partnership with Tracy, and he is at first rejected (when the gunfighter tricks the posse and then sends Kitosch off with Don Jaime's horse) and then used (as bait in a trap for a sheriff). In these episodes the tutor shows his mastery in deviousness, and the tutee is finally accepted after expressing some deviousness of his own (letting Tracy follow the wrong road and waiting at its dead end). Similarly the relationship ends when the tutee defeats his tutor with his own trick (a hidden derringer). Also, there is no "paternal" shooting lesson. Both men show off in their shooting competition — at Tracy's collection of sheriff stars!

Kitosch shares with Scott Mary a limiting social situation, and they both take up company with a notorious gunfighter, whom in the end they kill to protect/avenge someone who is part of the old order. In the beginning Don Jaime is similar to the bad city fathers of *I giorni dell'ira*. He is a negative authority when he brands the hero, and when he sends his men after him. Don Jaime also reigns over the town, where Kitosch is refused a horse and the sheriff jails him on a pretext. Yet in the end it is to save Jaime's life that Kitosch kills Tracy, as Scott kills Talby to avenge Murph. Before the branding in *Il tempo degli avvoltoi* Kitosch takes his punishments with good humor, and in the end the rancher honors his promise of safe conduct. In terms of *I giorni dell'ira*, Don Jaime's character thus represents a merging of good (Murph) and bad (city fathers) in an established order that Kitosch, like Scott, ultimately abandons.

Kitosch is a womanizer. The whipping and branding take place when the Don prevents his access to women. His partnership seems to bring him restitution, as he is seen enjoying himself with drinking and prostitutes— making Kitosch one of the few Italowestern heroes contradicting the conclusion made by Frayling (and others) that "The 'hero' does not spend his dollars."[3] That this happy state is aborted when Tracy starts a fight with a prostitute is not a coincidence, because Tracy is associated with the destruction of women. The coffin on his wagon does not contain gold or weapons but his dead mother, he tortures and (probably) kills his afflicted wife, whom he earlier had brutalized, and later he kills a woman who is in love with Kitosch. Thus, like Jaime, he separates the hero from women. In this respect, he is like Ryan and Talby who, each in his own way, emerge as a party to the tutee's opponents.

Tracy — whose disgust for women causes the loss of their booty — represents a reversal of the tragic mercenary, whose quest for money brings the loss or brutalization of his woman. When he agrees to leave with the wife of Don Jaime, who promises him her husband's money, the implication is not a rejection of misogyny, but that he, in this larger-than-life femme fatale, recognizes a partner as ruthless as he is.

If Kitosch values women and a good time, retribution dominates for Tracy vis-à-vis Big John (as for Kitosch when he beats Don Jaime down). When Tracy prepares to draw on Kitosch, one cannot be sure whether the dominating motive is to get rid of the contender for the money or to kill him for ending the partnership. He no doubt intends to kill Kitosch in their ensuing fight, so in this case function 4 in the plot occurs at (what seems to be) the end of the partnership, though afterwards Tracy aborts his retribution for a money motive.

Kitosch leaves after rejecting the selfish evil womanhood of Jaime's wife (the only woman remaining), the selfish (insanely) evil partnership of Tracy, and the monetary motive (the ransom). The former evil authority, Don Jaime, takes on a servant position when he helps Kitosch up on his horse. However the ending is not an apotheosis of the hero, as he leaves wounded (possibly fatally). Don Jaime calling out after Kitosch brings to mind the ending of *Ciak Mull*, when Caldwell (who, somewhat like Jaime, has in turn taken the position of evil authority, good authority, and finally also false, "illegitimate" authority) similarly calls after the leaving "prodigal son." Likewise, the hero of *Shane* leaves wounded (possibly fatally) after saving the life of his "employer" Starret, and implicitly rejecting the love

Unstable partnership of mixed gender: Larry Blackie (Robert Woods) and Belle Starr (Elsa Martinelli) in ***The Belle Starr Story***.

of Starret's (good) wife, and with a filial, not a parental, figure calling after him in vain.

The dark confusion of the ending resonates with other moments of the pathetic in the story: The almost blind Traps threatened by Tracy's lamp in the dark room and subsequently abandoned among the flames; and Tracy's epileptic fits, tied to outbursts of destructive obsession (his possession by the devil, as the priest calls it). It occurs when Kitosch stops him from tormenting Traps, shoots Big Jim while Tracy is crucifying him, and downs Tracy during their fight.

The "Social Bandit" Story

Enter the Revolution

When Damiano Damiani (director) and Franco Solinas (script) with *Quién sabe?* (1966) introduced the revolution in Mexico as the scene for a Spaghetti Western, they also brought important modifications to the legacy of *Fistful of Dollars* and *Few Dollars More*.[24]

In this story a protagonist with no self-confessed name, but called Nino by his partner-to-be Chunco, uses cunning to gain entrance to one camp, the revolutionaries, because the opposing camp, the army, has paid him to kill the leader Elias. This is infiltration as motif rather than the full plot, as he does not attempt to manipulate the two camps against each other to further his own gain. Instead he fulfils his contract with the army to the full.

On the other hand, Nino develops an unstable partnership relation to Chunco, who is a Mexican, and at least associated with the "gang" that Nino infiltrates:

- They save each others lives
- Nino shares the money for his contract with Chunco
- In the end Chunco kills Nino

Chunco is another Gian Maria Volontè performance, with much in common in looks, speech and demeanor with his Ramon and Indio characters. Only, instead of having his gang infiltrated by one or two Anglos, this time he strikes a partnership with Nino, who is a lone Anglo in Mexico. To complete this transformation of the ethnical code, in *Quién sabe?* it is Chunco who gets a second motive, associated with the cause of the oppressed peons, and also the one who survives in the end. The Mexican character in the constellation is promoted to the position of main hero. This is unlike the "unstable partnership" films discussed so far, where the hero has been an Anglo, in most cases seconded by an Anglo (sometimes a government agent) but in some cases by a Mexican, who then usually proves deceitful.

The Political Theme

In *Quién sabe?* some of the plot functions acquire a different meaning vis-à-vis the other "unstable partnership" films, because of realignments on the good/bad dimension. Nino does not infiltrate the band of the villain, like Monco does, nor is he a government agent out to recover loot stolen by the villain like the sleeping partner protagonists, because he is in fact working *for* the villain, not Elias but the government and especially the army. This is established by the executions in the introductory scenes and the (reported) massacre of the people of San Miguel.[25]

State power is here portrayed as bad, as the destroyer of innocents,[26] while the characters most unequivocally portrayed as good — Elias and, to a certain degree, Chunco's brother Santo — are fighting to replace it with another government. This way *Quién sabe?* introduces a political code dimension of state apparatus versus armed opposition, where the first position is associated with the interests of the wealthy (the bourgeois characters on the train, and the landowner) and the second one with the poor (the peons at the train stations and in the village).

One example of how the political dimension changes the meaning of a situation is when Elias sentences Chunco to death for deserting the people of San Miguel. It is common in the infiltrator stories that the hero is faced with, and narrowly escapes, death from the band that he is infiltrating. In *Quién sabe?* he accepts the verdict and does not try to avoid it, because he finds it just. Moreover, when he next time meets the man who has saved him from the sentence — by killing his brother/executioner and Elias — he intends to kill him but is temporarily won over by the prospect of an equal money-oriented partnership. After his encounter with the shoeshine man at the railway station, and when he has seen how Nino treats the people there, he regains his commitment to the poor Mexicans and shoots Nino.

The Nature of Partnership

Chunco accepts Nino in his gang and later kills one of the other gang members to save him, saying that he does not know why. He also nurses Nino back to health when the Anglo gets sick. Nino in his turn saves Chunco from the execution and shares the reward with him, though there is no selfish reason or explicit agreement to do so—except maybe that the Mexican has saved his life. Homoerotic attraction as an explanation has meager support in the explicit content of the syuzhet. Chunco's killing of Nino would be hard to explain as a crime of passion. For Chunco, I suggest his conflicting interior motives. Nino does not kill Elias because of sympathy for the cause of the authorities—he treats the representatives of the army who pay him with a slight disdain—and he shows no interest in sensual pleasures such as drinking or women. Perhaps it is his single dedication to monetary value that attracts Chunco, who robs the weapon transport for money, but keeps this issue fuzzy in respect to his politically dedicated brother. Conversely, Chunco also hates the repressive authorities and becomes a political hero, so—as it happens in Italowestern partnerships—he gets a second motive.

In the "unstable partnership" plots discussed earlier, a different second motive for at least one of the partners usually means that they can avoid a deadly confrontation. In this case it is precisely the existence of a second, non-monetary motive that is its cause. Chunco must kill Nino, who has killed revolutionaries and despises the ordinary people of Mexico, because his heart says so. It is his gut political feeling, that earlier has surfaced in his assertion that the Mexicans have no less value than Nino, and in his "ethical" reaction to his own death sentence.

Specialists, Bandits and Revolutionaries

In Sergio Sollima's *Corri, uomo, corri* the knife specialist Cuchillo is hired to help the revolutionary poet Ramirez bring back the gold of Juarez, which he has hidden in the United States. Also looking for the gold are the bandit Reza, the sadistic government agent Savigny and the mercenary Cassidy. Ramirez is killed when he protects a woman from the men of Reza, but Cassidy eventually helps Cuchillo defeat the others and send the gold to the revolutionary General Santillana.

In the same year, 1968, *Il mercenario*, by Sergio Corbucci, debuted. The Mexican mine worker Paco joins the revolution, assisted by the Polish mercenary Sergei, who works strictly for money. Paco turns into a dedicated nationalist revolutionary under the influence of Columba, who is the daughter of an insurgent, but when he breaks the partnership with Sergei, the result is military disaster. After defeating the sadistic mercenary Curly, and being saved from execution by Columba, they part as friends.

In Corbucci's successor film *Vamos a matar, compañeros* from 1970, the corrupt revolutionary General Mongo commissions the Swedish mercenary Yod to bring back nationalist intellectual Xantos from the United States, as he knows the combination to a big safe, the contents of which Mongo is after. He sends along his underling Vasco to keep an eye on Yod. Inspired by Xantos, Vasco joins with the student activist Lola and her friends to fight Mongo, as does Yod. However, the safe contains only a sickle, earth and a sheath, and Vasco and Yod fall out because of the latter's demand for remuneration but rejoin to fight Yod's old mercenary enemy John the Wooden Hand (who lost his hand because of Yod), and later the army.

Corri, uomo, corri, Il mercenario and *Vamos a matar, compañeros* appear as close variations on the same story, with similar constellations[27]:

Table 7A. Armature Constellation of Three Political Spaghetti Westerns

	Mercenario	*Compañeros*	*Corri, uomo, corri*
Non-Mexican money-oriented specialist	Sergei Kowalski, Polish mercenary	Yod Petersen, Swedish arms dealer	Cassidy, former American sheriff
Non-Mexican sadistic money-oriented specialist	Curly	John the Wooden Hand	Savigny
Mexican bandit-revolutionary (peon)	Paco	Vasco	Cuchillo
Money-oriented "general"/gang leader	None	Mongo	Reza
Revolutionary idealist (bourgeois intellectual)	Father of Columba (deceased)	Xantos	Ramirez, the printers
Young woman revolutionary	Columba	Lola	(Dolores)
Revolutionaries	Paco's men (peons)	Xantos' followers (students)	Santillana and his revolutionary soldiers
Big-money bosses	Garcia	Oil barons (U.S.)	Bennington
Oppressive forces	The Mexican Army	The Mexican Army	The Mexican Army

Il mercenario: back of video sleeve with top picture featuring hero specialist Kowalski (Franco Nero), left, and social bandit Paco (Tony Musante).

The nine character types in table 7A emerge as doublings of four constellation positions.

1. The money-oriented Gringo specialist has an evil double — another foreign (non–Mexican) specialist who is a sadistic destroyer of innocents closely related to the oppressive government (Savigny), or at least commissioned by it (Curly, John).

2. The Mexican protagonist wavering between self-enrichment and social responsibility also has an evil double — an irredeemable egotist and a killer of the defenseless in a more or less transparent revolutionary cloak. Mongo — like Major Jackson — practices the sadistic game of sharpshooting at human targets, this time at revolutionary students instead of peons. Reza has innocent villagers killed to make Ramirez talk.

3. The "revolutionary cause" is doubled into idealist revolutionary leader — depicted as a bourgeois intellectual scientist (Xantos) or poet (Ramirez) — on one hand — and his younger, more activist followers, embodied by (Columba), or led by (Lola), a young woman on the other.

4. The oppression is doubled into the vested interests, landowners (Garcia) or foreign businessmen, on one hand, and their brutal military arm on the other.

Relationship to the "Unstable Partnership" Plot

Clearly, the relation between the Gringo specialist and the bandit/revolutionary is an unstable partnership. In *Corri, uomo, corri* Cassidy and Cuchillo are originally contenders that in Burton City are forced to work together against the threat of Reza. In *Il mercenario* Sergei and Paco form a business partnership that Paco breaks several times because of his commitment to the revolution. When Sergei instead turns Paco in (to cut his losses), he is also put in front of the firing squad, so they must cooperate again. In *Vamos a matar, compañeros* the company of Vasco is forced upon Yod when he accepts a mission from Mongo to bring back Xantos. They concur to protect Xantos — Vasco because he is impressed by his message, Yod because he is after the contents of the safe. When Yod steals a holy statue (to cut his losses), they fall out again but cooperate against John, and later against the army.

In *Corri, uomo, corri* the partners converge in motivation (to bring the gold to the revolutionaries) even if they separate. In the Corbucci films, as in *Quién sabe?* they diverge, as the bandit becomes committed to the cause, while the specialist remains indifferent. Especially the money orientation of Sergei is stressed over the brink of (conscious) parody, when in the heat of battle he demands payment in advance to assemble the machine gun and then again more money to fire it. The ending of *Il mercenario*, where the couple separate as friends, represents a certain reconvergence compared with Damiani's version, where Chunco kills Nino. This is still stronger in *Vamos a matar, compañeros*, where Yod turns back to help the revolutionaries fight the army detachment.

In the general "unstable partnership" plot there are two main protagonists—"A" as the duped avenger/infiltrator/outlaw and "B" as the agent/deceitful partner, revealed to have a second motive. For *Quién sabe?* Chunco is the main hero (A), and Nino the deceitful partner (B)—and an agent to boot. However, it is Chunco, the "A" hero, who wavers between two motives. Similarly, Paco and Vasco vacillate between monetary values and commitment to the political cause.

In *Corri, uomo, corri*, both Cassidy (B) and Cuchillo (A) get a second motive, the latter as he first is hired to help Ramirez but later rejects an offer from Santillana for a percentage of the gold (though he accepts having a square with his name in the city the general will name after Ramirez!).

We have earlier encountered "A" protagonists who get a second motive in the form of a Marisol woman and/or her child. Accordingly, young Latin women argue the case for the revolutionary cause in the referenced Corbucci films. However, of equal importance is that other face of revolutionary idealism, the intellectual father figures. The thematic role of the Marisol woman might also be absent, as in *Quién sabe?* or indeed in *Corri, uomo, corri*, where Dolores instead conforms to the thematic role of lower class firebrand, quite different from the intellectual "rebel girls" Lola and Columba. She "betrays" Cuchillo to Savigny for $1,000 to stop her lover from laying his hands on $3 million, which would put him out of her reach—that he would give it away to the revolution does not enter the mind of this down-to-earth proletarian. She retorts Cuchillo's parting suggestion—that they will meet in Ciudad Ramirez in the square with his name—with, "Now I have dollars, house and stable, you will come to me!" This is an inversion of Paco's (erroneous) interpretation of Columba's "betrayal" of him and Sergei to the authorities: "When the revolution is poor, they can use 60,000 pesos. Poor bandits like me, you can find as many as you want."

Compared with the "unstable partnership" plot, the two faces of the "revolutionary cause" in these films make a fourth position (D), whose characters articulate a political code dimension—of an oppressive state associated with the rich, versus the poor masses, and about political rights and peaceful versus violent methods of change.

In *Quién sabe?* this cause is represented, though perhaps less eloquently articulated, in the characters of the leader Elias and the rebel monk Santo—but most of all in the "heart" of Chunco himself. In the same vein Cuchillo tells Cassidy that he shouldn't kill for money, but "with a feeling."

The "Social Bandit" Variation

These stories of specialists, bandits and revolutionaries represent an important alteration of the basic "unstable partnership" plot—the *social bandit variation*—distinguished by the changed motive of "A" and added functions related to the presence of the "revolutionary cause" (D) position in the constellation[28]:

"Unstable partnership" plot	*"Social bandit" variation*
1. A wants an object.	A is a social bandit.
2. B wants an object.	B is a non-political specialist working for money.
3. C controls the object(s).	Society is exploited and terrorized by C.
4. A and B have a fight.	A and B have a fight.
5. A and B form a partnership.	A and B form a partnership.
6. A/B tricks B/A.	A/B tricks B/A.
	D is an idealistic revolutionary.
	A and/or B protect D.
7. A and/or B fight C.	A, B and D fight C.
8. B has a second motive.	A joins with D.
9. A and B get their object(s).	B still works for money.
10a. A and B leave together.	B stays with A and D.
10b. A and B separate.	A and B separate.

As in the variants described earlier, 10b includes the possibility that "A" kills "B" (*Quién sabe?*). The functions involving "D" might also be described as a decking out of the standard function 8. On the other hand, the political idealist, who often is older than the other protagonists, becomes an heir to the old man in the *Fistful of Dollars* films—though reversed, as he preaches idealism, not cynicism.

This variant is unlike the "sleeping partner" variant, as both "A" and "B" are equally active, and there is no hidden motive from "B." Nino in

Quién sabe? might seem to occupy the "B" position in a "malignant partner" variant, but this is true only in a weak sense — his hidden machinations use Chunco (A) as a means but are directed against Elias, not against the bandit.

The Other Westerns of Sergio Sollima

Before *Corri, uomo, corri* Sergio Sollima directed and co-wrote *La resa dei conti* and *Faccia a faccia*, both recognized as political spaghetti Westerns, even though they are not directly connected to the revolutionary struggle in Mexico.

For the major part of *Resa dei conti*, the Anglo lawman Corbett tries to bring in the Mexican Cuchillo — most probably the same character as in *Corri, uomo, corri*, though his girlfriend here is named Rosita — for having raped and killed a 12-year-old girl, until he realizes that the real culprit is the presumptive son-in-law of Broxton, the very man who set him on Cuchillo's trail.

Here the typical "malignant partner" plot — where an Anglo hero out for personal revenge (or vindication) is assisted by a Mexican partner who is really one of the guilty parties and in the end is killed — is inverted. An Anglo hero out to solve a crime he has no personal interest in is hunting a Mexican who is really innocent, and who in the end kills the (real) guilty party!

Corbett is presented as a master of cunning in the typical bounty killer introductory scene, when he catches his prey off guard by pretending to be their liaison. However, in the main story he is not only manipulated by Broxton — he also usually comes out second when tangling with Cuchillo (and Rosita). For example, in their first encounter Cuchillo escapes by stealing his horse, and then he side tracks Corbett by giving it away, together with his clothes, to an outlaw, adding further insult by leaving the sheriff's star as garter embellishment for a prostitute! In the end Corbett sees through Broxton's deceit, though, uses the real culprit to lure out Cuchillo, and then supervises a duel between the two.

Political idealism (the "D" position) is represented by the teachings of Juarez (an absent intellectual father figure — like Columba's father), as Cuchillo tells Corbett that he knows just one law — "The one that says most of the world's two parts, the masters' and the poor peons'. In my country we lived under such a law. No one ever knew who wrote it, but we lived under it. Then one day ... Juarez ... said we should change it. Everyone should be nice, and people should stop hating each other, and that the peons were free. Oh boy, we thought that it would work for a while, but nothing really changed." Later Cuchillo's description of the two parts is unwittingly corroborated by the landowner Don Serrano when Broxton says about Cuchillo, "He's a Mexican just like you are," and gets the reply, "Oh no, this man's a poor peon." If Broxton and Serrano together flesh out the constellation position of ruthless vested interests, the corrupt state apparatus is represented by Captain Seguro, who detests Cuchillo for being a Juarista but on the other hand orders closed eyes and ears when men of Don Serrano disturb the peace.

Corbett also has an evil double in von Schulinberg, Broxton's Austrian bodyguard with a dueling track record of "13 widows." Cast in the Erich von Stroheim mold of arrogant aristocrat *übermench*, this character also signals a political context, as the historical Juarez fought a usurping emperor of Austrian origin.

Even though Broxton has promised to make Corbett a senator, the story never suggests that Corbett has another purpose than to catch the man he thinks has committed a hideous crime. Instead of a conscious second motive, he eventually shifts his target to the real perpetrator. However, from a political perspective he goes from being a manipulated minion of the wealthy to becoming their enemy, in the name of justice. Cuchillo, on the other hand, is from the beginning the knowledgeable partner — and the unjustly accused. Unlike Chunco he does not kill the gringo that is in the wrong, because he couldn't kill a man in cold blood. To temper this revelation of "heart," he adds, "If I kill you, they will send a smarter man!"

Faccia a faccia also revolves around a partnership, between the Eastern intellectual Brad Fletcher and the Western bandit Beauregard Bennet. The latter character, name notwithstanding, is a Mexican, and he is again played by Tomas Milian with the same Latin flamboyance that he unleashed in his Cuchillo character and that further evokes Gian Maria Volontè's Latin bandits. In this film, Volontè himself appears as an Anglo, Fletcher. Their relation evolves like this:

1. Fletcher (inadvertently) saves Bennet from the sheriff by supplying the gourd of water that the bandit uses to knock out the guard.
2. Bennet (inadvertently) "saves" Fletcher from his illness by forcing him to test his physical limits.
3. Fletcher kills a man to save Bennet at Purgatory City and then chooses to follow him.
4. Bennet (mistakenly) follows Fletcher's advice to trust his brain more than his heart, and accepts the Pinkerton agent Siringo into his band.
5. Fletcher acts like an outlaw when he takes a woman by force and outfights her man, and is accepted as a full member of the band.

6. Bennet tests Fletcher's guts with a fake gunfight and then follows his plan to rob the bank at Will Creek.

7. The Will Creek robbery goes awry when Bennet does not kill a Mexican boy who sounds the alarm. Bennet is captured, Fletcher escapes with the loot, and the others are killed.

8. Fletcher takes control of the outcast community Puerta del Fuego, which consequently is sacked by vigilantes.

9. The two rejoin, and Fletcher has plans for another band. When Fletcher is about to kill Siringo after the latter just has saved them from the vigilantes, he is shot by Bennet.

There is a recurring American Western story line of the cultivated but effeminate Easterner morally and emotionally reborn when confronting the West, or alternately of the flawed gentleman turned into a tragic outlaw represented by Hatfield in *Stagecoach* and Doc Holiday in *My Darling Clementine*—"refugees from the East" in the terminology of Cawelti.[29] There is a light-hearted treatment of these themes in the mold of the Trinity constellation/plot in *Man of the East*.[30] However, the main Italowestern counterpart to the Eastern hero is that gentleman specialist from Carolina, Mortimer, and his host of followers—through a mirror darkly, though, as his Eastern heritage is a variant style and a superior technology of destruction and death rather than cultural refinement.

Brad Fletcher represents a still more sinister rereading of this character—the intellectual outlaw who starts out upholding the values of democracy and justice (approximately like Elias in *Quién sabe?*) but whose scholarly background does not temper ruthlessness. It fosters it, and he becomes as coldhearted as Nino. He scorns Bennet for not killing the boy, and his actions bring destruction and death to Puerta de Fuego, of which he earlier said that he had never seen people so "happy, living and free." His antagonist, Annie, remarks that it is a great difference between him and Bennet when they do the same thing.

In this story the Nino character is doubled into the ruthless, money-oriented Fletcher and the proper secret agent Siringo, who infiltrates Bennet's band in order to catch him, but in the end—like his agent colleagues in "unstable partnership" films such as *I corvi ti scaveranno la fossa* and *Un fiume di dollari*—fakes the death of Bennet instead of bringing him in.

Bennet, on the other hand, goes from a money-oriented bandit (like Chunco before the San Miguel sequences) to assuming the moral values that Fletcher expressed in the beginning. After sparing the boy, he refuses to buy his freedom by leading the vigilantes against Puerta de Fuego, and at the final confrontation—which replays the ending of *Quién sabe?*—he kills his partner and friend, who has shown no concern for the poor and the innocents, because his "heart said so."

This unusual breadth of character development (for the genre) is reflected story-wise by the "social bandit" variant's being played out in several models, each with the constellation positions distributed differently among the characters.

Table 7B. Models of the "Social Bandit" Plot in *Faccia a faccia*

Scope of the model	Social bandit A	Specialist B	Oppressor C	Idealist D	Victims
Model 1: Up to their arrival in Puerta del Fuego	Bennet	Siringo	Bosses in Purgatory City	Fletcher	(Victims of) the stagecoach robbery
Model 2: On to the capture of Bennet	Bennet	Fletcher (and Siringo)			Juan in Will Creek
Model 3: On to the end	Bennet	Siringo	Fletcher, vigilantes	Annie	People of Puerta del Fuego

In model 3, Fletcher comes out as a mixture of the "bad" double of the bandit — the egotistic and ruthless leader like Reza or Mongo — and the bad Anglo specialist, like Curly/John in the Corbucci films. Bennet's character development, on the other hand, means that he eventually, as a "social bandit" "A" hero, joins the "D" position, which Fletcher by that time has left (plot variant function 8).

The whole story is set not in revolutionary Mexico but in a prejudiced and evil Anglo society: In Purgatory City the two bosses manipulate people to fight and watch "the show" together, and the leading citizens in Silvertown offer their vigilantes a bounty for each man, woman and child killed in Puerta del Fuego.

Faccia a faccia was made in 1968, in a time of large strikes among workers and political radicalization among students, spilling over for some into armed uprising, even terrorism. From the atmosphere of the day a message for the film can be constructed — of the limitations of intellectuals (or a strict intellectual attitude) as leaders or providers of political guidelines among the masses.

Other Social Bandit Variations

Killer Kid

In this *Quién sabe?* remix, an agent for the American army posing as a criminal infiltrates the band of a Mexican revolutionary, just like Nino does, though not for a "wet job," but to destroy stolen U.S. Army guns to avoid an embarrassment for the American government.

Vilar, the unreliable "commander" of the revolutionary El Santo, is a variant of the social bandit Chunco, a greedy bandit-revolutionary who in the end also chooses the revolutionary cause before riches. The hero Morrison/Killer Kid and Vilar never ally in a partnership, which makes Morrison more of a lone infiltrator hero who gets a second motive after contact with El Santo, and especially his activist follower/daughter Mercedes.

She is thus fit to play the part of the idealistic activist brother of Chunco in an emotionally loaded walk of execution that is lifted from *Quién sabe?* The would-be executioner and executed are not brothers this time, but lovers, and the latter position is taken by the gringo agent (Kid), who in the first film (as Nino) is the ambusher—a position here taken by other gringos (men of the smuggler Burns).

After the aborted "execution," she lets him live to save her father and the revolution. And their love relation indeed becomes a partnership, as she dies fulfilling his mission of destroying the guns, and he promises to her he'll lead the revolution "for them and for you." The story represents a partial model of the "social bandit" plot, with Kid embodying both "A" and "B," and an ending combining functions 10b ("D" as El Santo/Mercedes dies), and 8b (Kid becomes "D" as their successor).

Tepepa

The hero of *Tepepa*, on the other hand, represents a combination of the "A" and "D" positions. He is consistently shown opposing the landowners and the army, never wavering toward any monetary motive, and with a shorthand political program, always adding "tierra y libertad" when saying his name, and he is loved by the people, who brings him food when he is in prison. The other possible "D," Madero, has the outer trappings of an intellectual father figure but is a bourgeois politician who quickly forgets those that have brought him to power and signs Tepepa's sentence of death, thus merging with the oppressors (C).

In the "B" position is the Englishman, Pryce, and the specialist competence that Tepepa needs in this story is that Pryce can write, as Tepepa's friend the priest has been killed by the rurales. The hidden agenda of the gringo is a vengeance motive similar to Mortimer's in *Few Dollars More*—Tepepa has raped Pryce's fiancée, an upper-class woman who then took her life. Pryce, who is a doctor, kills him with a scalpel on the operating table.

If Tepepa is killed like Elias, his aspect as "Chunco" is relayed by the boy Paquito. Like Chunco, he in one sequence is dressed in city clothes and ready to leave for the United States with the gringo, and—following the advice of Chunco to the shoeshine man in the concluding scene of *Quién sabe?*—he does "buy dynamite" for his father's Judas money. Furthermore, Paquito in the end kills his gringo "partner." The boy also has a prototype in Damiani's film who several times asks Nino what he thinks about Mexico—just like Paquito—and always gets the same answer as Paquito from Pryce—that he doesn't.

The rape that eventually seals the fate of Tepepa is downplayed—first by a clownish act when Tepepa sits down in her tub with his clothes on, secondly as the rape itself is not shown on screen, and thirdly that her subsequent suicide is also registered indirectly.[31] Incidentally, the cross-class rape motif gets a still more burlesque—and non-tragic—treatment in the introductory sequence of Leone's *Duck You Sucker*. One of the passengers in the wagon is a middle-aged bourgeois woman who somewhat too enthusiastically, and with gleaming eyes, describes the filthy promiscuity of the lower classes. During the robbery, Juan—after drawing out of her husband that he cannot help her conceive—shoves her into a cattle bin using a twig, thus metaphorically making her earlier talk about animal lusts come true. In a self-ironical reference, Leone has the shoving take place in a circular arena, a similar scene to the dramatic settings in his earlier Westerns, especially *The Good, the Bad and the Ugly*. In the bin the victim puts up a somewhat compromised resistance when Juan exposes himself, and then there is an edit to after the act, when he with certain gentleness removes her jewelry and says thank you, with a smile, before literally dumping her together with the male passengers—who are totally naked.

Tepepa is already a true revolutionary, and his female companion, who dances at the fiesta dressed in bandoleer and is shot down as she drives goats carrying explosives against an army column, does not need to formulate a political agenda for him. I will refer to the thematic role of armed guerrillera as "rebel girl." Idealists such as Columba and Lola also become rebel girls.

Un esercito di cinque uomini

The Dutchman—a former outlaw—gathers a group of specialists for a caper to rob a heavily guarded army train with a shipment of gold, destined for the dictator Huerta, with the hidden intent to deliver the main part of it to the Mexican revolutionaries. In this version the money-oriented

7. A Partnership Without Tricks   187

Unstable partnership in *Vamos a matar, compañeros*: video sleeve featuring social bandit Vasco (Tomas Milian), left, and specialist Yod (Franco Nero).

specialists (B) eventually are persuaded to join the revolutionary cause, though not by the intellectual revolutionary leading the Mexicans but by their mercenary (gringo) leader, who was converted pre-syuzhet by the tragic fate of a revolutionary woman (his wife) and her family and is hiding the political motive under a money-oriented surface to ensure the support of the others.

THE BOUNTY KILLER

The Bounty Killer is mostly a tightly narrated kammerspiel between three main protagonists—the wanted José Gomez, the bounty hunter Luke Chillson, and Ethel Novak, who runs an inn in a small village. Ethel helps José escape from a prison transport. Chillson learns about this and arrives at the village to wait for the Mexican. He captures him, but the villagers help José get the upper hand. When his men arrive, José demands money and supplies, and he declares that Ethel shall follow him to Mexico. However, she frees Chillson, who kills the bandits and leaves with the corpse of José.

José Gomez is known in the village as a local boy who was unjustly sent to prison. One of the citizens says, "Only the rich have to be careful with a man like José, not the poor. He is one of us." However, in a reversal of La resa dei conti, where the Anglo lawman mistakes a social bandit for a murderer, here the Anglo hunter is right—José Gomez has developed into a robber and a killer. The two men are vying for Ethel to confirm their definitions of themselves and each other.

The young, unattached cowboy who becomes a victim and the former gunfighter (Ethel's father) who reluctantly goes into action both represent hybridizations of motifs well known from American Westerns.

The "Social Bandit" Films as "Critique" of Their American Counterparts

Frayling suggests that especially the scripts written by Franco Solinas (*Quién sabe?*, *La resa dei conti*, *Il mercenario* and *Tepepa*) show a higher degree of political ambition than Hollywood treatments of the Mexican revolution, and he refers to certain political themes. Are there also differences regarding constellation/plot? [32]

Richard Slotkin describes the character gallery of *Viva Villa* (1934) and its followers.

- The "Christ-fool"—a sacred martyr for democracy, personified by the Mexican President Madero
- The oppressive dictator and "bad" aristocrat personified by Huerta, who murdered Madero and made himself dictator

- The peasant revolutionary (personified by Pancho Villa), who "expresses both the legitimate aspiration of the peasantry and their terrible rage" and so is justified in breaking some rules, but who might also pervert their revolution "through terror and excess."[33]

The U.S. postwar shift to the right was reflected in the "substitution of a glamorous and/or hard-bitten professional" for the populist rebel hero.[34] This North American mercenary eventually appeared in the Mexican environment in *Vera Cruz* (1954), which created a subgenre that Slotkin names "the counter-insurgency Western," which had its apex in 1960 with *The Magnificent Seven*.[35]

As described by Slotkin, the mercenary hero (Ben Trane in *Vera Cruz*, Chris in *The Magnificent Seven*) combines an idealistic cause (that develops out of sympathy with the oppressed Mexicans, and/or as professional respect for their courage) with gunfighter expertise and thus merges traits of the "Christ-fool" and the bandit rebel of the earlier films. Indigenous bandit/guerrilla leaders in their turn appear either as (more or less) inefficient "Maderos" (*Vera Cruz*) or rapacious "Huertas" (*The Magnificent Seven*).

How do these two Hollywood versions of the Mexican revolution compare with the Italowestern "social bandit" plot? Wallace Beery's Pancho Villa in 1934 — a "scruffy, ruthless bandit with a heart of gold" and "a slob, a womanizer, a buffoon, alternating between indolence and violent action, emotionally erratic and subject to fits of unthinking cruelty"[36] — seems closely related to the Italowestern social bandit. You also recognize the intellectual "Christ-fool" and the ruling-class oppressor. However, the "social bandit" plot adds a gringo expressing unbridled self-interest organized through market relations, representing a less benevolent aspect of gringo society.

In contrast to the "counter-insurgency" version, this same gringo does not replace the indigenous social bandit as savior of the peons. Instead they occupy the same scene, both cooperating and playing out their respective "solutions," with the "cause," "heart" or "dream" of the social bandit prevailing — in one way or the other — at the end of the story.

Also, the gringo is not, and does not, become any "chivalric" or "responsible" mercenary of the Ben Trane or Chris type but remains the money-oriented "true mercenary" (like Joe Errin in *Vera Cruz*). Furthermore, North American economic interests are often directly associated with the oppressor position — for example the oil barons hiring John to assassinate Xantos in *Vamos a matar, compañeros*, the alliance of Broxton/Serrano in *La resa dei conti*, and (weaker) Pennington's attraction to the gold in *Corri, uomo, corri*.

Thus, in comparison with the constellations in the Hollywood Western as described by Slotkin and Frayling, a "critique" of the Hollywood Mexican Westerns does indeed materialize in the "political" spaghetti Westerns. A snapshot comparison: The closing scene of *Guns of the Magnificent Seven* — where the leader of the mercenaries presents a little Mexican boy with a wooden sword, and the boy tells him that his name is Zapata — contrasts with the ending of *Tepepa*, where Paquito shoots Pryce after the Englishman has taken his revenge on Tepepa. Another rebel asks, "Why, didn't you like the gringo?" and the boy answers, "No, that gringo didn't like Mexico!"

A "Critique" of the "Social Bandit" Plot

Duck You Sucker

Leone's fourth Western, *Duck You Sucker*, is characterized by Frayling as a "criticism" of the Italian political Western.[37] The story shares the constellation positions of the "social bandit" films, the "criticism" supplied mainly by significant changes in their meaning.

The setting of an oppressive class society is effectively depicted in the introductory episode, with extreme close-ups of the faces and especially mouths of the passengers as they devour food and insult the extra passenger Juan (whose bandit family is soon to take over the coach). The face of oppressive authority is doubled along familiar lines in the governor, whose portraits reside over a reign of terror and who appears in person when trying to skedaddle with the spoils, and the commander Don Toruiz, with the familiar Prussian comportment. However, the (Irish) gringo specialist, Sean, is a political activist who rejects Juan's suggestion of a partnership as bank robbers, saying that he prefers "killing uniforms to be a chicken thief."

Conversely, the bandit Juan never becomes attracted by the prospects of the revolutionary movement, as is understood by the vehement description that he gives to Sean:

> The people who read the books, they go to the people who don't read the books, the poor people, and say "Ho, ho! The time has come to have a change." So the poor people make the change. Then those who read the books sit around the polished table and they talk and talk and talk, and eat and eat and eat. But what have happened to the poor people? They are dead!

He is hailed as a revolutionary hero by (his own) misunderstanding, at least initially manipulated by Sean to break into a bank that now is a political prison. In the process Juan loses what he really valued, his bandit family.

The doctor Villego occupies the position of intellectual revolutionary. Neither the embodiment of a noble cause (as in *Vamos a matar, compañeros*) nor a traitor to the peons (as in *Tepepa*), Villego is a competent revolutionary who breaks under torture and is observed by Sean fingering his comrades for execution. In a final act of manipulation, Sean brings him on the train rushing into the one carrying Toruiz and his soldiers, thus making Villego the second man who Sean turns into a revolutionary hero.

The Sean character, the political (and technical) specialist outsider, has no real counterpart in the political films discussed so far. He rather simulates the political position of their directors/scriptwriters, attempting to push their "social bandit" hero to embrace the political cause. That operation fails in this story, though, because the cause is described as basically consuming the ones for which it is fought, and its proponents Sean and Villego as characters are less clear-cut and more tainted by their choices.

This is fundamentally more pessimistic than the disillusion of Cuchillo in *La resa dei conti*, or even the treason of Madero and death of the hero in *Tepepa*. In these cases there remains at the end a character — Cuchillo and Paquito, respectively — who personifies hope and some kind of direction, while the "general" Juan crying "What about me!" at the end of *Duck You Sucker* rather embodies the helpless individual caught in the midst of revolution — and "revolution means confusion," a quote from Sean that Leone uses for a description of its message.[38]

That there is a massacre of kin (Juan's sons), and not of a social collective (such as the hacienda peons in *Tepepa*), further differentiates *Duck You Sucker* from the typical "social bandit" films. "Social" massacres in the form of abundant executions do take place in Leone's film, but they are part of the setting rather than directly influencing the characters. Generally, the revolution in *Duck You Sucker* is presented as an urban concern, involving urban types of characters such as Villego and Sean. The cheering masses also are a part of the urban setting, and not the countryside poor following Tepepa and Paco, or being left behind by Chunco.

... AND THE COMEDIES

The revolutionary gringo manipulating a mercenary bandit to become an unwilling revolutionary recurs in Duccio Tessari's *Viva la muerte... tua!*, though largely in a comedy mood. For one, it features a hero pair out to find the whereabouts of a treasure by instructions that are tattooed on men's asses. As in the "malignant partner" story *... dai nemici mi guardo io!* discussed earlier, it turns out that the Mexican partner Lozoya secretly harbors one of the clues!

Again the gringo hero Orlovsky (Franco Nero, who did Sergei and Yod as well as Django) is a European visitor, from Russia. He is a con artist who, wearing priestly disguise, learns from a dying man about a treasure in a village. Similarly to the setup in Leone's *The Good, the Bad and the Ugly*, he must cooperate with Lozoya (played by Eli Wallace, Tuco in the latter film), who knows which asses give the location within the village. Both partners lie to and swindle each other to find out what the other knows and beat him to the treasure.

This brittle partnership is further complicated by Mary, who is Irish, like Sean in *Duck You Sucker*, though she is a journalist instead of an explosives expert. She encourages Lozoya, being mistaken for the legendary revolutionary El Salvador, to start an uprising—according to Orlovsky's accusation just for the sake of getting a story. A more solid pretender to the position of revolutionary idealist is Lozoya's sister Lupita. Her husband was a revolutionary killed by the military, and when she wouldn't inform on his friends, her tongue was cut out. When the soldiers kill Lupita and her son, Lozoya/"El Salvador" gets a genuine second motive—"to kill as many regulares as there are hairs on my sister's head." After staging an uprising against the brutal army commander (Huerta, of course, in a delightfully sleazy performance by Eduardo Fajardo, also Major Jackson in *Django*), "El Salvador" gives away the treasure to the people and is consequently sold to the army by Orlovsky and executed. However, this is all a ruse, and Huerta and his men are blown to pieces by the Russian. Finally, the two scoundrels share the reward money, and Lozoya expresses relief to be "an honest bandit" again.

The rebel girl Lupita and money-oriented gringo Orlovsky are clearly characters out of the "social bandit" variant, as is the handicapped and rapacious sheriff Randall, with his grudge toward Orlovsky a retake of John the Wooden Hand in *Vamos a matar, compañeros*. Mary and (most of the time) the "honest bandit" Lozoya rather belong to Leone's disillusioned variation, though pictured in a comedy mode. The result is a lighthearted affirmation of egoistic money orientation and an ironic undermining of the revolutionary "cause." A place is left for earnest (and tragic) idealism, though it must coexist with comedy low enough to include the dropping of pants. The conclusion, which shows the bandit and the gringo together pursuing a monetary motive, constitutes a rare (and inverted) occurrence of the 10a function in the "social bandit" plot.

In Corbucci's *Che c'entriamo noi con la rivoluzione?* released one year later, the priest Albino and the stage actor Guido are brought into an involuntarily partnership, when the revolutionary Peppino (a third Italian!) uses a theatrical performance to smuggle revolutionaries into Vera Cruz for a coup. Once more the focus is on comedy (for example, Albino is unaware of the uprising because he has plugged his ears and can't hear the shots), as well as on acting and staged illusions, but there are also moments of true pathos more prominent than in Tessari's film.

The scene where the revolutionaries are betrayed and massacred by the army colonel Herrero recalls the fate of the outlaws in the same director's highly pathetical *Il grande silenzio*.[39] In the final scene Guido, after seeing Albino executed, incites the crowd to rebellion (instead of impersonating Zapata and denouncing the revolution as he is supposed to) and dies in the arms of the priest (who was executed with blanks!), saying, "What a finale."

Somewhere in between comedy and pathos is a curious episode about a group of men that is paid by the military to chop off the hands of peons (and who kill an army representative who wants to lower the sum). Led by an ugly matriarch — who makes the priest have intercourse with her[40] — they are somewhat reminiscent of the Camiseros clan in *Professionisti per un massacro*. The band is attacked and killed by peons (with chopped-off hands), who carry death's head masks and shout, "Viva Zapata." Otherwise, there are neither oppressed peons nor wavering social bandits in this film, and the Peppino character is certainly a chip off the Sean block.

The "Social Bandit" Plot Together with Other Plots

REQUIESCANT

Requiescant features film director and author Pier Paolo Pasolini in a minor part as a revolutionary man of the church. Storywise it provides an amalgamation of the "prodigal son" plot and the "social bandit" variation.

Requiescant is a prodigal hero whose real father, a leader of the Mexicans, was killed by Ferguson. The latter is a clear-cut evil authority who upholds a reign of terror over the people (Mexicans) and over his wife, Ethel. His man Light is an evil equivalent and pimp who has taken possession of and eventually kills the old flame of the hero. The hero even finds a positive equivalent, a "sister," in Ethel, whose parents also were murdered by Ferguson. There is also a homoerotic bond hinted at when Ferguson tells Light that he is a good boy but should get rid of the women he is keeping, and also adds that he himself married only to get an heir.

Somewhat like Chuck Moll, the hero is raised without knowledge of his (Mexican) heritage, and he must return to the place where he lost it, the place of a massacre, to get it back. Added to the "prodigal son" setup is a social-ethnical dimension, as it is the rights of the Mexican working class that have been usurped, and they are ready to start, or rather continue, an armed uprising.

I CANNONI DI SAN SEBASTIAN

The hero in this story acts as a social bandit when he is greeted as a savior by a village of peons and eventually takes responsibility for them.

Dressed and recognized as a priest, he is also an infiltrator, and when he decides to fight, he uses cunning and manipulation to bring the guns and the villagers together. Moreover, his change from freewheeling bandit to community leader under the largely post-mortem influence of Father Lucas can be compared to the influence of the revolutionary idealist on the social bandit. The "social bandit" pattern is also recognizable in the setting, a Mexico where the "betters" do not care for the poor people.

On the other hand, the hero does not fight oppressive government forces but the Yaquis, who will attack the peons whenever they gather at the village with a priest in the church. The issues at stake — reorganizing village life instead of hiding in the mountains, the building of a dam, raising a crop and harvesting, taming a wild horse — are all acts of civilization and social progress, as against the forces of wilderness represented by the Yaquis, turning the bandit-cum-priest of San Sebastian into a hero of Wright's classical plot.[41]

The classical slant is further enhanced by the character of Teclos, the half-breed. While the Yaqui chief appears as an honorable, though terrible, enemy, Teclos is the real villain, who deceives the villagers, tortures the hero, and counteracts his mission of peace, and so is instrumental in bringing about the final confrontation. The treacherous half-breed belongs in the gallery of stock characters of the American Western and of the Imperialism films at large.[42] In the spaghetti Western, on the other hand, the ethnic/cultural crossover, especially of the Anglo-Mexican kind, is predominantly a hero trait — as witnessed by Joe and Angel Face, by Django appearing in Union garb among post–Confederates and Mexicans, and by his female equal Maria's combining "the worst" of Anglo and Latin blood.[43]

IL PREZZO DEL POTERE

Despite its political theme — a Western allegory of the Kennedy murder — *Il prezzo del potere* develops mostly as a basic "unstable partnership" story, supplanting gold for documents containing "political dynamite," that the partners want to use differently. Bill (A) wants "justice" and the people to "know the truth" especially since the assassins also killed his father. He fits fairly well among Giuliano Gemma's line of vindicative characters. The presidential aide Macdonald (B) is a government representative wanting to use the documents for political ends (in this case to ensure a civil rights policy). As in a normal "sleeping partner" variant, the "A" hero lets the agent leave with the treasure, though other happenings are less common for that variant — MacDonald is more active than the typical agent, and there is a fight between the heroes. In fact, they raise guns against each other almost every time they meet.

The story differs from the "social bandit" films in that the oppressed

Il mercenario: video sleeve featuring evil specialist Curly (Jack Palance).

social group, the African Americans, do not appear as a collective entity. They are abstracted into the character of Jack, who is framed for the assassination and consequently murdered. Furthermore, the only other African American character, a singer who is bribed to witness against Jack, is neither a rebel girl nor a Marisol woman.

ODIO PER ODIO

The partner relationship in *Odio per odio* somewhat recalls Corbett/Cuchillo in *La resa dei conti*: Jeff (in this case not a sheriff but a bank robber), harbors a suspicion against Miguel (for betraying a trust concerning the family of the Anglo) — though here the spectator knows from the outset that it is false.

Even less politically articulated than the "Juarista" Cuchillo, Miguel mines gold that is used by Coyote to buy peons free from their American padrones, and Coyote hints to others that he is a son of the revolutionary Carranza. Coyote fills the role of the idealist, and his handicap (a limp) somewhat evokes the otherworldliness of the idealist, though he eventually emerges as a leader in battle. The peons, who do not materialize until the end, earlier "appear" when Miguel recounts their names — once telling the pilfering assistant that their eyes see him, another time as cunning tactics when fighting the villain Moxson's men.

Still, this hybrid "social bandit" plot lacks both a gringo specialist (Jeff is never directly involved in the mining/liberation context) and any agents of social oppression (the padrones exist off-screen). It is connected to the Jeff/Miguel relation in the following ways:

- The "egotistic" motive of Miguel — to leave for New York to pursue his artistic talents — becomes substantiated in his bank deposit, which in its turn is taken away by Jeff. Thus, at least metonymically, the gringo is connected to a non-altruistic (though not monetary) motive in opposition to the socially responsible one.
- Moxson abducts Jeff's money and family, and he tries to take the gold meant to liberate the peons.
- The peons arrive to assist the partners in the showdown.

Finally, the moments of the pathetic in this story are primarily connected not to the Latin/social part of the syuzhet but to the deprived hero outlaw with an affliction (malaria) and an unknowing daughter, resembling *Minnesota Clay*.

LA BANDA J & S. CRONACA CRIMINALE DEL FAR WEST

This Western "Bonnie and Clyde" emulation tells, mostly in a humorous vein, about Sonny, niece of the deceased gravedigger, who teams up with the outlaw Jed. Plotwise it represents an interleaving of the tutorship and the "social bandit" constellation/plots. *The tutorship story* comes through like this:

- Sonny insists on a partnership, probably for similar reasons to Scott Mary — to find a better life.
- She is at first roughly treated by Jed — she is beaten, robbed and left behind.
- She then saves him — by shooting a man.
- She attains a partnership — they marry and rob together.
- She gets wise to him — when he abandons her for a woman with larger breasts(!)
- She finally gets the upper hand by turning Jed's own tricks against him:
- When he cheats on her and she robs him (and other guests), it recalls the scene where he teaches her to win at the casino.
- When she betrays his whereabouts to Franciscus and the sheriff, it recalls when he left her to be caught by the law at their first stagecoach robbery.
- In the beginning she wants to buy a gun and be just like Jed; in the end she refuses his life of "killing and stealing."
- His demand that she should follow him "like a dog" is turned back on him in the closing scene.

In addition, Jed is a social bandit. He hates the rich (as well as virgins!) and robs only them, because, "What can one rob from a poor man?" He is thus mainly money-oriented, and — like Chunco — he deserts the peons of a village after ridding them of their oppressors. Consequently, they must abandon their homes, and he is struck by guilt. In the "social bandit" constellation Sonny is the idealist. She refuses to kill the stage passengers and later the blind Franciscus, because, she says, "I am not an animal." (When Jed says, "Worse, female!" she agrees and walks away, and he must follow.) Like Brad Fletcher in the first part of *Faccia a faccia,* her teaching is about moral responsibility, not political. Also the threat against the villagers comes from the thugs of a landowner, not soldiers of the state. This constellation also has a place for their nemesis, the law man Franciscus, in the ranks of the vengeful specialists, such as John the Wooden Hand in *Vamos a matar, compañeros.* He has lost his position as a prison warden due to Jed, and he furthermore incurs a physical affliction (blindness) because of the heroes.

LA COLLERA DEL VENTO

This story implies a Spanish rather than Mexican setting. With professional assassins, an oppressive landowner, poor farm workers, an intellectual revolutionary, and a rebel girl, it amply fulfills the criteria for a "social bandit" constellation, though. The hero is initially a Nino character who kills a labor organizer, but impressed by the latter and by a young woman among the farm workers, he starts helping them with advice. However, he is seconded not by a social bandit but by a partner—"friend, maybe he's a brother; we came to the orphanage the same day"—who is killed by the landowner to cover his tracks, and thus vengeance becomes a second motive doubling the social one. Like most other money-oriented specialists, Marco does not join the revolution/social movement—in his case because he is a murderer whose past will catch up with him. It is not illogical that he dies in the end.[44]

PREPARATI LA BARA!

That the malefactor Barry in this vengeance story commits his deeds to finance a political career does not make it a "social bandit" story.[45] However, Garcia puts forth a social aspect when he refers to poverty to explain his treachery. Also, he has a wife and child, rare attributes of money-oriented partners. Rather, we have a Mexican "bandit" torn between a monetary motive and a "cause"—here criminal justice. In addition, as a Mexican wife who has her husband removed by the villain (hanged, as is believed, on a trumped-up charge), and then submitting to the same "fate" herself, she qualifies as a Marisol woman, and like a rebel girl she actively fights the villain (by getting Django out of Barry's clutches). Finally there is a gringo using special methods and tactics (the fake hanging by a hook, the psychological warfare of the "dead" appearing to terrify those giving false testimony). These fragments from a "social bandit" constellation are planted in a gringo environment and a vengeance constellation/plot, in another example of hybridization.

"SOCIAL BANDIT" MOTIFS

Django was released the same year as *Quién sabe?* and resounds with political motifs, including cast-out Mexican revolutionaries planning to buy machine guns and return, and Confederate renegade leftovers in KKK-style hoods. Django himself voices democratic opinions, but his second, non-monetary motive concerns personal revenge and not social justice.

Most of the "prodigal son" story *Texas addio* transpires in Mexico,[46] where an execution is shown with a drunken alcalde signaling the killings by "plopping" the cork of his canteen and laughing. Delgado's reign of terror is part of a general oppression that must be dealt with by an armed uprising. The hero Burt saves the life of the intellectual revolutionary Hernandez and later reluctantly does a short stint as military advisor to the revolutionaries when they destroy Delgado's men, before going on with his personal motivations. A similar association between the violence of the usurper and political coercion is hinted at in *Vendetta* when Mexican villagers hide African American slaves escaped from Cobb. His minion Gomez makes an inefficient appeal warning them about "rebellious ideas" before Cobb applies more severe coercion.

The Mexican revolution plays a conspicuous part in the second Carrancho film, *L'uomo che viene de Canyon City*.[47]

In an early sequence in *Gringo*, the hero belongs to a Mexican guerrilla band that is destroyed by the army. There is no explicit linking to the social motif of racial prejudice in the rest of the film, which takes place in the United States, but possibly the dying words of the guerrilla leader urging Gringo not to make the same mistake as he did explain Gringo's initial preference for legal means.[48]

The Physical Pair of Colizzi

The three Italowesterns scripted and directed by Giuseppe Colizzi belong to the most commercially successful films of the genre, and they also established the actors Terence Hill (Mario Girotti) and Bud Spencer (Carlo Pedersoli) as a protagonist pair. Their cooperation continued in the blockbuster Trinity series of Enzo Barboni.[49]

Dio perdona ... io no!

In *Dio perdona ... io no!* the gunfighter Cat and the insurance agent Earp Hargitay track down the supposedly deceased gang leader Bill San Antonio after a train robbery. They get away with the loot, but then they fall out (because Cat wants more than the percentage offered by the insurance company) and are captured by Bill. In the end Bill is blown up by dynamite, and Cat leaves with the gold and the wounded Earp.

The story reads like a seamless medley of "unstable partnership" variants. The false death of Bill San Antonio and its immediate consequences represent a chronological reversal of the "malignant partner" variant, where a "B" partner helps an "A" hero fight a succession of "C" villains before finally being revealed as another "C" and killed. In this story Bill (B) is first "killed" by Cat (A) but before he has instigated his men (C) to successively search out A for a monetary reason (by leading them to believe that Cat has taken the booty). The underlying motivation of "B"—to manipulate a fight between his former accomplices and the hero for monetary reasons (the gaining or keeping of riches)—is common to both cases. Additionally, it recalls Indio's device to make his gang fight the two bounty killers while he skips with the booty, and thus unveils an analogue between this episode in *Few Dollars More* and the "malignant partner" variant.

The next phase of the fabula (which is the first part of the syuzhet), is instead a "sleeping partner" variant, with Earp as the agent (for an insurance company) out to restore robbery loot. Following at a distance, he lets Cat ferret out the position of the gold. The following fight between them might be interpreted as an instance of "unstable partnership" plot function 4 and heralds the last metamorphosis of their relation into a "congruous partners" variant, though initially a rather weak version. They are tortured and gets out of the situation separately, and Earp interferes in the concluding duel between Cat and Bill as an independent contender for the gold, not as a supporting observer. In the last scene the partnership is confirmed by Cat when he brings Earp to safety and then takes him to a doctor, though a future conflict remains a possibility.

It is also a reversal that instead of the hero, the villain is believed dead — and becomes maimed (in hands and legs). Ethnically, there is a Mexican village terrorized by the second gang of Bill (also mostly Mexicans). A marginalized character in the village, a drunk carrying glasses and hat, this time is an informer to the villains and not a helper to the hero. Less surprising is that an old man who is friendly to Cat in an earlier scene is an undertaker!

I quattro dell'Ave Maria

This is a direct sequel as the protagonists, now called Cat and Hutch, collect the reward for the robbery loot and blackmail Bill San Antonio's partner, a banker. However, they are robbed by Kakopoulous and — trying to regain their money — get involved in his vendetta against three treacherous former partners, of which the banker was the first.

Cat and Hutch continue as congruent partners, a doubling in the "A" position of an "unstable partnership" plot with Kakopoulous as "B," and his partners as "C." It is a chronologically reversed "malignant partner" variant, insofar as Kakopoulous surprisingly raises his gun against his partners at the beginning of their relationship and not at the end, when he stays with them. Otherwise, the trio typically encounters one of Kakopoulous's treacherous partners after the other — the aforementioned banker even before the partnership.

In the Mexican episode of *I quattro dell'Ave Maria* the "social bandit" constellation of specialist, social bandit, political idealist, and repressive army is mostly absent — except for greedy "revolutionary" commanders and possibly Cat as a snapshot specialist when he manipulates one of the commanders against the other and lends a hand at the machine gun.

La collina degli stivali

In this story, the congruous couple teams up with the African American gunfighter/avenger Thomas. Cat and Hutch have an altruistic motive: to help small prospectors against mining boss Fisher.

The campaign to undermine Fisher's reign of terror is well organized in caper style and also uses a circus to agitate for resistance, including a pantomime "freely adapted from ... Mr. William Shakespeare." "Social bandit" ingredients are totally missing though — the ethnic-cultural environment is strictly Anglo, and Fisher is just a traditional big-boss villain. Compared with the usual big boss versus farmers situation, the prospectors voice no interest in bringing in civilized society. This oppressed collective that finally rebels somewhat recalls the old sidekick men being left in charge at the end of *Fistful of Dollars*. Families are only occasionally talked about or glimpsed, and the women that are active in the story are the circus's cancan dancers.

The Physical Pair

The Colizzi "unstable partnership" films present clever variations on different kinds of partnerships, but not any constellation/plot variant of their own. Most original is that the protagonists Cat and Hutch are differentiated by a code of physical and personal characteristics.

Cat is characterized as *agile*:

- He is named after an agile animal and is feline in his dislike of water and inability to swim. Hence Earp/Hutch must take him on his back when swimming across the river in *Dio perdona ... io no!* In a sneaking scene in the same film, he even averts suspicions by throwing out a cat.
- He is seen climbing walls in *Dio perdona ... io no!* and *I quattro dell'Ave Maria*.
- In the first film he fights the stronger Earp by swinging in a tree and kicking.

Hutch is characterized as *strong*:

- He carries the large, heavy box with the Antonio gang's gold in *Dio perdona ... io no!* and later he cracks the thick beam he is tied to.
- In *I quattro dell'Ave Maria* the others put the unknowing Hutch

against the prizefighter Tom Glancingglove. He is struck down twice, and then they clobber each other until Tom faints while standing and is pushed over.

These differences are highlighted in the rumble in *I quattro dell'Ave Maria* that is started when Hutch throws away a dove to be used as a prop when he has his picture taken — and someone shoots it down. When a man with an iron rod attacks Cat, he holds a hat in front of the face of his adversary and hits him in the stomach. Hutch is jumped by a heap of men that are cast aside when he rises. The differences are also reflected in the weapons that they use — Cat is agile with the knife, while Hutch's choice weapon in that same film is a seven-barrel rifle — "a people leveler."

Added to these physical differences are contrasting personality traits. Hutch is wrathful and emotional. In *I quattro dell'Ave* Maria, after they have been robbed by Kakopoulous, he smears sand in his face and begs Cat to kill him — though when Cat does take aim, Hutch stops and asks if he has "gone loco!" Cat is ironic and deliberate, as shown in the special "burning fuse"

The Bud Spencer hammer blow — here as Hutch in *I quattro dell'Ave Maria*, and later employed as Bambino in the Trinity movies.

duel he sets up for Bill San Antonio. Generally he is the one with the plans. His maiming of Bill also shows him to be more ruthless. In *I quattro dell'Ave Maria*, Cat tells Kakopoulous that he will kill him if he doesn't show up with the money, and Hutch adds, "He is not like me, you know. He'll do it!" Of course, the contrasts cool and emotional are not unusual in the spaghetti Western, but they are usually depicted as a differentiation in cultural style (gringo/Latin) rather than as purely personal.

CHAPTER 8

Stories of Betrayal

The Good, the Bad and the Ugly
and the Deterioration of Partnership

Compared to *Few Dollars More*, Leone's next film, *The Good, the Bad and the Ugly*, shows a similar set of actors in a similar constellation, with Eastwood playing a laconic marksman who at least in the final scenes dons a poncho, Van Cleef being a calculating manipulator wearing a suit and smoking a pipe and Eli Wallace supplanting Volontè as the flamboyant Latin member of the threesome.

Angel Eyes,[1] the Van Cleef character, is hired by Baker to find information from Stevens and then kill the latter. He learns that a cash box of $200,000 in gold is involved and shoots Stevens (and his young son) after accepting his money (a larger sum) to kill Baker, which he does.

The other two protagonists, the Mexican Tuco and the Eastwood character called Blondie (by Tuco), run a scam where Blondie delivers the wanted Tuco to get his bounty and then saves him from hanging by shooting off the rope. Eventually Blondie breaks up the partnership and leaves Tuco to a hard, though not impossible, walk through the desert, while he himself goes on to continue the same business with another wanted partner.

By accident, Tuco learns the name of the graveyard where the cash box with gold is buried, and Blondie learns the name on the grave. Tuco quickly renews the partnership and helps Blondie (whom he was about to kill) to recover. As soon as he has all the information that (he thinks) is needed to find the gold, Tuco breaks this second partnership and rides ahead.

In the final three-way showdown — which brings the demise of Angel Eyes — Blondie has secretly emptied Tuco's gun, and the stone that he sets as the prize of the duel, with the name of the grave written on it, is blank.

Cumbow quite accurately describes *The Good, the Bad and the Ugly* as about jokes and betrayal.[2] In the duel, Blondie can claim that his writing is no lie, as the gold in fact is in a grave marked "unknown" beside another grave. This is actually a betrayal in the form of a joke. Another one, still more cruel, is Angel Eyes' mercenary work ethic ("Once I'm paid, I always see the job through") when he kills both Stevens and Baker — in fact to eliminate competition for the gold!

Jokes and surprises are played on the characters by other characters. Tuco buys a gun and then uses it to rob the store. The exhausted Blondie on his sick bed beckons Tuco to come near just to splash water on him and then says "I sleep better knowing my good friend is by my side protecting me." There is also a running gag about "two kinds of people."[3]

Jokes are played on the spectator by the syuzhet, for example in the sequences starting with Tuco's horse being shot from under him by bounty hunters, who are interrupted and killed by Blondie. In the next scene Tuco curses and spits on Blondie as he takes him in to a sheriff and collects bounty. In the following scene Tuco is to be hung but is saved by Blondie, who shoots off the rope and helps him get away. Only now the spectator realizes that this is not the first time they have worked this scam. Likewise, in the opening of the film, one man advances against two others in what obviously is a walk-down to a duel. Only, once they have drawn their guns, they together storm through a door in an assault against Tuco, who emerges victorious from the window.

Tuco and Blondie, disguised in Confederate grey, cheer an approaching troop of grey soldiers. Tuco cries, "God is with us, because he hates the Yanks too!" but Blondie comments, "God's not on our side, because he hates idiots also," as he has discovered that the "grey" uniforms are Union blue covered with dust. This is a joke played by the syuzhet on the characters.

An important difference, compared with earlier Leone Westerns, is the disappearance of the non-monetary motive. The three protagonists are one-sidedly and instrumentally motivated by money. Tuco's revenge motive quickly fades away when he learns about the $200,000. Certain war-related situations in the story, when we see masses of men gathered to a joint destiny — the retreat of Sibley's army, the church hospital, the prison camp, and of course the slaughter at the bridge — do contribute to an epic setting full of pathos that cannot help but influence its overall reception. None of the three protagonists has any motivation relating to the war, though, either as patriots, professionals or pacifists. The war rather acts like an impersonal "manipulator" against the main characters of the story, surprisingly turning the odds to their benefit or disadvantage.[4]

Traits such as manipulation and expertise that are prevalent in earlier Leone films also appear in *The Good, the Bad and the Ugly*. There is true expertise in the scene in the hardware store when Tuco assembles his super revolver using parts from different models, but the traits of expertise from *Few Dollars More* also appear in twisted and parodic forms—Angel Eyes' "professional" work ethic, and Blondie's pretended "bounty hunting."

Blondie and Tuco perform an inverse manipulation when blowing the bridge to get the two armies to stop fighting (and march away). It is also manipulative when Tuco sends his men to (unsuccessfully) attack Blondie through the door while he himself appears from the window to get the drop on his quarry. Likewise, the reason for Blondie to make Tuco at first dig up the wrong grave is hard to explain, except as a way to "smoke out" Angel Eyes' (suspected) presence on the scene.

Betrayals (and jokes) appear in Leone's earlier Westerns. However, as the Leone-Eastwood film trilogy progresses, the betrayals deepen and the partnerships deteriorate. In the midst of manipulations and tricks in *Fistful of Dollars*, the Baxters and the Rojos are family-based gangs that stick together internally. In *Few Dollars More* Indio betrays his own men, and a partner has earlier betrayed him to the law, and there is the possibility that the bounty killers will "end up shooting each other in the back." However, Monco's failed attempts to pull fast ones on Mortimer are benign compared with what happens in the Blondie/Tuco partnership.

Variations on The Good, the Bad and the Ugly

Betrayal for the reason of monetary gain also is the dominating feature in a series of films directed by Enzo Girolami in 1967 and 1968. The first was *Vado, l'ammazzo e torno* in 1967. It begins by "burying" look-alikes of the heroes of *Few Dollars More* and *Django*,[5] and then proceeds to monetary motivations and multiple betrayals according to *The Good, the Bad and the Ugly*. Again, the major contenders are three—the bounty killer Stranger, the bandit Monetero and the bank official Clayton—and their prize is a shipment of gold. However, this time one cannot qualify any one of these three protagonists as better, worse (or, for that matter, uglier) than the others. They show no qualms about hurting or killing contenders for the gold in an open fight, but unlike Ramon, Indio and Angel Eyes, they are not "destroyers of the innocent." This leveling "goodness" brings them their reward in the end, when their three-way confrontation climaxes with a surprise sharing of the disputed booty, expressed by a variant make-believe gunfight, when they jointly turn their fire against the inanimate gold that really had been "manipulating" their movements so far—and the joke is played on the expectations of the audience.

In *The Good, the Bad and the Ugly*, traces of blood on the floor bear witness that Tuco has been tortured by Angel Eyes, and the hardships of Blondie when submitted to the heat of the desert by Tuco are explicitly revealed to us. In *Vado, l'ammazzo e torno* the only scene of torture is when Monetero gets whipped on the orders of the army captain. This signifier of brutality and pathos is here blunted, in the sense that (1) the victim is not the hero, and (2) the person responsible is not any of the protagonists. Spectator excitement is instead fueled by the twists and surprises of the syuzhet and the constant betrayals and double-crosses revolving round an object of desire, changing from the gold proper to the amulet (which is a trace to it) to the ledger of shields (which explains the amulet) to the false gold at the hiding place and finally back to the real gold.

If Tuco and Blondie enter and betray partnerships with each other more readily than the protagonists of *Few Dollars More* (including the enforced, and short-lived, partnership of the "good" Blondie with the "bad" Angel Eyes), the ethics of partnerships in *Vado, l'ammazzo e torno* are still more liberal — shifting from Clayton/Monetero (preceding the syuzhet) to Stranger/Monetero to Stranger/Clayton to Clayton/Monetero again up to the final three-way understanding. In *Few Dollars More* Indio betrays his band, while in *Vado, l'ammazzo e torno* the bandit "lieutenants" Pajando and Paco make betrayals more evenly distributed among the characters.

Similar to the "unstable partnership" plot, partnerships are often preceded by a fight. Stranger hits Monetero when he comes to his cell dressed as a monk, Clayton and Stranger have a fistfight before allying, and the second alliance of Clayton/Monetero takes place after a chase and fight between the former and Monetero's gang. The final three-part deal is even preceded by a shootout — against a fourth party.

In some of the fistfights, acrobatic feats of the protagonists add a lighter ambience, especially in the Turkish bath fight, where their foes are being beaten down into bathtubs that fall apart or into cupboards with towels, or overcome by steam from a pipe. The sequence is also backed by soundtrack circus music.

The following year Girolami released *I tre che sconvolsero il west*, which very much reruns the situations from the earlier film. Again three men vie for loot. In the end, there is not a three-way duel but another metaphoric twist to what *The Good, the Bad and the Ugly*; *Vado, l'ammazzo e torno*; and this film really are about. During a running fight the protagonists Moses, Kean and Clay in turn grab the bag with the money and run only to be felled and deprived of it by one of the others, until they face a gun — held by a fourth contender! Then the four of them leave together to spend the money "where there are women." While one could argue a case for Stranger's being the main protagonist of *Vado, l'ammazzo e torno* — in terms of screen exposure and steering of the action — *I tre che sconvolsero il west* is still more leveling, as there really are no reasons, in terms of story or otherwise, to post one of the three main characters as the hero more than any of the others.

The two Anglo characters in these trios are sporting Mortimer's city-oriented dress and style code. They have neither the unshaven looks nor enigmatic demeanor of Monco or Blondie, nor do they use any Anglo-Latin cross-dressing. Still, Latin ambience stays strong in both films, embodied in bandit gangs, and with *I tre che sconvolsero il west* also in Mose's wily girlfriend Rosita.

The main characters of *I tre che sconvolsero il west* are generally less in control of things than those in the first Girolami film, or the masters of cunning in *The Good, the Bad and the Ugly*. Kean is caught in his own priestly disguise when forced to perform a funeral rite, Moses does not have a clue about the real fortune hidden in the stagecoach that he robs in the beginning, and Clay gets into a panic when Rosita fakes being in labor (the booty is hidden under her skirt). Later, as the supposed "father," he must seek refuge from her irate family in the church, only to be knocked down by the padre — another one of her brothers! There are also other instances that make for more light comedy and less cruel jokes, though all violence in this film is certainly not confined within the bounds of good humor.

The Betrayal Constellation/Plot

These three stories mainly depict several characters, vying for the same monetary object. To this is added a series of partnerships among all of them. Each relation among the leading characters obeys the following functions from the "unstable partnership" plot:

1. A and B both seek a valuable object.
2. A and B have a fight.
3. A makes a deal with B to find and share the object.
4. A/B betrays B/A, which breaks the partnership (for this time).

While the "unstable partnership" plot discussed in the preceding chapter usually outlasts the whole syuzhet, this *betrayal constellation/plot* in fact replays parts of the former plot over and over again, as partnerships are formed and reformed successively between each pair of main protagonists. When one partner tricks another, the betrayal ends the partnership (temporary or for good) and another partnership is forged with another protagonist. Consequently, betrayals are manifold. Furthermore, the two partners both have the same kind of motive, which is monetary.

Capers

The attack of the band of Monetero on the train in *Vado, l'ammazzo e torno* is a true caper — one part of the gang robs a train wagon containing the money, a wagon that earlier has been uncoupled by Clayton from the other wagons with the escort, which is pinned down by the rest of the gang.[6] This also goes for the snatching of the bag with stolen money while the army and the bandits fight about it in *I tre che sconvolsero il west*, and even more so the bank robbery — with a guarded safe open only three minutes. There also appears a time bomb in this story, for further anachronistic reliance on precision.

A Professional Plot?

In 1968 Girolami made another version of the betrayal story, this time with another story angle and, at least partly, another mood. In *Ammazzali tutti e torna solo*, the Confederate army general Hood employs the civilian Clyde MacKay and his group to bring in a treasure of gold coins — disguised as dynamite — from a Union army fortress. They are at first accompanied by Captain Lynch, who later on reappears as a *Union* captain at a prison camp, where most of the group members are brought when they are captured after the raid. As the story develops, Lynch and the members of the group trick, betray and kill each other until only MacKay is left to collect the treasure — which he had hidden near its original position.

Clyde's companions are Dekker, an explosives expert with a bazooka-like special rifle, Blade, an acrobatic Indian knife specialist, Kid, a still more acrobatic, blond youth dressed in black, and Hoagie, who uses a slinglike weapon. Bogard, finally, is the bulky muscleman with an animal laugh.

Now, the bringing together of experts to combine their specialties in some caper-style effort constitutes a popular culture motif — introduced to the American Western environment in *The Magnificent Seven*, which has a fabula closely complying with Will Wright's professional plot.[7]

In this context, the most relevant functions of this plot are

2. The heroes undertake a job in return for money.
6. The heroes all have special abilities and a special status.
8. The heroes as a group share respect, affection and loyalty.
12. The heroes stay (or die) together.

There are a number of Italowesterns that follow this plot, or the main part of it.

- *I cinque della vendetta*— Five friends of the late Jim Latimore gather to mete out retribution to his murderers. Afterwards one stays with his widow, while the other three survivors part, though not together.

- *Oggi a me ... domani a te*—The deprived hero Bill Kiowa gathers a group of gunfighters to avenge himself on the bandit Elfego Baca, who has killed his (Indian) wife and fabricated the evidence that sent him to prison. After Baca and his gang have been eliminated during a night time sneak fight in a forest, the group leaves together.
- *Un esercito di cinque uomini*—In this caper movie, the group does not stay (or die) together outside of society. In the concluding scene it joins another kind of society, of Mexican revolutionaries, including women and children (see chapter 7).
- *La spina dorsale del diavolo*—The U.S. Army assembles an irregular force to cross the Mexican border to destroy the band of Apache chief Mangus Durango at its mountain stronghold. The commander is Victor Caleb, a deserter waging a private war against the Apaches, who have killed his wife. After the mission is completed, Caleb still cannot be pardoned, but the others report him as fallen in battle.

Evidently the members of the groups above (whose number curiously often seems to be five) are profiled both by differences in cultural and personal style—city suits, buckskins, womanizers, gluttons, ethnics—and differences in technical competence — acrobats, strong men, explosives specialists, experts at special weapons, etc. Technical competence is stressed least in *I cinque della vendetta* and the most in *La spina dorsale del diavolo*. It might be significant that the strong American presence in this production coincides with a particular stress on the melding of the group into a team and overcoming personal differences, while the other stories rather stress the differences in style of the men, and how their skills contribute to the accomplishment of the task.

However, *Ammazzali tutti e torna solo* is *not* another instance of this subset of the professional plot, but rather a deconstruction of it! Of course, there are correspondences, especially in the first part when we are treated to a series of caper episodes to convey the individual skills of the group members and their well-timed cooperation. What is missing is the recruitment of the different members of the group. We come to understand that this fact leaves more screen time to show their secession.

The first hint comes when Clyde is ordered by Hood to kill his companions when the mission is completed. He does not voice any protests. Even if he doesn't actually try to go through with it, he has no qualms about skipping with the money either. In this case it is the leader with a hidden motivation who betrays the group — what might be called an inverse infiltration.[8]

Later the group is easily manipulated by Lynch into killing Bogard. Dissolution continues when Dekker prefers joining with Lynch to get a head start instead of assisting his companions against the soldiers. In the conclusion, Hoagie and Clyde have no qualms about confronting each other. So "respect, affection and loyalty" among the group members cannot compete with the lure of gold.

From the prison-camp episodes onward, partnerships in *Ammazzali tutti e torna solo* regularly end with the death of one (or both). Finally there is only Clyde left standing to collect. For a moment it seems that Lynch with his dying shot has blown up the gold, but Clyde has the major part of it safely tucked away. Thus, the money motive prevails, with the hero diving for gold hidden in the water instead of (inversely) showering in gold, as in *Vado, l'ammazzo e torno*.

However, there are mechanics of implacability at work here lacking in the other two Girolami films, where finally enmity is not great enough to forbid the three main protagonists from sharing the fortune.

In *The Good, the Bad and the Ugly*, Angel Eyes is shown committing more repugnant acts than the others (disregarding the list of crimes read out at the hangings of Tuco!). Consequently, Blondie kills Angel Eyes but leaves Tuco with a smaller part of the money. *Ammazzali tutti e torna solo* singles out Lynch in a similar way—not just because he, like Angel Eyes, appears as a false officer in a camp for war prisoners. He also sets up Bogard to be killed by the others, and later he leaves Dekker to drown. However, even before these acts, Clyde hates Lynch's guts, and when the latter in the prison camp comments on his change of uniform ("Uniforms don't make any difference, I've had many. It's only money that counts"), Clyde refuses the suggestion of sharing the gold and retorts, "As a Southerner you made me sick, as a Northerner you make me vomit." And he sticks to this refusal in spite of being subjected to beating and a torture of heat.

Besides having a "bad" character set up to be obliterated, *Ammazzali tutti e torna solo* shares with *The Good, the Bad and the Ugly*—and with most deprived-hero films—an emphasis on physical hardships, which are played down and accorded a secondary place in the other two Girolami films. I am referring to the trek through the sand-colored desert landscape, and the iron hot box used to scorch prisoners in the sun. Also to the fights that take place among humble, unpainted interiors (there are no Turkish baths in sight here), the prison camp quarry, and the nature of the killings—drowning, being crushed by falling objects, or being impaled by a board. This invokes a sense of "seriousness" and pathos in a story without a competing non-monetary motive to attach the pathos to. Unlike *The Good, the Bad and the*

Ugly, the Civil War backdrop is not turned into any pathetic theme of massive waste of human life.

Parameters of the Betrayal Story

La più grande rapina del west was made the same year as *Vado, l'ammazzo e torno*, also with George Hilton, who played Stranger in the latter movie, though here as Billy Rum he is closer in dress and character to Hilton's character Jeff, the drunken half brother and good equivalent of the "prodigal son" hero in *Tempo di massacro*. Here he is introduced having a friendly drinking and thrashing bout with his friend Mark until Billy is locked up by his brother, the sheriff. Billy uses a secret way out from the cell to regain his bottle and returns behind bars again.

Things take a turn for the worse when a man dressed as a priest appears in town together with a woman, Moira, and a statue of St. Absalom, containing the loot from a bank robbery. Soon the rest of the bandits follow, led by Jarred. Several citizens are killed, including the sheriff. The scenes between the sheriff and his freewheeling brother recall the relations between American-style heroes and their trickster doubles in earlier Italowesterns such as *Uno straniero a Sacramento* and *Johnny Oro*. Mark, who attempts to get help from the outside, also displays U.S. Western looks and demeanor. The interventions of these "American" characters are short and unsuccessful, however. The sheriff is surprised by a bandit hidden behind the back of a swiveling chair and is shot with a gun under the table, both typical tricks of the *hero* in post–Leone spaghetti Westerns.

From his cell Billy sheds tears for his brother, and after slipping out and burying him at night, he declares vengeance. This suggests a deprived hero story, which is further strengthened by the malefactor character of Jarred, who thwarts the "clean job, no killings" designs of the priest both at the robbery and in the town, where he plans a massacre to leave no witnesses.

Jarred intends to get all the gold and fool the rest, but so does the "priest" and also some of the gang. The priest is an infiltrator who betrays the band that he has joined. Billy is ostensibly locked out of the action but secretly gains access to it and is thus something of an infiltrator too. Just like Billy regularly slips out of jail, so the priest at night slips away from the sleeping Moira to prevent the arrival of the guide that was to lead the gang through the desert. Later, when Jarred has arrived, he uses the cover of darkness to secretly meet Moira (who is Jarred's woman). Both protagonists also use manipulation against each other (and Jarred) to get to the loot.

The significance of information handling — Miguel Rojo's dictum from *Fistful of Dollars* about "a mere scrap of information" — is confirmed by the key importance of the telegraph. The messages must be acknowledged to avoid the attention of the posse. Eventually the telegraph operator is shot, and the posse arrives. Then suddenly Billy appears wearing a sheriff star and (temporarily) gets rid of Jarred's band (which acts the part of the male population of the town) by forcing them to join the posse out looking for them, thus clearing the way to the loot. This represents a peak of recursive infiltration tactics within the genre — only comparable to the scene of the "widow" in *I crudeli*.[9]

In *La più grande rapina del west* the betrayal context is set from the beginning by the caper-style bank robbery. It continues with the priest undermining the plan of Jarred and eventually overshadows the deprived-hero and "ersatz American" elements of the story, as Billy's actions focus on keeping the gold from the priest and Jarred rather than exacting vengeance. A remarkable scene carrying this ambience is where Billy appears in the dark behind his girlfriend Jenny and knocks out a rapist bandit without Jenny's understanding what is going on.

Professionisti per un massacro is a betrayal story involving a Confederate major, Lloyd, who deserts with a shipment of gold, and an officer (and Union spy) sent to retake it. The officer is assisted by three soldiers who otherwise would have been executed for theft — Ramirez, Chattanooga Jim and the defrocked priest Donney, with the Mexican clan of the Camiseros being another interested party.

Significant is the fight between the trio and the deserters inside the Camisero storehouse, a vicious struggle that also is tinted with parody because it must be kept silent, being fought on the premises of a third hostile party. It is even interrupted once when Mexican guards approach outside and then resumed when they go away. When Ramirez fires his gun and so breaks off the fight, it's really an act of manipulation to make the renegades withdraw before the Mexicans.

Among the Camiseros, in their turn, the leader kills one man for touching the gold, and later sets a gold bar as a prize for a sadistic contest — to try to shoot a man in the head before he ducks into a big jar — and wins it for himself by cheating (shooting through the jar), after which his matriarch mother approvingly tells him that he is the best.

However, even though it is greed that keeps the trio partners in crime (epitomized by the knack of Donney to "sniff" gold, while the Camisero matriarch licks it!), it does not destroy their steady, congruent partnership. The three are presented as a group of specialists — horse thief, bank robber, dynamite artist — but unlike MacKay's group in *Ammazzali tutti e torna*

Billy Rum (George Hilton), "Priest" (Hunt Powers) and Jarred (Walter Barnes) — greedy betrayers portrayed on video sleeve for *La più grande rapina del west*.

solo, they are still together when the syuzhet leaves them (with the gold, but pursued by the *Mexican* army).

Here is a man in uniform switching sides, though for reasons of duty, and another deserting for self-interest — in effect two variations on Lynch (and Angel Eyes)! However, the master manipulator is Sibley, the general who composes his "task force" to use the criminal skills of the three, and at the same time disclose a traitor within his ranks.

In *Un treno per Durango* Gringo and Luis are two not very successful thieves who get involved in the quest for a safe full of gold. These two heroes are less accomplished, and consequently presented in a more comical vein, than the trio in *Professionisti per un massacro*. They become the dupes of Brown, who takes an observer stance and appropriately pretends to be a government agent, and Helen — two master manipulators working the "one from the outside and one from the inside" tactics against a gang of bandits, as well as against Gringo and Luis. At the end there is a walk-down parody when Gringo and Brown advance toward each other, guns raised, with a build up of corridalike music, close-ups and other obtrusive camera angels, but both of them are out of bullets, and when in close firing range, they both at the same time raise their hands and surrender! Everyone is driven by greed here, including the revolutionary general and the common people of the village, who fleece Gringo and Luis. And of course, the romantic interest turns out to be only a tender trap. Still, even if Gringo and Luis are left arguing at the end, the partners that started together stick together in this story — both pairs of them!

Il momento di uccidere involves two gunfighters, Lord (again George Hilton) and Bull (Walter Barnes, who was Jarred in *La più grande rapina del west*), called in by Judge Warren to locate a Confederate war chest.

Up to the concluding scene, this seems to be a story of how an evil brother succeeds his older good one, how he kidnaps and threatens his crippled niece Regina to find out about a hidden treasure of gold, and how two gunfighters together with a faithful retainer in the family thwart these plans, save the maiden and recover the gold. There is also a hint of romance between the girl and one of the strangers, but the retainer warns her that he is interested only in the gold. There is also a taint of a prodigal daughter plot, with Regina losing her good father and in return is displaced from her home and ill-treated by an evil authority, her uncle; and equivalent, her cousin Jason Forrester. The latter is presented with all the sadistic trimmings, as he has fits of rage, scars people with burning cigars and whips, terrifies an African American (servant/former slave?) with target practice, and turns his crippled cousin over to his men after a sadistic game where she is led to believe that she can escape.

However, in the final scene Trent, the faithful retainer, turns out to be the master manipulator of the plot who has made a deal with Forrester and then deviously uses Lord and Bull to eliminate his partner: When the two heroes seem to have left, he proceeds to strangle Regina to have the gold for himself but finds that he is strangling a doll in Regina's wheelchair. She is not the crippled, good, helpless damsel in distress with a sweet eye for the hero that she seems to be. Instead, the lady is an impostor who now is standing and holding a gun. She kills Trent, but her relishing the gold is interrupted when she hears from the clavichord the same tune that she earlier had played — Lord and Bull are back.

Lord is also a manipulator. He steals the book that is a clue to the gold from Forrester's house and then suggests to him a 50–50 partnership. He arranges a night time meeting, where he and Bull forestall an ambush prepared by the Forresters, and then humiliates Jason to make him do something unplanned — have "Regina" write a letter demanding a return of the stolen book, thereby revealing that it is the Forresters who hold her. But that handwriting also discloses the false Regina to him.

With the true aims of Trent and "Regina" uncovered, the betrayal story triumphs over any contending plots. Everybody is in fact vying for the gold. Even the judge that called in Lord and Bull wants the gold for "the revenge of the South," and he sends Trent to look for Regina because she is a clue to the gold. Among the unstable partnerships originating from the betrayal constellation, Lord and Bull compose a steady, congruous one — "They are Lord and Bull, and where those two hang out, there's bound to be some killing."

Ognuno per sé has an unusual casting constellation with distinct Hollywood veterans Van Heflin (who plays Starret in *Shane*) and Gilbert Roland as the older protagonists — the prospector Sam and his old friend/enemy Mason — and equally distinct European Western stars George Hilton and Klaus Kinski as the younger ones — Sam's ersatz son Manolo and the latter's sinister consort "the Blond." It is an obvious variant of *The Treasure of the Sierra Madre* — John Huston's paradigmatic tale of the pervasive, and destructive, influence of gold on human relations. The two stories also share a robbery by a ragamuffin band that is concerned with tangible things such as food and animals and is ignorant about gold. The ending, where Sam keeps the gold but loses his friends, is an inverse in still darker mood than the template film, where two surviving gold miners stand united in laughter as the wasted gold dust blows back toward the mountain (compare this to the concluding carnivalistic scene of *La più grande rapina del west*, where an accidental explosion sends the gold raining down over the citizens, while the priest and Billy, together with their girlfriends, laugh and say, "St. Absalom fooled us all!")

The characters are essentially money motivated, the main exception being Annie, a saloon girl who takes Sam into her care and bed even though she regards him as only an unsuccessful gold miner. Sam talks with fervor about the joy of finding gold, and the earlier story of Mason and Sam involves a theft of army money. The Blond is a murderer and ready to kill both Sam and Mason for the gold, while Manolo wants to spare Sam. Mason is promised an equal part of the gold but hires the Brady brothers to get it all on the way back (or possibly just to get Sam killed). The brothers are professional killers who turn on their employer when they realize that gold is involved. Lastly, the owner of the general store runs a scam by sending men to ambush the miners who buy their supplies from him.

This film represents a forceful treatment of the betrayal story in the mode of tragedy and the pathetic, like the "tragic mercenary" variation in the bounty killer films. This calls for a non-monetary motivation — in this case trust and friendship. Annie tells Sam Cooper that he is all alone. He refutes her by bringing from his past people to whom he has had a relation, Manolo and then Mason. These earlier relations both have flaws though, and the presence of the gold turns the flaws into disaster, leaving Sam with the gold but depriving him of both the "son" found again and the friend found again. His relationship with Manolo is also a version of the standard story of the paternal relation of an older and a younger man endangered by an erotic diversion, in this case of a homosexual kind, as the scenes between Manolo and the Blond very clearly suggest.[10]

The Sartana/Sabata Cycle

Sartana, Sabata and the "Specialist Betrayal" Plot

The same ambience as in *Vado, l'ammazzo e torno* is to be found in Gianfranco Parolini's *Sartana* (1968). The bankers Stoole and Hallman officially send a shipment of gold with a stagecoach that is held up, but in fact they tuck it away and then proceed to claim insurance money for the "stolen" shipment. The remainder of the film constitutes an almost delirious row of betrayals and counter-betrayals involving the bankers, the Mexican landowner/gang leader Tampico, the outlaws Morgan and Lasky, Hallman's wife, the widow of the town mayor, and in the thick of the action the mystical black-clad hero Sartana, unnerving everybody and turning people against each other (when they don't accomplish this by themselves). Just as betrayal is piled on betrayal, chases and massacres abound. During the 90 minutes of the film, at least 80 persons are killed, including all the named characters except Sartana and his sidekick Dusty. The frenzied action is enhanced by frequent doubling: The hero is believed dead twice; he thrice terrifies Lasky using a melodic watch. There are two massacres with a machine gun; there are two attacks on the gold shipment, first by Tampico's man Moreno and then by Lasky (doubling along ethnic difference). Also, the coveted gold is replaced with stones twice. The final confrontation is also a doubling, or rather a prolongation. First Lasky shoots Sartana, but like Ramon in *Fistful of Dollars*, he is defeated by his own predictability, as he always shoots people in the forehead and Sartana wears a shield under his hat. Later comes a special loading duel with Lasky cheating by keeping a bullet in his revolver, but he is still defeated by Sartana, who has an extra chamber in his derringer. The derringer recalls Mortimer in *Few Dollars More*, where he produces such a deadly, though distinctly unfair, surprise from up his sleeve against a dangerous opponent. Like Mortimer and Joe, Sartana is a master of cunning, but unlike them, he discloses no secondary motive besides the gold sand in those bags. Some mystery remains though, as to whether he wants it for himself, like all the others, or is an agent of some kind who will deliver the gold (hidden in a hearse) to its original destination.

The Carmineo/Parolini Cycle

Similarly to *Django*, Parolini's *Sartana* established a film cycle where the core consisted of a series of films made by Parolini (under the alias Frank Kramer), with a hero mostly called Sabata, and a parallel series made by Giuliano Carmineo (under the alias Anthony Ascott or Ascot), with a hero mostly called Sartana.[11] Commercially, these films were successful, especially the first *Ehi amico ... c'è Sabata, hai chiuso!*, which starred Lee Van Cleef (while Sartana and his successors were played by John Garko or George Hilton).

- *Ehi amico ... c'è Sabata, hai chiuso!* (*Sabata* for short — Parolini, 1969) — Independent operator Sabata thwarts a bank robbery and proceeds to blackmail the instigators. The gunfighter Banjo, hiding out as a musician/pimp, hires out his services to both sides.
- In *Sono Sartana, il vostro becchino* (*Sono Sartana* for short — Carmineo, 1969) — Sartana is framed for a bank robbery, and eventually uncovers the banker as the real culprit. The hero (and his partner Buddy Boy) leaves with all the booty.
- *Indio Black, sai che ti dico ... sei un gran figlio di ...* (*Indio Black* for short — Parolini, 1970) — Indio Black (called Sabata in non–Italian

language versions) is enlisted to hijack a shipment of gold during the Juarez revolution, but he and the revolutionaries escorting him take it for themselves.
- *Buon funerale amigos ... paga Sartana* (*Buon funerale* for short — Carmineo, 1970) shows Sartana helping the niece of a murdered miner against a banker who is after her claim. However, it turns out that the niece and Sartana both are con artists who also try to swindle each other.
- In *C'è Sartana ... vendi la pistola e comprati la bara!* (*Vendi la pistola* for short — Carmineo, 1970) Sartana, who is a bounty hunter, discovers that mining town boss Spencer stashes the miner's gold away for himself and has Manti's bandits pretend to "rob" the transport. Other interested parties include Spencer's right-hand man Baxter, the saloon owner Trixie, and the gunfighter Sabata. In the end Sartana and Sabata take the gold and leave together after the former has "killed" the latter in a fake gunfight.
- *Una nuvola di polvere ... un grido di morte ... arriva Sartana* (*Nuvola di polvere* for short — Carmineo, 1970) — Grant Fuller, who is suspected of being behind the disappearance of large sums of both counterfeit and real dollars, sends for Sartana, who springs him loose and then goes to town to find the money. Other interested parties are the sheriff Manassass Jim; the band leader Monk; the beautiful widow Belle; the government agent Sam Putnam; a young lover of Belle pretending to be Sam Putnam(!); and gambling house owner Nobody. They all perish, last of all Fuller himself, who is killed by Sartana after involuntarily giving away the hiding place.
- *È tornato Sabata ... hai chiuso un'altra volta!* (*Tornato Sabata* for short — Parolini, 1971) — Sabata discovers that Mayor McCintock of Hobsonville, who collects extra taxes to finance a great building scheme, deposits counterfeit bills in the bank and uses the real money to buy gold for himself. Sabata proceeds to blackmail the mayor, and at the end he and his friends leave with the gold, after thwarting an attempt by the saloon owner Clyde to take it for himself.

The films stayed true to the original concept in terms of abundant betrayals and elaborate tricks and trick weapons. In Parolini's *È tornato Sabata ... hai chiuso un' altra volta!*, Sabata wields a derringer with an extra four-barrel magazine to fire from the end of the butt, but he also uses

- An extra derringer held with a magnet under his boot.
- A Winchester arranged under the table to overcome some gunmen that appear in his hotel room.

- A cigar to blow arrows with.
- A small "lemon-squeezer" gun with a round magazine.
- A derringer built into an adversary's army medal, his "good-luck charm" (which he has gambled away to Sabata), used to overcome that same adversary.

In *Nuvola di polvere* the hero carries a "silver" watch of lead on a chain that he uses in a steam-bath fight to snatch off a pipe and fill the room with steam to confuse his opponents. In the same film he breaks out of his "tiger cage" jail hole by blowing poisoned darts, employing a small pipe that he kept hidden in his shoe heels. Most imposing (and absurd) is a church organ, the pipes of which are usable as cannons or machine guns. He also uses a mechanical "robot," presented to him by an old man sidekick, to divert his opponents.

Tricks in the Sartana/Sabata films are often associated with gambling, and there are mirage situations involving mirrors and paintings, complicated set piece traps, and disguises.

The "Specialist Betrayal" Constellation/Plot

The predominance of special weapons and tricks in the core Sartana/Sabata films, compared with the betrayal films discussed earlier, justifies the addition of a corresponding function to the betrayal plot:

1. A and B both seek a valuable object.
2. A makes a deal with B to find and share the object.
3. A/B betrays B/A.
4. A fights B using special weapons or methods.

The new function 4 is especially relevant to those plot models where A = the hero. I designate these functions and their associated constellation positions as the *"specialist betrayal" constellation/plot.*

The "specialist betrayal" plot is straightforward in the sense that the Sartana/Sabata hero will almost always have only one (monetary) motive. On the other hand, the constellation that he faces grows in complexity. Most noteworthy is the position of the equivalent, e.g., Lasky in *Sartana*, who similar to the hero operates alone, independent of the "two" camps (the initial gang(s) of Lasky are soon wiped out). These hero/equivalent relations differ from the (more or less stable) hero/partner relationship in the "unstable partnership" stories. The partner displays a contrast in style, motivation and/or in other ways significant for the story, while the equivalent is similar to the hero, having the same motivation through and through.

There is a special ethnic coding relevant for the equivalents—played by William Berger (Lasky in *Sartana* and Banjo in *Sabata*), Klaus Kinski (Hot Bets in *Sono Sartana*), Dean Reed (Ballentine in *Indio Black*), Reiner Schöne (Clyde in *Tornato Sabata*) and Charles Southwood (Sabata in *Vendi la pistola* and Archie/Alexei in the Hallelujah films). They are blond and blue-eyed, as compared with the more or less darker complexion of the hero. Both hero and equivalent are gringos, but there is a relation of South European countenance (hero) versus North European (equivalent), which also in most cases corresponds to the nationality of the actors. The most prolific Sartana actor, Gianni Garko, is himself rather blond, but the coding holds even when he plays against the blond Berger (and the reddish Piero Lulli in *Nuvola di polvere*), because Sartana is seldom seen without his dark clothes and hat. This represents a reversal of other partnerships in spaghetti Westerns where a deceitful partner to the Anglo hero usually is a Latin of darker complexion.

The deprived hero (like Django) did usually face a town boss *or* an outlaw as his principal enemy, while the constellation of the Sartana/Sabata films in fact merges both corresponding theme-stories—the machinations between bandits and bounty killers or mercenaries are captured in the hero/equivalent relation, but there is also a big boss with bad cronies—or several bosses betraying each other, and also an ethnically distinct gang leader with his own conflicting agenda. There are also short but distinct appearances of outside specialists brought in by some boss to challenge (and be disposed of by) the hero (or the equivalent).

The "Specialist Betrayal" Plot Together with Other Plots

CAMPOSANTO

The main story of *Gli fumavano le colt ... lo chiamavano Camposanto* (*Camposanto* for short) does not differ much from some traditional American Western stories, such as *Shane*, concerning mysterious helpers who support farmers and families against big bosses and give shooting lessons to their sons.

Its correspondence to the earlier Sartana/Sabata films lies in a chain of interleaved episodes concerning the relationship between the hero Camposanto and his equivalent "Count," another expert gunfighter who is hired by the boss to kill the same young men that Camposanto protects.

These two mercenaries know and appreciate each other. Count is the only character ever to be told why Camposanto has helped the McIntyre sons (their father had earlier saved his life). When they separate, Count says that Camposanto is too much like him.

As they find themselves on different sides, they maneuver to avoid a direct confrontation, even though they calmly discuss the possibility. For example, Count uses his special sign — the shutting of his silver cup — to inform Camposanto that an attempt on his life is on the way. When the latter thanks him, Count replies that the elimination of other gunmen will drive up his own price. Later Count, after negotiating a higher price, undertakes to keep Camposanto away until sunup, while the villain besieges his friends. Count holds him down in a ravine with shots from his telescopic sight rifle. At sunup Camposanto uses a mirror in his watch to spot a hornet's nest and shoot it down on the Count so he can reach his lair and get the drop on him. Count calmly remarks that he has accomplished what he promised.

After Camposanto ostensibly has taken the booty for himself "for expenses," Count is suddenly there to take care of his own interests — now that there are no more customers. Camposanto refuses his 50 percent offer. After an introductory ceremonial comparable to the one in *Vendi la pistola* (shooting at each other's feet, Camposanto's lighting a match for a "last cigar" to Count, throwing a coin that, when it stops spinning, is a signal to shoot), they both turn and shoot down stones to kill the villain, who has been aiming at them. Camposanto then discloses that the coveted bags contain only stone — the money has been hidden in the bandage of one of the others that he chased away.

Spirito Santo

Spirito Santo in *Uomo avvisato mezzo ammazzato ... parola di Spirito Santo* (*Spirito Santo* for short) is played by certified Sartana John Garko, and is yet another hero from the same mold. He is dressed in white instead of black and has a suit and a long coat, which sometimes covers surprises, such as a lot of mirrors or a shield made up of golden lead. He is accompanied by a dove that he calls Eagle — "she is convinced that she is." He has won prospecting rights to half of a gold mine in Mexico. To get his claim confirmed, he finds it necessary to join the former leader Don Firmin and his daughter Juana in a counterrevolution against the military usurper Ubarte. Thus, like in *Indio Black*, the Sartanian hero is inserted into a "social bandit" story, though this time the constellation/plot interleaving is more complex. It can be divided into at least three stories:

- *The Juana Story*—A "social bandit" story featuring an idealist revolutionary (Don Firmin), a beautiful rebel girl (Juana), a gringo specialist mercenary (Spirito Santo), and an evil military dictator (Ubarte). A glaring omission for a "social bandit" story is the absence of the social bandit himself, though. Juana is a strong-willed organizer and leader, and there is no love interest between her and the specialist[12] but instead a tug of war concerning his relationship to the revolution. Eventually he comes around to helping her, but he never wavers in this instrumental attitude, even if he is visibly moved by the fate of some slain Firmin supporters. Also there is no departure ceremonial between Spirito and Juana. Obviously, their relation does not conform to the template partnership between a sophisticated, money-oriented specialist and a rough, emotional guerrillero. On the other hand, the relationship between the elegant Spirito Santo and the ragged Chicken Little — who also joins with Juana's cause — at least corresponds to the sophisticated/unsophisticated code,[13] but Chicken is a gringo and a dynamite expert, not a Latin revolutionary. His discord with Spirito Santo does not concern the revolution.

- *The Spirito Santo Story* — A "specialist betrayal" story with a gold mine as the object. The motivation for Ubarte's seize of power here is to get forced labor to exploit the mine together with the (part) owner Samuel Crow. Spirito Santo considers himself the co-owner of the mine and eventually finds that he must help in the overthrow of Ubarte to get to it. Ubarte and Samuel betray each other over the gold, but Spirito Santo is the one who gets it. Juana also has a place here as a female betrayer, though with a non-monetary, political motivation. She offers information about the location of the mine if Spirito Santo joins the revolution, not bothering to mention that her father has forgotten where it was! Besides the hero, one recognizes the constellation positions of the big boss (Ubarte), the challengers (Crow's family) and even, in just one scene, a helper (the engineer Hernandez — again Franco Pesce from *Sartana* and *Buon funerale*). However, also in this story something essential is missing, namely an equivalent. There is a contender — the swindler Samuel Crow, who masterminds Ubarte's secret mining operations and swindles him out of the gold and also counters Ubarte's own betrayal against him with the help of his brothers. However, he is part of a collective of evil brothers and not quite as independent as the hero, even if he shows a certain unwillingness to share the gold with them. Furthermore, there is none of the more or less deadly maneuvering indicative of the hero/equivalent relationship, as the hero and Crow don't meet face to face until the reckoning.

Maneuvering abounds instead in the relationship between Spirito Santo and Chicken Little (who is the only character who knows Spirito Santo from way back, calling him "Harold"). In the end the reformed gunfighter Chicken goes back to his old ways and covets the gold, but he is easily fooled by Spirito Santo and left with a substantial though minor part of the precious metal. He shouts curses and appeals after the departing hero in the manner of Tuco in *The Good, the Bad and the Ugly* and Parolini equivalents such as Ballentine in *Indio Black* and Clyde in *Tornato Sabata*. However, there are arguments against Chicken as an equivalent. He does wear a suit, but it is the black plain suit and slouch hat of the religious man and not an elegant city dress (while Samuel wears cowboy dress). More important, he is an easy mark for the hero in betrayal work. First, when it dawns on Chicken that the gold is in Ubarte's headquarters, Spirito has already for some time been looking for Hernandez, who has the plans for the building. Second, suggesting that Spirito Santo himself should go looking for the gold in the house lures Chicken into going so the hero can find the real entrance, which is in the courtyard.

- *The Chicken Little Story* — Some aspects of the Chicken Little character have not yet been under consideration. He is sturdy, strong and a Christian proselyte. Also, his cooperation with Spirito Santo is forced upon them by Juana, and before they set off to Mexico, Spirito Santo makes considerable, though failed, efforts to wriggle himself out of it. These aspects all conform to the Trinity constellation/plot.[14] The Trinity partnership pair consists of a big strong hero and a smaller quick one, and actor Chris Huerta comes off well as the strong man Chicken. Other constellation roles in the Trinity films are an evil big boss (here Ubarte), and a harassed group of Christian pacifists (the pastor who has converted Chicken is an extremely weak version, as he isn't a victim). What is lacking in *Spirito Santo* is the quick partner. Spirito is a partner quick in his thoughts and on the draw, but otherwise he is very different from the lazy and raggedly dressed Trinity. Just as Chicken won't do as a guerrilla bandit in the Juana story or as an equivalent in the Spirito Santo story, Spirito Santo is unfit as a Trinity character in the Chicken Little story.

In the interweaving of these three stories, where each one left to itself would be a lopsided and weak version, different scenes belong to the realms of different stories, while others constitute meeting places for all three. In the confrontations between the revolutionaries and the military, the situation as such belongs to the Juana story (mercenary specialist Spirito Santo helping revolutionaries destroy troops of the oppressive government); the convoluted and outrageous nature of Spirito Santo's methods belong to the

8. Stories of Betrayal

Spirito Santo story; and some episodes during the fights against the military featuring Chicken's strength, and some where opponents are immobilized in a non-lethal and comical way (like when government soldiers are knocked out one by one when running out through a door), are part of the Chicken Little story.

In *Spirito Santo* parts of this "specialist betrayal" constellation/plot lean toward surreal effects, and parts of the low-comedy Trinity constellation/plot share space with very serious and tragic parts of the "social bandit" story. Innocent people are raped and massacred in the Juana story while in other episodes people are fed manure as torture, hens are fed explosives to hatch exploding eggs, or we are invited to have fun at a fat man in drag. This lack of congruence makes the syuzhet even more surreal than perhaps was intended.

The Hallelujah and Tresette Films

Carmineo continued with George Hilton as a costume-clad hero in *Testa t'ammazzo ... croce sei morto ... mi chiamano Allelujah!* (1971), *Il west ti va stretto amico ... è arrivato Allelujah!* (1972), *Lo chiamavano Tresette ... giocava siempre col morto* (1973), and *Di Tresette c'è ne uno ... tutti gli altri son nessuno* (1974). Under the Trinity spell, these films gradually supplant

Expert trickster Tresette (George Hilton), left, and strong partner Bambi (Chris Huerta) in *Lo chiamavano Tresette ... giocava siempre col morto.*

deadly violence with humorous brawls and, furthermore, in the Tresette films the equivalent is replaced by a strong partner (again played by Huerta) in the constellation.

The Sartana/Sabata Cycle with Other Directors

Compared with the films with a hero named Django, the films of the Carmineo/Parolini core seem less disparate.[15] However, when taking into account films with heroes (or titles) using the Sartana/Sabata/Spirito Santo label that are directed by others, the disparity instead becomes greater. The constellations, codings and plots in themselves can be very different indeed. Instead of acclaiming the money-motivated betrayer, they might portray an initial steady pair destroyed by such a character, as in *Arriva Sabata!* and *Lo irritarono e Sartana fece piazza pulita*. They might portray the hero as an unselfish crime fighter as in the Sartana films of the ill-reputed Demofilo Fidani—*Passa Sartana ... è la ombra della tua morte, Arrivano Django e Sartana ... è la fine!* and *Quel maledetto giorno d'inverno ... Django e Sartana all'ultimo sangue*. The Sartana character might also be a deprived avenger (*Sartana non perdona*), a Mexican bandit in a traditional U.S. "gunfighter" theme-story (*Prima ti perdono ... poi t'ammazzo*), an army officer on a mission (*Spirito Santo e le cinque magnifiche canaglie*), or a Trinity-style hero (*Trinità e Sartana figli di ...* and *Allelujah e Sartana figli di ... Dio*). The only characters somewhat retaining the feeling of the original cycle are in *Django sfida Sartana*—coupled with a vindicative Django—and *Sartana nella valle degli avvoltoi*—though its arduous wilderness trek disagrees with the predominantly urban environment of the core films.

Is this the reduction of the trans-story hero to the unabashed use of "Sartana," "Sabata," "Spirito Santo," etc., as commercial signals employed to lure the spectator to any kind of content (albeit still of a Western kind)? Well, not quite! It is noteworthy that—only *Sartana non perdona* apart—these heroes do not operate in any of the two main schemas that Frayling recognized for plots in the Django films—those of the avenger and the bounty hunter.[16]

The Betrayal Constellation/Plots and the Retreat of the Pathetic

Vestiges of the Non-Monetary Motive

Among the films discussed so far in the context of the betrayal and "specialist betrayal" plots, non-monetary motives and pathetic moments play a mayor part in *Ognuno per sé*, with its several models of non-monetary-based relations between men destroyed by greed, and they also decide the conclusion of *Arriva sabata!*, with the disputed fortune consumed by fire and the surviving Sabata alone — after the deaths of the old friend who had betrayed him once and the new friend who had betrayed him all along. In both these cases of a betrayal plot with a tragic outcome, the destruction is wrought upon friendships between men. This is different from the stories of the tragic mercenary, where it usually is a loved one or a family member that is victimized.

It is true that in *Ognuno per sé* Sam claims to have raised Manolo as his son, but the backslapping nature of their reunion — joking, pranking, getting drunk, is more manly (or should one say boyish) than parental. In this story there is also a love relation between Manolo and the Blond, and homoerotic attraction might also be cued from the scene in the bedroom where Sam punishes Manolo for that relation. However, among these money-hungry men there is no character analogue to the non-monetarily motivated and victimized woman of the tragic mercenary constellation. Furthermore, the only relation that is openly (homo)sexual is not directly dissolved by greed, as Manolo dies when avenging the death of the Blond,[17] though it is their common avarice that leads up to the situation.

Up to the confrontation between the two partners, *Lo irritarono e Sartana fece piazza pulita* seems imbued with a similar message about the evil of riches, but it is turned into an ironic ending, featuring a *ménage à trois* of swindlers.

In other films discussed in this chapter, the pathetic moments, where they remain, are relegated to others than the main characters, and to a marginalized position in the story. In *Un treno per Durango* two bandit brothers are manipulated by Helen to kill each other, and her partner Brown rings the church bells to drown out their words and stop them from reconciling. The duped hero couple survives and stays together, though. In *Professionisti per un massacro* the rage and despair of Primero, and his matriarch mother, when his brothers one by one return in coffins, are moments of pathetic emotion. However, they are not innocents whose fate will motivate the actions of the hero. Also, the interesting character of the surviving daughter, who blames the heroes for the massacre of her family and consequently saves the real culprits from an ambush, is promptly propelled out of the story.

Among the Carmineo/Parolini films, a potential challenge to the monetary motive is to be found in *Indio Black*, mostly embodied in Escudo, who at first questions the services of a mercenary like Indio. This tentative expert/"social bandit" relation dissolves with their unanimous decision to disregard the revolution and keep the gold — without any fight or any ensuing deaths of loved ones. Furthermore, Escudo's pathos is ironically undermined as his heroic lamentations over dead comrades-in-arms always are cut short by sudden considerations for the gold.

The Triumph of Greed and Its Consequences

The near-hegemony of greed as the motivating force brings consequences in the areas of violence and action.

In the mainstream Italowesterns discussed so far, there are characteristic forms of violence — which also are important narrative moments of the pathetic:

- Massacres and atrocities committed against the innocents.
- Sadistic games.
- Physical sufferance of the hero — usually by extreme forms of violence directed against his body.
- Psychological sufferance of the deprived hero — the death of the loved ones of the avenger and the tragic mercenary, destruction of the familial position of the prodigal, or of the social position of the vindicative hero.

These moments — which in stories of deprived heroes are reinforced up to (and sometimes beyond) the limit of the absurd — serve to engage and awe the audience, as well as to supply non-monetary motives. Consequently, in the betrayal stories, where there are no non-monetary motivations to be fired by such moments, they are missing, or their impact is lessened. When innocent bystanders get in the way and are quickly disposed of (such as the stagecoach passengers in *Sartana*), the syuzhet does not cue us to attach any emotional significance to them. Typically, the only notable exception to this expediency is related to the hybrid "social bandit" story in *Spirito Santo*.

In Leone's films, an important contribution to the pathetic mode is made by the larger-than-life confrontation scenes, where the flow of action halts for a build-up of emotional tension with music and a montage of camera shots displaying the reckoning between characters. Similarly staged confrontations appear often in the films of the deprived heroes, but they are missing in the betrayal films, where they are not inserted to cover a trick or for purposes of irony, such as in *Vendi la pistola* and *Camposanto*, or again relegated to the equivalent as in *Sabata* (Banjo versus the Clantons).

Without recourse to such moments of the pathetic, the betrayal stories instead employ an excess of action and intrigue to engage and awe the audience:

- A more complicated and crowded constellation of characters.
- A syuzhet more closely packed with actions and confrontations.
- An armory of special weapons more numerous and more surprisingly special.
- A game of still more complicated and interlocking manipulations and tricks, employed not only by the hero and the main villain but also by the equivalent.

The hero's equivalent (in the Sabata/Sartana films), so like the hero in motives and cultural style, also replaces the partner who sometimes was different from the hero in motive, and almost always in style. The equivalent creates a friction with the hero by being too much alike — just as manipulative, just as greedy — rather than being too different — and their crossing feints and manipulations significantly contribute to the "thick of the action" in these films.

Mystery and Surprise

With the lack of a second, non-monetary motive also disappears most of the mysteriousness shrouding earlier Italowestern heroes. One aspect of his mysteriousness is somewhat retained though — the unpredictability. Like Joe's poncho and Django's coffin, the cape of Sartana is covering many surprises. A trick, a mirage, and a concealed or unforeseen weapon — these are methods frequently employed by betrayal plot heroes. Still, there is a subtle difference compared with some of the surprises dealt out by earlier Spaghetti Western heroes — Joe's rejoining the Rojos after learning from Silvanito about Ramon's destruction of the family of Marisol, Ringo's bargaining with Sancho for a better deal than with the sheriff, and Django's rejection of Maria for the Mexican girl as his consort. Such actions are all the more intriguing as they seem to rebel against the expectations of the spectator concerning the right thing to do — at least until they are revealed as masterstrokes of cunning. However much we might enjoy being surprised by the tactics of the money-motivated heroes in the betrayal stories, they seldom offer such plays at the outer limits of the nice/not nice distinction. Closest is probably MacKay's acceptance without objections of the demand echoed in the title of *Ammazzali tutti e torna solo* ("Kill them all and come back alone"), and this occurs in a film that in other respects is closer to the deprived-hero films.

Eastern City Style and Costume Ball Ethnics

Joe, Django and their ilk act predominantly in urban arenas, but these are wretched villages with shattered social lives, whose simple saloons or cantinas with scant interiors fit the heroes' own dusty and ragged — though colorful — appearances with ponchos, fur-lined leather vests, etc. Not even the larger urban centers shown in *Few Dollars More* or *The Good, the Bad and the Ugly* offer the saloons with elegant interiors, cancan dancing and occasional Turkish baths signifying the civilized Eastern city style of the main characters especially in the Sartana/Sabata series. They dress in suits and use weapons fitted to such environments, such as small derringers or casual objects close at hand. However, behind the civilized veneer, law and order are still marginalized, and the church serves only as an alternative battleground.

Now, while the elegant veneer of the hero and the lack of non-monetary motives might account for the reluctance concerning degradation and torture in these stories, no such "internal" narrative reasons suffice to explain another development, especially in the "specialist betrayal" films: namely an overall lessening of the importance of the Latin cultural style and its replacement by *costume ball ethnics*. This term indicates that, unlike the Latin/Anglo one of the deprived-hero films, this ethnic difference does not cut across any other code dimensions. The Scottish or Russian identity of the equivalents in the Hallelujah films, or the Irish one of the boss in *Tornato Sabata*, mean nothing beside details of looks, speech and demeanor. The Austrians in *Indio Black* represent the exception, as they embody colonial repression in a "social bandit" story environment and consequently are set off by their aristocratic arrogance and ruthlessness—from the sadistic games of Skimmer through the secret-agent assassins in bowler hats on down to the soldier who mows down his own comrades with a machine gun. Then again, in *Il west ti va stretto amico ... è arrivato Allelujah!* the same Teutonic military style is only a target for spoofing.

CHAPTER 9

Triumph of Comedy

The most dramatic turn in the Spaghetti Western genre after the breakthrough of *Fistful of Dollars* and the huge success of its follower, *Few Dollars More*, came about with Enzo Barboni's *They Call Me Trinity* (1970), below called *Trinity 1*, and *Trinity Is Still My Name* (1971), below called *Trinity 2*. As in the case of Django and Sabata/Sartana, the commercial success spawned a trans-story Trinity hero in films from other directors and performed by other actors. Even in films without any hero named Trinity, similar *post–Trinity* story lines were employed.

Trinity — The Comical Deprived Hero

The man dragging a coffin through a dirty and barren landscape in the opening shots of *Django* might stand as a figurehead of the Italowestern deprived hero, haunted by inner demons and outer fiends. By coincidence or by design, the opening of *Trinity 1* presents the inversion of that situation — a hero resting in a litter that is being dragged by a horse through the wilderness.

Dirt and Smell

Compared with the Django hero, Trinity's clothes are still dustier and even torn, and his countenance is still more ingrained with dirt. This outer signification of the torment of the deprived hero might easily be turned into humor when overdone, and especially when it is accentuated, as in this case, by that real-world companion to dirt, smell.

In *Trinity 1* the deputy (and old man) Jonathan refuses to touch Trinity because of the way that he looks and smells when he has just arrived. His brother Bambino had been in the same state when he arrived in town —

"Had to use three pieces of soap just to see the color of his skin!" Trinity finishes Jonathan's last piece of soap in his bath —"I ain't seen so much dirt since the overflow of the Pecos"— and then the poor man has to watch him put on his dirty duds again. In *Trinity 2* Pearl recognizes the presence of her son Trinity by his smell, and she complains about how hard it is to get Bambino into a bath.

In the post–Trinity films, the dirt and smell aspect of the original Trinity/Bambino pair is fully retained only in *Tedeum*, where the father of the hero goes under the name Stinky Manure, and his wife doesn't mind shoes and pipes spicing her pot of beans. Similarly, in *Buddy Goes West* an old man is put into a water barrel and the enterprising Chinese cook uses the water thus seasoned as onion soup, which scares off the visiting health inspector.

Gluttony

Hunger might be used as a mark of suffering, but similar to dirt it is here exaggerated — into grotesque gluttony. In the opening sequence at the cantina in *Trinity 1*, the others watch with fascination as Trinity devours a whole pan of beans, a large piece of bread and one whole bottle. Bambino slaps at Trinity's hand when Jonathan serves the food, and the brothers are very attentive to how much food the other takes. It is also the free meals that catch Trinity's interest when Bambino enumerates the advantages of being a deputy sheriff. At the dinner by the farmers, Trinity, who is eager to make a good impression on the farmers' daughters, halts Bambino when he has taken his fourth full scoop from the pot.

In *Trinity 2* all members of the family launch themselves on a fried bird, with lines like, "Looks like an eagle," "Eat your own food, dam' it," and belching. When the brothers later dine in a restaurant, they stop the waiter from taking away the remaining roast, and from then on Bambino takes a good grip on it every time a waiter approaches. In many spaghetti Westerns, the table manners mirror the crude environment, and one might eat with a spoon (like Joe)— sometimes even a wooden one (like Django)— but here the bare hands are used, accompanied by loud smacking that the other patrons of the restaurant abhor.

Post-Trinity characters such as Smith in *Così Sia* and Buddy in *Storia di karatè, pugni e fagioli* and especially *Buddy Goes West* stand out as masters of voraciousness. The latter has an eating contest with the sheriff where they devour a whole turkey, among other courses. When the sheriff finally gives in and goes to throw up, Buddy orders a bunch of bananas for dessert!

Unpredictability

Joe in *Fistful of Dollars* acts against advice or commands given to him, and against the spectator's immediate expectations. The Trinity films take this game of unpredictability one step further, because Trinity tends to act according to advice or commands when the spectator expects him to disobey. When he arrives at the confrontation between the three men and Bambino in *Trinity 1*, Trinity heeds their warning to take off his gun belt, and then he leisurely stands watching. Likewise, apparently docile, he lets the bounty hunters in the opening of *Trinity 1* inspect him, and those in the opening of *Trinity 2* question him. When Wildcard Hendricks in the second film accuses him of cheating at cards, he answers with an amiable and vaguely confirming hum. In all these cases the opponents fail to observe the taunting veiled behind the blue-eyed openness and have to pay (more or less dearly) for it.

A Comical Unstable Partnership

In *Trinity 1* an unstable partnership is established between the brothers:

- Bambino at first wants Trinity to leave before he messes up an intended theft of horses from big boss Harrison. Later he offers Trinity a deputy position.
- Trinity refuses, but after meeting with the farmers' daughters, he changes his mind. The now unwilling Bambino deputizes him under the threat of otherwise being disclosed as a horse thief.
- Bambino forbids Trinity to approach the newly arrived gunfighters, but Trinity disobeys him and scares them away. Bambino now escorts him out of town, and they have an ersatz shootout.
- Trinity joins the farmers and swears to Bambino that he will marry and settle down (thus getting off his brother's back for keeps) if Bambino helps them against Harrison.
- After running off Harrison, Bambino finds that Trinity has given the stolen horses to the farmers and parts with him in a rage.

In the second film the same characters are forced into a partnership at their father's (faked) deathbed.[1] Bambino's attempts to educate his younger brother on the path of crime are sabotaged by Trinity, but in the end he gets to reproach Bambino because they must give up the money when the latter is close to being recognized by the Rangers.

Unstable partnerships prevail also in the post–Trinity films. In *Carambola* Len rejoins Coby only after he is made to believe that he has killed

Trinity (Terence Hill) enjoys his comfy saddle in *Trinity Is Still My Name.*

someone. In *Buddy Goes West* Cocoa follows the unwilling Buddy around because he considers him a blood brother, on account of a blood transfusion! In *Un animale chiamato uomo* Bill repeatedly takes advantage of John, who with apparent relief makes a cup of coffee after Bill is jailed, and spits it out when he is immediately released. Trinity several times refuses cooperation with Sartana in *Trinità e Sartana figli di...*, and later the pair rides away from Buck Ben Bolt only to realize that it is he who has the money. Like his namesake, Trinity in this film also repeatedly gives away their booty. Buddy and Sam in *Storia di karatè, pugni e fagioli* are more of a steady pair (even if Sam grumbles that Buddy has traded their guns for food) but they ally with a con man, Colonel Quint, and when they accidentally save the life of Mokkaido, he gratefully forces his unwelcome services (such as cooking rice) on Buddy.

If the pair converges to lay their hands on some booty, each one fears that the other will skip with it — this is relevant for Hallelujah and Sartana in *Alleluja e Sartana, figli di ... Dio*, for the hero and the monk in *Tedeum*, and for Slim and the pizza baker/preacher in *Posate le pistole ... reverendo*. Jesse and Lester in *Jesse e Lester, due fratelli in una posto chiamato Trinità* might be half brothers, but what really keeps them together is their inherited mine, even if they disagree whether to build a church or a brothel for the profits. Smith in *Così sia* wants to build a school with the money that he has swindled from Horatio, and Horatio sells Smith's church to someone who wants to build a saloon.

Properties of the Comedy Pair

THE LAZY

While Trinity lies sleeping or yawning on his litter at the beginning of *Trinity 1*, the title song suggests he looks like "a sleepy-type guy," slow to react. When Bambino asks him why he doesn't show any ambition — "rustle cattle, hold up a stage, play cards" — Trinity retorts that he is "too busy doing nothing." In both stories, Bambino shows more purpose, but still he gets noticeably irritated in *Trinity 1* every time the actions of Trinity vis-à-vis Harrison's henchmen oblige him to act out his role as sheriff. Jonathan deplores the "bad luck" of the sheriff— when something happens he is always somewhere else!

... BUT QUICK

The next line of the title song promises we'll change our minds about Trinity when we "see him use a gun," and indeed Trinity is capable of a remarkable speed of movement when required. It is exaggerated into superhuman parody, especially in the second film in the "duel" against the notorious Wildcard Hendricks, where he repeatedly slaps Hendricks, draws, holsters and slaps him again before the latter has a chance to draw. The same agility and speed are shown in the card game preceding the confrontation, and in brawls—where he uses acrobatics, or ducks to make two opponents hit each other.

Trinity shows trickster traits also in other respects: He is simultaneously cunning and ignorant; he makes fun of people and likes mischief. His eyes glow with expectation when he hears that two professional gunfighters have arrived (to kill him and his brother)—and the ensuing confrontation ends with their rushing out in their underwear, not taking time to mount their horses because, "He said 10 seconds!" While his followers in the post–Trinity Western fail to reproduce his particular brand of mischievous laziness, at least many of them are con men, a "profession" often associated with trickster activity.

THE STRONG

Bambino is physically an opposite of Trinity. He is a huge and strong man who lets his big fist fall like a sledgehammer on the skulls of his opponents. A typical moment in a brawling scene is that a dozen or so opponents jump Bambino, and then the whole bunch is thrown aside as he straightens out. Another is when an opponent from behind breaks a chair or a table over his head, and Bambino slowly turns around and looks at the poor villain like he was an annoying insect before he clobbers him. As Bambino, the actor Bud Spencer (Carlo Pedersoli) excels in slow, pausing reactions somewhat reminiscent of Oliver Hardy.

While Trinity's normal mood is a vaguely taunting friendliness, Bambino is surly—and Trinity gives him plenty to sulk about. In *Trinity 2* Spencer gives a peak performance of slowly mounting irritation as he waits hour after hour for Trinity, regularly putting back the hands of the clock on the wall (because the cantina is to close at midnight) and, when he temporary leaves (to lock up disrupting bad men), always pausing in the door to stare at the cantina owner and ask for the time, ensuring that the man will not take the opportunity to close shop.

Motivation

The motivation of Trinity in *Trinity 1* seems to be "doing nothing" and, as a second motive, love. Moreover, when he finds that love of a farmer's daughter (or two) is associated with toiling, he returns to the first motive. In *Trinity 2*, besides a very similar love interest, he shows interest in money.

When Parker offers Bambino $2,000 "to keep his eyes closed," Trinity reminds him that they have four eyes, and thus gets the sum quadrupled. He also suggests that they collect bounty on the Smith brothers, and it is he who finds out about the money at the mission. In this film the two motives do not enter into conflict.

If there is an "internal" conflict of motives for Trinity in the first film (laziness versus love), there is also an external conflict between the pair of heroes, manifested when Trinity gives away the horses that Bambino has managed to steal to the farmers because, "It's only right that these people get paid back for damages." In the second film the stagecoach holdup might be interpreted as playing out a similar procedure, as he robs only Bambino. Inversely, it is the suspicions of the Ranger captain toward Bambino that causes them to lose the smuggler's money.

The Wannabes

Spencer's massive build and Hill's impertinent smile and stingy blue eyes, plus their common talent for play with facial expressions, made them a hard act to follow in the post–Trinity films. Len and Coby in *Carambola* come closest in looks, if not demeanor. Chris Huerta as Buddy in *Storia di karatè, pugni e fagioli* is burly, though not as huge as Spencer, and wisely supplants the slow irritation game of the latter with an energetic performance. He excels in the area of gluttony, though. Huerta plays basically the same character in the *Spirito Santo* and *Tresette* films of Carmineo.

In *Si può fare ... amigo!*, Coburn is played by Bud Spencer and is very close to Bambino (like Buddy in *Buddy Goes West*)—though Trinity is replaced by the pimp Sonny, who is quick (with the gun) and surely an unwanted partner, as his plan is to make Coburn marry his sister (to make her an honorable woman) and to immediately kill him afterwards. The boy Chip—whom Coburn unwillingly has taken on—carries the unpredictable property of Trinity, as he turns down several generous offers for his shack on a muddy piece of land, as it turns out with good reason when oil is found there!

Man of the East, featuring Terence Hill, is conversely a Trinity film without Bambino. Bull, one of the gang trying to raise the hero into a Westerner, fills in the place of the strong, but has forgettable facial play and less volume.

Trinity (played by Harry Baird) in *Trinità e Sartana figli di ...* has the distinction of being the only black-skinned hero in the Italian Western, the joke being that he is called Trinity because he comes from Trinidad!

The Trinity Constellation/Plot

The Trinity Plot

A common plot for the Barboni Trinity films and their followers can be constructed as follows:

1. A is strong.
2. B is quick.
3. A has a grudge against B.
4. A and B must work together.
5. A (and B) look for something valuable.
6. A and B appear under false pretenses.
7. A and B act in unsophisticated or unconventional ways.
8. Some big boss in alliance with bandits threatens a marginal group.
9. B (and A) protect the group.
10. A and B fight the villains.
11. A and B capture the valuable object.
12. A/B causes the object to be lost.
13a. A and B stay together.
13b. A and B split up temporarily.

The Trinity Constellation

RELIGIOUS GROUPS

In both films there are religious communities that refuse to take part in killing. They can be persuaded to take a slug at the villains, though, providing a plausible pretext for having comical violence without bloodshed. They also represent a continuance of the Italowestern interest in socially marginal characters rather than mainstream society. It is such groups, not the average citizens, that the brothers help and inspire to take part in brawls. It thus follows a certain logic that the settler father in *Trinity 2* is too "normal" to take part in the concluding free-for-all fight — every time that he tries to step in, he is immediately decked.

Even after the two Trinity films proper had established the pattern of brawls rather than massacres, there was a remarkably frequent use of religious characters in the post–Trinity films. Religious pacifism sometimes still comes into play (such as when Jesse discloses that he has taken the bullets out of the gun Lester is pointing at the bandits), but the usual context is that one of the heroes is religious, which provides disjunctive motivations for the pair, or they might be falsely religious as part of a scam, as in

Tedeum and *Alleluja e Sartana figli di ... Dio.* In *Man of the East* one of the outlaw "godfathers" of the Eastern hero is a preacher (and even knows how to read!). *Si può fare ... amigo!* offers a change of pace, as it is the villain who is (disguised as) a priest.

THE LAWMEN

The Trinity films bring a change of pace in treating the institutions of law, generally nonexistent, weak or corrupt in the stories of bounty hunters, deprived heroes and also specialist betrayers. This is most evident in *Trinity 2*, where the Texas Rangers stand for an authority not to be ducked or challenged. The town sheriff also appears strong, until the moment it is disclosed that he is taking orders from boss Parker. From that moment on, he behaves confusedly, and soon makes himself scarce. In earlier Italowesterns an honest sheriff would rather be weak, while a strong sheriff most probably turns out to be a criminal big boss, or at least the partner to one.

In *Trinity 1* the lawman, who step by step is crippled by Bambino and his mates because of misunderstandings—"We were just going the same way, but we didn't know"—might not seem very impressive, but at least he is persistent and his approach eventually means that they must run. Additionally, those strong Rangers are referred to also in this story.

BOUNTY KILLER ADVERSARIES

While the law is respected at least when it is around, bounty killers and paid gunfighters—the chosen professions of so many spaghetti Western heroes—are ridiculed. In *Trinity 1* two arrogant gunfighters dressed in black suits (one is named Mortimer) are run out of town in their underwear. In *Trinity 2* a party of bounty hunters (this time dressed in standard Western outfits) are tricked and robbed thrice, first by Bambino, then by Trinity, and finally by their parents!

Similarly, in several of the post–Trinity films, bounty killers or hired guns dressed in black suits in the Sartana/Sabata tradition turn up only to get flattened by the hero(es). An especially unfortunate pair emerges in *Man of the East*:

- The two men tell an innkeeper about the Englishman's being dead and his band scattered. When they say something disparaging, the hired hand at the inn—up till then believed to be mute—suddenly states, "The Englishman was a scholar and a gentleman." Realizing that this is Bull from the gang, the two stand up and threateningly twist their holsters until he raises his hands up in the air.

Satisfied they sit down, but he brings down his hands on their heads and bangs them at the table, knocking them out and breaking the table in the process.
- The two bounty hunters, one bandaged, enter a saloon where Bull stands as winner after a big brawl. They ask where his partners Preacher and Monkey are, and he answers, truthfully, that they are right behind them. The bounty hunters are disarmed and robbed. Bull asks for a table to be fetched. He makes a sign, the two men dutifully bow their heads and he brings down his hands on their heads and bangs them at the table knocking them out and breaking the table in the process.
- The two bounty hunters, both with heavily bandaged heads, enter and surprise Bull and Monkey, but Preacher enters behind them. They are disarmed, and Monkey pointedly knocks at a solid table. One of them asks for another solution, and while Bull plays a wretched tune on the violin and Preacher sermonizes, "Giveth everything that you got in your pockets and get out of here or we break every bone in your head," they put their money in Monkey's hat and leave.

BOSSES AND BANDITS

In *Trinity 1* and *Trinity 2* the villainous bosses and bandits are but slightly touched by the comedy mode, even though the unfortunate Mezcal mistakes Bambino for someone who will turn the other cheek. This kind of burly Fernando Sancho–type bandit suffers a parodic inversion in *Trinità e Sartana figli di ...* and *Alleluja e Sartana figli di ... Dio*, where Alan Abbot plays a Mexican bandit leader that is diminutive, thin and hysterically choleric.[2] The latter film also features costume ball ethnics in the form of Scotsmen.

FEMALE INTEREST?

The women that the original Trinity courts, with pubertal shyness, are farmers' daughters cut and dried from (very) traditional American Westerns. The only other woman of significance is the saloon girl/mother of the heroes in *Trinity 2*. Besides farmers' daughters there are also prostitutes in similarly passive roles in the post–Trinity films, but few Marisol women. Active con women of the type encountered in the betrayal plots are the beautiful, and thieving, school marm in *Così sia* as well as the strong Betty and the sweet Wendy in *Tedeum*. The only non-trickster female who appears on equal footing with the male heroes is Yvette in *Un animale chiamato uomo*, a female doctor who can find work only as a dancer/prostitute!

Codes in the Trinity Stories

The Unsophisticated

In *Trinity 2* the heroes show themselves totally unaware of proper restaurant procedure. They say, "Give us something to eat!" when the waiter starts describing the menu, and when he pours a sip of wine for tasting, Trinity grabs the bottle. Later they draw their guns at the sound of a champagne cork and strike down the waiter when he lights the dessert.

Similarly, in their first visit at the mission, Bambino turns out to be totally ignorant about the hows and whys of confession, and he ends by breaking the confessional and almost slugging the priest. When the monks refer to Lucifer, Trinity believes that he is "a professional from back East," and suggests that the monks should tell him to go to hell! In the first film Bambino is shown sleeping on the floor beside his bed, with his saddle for a pillow.

These jokes position both brothers on one pole of a "sophisticated/unsophisticated" code of manners that also is used in some "social bandit" films, e.g., *Vamos a matar, compañeros*, where it distinguishes the uncouth bandit from the specialist, who knows the ways of bourgeois society, in situations that are vehicles for humor. In the Trinity films typically both heroes are unsophisticated, though.

Also, when Bambino tries to teach Trinity the basics of being an outlaw, his brother acts awkwardly. On the other hand, at the poker game in the same film, it is Trinity who is the expert, and Bambino who breaks decorum by guffawing when his brother does well.

Violence

The retreat of the mode of the pathetic, already evident in the betrayal films, is accomplished in the Trinity films, with their heavy reliance on different flavors of comedy. The big massacre, the merciless beating of the hero, the terror and murder of the innocents—all this disappears, as does the mystery related to the hero.[3] *Trinity 1* is a transition film in this respect. In the opening sequence, Trinity releases the wanted Chico from two bounty killers. After Trinity has left, they open the window to shoot but are felled by "miraculous" shooting from Trinity, backwards without looking. In the next scene three men are killed by Bambino in a classic stand-up gunfight. When Trinity later confronts Harrison, one henchman draws behind his back and is shot out the window, and another, who aims at him from above, is shot in the crotch (neither wounds deadly). This episode offers the last gunshot wounds in the two "genuine" Trinity films. From that point on, big brawls replace big massacres. Sadistic play is still present when the bandit Mezcal visits the farmers and first slaps his own men because they lack courtesy for the hosts, and then slaps a host for not having wine to serve. The major hires Mezcal to kill the farmers, which is an important fact in the plan of the brothers.

TRINITY: Would you kill women and kids?
BAMBINO: Hmm. Not kids anyway.
TRINITY: See? If you wouldn't, the major certainly wouldn't.

This would indeed be an unexpected delicacy of mind for a big boss in an earlier type of Italowestern! Still, a big massacre in the "old" style is still a possible alternative in *Trinity 1*. It is, however, realized only as parody when the captured bandit Emiliano and the brothers rustle the horses of Harrison:

HARRISON'S GUARD: Any killings?
EMILIANO: Todos muertes!
GUARD: All dead?
EMILIANO: Children, women, old ladies, all dead.
GUARD: Holy ... Killed them all?!
EMILIANO: Cats, dogs, everybody!
GUARD: What a massacre!
EMILIANO: Sí. It was a nice massacre!

In the introductory scene of *Trinity 1*, the wounded Mexican Chico is taunted by his gringo capturers, and later Trinity refers to racism — "You know how it is, the Mexicans are always wrong!" — when he has Bambino write out a pardon, claiming (over Chico's own objections) that there were witnesses to self-defense. For the rest of *Trinity 1*, this theme of social victimization is dissolved into parody as Chico is dead drunk every time he is to be released from the cell where he is supposed to sober up.

In *Trinity 2* no one suffers death or serious damages. Boss Parker tells his partner that government agents (that is, Trinity and Bambino) are not killed but bought. The bandits' violence and threats toward monks and peons are related rather than actually shown on-screen. Furthermore, in the first film Trinity shows genuine aggressiveness in the confrontations with Harrison and his men. This has no real counterpart in *Trinity 2*.

Because they appear in a tradition of violent spaghetti Westerns, the two Trinity films need narrative motivations why gunfights are put aside for brawls without shooting irons. Besides the pacifism of the religious groups that they protect, the brothers might accept a challenge to fight without weapons (*Trinity 1*), or follow an ordinance from the sheriff to take off their guns in the saloon (*Trinity 2*).

9. *Triumph of Comedy* 243

The post–Trinity films reproduce the wavering attitude toward violence of *Trinity 1*. While all of them shun torture, massacres and specialist weapons, *Jesse e Lester, due fratelli in una posto chiamato Trinità* and *Un animale chiamato uomo*, for example, include the final killing of the villain (and perhaps his henchmen), while others are completely safe for family audiences in this respect.

Cunning

While the code of violence is thoroughly revised, the code of cunning remains largely unchanged. In addition to his unpredictability, Trinity shows skill in manipulation. In *Trinity 1* he several times gets his brother to do what he wants by declaring that he knows that Bambino thinks that way. At the fight in the saloon, he strikes the first blows and then sits down smoking while Bambino fights the nine opponents.

In *Trinity 2* he promises the bounty hunters that he will spare the life of the last one standing, and then disappears while they fight. In the preceding episode Bambino scares the same men by pointing his gun. They calm down when he tells them that the weapon is empty and lend him ammunition, which he uses to hold them up. Bambino's plan for the stagecoach holdup includes infiltration (Bambino travels as a passenger) and a faked duel between the brothers. Moreover, their father pretends to be on his deathbed to convince the two brothers to work together.

In the post–Trinity films there is also manipulation, performed by the quick partner—Horatio, Slim, Bill and Coby—toward the strong partner (where such a distinction can be made) as well as against others. The partnership of Sam and Buddy with Quint in *Storia di karatè, pugni e fagioli* is preceded by mutual acts of swindle.

Personal Style

Using the terminology of Frayling (and Eco), the "continuous series of connotations" of the Trinity hero would be the laid-back style interspersed with unexpected quick movements and actions, the taunting smile and a somewhat disturbing clear-blue gaze—which actor Terence Hill (Mario Girotti) employed earlier to good advantage as Django in *Preparati la bara!*

The dress is also significant and represents a reversal compared with the hat brims and covering garments in the form of ponchos and overcoats veiling Joe, Django and Sabata/Sartana. Trinity wears trousers and an under-jacket with arms, unbuttoned by the neck. He signals a supreme

Trinity wannabe — video sleeve for *Così sia*.

transparency (including holes in the jacket!) with no need of protection, and at the same time he renounces any claims on the mystery surrounding earlier spaghetti Western heroes.

Low Comedy

Besides the "dirt and smell" jokes, low comedy is featured with the farting baby in *Trinity 2*, the birthmark on the rear that identifies the brothers in *Jesse e Lester, due fratelli in una posto chiamato Trinità*, and bandits in long johns in *Tedeum* and (interminably) in *Così sia*, which also contains jokes of comparable subtlety about homosexuals. Also, there is the unfortunate snake that the monk flattens when it crawls over Wendy's behind in *Tedeum*.

The Trinity Story in the Context of the Spaghetti Western

The aforementioned depreciation of betrayal story specialist gunfighters is in tune with Trinity as a manifestation of the deprived hero in the comical mode. Furthermore, as described by function 12 of the plot, the valuable object does not land with the protagonist but ends in the hands of some kind of rightful owners or good cause (the rangers, the settlers), just as happens in most of the deprived-hero stories and the infiltrator films in general. Alternatively, it is squandered by bad luck or incompetence. Lester wastes the income from his and his half-brother's mine by doing the conventionally appropriate, which in the context of the film amounts to disaster, like sending gold with the transport (that always gets robbed by one of the two bandit gangs) or putting money in the bank (that gets robbed and goes bankrupt). He also steals Jesse's money to stop his bordello project. Buddy in *Storia di karatè, pugni e fagioli* has traded his and Sam's weapons for some steaks and a sack of beans ("They were wonderful, Sam ... tasty, tasty").

When Trinity approaches the bounty hunters in the first film accompanied by tension-building music reminiscent of Django or Sartana films, it stands out as a conscious reference because this kind of music is not otherwise used in *Trinity 1*. The shift in substance of content is paralleled by a shift in musical style toward a light, easy-listening, slightly sentimental style epitomized by the title song of *Trinity 2*, composed by the DeAngelis brothers.

The Trinity Story in the Context of the Classic American Western

Traditional family values are sent up in *Trinity 1*, where Trinity convinces Bambino when he swears that their mother will become an honest woman if he lies! He also justifies his fight at the saloon by the fact that Harrison's men had called their mother an old whore. When Bambino replies that it is true, he retorts, "She ain't that old." As for brotherly love, when Jonathan wakes "the sheriff" to inform him that his brother has got into trouble at the saloon, Bambino's face lights up with wild hope as he asks, "They killed him?" only to revert to surliness when the answer is negative!

In *Trinity 2* the voraciousness of the family dinner is a hilarious inversion to the courteous dinner that Shane is treated to by the Starrets—"with the good plates and extra fork." Instead there is a gobbling and burping company in a tumbledown shack, with the mother of the house in a well-worn saloon girl's outfit talking about how the children enjoyed being at the wedding of their parents, the father worrying that the youngest son is late in becoming a famous criminal, and the older brother seriously considering drowning the younger in the bathtub.[4]

The conflict between the horse-breeding Harrison and the religious farmers in *Trinity 1* is not put forth as in a classical-plot American Western about the coming of civilized society. The farmers are not defenseless because they represent the good but weak dimension of society. They are a pacifist religious group, and so in fact belong to the marginal part of society.

Archaeology of the Trinity Story

Constellation Archaeology — The Colizzi Pair

Before becoming Trinity and Bambino, actors Hill and Spencer cooperated as Cat and Hutch in the Colizzi trilogy.[5] These heroes are differentiated on physical and personal codes, more than a little reminiscent of the quick/strong contrast in the Trinity stories. The rumble in *I quattro dell' Ave Maria* might just as well have appeared in the Barboni films. In *La collina degli stivali*, where Cat is met with irate suspicion from Hutch that he will "pull me into some crazy business," the tone of the Trinity/Bambino relationship is largely set.

However, in the Colizzi films the protagonists still use guns a lot and kill plenty of people. Compared with the Cat character, Trinity shows no ruthlessness, and his lazy disposition permits him to show agility only in brawling (and dealing cards).

Dress Archaeology — Men in Tricot

The dress code of Trinity — the tricot undergarment with long arms — has some significant precursors in the Italowestern. Jeff, the half brother of Tom in *Tempo di massacro*, wears this garment over his torso (including at least one tear). Jeff also displays definite trickster traits. For a large part of the film, he is consistently drunk, his contribution to the action being to start a saloon brawl, and to exhort Tom to leave. When Jeff eventually shows Tom the way to Scott's ranch and they have been turned back by his guards, Jeff suddenly asks Tom if he is willing to answer to Scott for the death of the men and then puts on a wrist protector, turns and shouts, "Hey, gentlemen!" Hanging sideways in the saddle, he rides toward them and shoots them down. Later he performs the same actions on another set of guards, including the "Hey, gentlemen!" line. In the final reckoning with Junior and his men at the ranch, it is Jeff who suggests that Tom attack from the outside and he himself from the inside. In the same type of dress, George Hilton plays a very similar drinking trickster character in *La più grande rapina del west*, where he even attempts a familiar move of the post–Trinity Western, to strike up an unstable partnership with an outlaw posing as a priest.[6]

Plot Archaeology — *Vivi, o preferibilmente morti*

Before Trinity, the Ringo/Gary characters played by Giuliano Gemma constituted the only Italowestern hero type stressing an open style instead of mysteriousness.[7] Another Gemma box office success, *Vivi, o preferibilmente morti*, released in 1969, one year before *Trinity 1*, conforms to certain aspects of the Trinity constellation/plot. Gemma plays Monty, a gambler in debt who must spend three months out West with his brother Ted in order to gain an inheritance. The latter is reluctant, and rightly so— Monty causes his house to burn down, and then initiates a series of unsuccessful projects to earn money enough to pay Ted's next mortgage. They rob a bank and come away with big sacks of nickels and dimes worth $30; they capture a bandit but he escapes and robs them of the bounty; and they kidnap the daughter of a rich man who turns out to be glad to be rid of her for a while. The proceedings recall ...*e per tetto un cielo di stelle*, also directed by Duccio Tessari, but without any deadly violence.

These brothers are not physical contrasts, like Trinity and Bambino, but they are reluctant partners who form a pair whose projects consistently end as comic failures. Moreover, the failures often appear as parodic versions of American and spaghetti Western episodes (the shooting out of the lamp in a house under siege, which causes the house to burn down; or bounty-hunting). It is even complete with the Rangers showing up to gather the bad guys and the gold, leaving our heroes empty-handed except for a thank you! I have already mentioned the parodic inversion of the make-believe duel,[8] which furthermore is presented in a Leone-style montage with close-ups. It also offers a dirt joke in a fight in a bathhouse, where one bad guy falls into a tub and turns the water brown.

Provvidenza — *The Expert Trickster*

The Comical Bounty Killer Hero

I have commented previously about the sad plight of the professional gunfighter in the Trinity environment. However, the Sabata/Sartana garb was not worn solely by ridiculed sideshow characters in the post-Trinity Westerns. The hero of Carmineo's *Tresette* films is such a trickster in a suit — a quick hero aided by his strong partner Bambi. Still more successful at the box office was another specialist trickster hero— Provvidenza.[9] This character was played by Tomas Milian in two films—*La vita a volte, è molto dura, vero Provvidenza?* and *Ci risiamo, vero Provvidenza?*

Provvidenza is a smallish bounty killer sporting a Charlie Chaplin–like outfit. He travels in a personal stagecoach that is full of gimmicky utensils. At the start of the story, he collects bounty for the bandit Hurricane Kid, then helps the outlaw escape (with a saw hidden in a bottle) and captures him to go to another state where there also is a reward to collect. Unlike the arrangement of Tuco and Blondie in *The Good, the Bad and the Ugly*, it is not voluntary on the part of the Kid, though. He overpowers his captor, changes clothes and (unsuccessfully) tries to collect the bounty on himself. There follows a quiz competition for the bounty money, which turns out to be counterfeit, and then contention for a bag of real money, involving also the mercenary saloon girl Stella (who gets her behind kicked whenever she makes a play for the money), a stone-drunk band of Southern renegades, and the sheriff who is behind the swindle. Provvidenza and the Kid form a partnership to share the bounty money, but in the end the latter finds himself tied up behind Provvidenza's coach together with the other wanted characters.

This film is rather reminiscent of the betrayal and "specialist betrayal" stories both with regard to its plot, with constant betrayals concerning an

9. *Triumph of Comedy*   249

object of value, and to the gadgets used by the hero. However, the Trinity influence surfaces with the unstable alliance between quick and strong partners and the fact that the money accidentally ends up in the hands of a religious congregation. There is even talk of the rangers coming!

THE STRONG PARTNER

Hurricane Kid is a slab off the Bambino block. When he jumps from the second floor into the saddle, the horse is pressed down into the ground by his weight, and when he rushes Provvidenza and misses, a cliff is broken into two. When he bathes in the river, the water turns black, and dead fish float up. His snoring is deafening. He is also gluttonous and unsophisticated — he puts eau de cologne into his nose and belches so Provvidenza's jacket rose explodes.

THE QUICK SPECIALIST

Provvidenza on the contrary is sophisticated. He is dressed in a black coat, grey-striped trousers with colored vest, and a multipurpose umbrella. He (and the Kid) occasionally appear in tricot underwear à la Trinity, though.

Provvidenza's coach has a mattress that rolls up automatically when he rises in the morning, an arrow to show direction and a catapult driver's seat. He whips the horses by pressing a button. He has a bag containing a hen that hatches eggs and a mail pigeon. The walls are decorated by flower pots and pictures of scantily clad old girlfriends. During a pursuit he uses his umbrella as a club to shoot off balls. From his wagon he also lets out tin cans, smoke, water and pies thrown by way of catapult.

In fights, Provvidenza uses the quick-evasion tactics of Trinity, and also his umbrella as a rapier. He and the Kid organize their partnership by chaining the bag with the money to both parties, and when the bills turn out to be counterfeit, they use the chain to fight their way out. When he plays billiards (with two captured renegades as a stake), he shoots balls at the heads of the opponents (one man gets an "8" imprinted on his forehead).

Provvidenza is the master of a rag-tag technology whose ingenuity manages to send up even the Sartana/Hallelujah series. As a trickster he is more multi-faceted than Trinity and indeed fulfills the full criteria of the anthropological trickster figure.[10]

- He is a shape-shifter over biological borders by acting like a bird (with a loose beak) sitting in a tree luring the Kid into a trap with a gun on a string. He moves like a rodent when he is to chew off a rope, and meows like a lovesick cat when the Kid finds him in bed instead of Stella.
- He is a shape-shifter over national borders—he is Italian when he sings an Italian song to help confuse the Kid when they are sharing

the money, German when marching or making a Hitler salute, and he appears as a yogi. He speaks French, and sometimes Chinese, while playing billiards. He wears a suit made by a British tailor, and when it is time to solve a mystery, he smokes a curved pipe and sports a high English accent. He says, "Thou stinketh" in old English.
- He is a situation inverter — he uses his umbrella as a parasol and gives Stella a water lily to avoid her questions about sharing the money. He breaks out in opera and operetta arias several times. He also, anachronistically, says, "Be with you in a minute" like a television announcer before passing out, and sings a "Money cha-cha-cha." Provvidenza keeps his bowler hat on. He wipes sweat off it, scratches his head on it, and takes off the brim to make it into a bathing cap.
- He is ambiguous and anomalous. He smacks with his mouth and gives out a silly little laugh. He hides money in the crotch of his pants. When the Kid knocks him out, he dances, takes off his coat, and shadow boxes for a spell before passing out.
- He is deceiver and a trick-player. He uses escape-artist techniques when he is tied up. When playing poker, he picks out cards from the other player's arm and collar (and ear!) with the gestures of a magician. When in jail, they are handed food in a pan by the handle through the bars. The Kid cannot get the pan through the bar without spilling the food, but Provvidenza bounces the food over the bars and into his mouth. When the Kid hands him his pan to do the same, he puts the two pans together and takes them through the bars without spilling, but eats it all before handing the Kid the empty pan!

Provvidenza displays parodical expertise, as in the bounty hunter quiz set up to decide whether he or the Kid is the real Provvidenza, and when he flaps a stock of money and hears that $10 is missing. He can tell from rustling a bill that it is counterfeit and bites the head of a porcelain figure and tastes that the china is false. There are parodic fighting scenes, such as when he dances the tango and says "no violence" (with an Indian accent) while hitting and kicking Hurricane Kid, and the parodic elegance of his morning toilet when he gurgles with liquid from a barrel that says "beer," sprays into his throat and tries to sing a note, and brushes teeth, face, clothes and shoes with the same big brush in front of the mirror. Memorable also is the Southern renegades' drunken salute to the flag.

The examples above are all taken from *La vita a volte, è molto dura, vero Provvidenza?* In the second film the stagecoach is replaced by a steam engine. Provvidenza falls in love with the daughter of a Chinese con man and in the end leaves in a balloon. Among other things the spectator is treated to a chase during a masquerade held in a skating ring (in a big tent in the middle of the prairie).

Fistfights and Brawls— A Barroom Chronicle

Saloon brawls in the traditional Western style appear in pre–Leone spaghetti Westerns such as *Gringo* and *Massacro al Grande Canyon* but are missing from Leone's template genre films, where direct contact violence appears as infliction of pain and torture on defenseless or almost defenseless victims.

In 1966, Sergio Corbucci and his cinematographer Enzo Barboni presented a new concept of the Western fistfight in *Django*, with the fight between the hero and Hugo's "Lieutenant" Ricardo. They slug and kick and sometimes hold each other while they continue to hit. Chairs and belts are used, and finally they wrestle for a rifle. Ricardo is pushed away and falls on a hatchet, and his death ends the fight after about two minutes. Compared with earlier Italowestern fistfights, this sequence leaves an extremely mobile impression. The camera — apparently handheld — shows the fighters at waist or shoulder height and follows their movements, sometimes trailing a single blow to its conclusion. These shots are interspersed with full shots from a very high angle and also views of the bystanders at close range as they watch and retreat somewhat not to get too close. These last shots are easily interpreted as subjective, from the combatants, though they might just as well "originate" from some abstract "focus of battle."

Corbucci/Barboni did not invent this whole visual "package." In *Il ritorno di Ringo* from the preceding year, there is a saloon "fight" when Rosita baits Esteban against Ringo. The camera follows Ringo closely at shoulder level while Esteban's men beat him around. Sometimes he gets in a blow himself, but mostly this is a scene of torture. A camera closely trailing the combatants is employed also in the concluding man-to-man fight between Ringo and Paco. This is a ferocious sequence where they kick and slug each other to almost absolute exhaustion, and it is spiced by the fact that Ringo's right hand is wounded, so once when he forgets himself and uses it in a blow, he is as hurt as Paco. At the end the two men barely have the strength to go for their guns that lie spread on the floor. Ringo then shoots Paco several times in his arms and shoulders. Compared with this struggle, the one in Corbucci's film adds the "subjective" shots framing the on-screen spectators, and the high-angle shots.

The moving-camera fight would be used in many spaghetti Westerns. In the saloon fight in *Tempo di massacro*, there is even one subjective shot where an opponent emerges and slugs at the screen! Also in episodes of beating and torture, the tormentors are shown from the point of view of the victim.

With or without a moving camera, the motif of a fight to exhaustion (ending in a standstill when both combatants fall down without any strength left) came to be used as a preliminary to a partnership between former opponents, thus representing the function 4 in the partnership plot, and the function c in the "tragic mercenary" plot.[11]

The Trinity Brawl

Trinity 1 carries a reminiscence of vile and dangerous fighting in the confrontation at the store, where one of the opponents swings an axe, even though no one gets hurt. The first typical Trinity brawl takes place later in the saloon, when the brothers are challenged to fight "like men" without gun and sheriff's star. Trinity, who accepts the challenge—"they are only nine"—asks Bambino if he will take them on alone, but Bambino yawns and says that he just woke up and that Trinity should take his share. Trinity then strikes two men, sits down smoking, and watches them all attack Bambino. The latter pushes the whole mass away and then emerges. During the rest of the fight the proceedings are that they take a punch at his body and he then hammers or slugs or elbows them down. The fight lasts only about one minute. The saloon fight in *Trinity 2* against the Smiths is twice as long but follows a similar trajectory. Bambino takes a hit without trying to avoid it and then slugs the man down, sometimes using a "hammer" fist directly on the head. In this case he once varies his tactics by grabbing an opponent's hand and using it first to hit another attacker, and then the man himself. Trinity, who does his part this time, ducks and avoids most blows before striking back. Sometimes he makes the opponents hit each other. In the concluding fight at the mission in the same film, where the brothers and the monks together fight the gang of Parker over a leather bag containing $50,000, he once throws the bag up in the air to make his hands free, strikes down a man, and then catches the bag coming down. The sequence also contains some typical Bambino scenes, as when he is beaten in the back or over the head with a wooden pole or thick plank and then turns around, visibly irritated, and strikes the assailant down. Another routine is when a whole group of men runs after him into a doorway, and then we see the whole gang being beaten back out at the same time, and he emerges.

Unlike the Django-style fight, these sequences are shown mostly in stationary medium shots, and never in close-ups. Also, dangerous objects are not used as striking weapons. The in-frame action is quicker and more densely "packed" than in the pre–Leone brawls, though.

The Carmineo Situational Fight

Just like in the Dollar trilogy, violence in the core Sartana/Sabata films involve firearms and deaths, not hand-to-hand fighting. Good-natured brawling gradually gained story space in *Tornato Sabata, Camposanto* and *Spirito Santo* to become dominant in the Hallelujah and Tresette vehicles— no doubt following the Trinity example. On the other hand, *Vado, l'ammazzo e torno* already featured acrobatic fistfights, as in a Turkish bath where guns were not carried.

Compared with the Trinity films, the comedy of mimics plays smaller part in the Carmineo confrontations, and instead the use of unexpected auxiliary objects is emphasized. In this respect the brawling in the later Carmineo films inherits the flair for variation and surprising tricks and feints from the gunfights of his earlier films. I will illustrate this with a closer look at a sequence in *Il west ti va stretto amico ... è arrivato Allelujah!*, where Hallelujah forces an encounter with boss Ferguson against the will of his three guards (here called X, Y and Z).

When Hallelujah enters the room from the street, the three guards treat him with a loud laughter, and at first he joins in. When he still insists on seeing Ferguson, and they proceed to throw him out, he first disables one by hitting his foot with a hat stand and uses the hat stand to shove away the two others so they trip backwards over the railing that divides the room and land back in the chairs they first were sitting in. Then he hits the first with the hat stand again on the foot and comments, while the man jumps up and down holding one foot, that he must have had bunions. When the man again approaches from behind, Hallelujah does a handstand and kicks him so he lands on the floor and knocks down a vase on his own head. The other two get up, collide inadvertently and then rush on Hallelujah, who ducks so one hits a pole with his head, is inadvertently hit by the other, then slammed against the pole again by Hallelujah and shoved onto the second. Now X and Z attack Hallelujah, who jumps over the railing, and when they jump after him, he jumps back again. Next they run through the two different gates in the railing to catch him, but he evades them so they collide. They both take a swing at him, but Hallelujah moves a brass lamp hanging from the ceiling so they both hit it and hurt their hands, and then he knocks each one of them down with it, commenting on how nicely the bell chimes.

He now encounters Y when going through the barrier and swings the gate at the latter's groin so he staggers off. Z now advances with his guard up, but Hallelujah bends his arm by the elbow, compliments his muscles, which makes Z look pleased, then takes Z's hat, puts it on his own fist and takes a swing at him. Then he puts the hat back on the head of the staggering man, who still makes an advance to grab Hallelujah. Our hero then hits Z's face a lot of times in the manner of working with a punching bag, with corresponding sound effects. He then finds that the man still stands because he is leaning against a chair, which Hallelujah takes away to make him fall. X has come to life again and attacks Hallelujah with a pipe taken from the stove. Hallelujah ducks and takes out a drawer, and he hits X with the back side of it several times before smashing it over his head, making him unconscious. Lastly, when leaving the room, Hallelujah gives a sympathetic word to Y, who cringes in pains from his groin.

In the beginning the three guards are characterized by mannerisms: One lights a match on his teeth, one picks his nose, and one cracks walnuts with his teeth. These are "reused" by Hallelujah during the fighting: The first one loses a lot of teeth (when accidentally hit by the second); as for the second, after he has been made unconscious, Hallelujah puts the man's finger into his nose and he picks it and smiles in his unconsciousness; when the third has passed out, Hallelujah uses his mouth as a nutcracker.

Terrence Hill as Cat in *I quattro dell'Ave Maria*, somewhat in between the earlier "Django" fighting style and the more relaxed style of the Trinity films.

9. Triumph of Comedy 255

Notice the use of unconventional striking weapons that are what I call *situational*, i.e., indigenous to the place of the confrontation — the hat stand, the swing door of the railing, and the drawer. I have already referred to Italowestern combats in barns or cattle sheds using close-at-hand work tools for weapons. However, hat stands, drawers, etc., are much further removed from the conventional sphere of violence compared with an axe or a hayfork, and their use as such brings or furthers a feeling of parody and comedy to the situations.

The example also features manipulation on a low tactical level, when the hero makes his opponents hurt each other by his use of evasions and other tricks. Remarkable — and more of an innovation in the genre — is also the transposition of objects into another realm of choreography, for example a head used as a punching bag or a nutcracker, — a kind of effect otherwise frequently used in silent and animated slapstick.

The Provvidenza films also stage fights in locales loaded with objects he finds ingenious uses for (e.g., a restaurant and a pool room). In contrast, the Trinity brawls employ objects sparingly — though in the mission fight, wet cloth, wetted loaves of bread and baking utensils are used to hit the bandits, and parts of the extended fight imitate a game of football or rugby.

The battles in the Trinity films are staged in rather bland environments: outdoors and saloons. The deprived connotations of the Trinity heroes, their lack of sophistication and small circumstances, also show in the small number of trinkets used as situational objects in the fights. What is generally true for the stories with Terence Hill and Bud Spencer as Trinity and Bambino is also valid for the fights — it is not any objects wielded by them that create the life and substance of the scenes, but the play of their bodies.

CHAPTER 10

Un Minuto per Pregare — Concluding Remarks

The Infiltrator Revisited

In Figure 10A various instances of infiltrator Spaghetti Western films are structured by the different constellation/plots where they belong, further distinguished by whether they (in the main) belong in the mode of the pathetic or the mode of the ironic.

Infringements of Genre Boundaries

The Italowesterns emerged in an environment that also produced horror films, musclemen epics and other sword-and-sandal films, as well as cloak-and-dagger pics, swashbucklers and other films of general adventure. Secret-agent films were made in great numbers concurrent to the Westerns. At Westerns' twilight, war films, martial arts films and pornos (soft- and hardcore) came in to vogue. These different kinds of films were often made by the same persons behind and in front of the camera, and not surprisingly, there are spaghetti Westerns whose stories are interleaved and hybridized (or possibly amalgamated in other ways) with stories typical of these other genres.

Gun and Sandals

In *Sansone e il tesoro degli Incas*, a Westerner named Samson gets involved with an ancient tribe of Inca Indians hidden in a mountain. The same influence from sword-and-sandal films is evident in *Tre pistole contro Cesare*, where an Anglo former sheriff, a Chinese martial arts expert and

10. *Un Minuto per Pregare* — Concluding Remarks 257

Figure 10A.
The Context of the Infiltrators

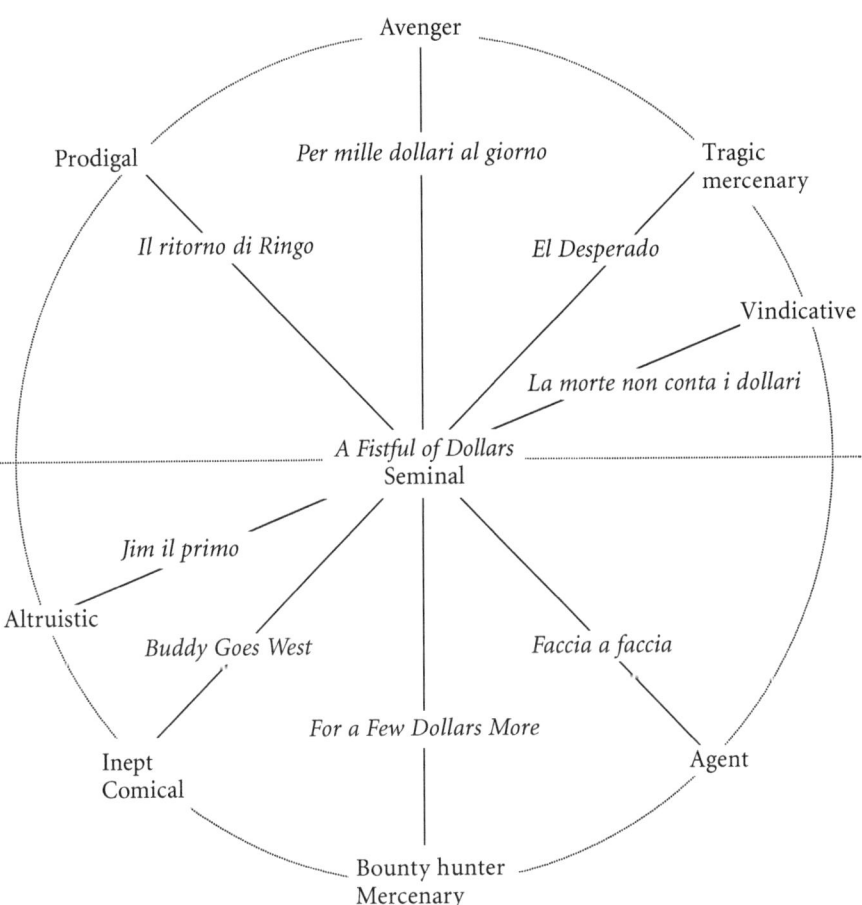

a Mexican magician (named Devereaux) convene to share an inheritance (revealed to be a bed made of gold). In the process they must fight big boss Julius Caesar Fuller, who dresses in a toga and lives in a Roman palace with local women performing erotic dances. He has a gang of thugs in Western outfits, though.

Shot, Not Stirred

Rocco in *Sugar Colt*, Slim Corbett in *Dio li crea ... io li ammazzo!* and Silver in *Il venditore di morte* are all introduced accompanied by beautiful women, and — in the latter two films — also in remarkably luxurious surroundings. These three stories are also otherwise heavily influenced by secret-agent films. The heroes work to uncover mysteries. Rocco — who somewhat anachronistically uses narcotic gas to loosen tongues — takes on his mission to fulfill the last wish of a friend and find his assassins, while the other heroes do it for money. There are no second motives.

Diverse Others

As El Desperado, a masked bandit à la Zorro, the hero of *Il magnifico texano* seeks the killers of his father and also helps oppressed Mexicans while otherwise posing as a fashion designer. *Una ragione per vivere ... una per morire* and *La spina dorsale del diavolo* both have former military men as heroes, and both employ the motif from the war film *The Dirty Dozen* (which is in itself an offspring of *The Magnificent Seven*)[1] — about an officer training a group of condemned men for a special mission — only in the first case the commander is also condemned, and in the second case he is the only one who is condemned.

In *Django il bastardo* some of the episodes have the ambience of a horror story, and at the end the hero/avenger suddenly disappears like a ghost.

Enter the Dragon

In *Ci risiamo, vero Provvidenza?* a Chinese villain sends his kung fu fighting henchmen against the hero, but they are bested by his Chinese engine driver. This is but one effect of the great influx of Asian martial arts films in the European popular film market around 1970. Several spaghetti Westerns included such heroes in their stories, such as *Il mio nome è Shanghai Joe, Che botte, ragazzi!* and, in a more comical vein, *Storia di karatè, pugni e fagioli* and *Il bianco, il giallo, il nero*. In these films, the Asian hero acts for non-monetary reasons. In *Là dove non batte il sole* one hero is a Chinese martial arts instructor looking for a sum of gold, though for reasons of family honor. He must team up with an Anglo thief/gunfighter with information about the money (clues are tattooed on the behinds of women — not men as in *Viva la muerte ... tua!*).[2] This film is something of a tutorship story, but it is inverted on the age code, as it is rather the Chinese who has skills to teach the Anglo (who indeed is played by Lee Van Cleef).

These obvious examples of cross-genre relationships represent only the tip of the iceberg. There are more subtle issues, such as the one raised by Sandro Graziani that the Leone hero, with his movements of well-calculated precision, is foreign to his historical time and rather reflects our time of electronics and programmed reactions—as the agent film does more openly.[3]

Transformations of the Spaghetti Western

My employment of the concepts of *armature*, *code* and—to some extent—*message* has been inspired by their use by Lévi-Strauss to describe mythical transformation systems.[4] Approximately, I would describe the transformations within the spaghetti Western films as follows. Compared with a classical Western, *Fistful of Dollars* and its immediate followers presented the change from a hero ending up fighting for the good values of society against the selfish money interests of a villain to a hero who was mainly driven by selfish money interests in a situation where those same good values of society had no real representative, and no relevance, and the villain represented an increased super-violence against the defenseless.

The stories of deprived heroes (such as Django) had a hero fighting for personal vindication or retribution against the same kind of super-violence, in the end deprecating a money motive for a non-monetary one. The later betrayal stories presented groups of heroes (or a specialist hero and an equivalent) and villains pursuing conflicting monetary motives using ingenious devices and stratagems, while the super-violence against defenseless groups was relegated to the background. They represented a similar transformation of the American professional plot, with the internecine struggle of a group replacing the forging of a group of professionals.

From *Few Dollars More* onward, the backbone of the genre was constituted by stories of the conflicts and alliances of two heroes, with one hero representing a selfish monetary motive and the other a vindictive or vindicative (or altruistic) one, and thus balancing the two tendencies.

A metacode of exaggeration is a common property of these stories, playing out at the same time in a rhetoric of the pathetic (the suffering of the hero and the massacre of the defenseless by a ruthless, sadistic villain), and a rhetoric of the ironic (the schemes and sarcasm of the hero exploiting the greed of others) and self-ironic (the unrealistic complexity of the schemes and ingenuity of the devices employed).

The second turn of the genre, constituted by the success of the Trinity films, in a way pushed these tendencies into a comical trickster mode—the

Kung fu-style bar brawl. Wang Ho Kiang (Lo Lieh) has it out in *Là dove non batte il sole*.

general mischief and puerile love of Trinity, the all-out anachronisms and trickster antics by Provvidenza and the combined incompetence and bad luck of the religious/con-man duo. However, traditional representatives of good societal values made a comeback in the form of religious settlers, or preachers intent on (or pretending to) build churches or schools. In this way the spaghetti Western would seem to take a turn back to the American classical plot — with important differences though, because this is a rhetoric of the comical where the upholders of societal values are slightly comical minority religious groups who are protected by the heroes on a whim, or because the latter fail in their monetary endeavors. Good society also reappears in the form of "the rangers" (or the army) — upholders of a non-corrupt societal order, though mostly at a distance or arriving in the last scene.

This partial "return" of the spaghetti Western to its point of departure rather neatly illustrates one of Lévi-Strauss's "transformation rules," namely that mythic deduction moves in spirals, and not in circles, so we never return exactly to the starting point.

10. Un Minuto per Pregare — Concluding Remarks

On the other hand, it is important to note certain limitations to this description of the spaghetti Western transformations.

This methodology belongs to the analysis of content and so can be equally well applied to films belonging to different genres but with similarities in content — or perhaps to describe transformations between whole genres. My section on genre boundary infringements earlier in this chapter should serve to stress this point. Still, for practical reasons, the present study is confined to the spaghetti Western film as defined in chapter 1.

Furthermore, any kind of story is in principle eligible for the application of transformation studies in this sense, regardless of media. Thus the comparison might as well include comics, books, graphic novels, etc.[5] On the other hand, any delimitation of a film genre by definition includes considerations concerning the form and substance of its expression. Thus, while I find the methods and concepts employed in this study valid and usable to elucidate modern popular cultural phenomena such as the spaghetti Western, I freely admit that for a full study of this cinematic phenomenon, they must be supplemented by analytical tools geared toward the study of expression.

As for the study of story content, there are also other approaches of a partly different breed, for example from the post-structural and post-colonial traditions, and no doubt these also could yield interesting results that will alter our current understanding of the spaghetti Western. I choose to pass on any "current best method" controversy, and just hope that my endeavors have brought some insights and perhaps also some pleasures to you, dear reader.

APPENDIX A

Top-Grossing Italian Westerns, 1964–1975

Income in thousands of lire, lowest to highest gross.

Title	Year	Director	Main actor(s)	Income
Corri, uomo, corri	1968	Sollima	Tomas Milian	1,000,146
Django	1966	Corbucci	Franco Nero	1,026,084
Viva la muerte ... tua!	1971	Tessari	Franco Nero, Eli Wallace	1,061,251
Carambola	1974	Baldi	Len Coby, Paul Smith	1,063,135
Vendetta	1967	Vancini	Giuliano Gemma	1,072,359
Il mercenario	1968	Corbucci	Franco Nero, Tony Musante	1,101,445
Faccia a faccia	1967	Sollima	Tomas Milian, Gian Maria Volontè	1,116,721
Ehi amico ... c'è Sabata, hai chiuso!	1969	Parolini	Lee Van Cleef	1,117,152
Wanted	1967	Ferroni	Giuliano Gemma	1,132,590
Amico stammi lontano almena en palmo	1972	Lupo	Giuliano Gemma	1,137,961
...E per tetto un cielo di stelle	1968	Petroni	Giuliano Gemma	1,145,950
Valdez il mezzosangue	1973	Coletti	Charles Bronson	1,162,429
Ci risiamo, vero Provvidenza?	1973	de Martino	Tomas Milian	1,171,839
Che c'entriamo noi con la rivoluzione?	1972	Corbucci	Vittorio Gassman, Paolo Villaggio	1,185,715
Cipolla Colt	1975	Girolami	Franco Nero	1,190,585

Title	Year	Director	Main actor(s)	Income
Vivi, o preferibilmente morti	1969	Tessari	Giuliano Gemma	1,202,368
Centomila dollari per Ringo	1965	de Martino	Richard Harrison	1,236,276
Arizona Colt	1966	Lupo	Giuliano Gemma	1,249,041
Da uomo a uomo	1967	Petroni	Lee Van Cleef	1,261,929
Il prezzo del potere	1969	Valerii	Giuliano Gemma	1,273,858
Per pochi dollari ancora	1966	Ferroni	Giuliano Gemma	1,309,699
Il ritorno di Ringo	1965	Tessari	Giuliano Gemma	1,317,664
Una pistola per Ringo	1965	Tessari	Giuliano Gemma	1,351,605
La vita a volte, è molto dura, vero Provvidenza?	1972	Petroni	Tomas Milian	1,399,979
La resa dei conti	1967	Sollima	Lee Van Cleef, Tomas Milian	1,440,849
Vamos a matar, companeros	1970	Corbucci	Franco Nero Tomas Milian	1,451,782
Keoma	1976	Girolami	Franco Nero	1,571,995
Adios gringo	1965	Stegani	Giuliano Gemma	1,577,007
Un dollaro bucato	1965	Ferroni	Giuliano Gemma	1,590,886
Si può fare ... amigo!	1972	Lucidi	Bud Spencer	1,598,524
La collina degli stivali	1969	Colizzi	Terence Hill, Bud Spencer	1,741,827
A Fistful of Dollars	1964	Leone	Clint Eastwood, Gian Maria Volontè	1,896,539
Il bianco, il giallo, il nero	1974	Corbucci	Eli Wallach, Giuliano Gemma, Tomas Milian	1,897,807
Una ragione per vivere ... una per morire	1972	Valerii	James Coburn, Bud Spencer	1,960,071
I giorni dell'ira	1967	Valerii	Giuliano Gemma, Lee Van Cleef	1,997,410
Dio perdona ... io no!	1967	Colizzi	Terence Hill, Bud Spencer	2,067,440

Top-Grossing Italian Westerns, 1964–1975

Title	Year	Director	Main actor(s)	Income
I quattro dell'Ave Maria	1968	Colizzi	Terence Hill, Bud Spencer	2,225,784
Duck You Sucker	1971	Leone	James Coburn, Rod Steiger	2,464,773
Once Upon a Time in the West	1968	Leone	Charles Bronson, Henry Fonda, Claudia Cardinale	2,503,669
Un genio, due compari, un pollo	1975	Damiani	Terence Hill	2,684,413
Sole rosso	1971	Young	Charles Bronson, Alain Delon, Toshiro Mifune	2,970,289
They Call Me Trinity	1970	Barboni	Terence Hill, Bud Spencer	3,104,061
The Good, the Bad and the Ugly	1966	Leone	Clint Eastwood, Lee Van Cleef, Eli Wallace	3,210,701
Man of the East	1972	Barboni	Terence Hill	3,367,119
For a Few Dollars More	1965	Leone	Clint Eastwood, Lee Van Cleef, Gian Maria Volontè	3,492,268
My Name Is Nobody	1973	Valerii	Terence Hill, Henry Fonda	3,620,446
Trinity Is Still My Name	1971	Barboni	Terence Hill, Bud Spencer	6,087,656

Source: AGIS

APPENDIX B

Films Quoted

The *Italian b.o.* column indicates box office success in Italy, by quartile of intake, i.e., Q4 represents the most commercially successful 25 percent of all Italian Westerns. Source is AGIS and, before 1965, Catalogo Bolaffi.

Films Quoted by Italian Title

Italian (alt. Spanish or French) title	English title*	Year	Director	Italian b.o.
5000 dollari sull'asso/ El rancho de los implacabales/Pistoleros de Arizona	Five Thousand Dollars on One Ace	1964	A. Balcazar	Q3
Acquasanta Joe	Holy Water Joe	1971	M. Gariazzo	Q2
Adios gringo	Adios gringo	1965	G. Stegani	Q4
Al di là della legge	Beyond the Law	1968	G. Stegani	Q4
All'Ombra di una colt	In a Colt's Shadow	1965	G. Grimaldi	Q3
Alleluja e Sartana figli di ... Dio	Hallelujah and Sartana Strike Again	1972	M. Siciliano	Q1
All'ultimo sangue	Bury Them Deep	1968	P. Moffa	Q2
Los amigos	Death Smith and Johnny Ears	1973	P. Cavara	Q3
Ammazzali tutti e torna solo	Kill Them All and Come Back	1968	E. Girolami	Q4
Anda muchacho spara!/ Il sole sotto terra	Dead Men Ride	1971	A. Florio	Q2
Un animale chiamato uomo	Animal Called Man	1972	R. Mauri	Q1

*The English titles are in many cases taken from Weisser, and may thus differ from the titles used in other countries, like England.

Films Quoted 267

Italian (alt. Spanish or French) title	English title	Year	Director	Italian b.o.
Arizona Colt	Arizona Colt	1966	M. Lupo	Q4
Arriva Sabata!	Sabata the Killer	1970	T. Demichelli	Q3
Arrivano Django e Sartana ... è la fine!	Django and Sartana Are Coming ... It's the End	1970	D. Fidani	Q1
La Banda J & S. Cronaca criminale del far west	Bandera Bandits	1972	S. Corbucci	Q3
Bandidos/Crepa tu ... che vivo io	Bandidos	1967	M. Dallamano	Q2
The Belle Starr Story/ Il mio corpo per un poker	The Belle Starr Story	1967	P. Cristofani*	Q1
Il bianco, il giallo, il nero	White, Yellow and the Black	1974	S. Corbucci	Q4
Black Killer	Black Killer	1971	C. Croccolo	Q1
Blindman	Blindman	1970	T. Anthony	N/A
The Bounty Killer/ El precio de un bombre	The Ugly Ones	1966	E. Martin	Q4
Un bounty killer a Trinità	Bounty Hunter in Trinity	1972	A. Massaccesi	Q1
Buffalo Bill, l'eroe del far west	Buffalo Bill, Hero of the Far West	1964	M. Costa	Q2
Buon funerale amigos ... paga Sartana	Have a Good Funeral, My Friend ... Sartana Will Pay	1970	G. Carmineo as A. Ascott	Q3
Cabiria		1914	G. Pastrone	N/A
California	California	1977	M. Lupo	Q4
Campa Carogna ... la taglia cresce	Those Dirty Dogs	1973	G. Rosati	Q3
O'cangaceiro		1969	G. Fago	N/A
I cannoni di San Sebastian	Guns for San Sebastian	1968	H. Verneuil	Q4
Captain Apache	Captain Apache	1971	A. Singer	N/A

*There is some controversy over who really hides behind the "official" director moniker Nathan Wich (given by A.G.I.S.) or Vich (given by Poppi-Percorari and Weisser). Weisser ascribes it to female director and scriptwriter Lina Wertmuller. Poppi-Percorari argues that she is the co-writer "George Brown" and so couldn't at the same time be director/writer Wich, whom they choose to believe is the otherwise unknown Cristofani, who is registered in the archives.

Italian (alt. Spanish or French) title	English title	Year	Director	Italian b.o.
Carambola	Carambola	1974	F. Baldi	Q4
C'è Sartana ... vendi la pistola e comprati la bara!	I Am Sartana ... Trade Your Guns for a Coffin	1970	G. Carmineo as A. Ascott	Q4
Che botte, ragazzi!	Return of Shanghai Joe	1974	A. Albertini	Q4
Che c'entriamo noi con la rivoluzione?	What Am I Doing in the Middle of the Revolution?	1972	S. Corbucci	Q4
Ci risiamo, vero Provvidenza?	Here We Go Again, Eh Providence?	1973	A. de Martino	Q4
Ciak Mull, l'uomo della vendetta	Chuck Moll	1970	E. Barboni	Q3
I cinque della vendetta	Five Giants from Texas	1966	A. Florio	Q3
El Cisco	Cisco	1966	S. Bergonzelli	Q3
Cjamango	Cjamango	1967	E. Mulargia	Q3
La collera del vento	Trinity Sees Red	1970	M. Camus	Q3
La collina degli stivali	Boot Hill	1969	G. Colizzi	Q4
La colt era il suo Dio	God Is My Colt .45	1972	L. Batzella	Q1
Une corde, un colt/ Cimiterio senza croci	Cemetery Without Crosses	1968	R. Hossein	N/A
Corri, uomo, corri	Run, Man, Run	1968	S. Sollima	Q4
I corvi ti scaveranno la fossa	And the Crows Will Dig Your Grave/ Gringo the Buzzards Are Digging Your Grave	1971	I. F. Iquino	Q3
Così Sia	Man Called Amen	1972	A. Cantabianco	Q4
I crudeli	Hellbenders	1967	S. Corbucci	Q1
Da uomo a uomo	Death Rides a Horse	1967	G. Petroni	Q4
...Dai nemici mi guardo io!	Three Silver Dollars	1968	M. Amendola	Q2
Dans la poussière de Soleil	Dust in the Sun	1972	R. Balducci	N/A
El Desperado	Big Ripoff	1967	F. Rossetti	Q3
Di Tresette c'è ne uno ... tutti gli altri son nessuno	Dick Luft in Sacramento	1974	G. Carmineo as A. Ascott	Q4

Films Quoted

Italian (alt. Spanish or French) title	English title	Year	Director	Italian b.o.
Diecimila dollari per un massacro	$10,000 Blood Money	1967	R. Guerrieri	Q3
Dio li crea ... io li ammazzo!	God Made Them ... I Kill Them	1968	P. Bianchini	Q3
Dio perdona ... io no!	God Forgives, I Don't	1967	G. Colizzi	Q4
Django	Django	1966	S. Corbucci	Q4
Django il bastardo	Django the bastard	1969	S. Garrone	Q3
Django kill!/Se sei vivo spara	Django Kill ... If You Live, Shoot!	1967	G. Questi	Q3
Django non perdona/Mestizio	Django Does Not Forgive	1965	J. Buchs	N/A
Django sfida Sartana	Django Challenges Sartana	1970	P. Squitieri	Q2
Django spara per primo	Django Shoots First	1966	A. De Martino	Q4
Django 2 — Il grande ritorno	Django Strikes Again/Return of the Hero	1987	N. Rossati	N/A
Un dollaro bucato	Blood for a Silver Dollar	1965	G. Ferroni	Q4
Un dollaro tra i denti	Stranger in Town	1966	L. Vanzi	Q2
Le due facce del dollaro	Two Sides of the Dollar	1967	R. Montero	Q3
Duell vor Sonnenuntergang/Ragazzi sparata a vista a Killer Kid	Duel at Sundown	1965	L. Lahola	N/A
...E per tetto un cielo di stelle	A Sky Full of Stars for the Roof	1968	G. Petroni	Q4
È tornato Sabata ... hai chiuso un'altra volta!	Return of Sabata	1971	G. Parolini as F. Kramer	Q4
Ehi amico c'è Sabata ... hai chiuso!	Sabata	1969	G. Parolini as F. Kramer	Q4
Un esercito di cinque uomini	Five Man Army	1969	D. Taylor, I. Zingarelli	Q4
Faccia a faccia	Face to Face	1967	S. Sollima	Q4
Fedra West/Io non perdono ... uccido	I Do Not Forgive ... I Kill	1968	J. L. Romero Marchent	Q1
Il figlio di Django	Son of Django	1967	O. Civirani	Q2
Un fiume di dollari	Hills Run Red	1966	C. Lizzani	Q4

Italian (alt. Spanish or French) title	English title	Year	Director	Italian b.o.
Un genio, due compari, un pollo	Genius	1975	D. Damiani	Q4
Gentleman Jo ... uccidi!	Gentleman Killer	1967	G. Stegani	Q3
Giarettiera Colt	Garter Colt	1968	G. Andrea Rocco	Q1
I giorni della violenza	Days of Violence	1967	A. Brescia	Q3
I giorni dell'ira	Days of Wrath	1967	T. Valerii	Q4
Il giorno del giudizio	Drummer of Vengeance	1971	M. Gariazzo	Q1
Giubbe rosse	Red Coat	1975	J. D'Amato	Q4*
Gli fumavano le colt ... lo chiamavano Camposanto	They Call Him Cemetery	1971	G. Carmineo as A. Ascott	Q3
Le Goût de la violence		1961	R. Hossein	N/A
Il grande duello	The Big Showdown	1973	G. Santi	Q3
La grande notte di Ringo	Ringo's Big Night	1966	M. Maffei	Q3
Il grande silenzio	Great Silence	1968	S. Corbucci	Q2
Gringo/Duello nel Texas	Gunfight at Red Sands	1963	R. Blasco	N/A
Indio Black, sai che ti dico ... sei un gran figlio di...	Adios Sabata	1970	G. Parolini as F. Kramer	Q4
Jesse e Lester, due fratelli in una posto chiamato Trinità	Jesse and Lester, Two Brothers in a Place Called Trinity	1972	R. Genta	Q3
Jim il primo	Last Gun	1964	S. Bergonzelli	Q1
Johnny Oro	Ringo and His Golden Pistol	1966	S. Corbucci	Q3
Keoma	Keoma	1976	E. Girolami	Q4
Killer Kid	Killer Kid	1967	L. Savona	Q3
Là, dove non batte il sole	Blood Money/ Stranger and the Gunfighter	1974	A. Margheriti	Q4
Lo chiamavano King	His Name Was King	1971	G. Romitelli	Q1
Lo chiamavano Tresette ... giocava siempre col morto	Man Called Invincible	1973	G. Carmineo as A. Ascott	Q4

Giubbe rosse is not part of the data that the quartiles are based on, but its box office intake would have placed it in Q4.

Italian (alt. Spanish or French) title	English title	Year	Director	Italian b.o.
Lo credevano uno stinco di Santo	Too Much Gold for a Gringo/They Believed He Was a Saint	1972	I. F. Iquino	Q2
Lo irritarono e Sartana fece piazza pulita	And Sartana Kills Them All	1970	R. Romero Marchent	Q3
Una lunga fila di croci	No Room to Die	1969	S. Garrone	Q3
I lunghi giorni dell'odio	This Man Can't Die	1968	G. Baldanello	Q2
El Macho	Macho Killers	1977	M. Andrei	Q1
Il magnifico texano	Magnificent Texan	1967	L. Capuano	Q3
Le maledette pistole di Dallas/Las malditas pistolas de Dallas	Damned Pistols of Dallas	1964	J. Maria Zabalza, P. Mercati	Q1
Mannaja	Man Called Blade	1977	S. Martino	N/A
El más fabuloso golpe del far west	The Boldest Job in the West	1969	J. Antonio de la Loma	N/A
Massacro al Grande Canyon	Massacre at Grand Canyon	1963	S. Corbucci	Q1
Il mercenario	A Professional Gun	1968	S. Corbucci	Q4
Mi chiamavano Requiescat ... ma avevo sbagliato/Mano rápida	Fast Gun Is Still My Name	1973	F. Brana	N/A
Mille dollari sul nero	Blood at Sundown	1966	A. Cardone	Q4
Minnesota Clay	Minnesota Clay	1964	S. Corbucci	Q3
Un minuto per pregare, un istante per morire/ Escondido	A Minute to Pray, a Second to Die	1968	F. Giraldi	Q2
Il mio nome è Shanghai Joe	Fighting Fists of Shanghai Joe	1973	M. Caiano	Q1
Il momento di uccidere	The Moment to Kill	1968	G. Carmineo as A. Ascott	Q3
La morte non conta i dollari	Death at Owell Rock	1967	R. Freda	Q3
I morti non si contano	Cry for Revenge	1968	R. Romero Marchent	Q3

*There is some controversy over who really hides behind the "official" director moniker Nathan Wich (given by AGIS) or Vich (given by Poppi-Percorari and Weisser). Weisser ascribes it to female director and scriptwriter Lina Wertmuller. Poppi-Percorari argues that she is the co-writer "George Brown" and so couldn't at the same time be director/writer Wich, whom they choose to believe is the otherwise unknown Cristofani, who is registered in the archives.

Italian (alt. Spanish or French) title	English title	Year	Director	Italian b.o.
Navajo Joe	Navajo Joe	1966	S. Corbucci	Q2
Una nuvola di polvere ... un grido di morte ... arriva Sartana	Light the Fuse ... Sartana Is Coming	1970	G. Carmineo as A. Ascott	Q3
Odio per odio	Hate for Hate	1967	D. Paolella	Q4
Oggi a me ... domani a te	Today It's Me, Tomorrow You	1968	T. Cervi	Q4
Ognuno per sé	The Ruthless Four	1968	G. Capitani	Q3
Oklahoma John/I ranch degli spietati	Man from Oklahoma	1965	J. Jesus Balcazar	Q2
Pampa salvaje		1966	H. Fregonese	N/A
Passa Sartana ... è la ombra della tua morte	Shadow of Sartana ... Shadow of Death	1969	D. Fidani	Q2
Per centomila dollari t'ammazzo	For $100,000 per Killing	1967	G. Fago	Q3
Per il gusto di uccidere	Taste for Killing	1966	T. Valerii	Q3
Per mille dollari al giorno	For $1,000 a Day	1966	S. Amadio	Q4
Per pochi dollari ancora	Fort Yuma Gold	1966	G. Ferroni	Q4
Una pistola per Ringo	Pistol for Ringo	1965	D. Tessari	Q4
Le pistole non discutono	Bullets Don't Argue	1964	M. Caiano	Q1
Il pistolero dell'Ave Maria	Forgotten Pistolero	1969	F. Baldi	Q4
La più grande rapina del west	Greatest Robbery in the West	1967	M. Lucido	Q4
Pochi dollari per Django	Few Dollars for Django	1966	L. Klimovski	Q4
Un poker di pistole	Poker with Pistols	1967	G. Vari	Q2
Posate le pistole ... reverendo	Pistol Packin' Preacher	1972	L. Savona	N/A
Prega per il morto e ammazza il vivo	Shoot the Living ... Pray for the Dead	1971	G. Vari	Q2
Preparati la bara!	Get the Coffin Ready	1968	F. Baldi	Q4
Il prezzo del potere	Price of Power	1969	T. Valerii	Q4
Prima ti perdono ... poi t'ammazzo	Dig Your Grave, Friend ... Sabata's Coming	1970	I. F. Iquino	Q3

Films Quoted 273

Italian (alt. Spanish or French) title	English title	Year	Director	Italian b.o.
Professionisti per un massacro	Red Blood, Yellow Gold	1967	N. Cicero	Q3
El proscrito del Río Colorado	Django the Condemned/Django the Honorable Killer	1965/ 1966	M. Dexter	N/A
I quattro dell'Ave Maria	Aces High	1968	G. Colizzi	Q4
I quattro inesorabile	Relentless Four	1965	P. Zeglio	Q4
Quei disperati che puzzano di sudore e di morte	Bullet for Sandoval	1969	J. Buchs	N/A
Quel maledetto giorno d'inverno ... Django e Sartana all'ultimo sangue	One Damned Day at Dawn ... Django Meets Sartana	1970	D. Fidani	Q2
Quella sporca storia nel west	Johnny Hamlet	1969	E. Girolami	Q3
Quién sabe?/El Chuncho	A Bullet for the General	1966	D. Damiani	Q4
Quinto: non ammazzare	Quinto: Fighting Proud	1969	L. Klimovsky	N/A
Una ragione per vivere ... una per morire	Massacre at Fort Holman	1972	T. Valerii	Q4
Requiescant	Let Them Rest/Kill and Prey	1967	C. Lizzani	Q3
La resa dei conti	The Big Gundown	1967	S. Sollima	Q4
Reverendo Colt	Reverend Colt	1970	L. Klimowsky	Q2
Ringo del Nebraska	Savage Gringo	1966	A. Roman	Q3
Il ritorno di Ringo	Return of Ringo	1965	D. Tessari	Q4
El Rojo	Rojo	1966	L. Savona	Q3
Sansone e il tesoro degli Incas	Lost Treasure of the Incas	1965	P. Pierotti	N/A
Sartana nella valle degli avvoltoi	Sartana in the Valley of Death	1970	R. Mauri	Q2
Sartana non perdona/ Sonora	Sartana Does Not Forgive	1968	A. Balcazar	Q3
Sartana/Se incontri Sartana prega per la tua morte	Sartana	1968	G. Parolini as F. Kramer	Q4

Italian (alt. Spanish or French) title	English title	Year	Director	Italian b.o.
Scalps!	Scalps	1985	B. Mattei	N/A
La Sceriffa		1959	R. Montero	N/A
Der Schatz im Silbersee		1962	Dr. H. Reinl	N/A
Se t'incontro t'ammazzo	Finders Killers	1971	G. Crea	Q1
Se vuoi vivere ... spara!	The Outlaw Rider/ If You Want to Live ... Shoot!	1968	S. Garrone	Q2
Sella d'argento	Silver Saddle	1978	L. Fulci	Q1
I senza Dio	Thunder over El Paso	1972	R. Montero	Q2
Sette ore di fuoco/ Aventuras del oeste	Seven Hours of Gunfire	1965	J. L. Romero Marchent	Q2
Sette winchester per un massacro	Payment in Blood	1967	E. Girolami	Q1
Sfida a Rio Bravo/ Desafio en Rio Bravo	Gunmen of Rio Grande	1964	T. Demichelli	N/A
Si può fare ... amigo!	It Can Be Done ... Amigo	1972	M. Lucido	Q4
Sono Sartana, il vostro becchino	I Am Sartana, Angel of Death	1969	G. Carmineo as A. Ascott	Q4
La spina dorsale del diavolo	Deserter	1970	N. Fulgozzi, B. Kennedy	Q4
Spirito Santo e le cinque magnifiche canaglie	Gunmen and the Holy Ghost	1972	R. Mauri	Q1
Storia di karatè, pugni e fagioli		1973	Toni Ricci	Q4
Uno straniero a Sacramento	A Stranger in Sacramento	1965	S. Bergonzelli	Q3
Sugar colt	Sugar Colt	1966	F. Giraldi	Q3
Il suo nome gridava vendetta	Man Who Cried for Vengeance	1968	M. Caiano	Q3
Tedeum	Sting of the West	1972	E. Girolami	Q4
Il tempo degli avvoltoi	Time of Vultures	1967	N. Cicero	Q3
Tempo di massacro/ Le colt cantarono la morte e fu ... tempo di massacro	Massacre Time/Colt Concert	1966	L. Fulci	Q4
Tepepa	Blood and Guns	1969	G. Petroni	Q4
Tequila!	Tequila	1973	T. Demicheli	Q2

Italian (alt. Spanish or French) title	English title	Year	Director	Italian b.o.
Testa t'ammazzo ... croce sei morto ... mi chiamano Allelujah	Heads You Die ... Tails I Kill You	1971	G. Carmineo as A. Ascott	Q4
Texas addio	Texas, Adios	1966	F. Baldi	Q4
I tre che sconvolsero il west/Vado, vedo e sparo	I Came, I Saw, I Shot	1968	E. Girolami	Q3
Tre colpi di winchester per Ringo	Three Graves for a Winchester	1966	E. Salvi	Q3
I tre del Colorado/ Rebeldes del Canada	Three from Colorado/ Canadian Wilderness	1965	A. de Ossorio	Q2
Tre dollari di piombo/ Tres dólares de plomo	Three Silver Dollars	1964	P. Mercati	Q1
I tre implacabili/ Tres hombres buenos	Magnificent Three	1963	J. L. Romero Marchent	N/A
Tre pistole contro Cesare/Tre ragazzi d'oro	Death Walks in Laredo	1967	E. Peri	Q1
I tre spietati/El sabor de venganza	Gunfight at High Noon	1963	J. L. Romero Marchent	Q4
Un treno per Durango	A Train for Durango	1968	M. Caiano	Q2
Trinità e Sartana figli di...	Trinity and Sartana Are Coming	197?	M. Siciliano	Q3
Uccidete Johnny Ringo	Kill Johnny Ringo	1966	G. Baldanello	Q3
Uccidi o muori	Kill or Die	1966	T. Boccia	Q3
Uomo avvisato mezzo ammazzato ... parola di Spirito Santo	Forewarned, Half-Killed ... the Word of the Holy Ghost	1972	G. Carmineo as A. Ascott	Q3
L'uomo che viene de Canyon City/Odio en la frontera	Man from Canyon City	1965	A. Balcazar	Q3
L'uomo dalla pistola d'oro	Man with the Golden Pistol	1965	A. Balcazar	Q3
Vado, l'ammazzo e torno	Any Gun Can Play	1967	E. Girolami	Q4
Vamos a matar, companeros!	Companeros	1970	S. Corbucci	Q4
Vendetta/I lunghi giorni della vendetta	Long Days of Vengeance	1967	F. Vancini	Q4

Italian (alt. Spanish or French) title	English title	Year	Director	Italian b.o.
La vendetta è il mio perdono	Shotgun	1968	R. Mauri	Q2
La vendetta è un piatto che si serve freddo	Vengeance Is a Dish Served Cold	1971	P. Squitieri	Q3
Il vendicatore di Kansas City/Sonaron cuatro balazos	Shots Ring Out!	1964	A. Navarro	Q1
Il venditore di morte	Price of Death	1971	E. Gicca Palli	Q2
La vita a volte, è molto dura, vero Provvidenza?	Sometimes Life Is Hard, Right Providence?	1972	G. Petroni	Q4
Viva la muerte ... tua!	Don't Turn the Other Cheek	1971	D. Tessari	Q4
Vivi, o preferibilmente morti	Alive or Preferably Dead	1969	D. Tessari	Q4
W Django!	Man Called Django	1971	E. Mulargia	Q2
Wanted	Wanted	1967	G. Ferroni	Q4
Il west ti va stretto amico ... è arrivato Allelujah!	Return of Hallelujah	1972	G. Carmineo as A. Ascott	Q4
Winnetou II	Last of the Renegades	1964	Dr. H. Reinl	N/A

Films Quoted by English Title

English title	Italian (alt. Spanish) title	Year	Director	Italian b.o.
Buddy Goes West	Occhio alla penna	1980	M. Lupo	N/A
The Charge at Feather River		1953	G. Douglas	N/A
Chato's Land		1971	M. Winner	N/A
Cut-Throats Nine	Condenados a Vivir	1971	J. L. Romero Marchent	N/A
The Dirty Dozen		1967	R. Aldrich	N/A
Drums Along the Mohawk		1939	J. Ford	N/A
Duck You Sucker/ Fistful of Dynamite	Giù la testa	1971	S. Leone	Q4
A Fistful of Dollars	Per un pugno di dollari	1964	S. Leone	Q4
For a Few Dollars More	Per qualche dollaro in più	1965	S. Leone	Q4

English title	Italian (alt. Spanish) title	Year	Director	Italian b.o.
Fun in Acapulco		1963	R. Thorpe	N/A
The Good, the Bad and the Ugly	Il buono, il brutto, il cattivo	1966	S. Leone	Q4
Gunfighters of Casa Grande	Pistoleros de Casa Grande	1964	R. Rowland	N/A
Guns of the Magnificent Seven		1968	P. Wendkos	N/A
Hannie Caulder		1971	G. Kennedy	N/A
High Noon		1952	F. Zinneman	N/A
I Spit on Your Grave		1980	M. Zarchi	N/A
Jesse James		1939	H. King	N/A
The Magnificent Seven		1960	J. Sturges	N/A
A Man Called Horse		1970	E. Silverstein	N/A
The Man from Laramie		1955	A. Mann	N/A
Man of the East	...E poi lo chiamarono il magnifico	1972	E. Barboni	Q4
The Man Who Shot Liberty Valance		1962	J. Ford	N/A
My Darling Clementine		1946	J. Ford	N/A
My Name Is Nobody	Il mio nome è Nessuno	1973	T. Valerii (and S. Leone)	Q4
Once Upon a Time in the West	C'era un volta il west	1968	S. Leone	Q4
The Savage Guns	Tierra Brutal	1962	M. Carreras	N/A
Shalako	Shalako	1968	E. Dmytryk	N/A
Shane		1953	G. Stevens	N/A
Stagecoach		1939	J. Ford	N/A
Singin' in the Rain		1952	S. Donen	N/A
They Call Me Trinity	Lo chiamavano Trinità	1970	E. Barboni	Q4
A Town Called Bastard		1971	R. Parrish	N/A
The Treasure of the Sierra Madre		1948	J. Huston	N/A
Trinity Is Still My Name	...continuavano a chiamarlo Trinità	1971	E. Barboni	Q4
The Troublemakers/ The Fight Before Christmas	Botte di Natale	1994	T. Hill	N/A
Vera Cruz		1954	R. Aldrich	N/A
Viva Villa		1934	J. Conway	N/A

Chapter Notes

Preface

1. Whether the later phenomena usually subsumed under the label of postindustrial and/or information society represents something radically new, or just another phase of industrialism, is outside the scope of this discussion. At least at a glance, they seem to include a still larger mass-mediated quota of cultural activity as a new mass medium, the Internet, comes to the fore.

2. *No Room to Die — A Structuralist Study of the Content of Spaghetti Westerns* (Department of Cinema Studies, Stockhom University, 2002).

Chapter 1

1. Rick Altman, "A semantic/syntactic approach to film genre," quoted from Altman (1999) p. 216ff. The article was first published in *Cinema Journal* 23, no. 3 (Spring 1984).
2. Altman (1999) pp. 62–68.
3. See Mendez-Leite p. 713, and Frayling (2000) p. 123.
4. Wagstaff p. 252. According to AGIS (General Association of Italian Spectacles), it earned more than 6 billion lire, not quite twice as much as the second most successful Italowestern, *My Name Is Nobody*.
5. Jean Mirty. *Dictionnaire du Cinéma*. Paris: Larousse, 1963. p. 276.
6. Ford. *Histoire du Western*. Paris: A Michel, 1976, ch 22. Frayling (1981) 1ff, Frayling (2000) p. 29ff, Hembus p. 677.
7. See Molinari.
8. See the bibliography, especially the entries by Baldelli, Joyeux, Frayling (1970), Lhassa, Jameson, Mengershausen, Pierre, Bädekerl, Baudry, Dumont, Graziari, Leperis, Gili, Bützov, Kaminsky, Sabatier, Wallington, Königstein, Kliess, Ferrini, Cawelti (1974) and Staig/Williams. The last work has the most comprehensive treatment of the music.
9. In the filmography of Eurowesterns edited by Weisser (which does include Zorro films), Sancho appears in 54 of the 558 entries!
10. Altman p. 221; Jim Kitses. *Horizons West*, Bloomington: Indiana University Press, 1969. pp. 10–14; Cawelti (1971).
11. However, Wright does use an "exclusive pantheon" argument when he refuses to consider the top-grossing *The Charge at Feather River* (1953) because it is an "awful Western," allegedly owing its commercial success to the current 3-D craze.
12. I choose this "top-grossing" limit not just because it is a nice even number, but also because the preceding 900 million to 1 billion interval is comparatively thinly populated. Also, using the combined taking from Italy, Spain, France and Germany (and possibly Britain) might have been a more valid measure.
13. Altman p. 210.
14. Wagstaff (p. 247) points out that the box office intake for spaghetti Westerns mainly shown in Italian third run

cinemas, where tickets were far less expensive, represented a far larger number of spectators than a comparable intake mainly coming from first run cinemas.
 15. *Westerns All'Italiana (WAI)* has been published since 1983 and edited by Tom Betts of Anaheim, California.
 16. Altman p. 217.
 17. *Shalako* (1968), and the 1971 "wave" of *Hannie Caulder, A Town Called Bastard, Chato's Land* and *Captain Apache; Dans la poussière de solei* (1972) and *Une corde, un colt* (1968). Lhassa (1983) credits Robert Hossein, the director/star of the last film, with directing a non-comedy Western already in 1961, *Le Goût de la violence* (p. 44).
 18. See "Before the Beginning?" in chapter 4.

Chapter 2

1. Mainly from the first two parts of his *Mythologiques — The Raw and the Cooked* and *From Honey to Ashes*.
 2. Wright p. 15.
 3. Ibid. p. 49.
 4. Lévi-Strauss (1979) p. 199.
 5. A fourth opposition, wilderness/civilization, which distinguishes the hero from society and villains, is also mentioned, but plays a marginal role in Wright's analysis.
 6. Wright, p. 132.
 7. Chatman, p. 26; Bordwell pp. 34–35, 49–50.
 8. The opening sequence of *Una pistola per Ringo* may be interpreted as a partly inverted variation on the conclusion of John Ford's *Stagecoach*. In Ford's story the Ringo Kid breaks out of jail, where he serves a sentence for killing a Plummer brother, and he seeks out the other three brothers because they have murdered his kin. In Tessari's version Ringo is acquitted of the charge of killing a Benson brother, and the other four brothers seek him out for murdering their kin — though they end up just as dead as the Plummers.
 9. The insider/outsider tactic is uncommon among the top-grossing Westerns studied by Wright. Its employment in the more humble environments of American "B" and serial Westerns is beyond the scope of this investigation.
 10. See "The Female as Involuntary Infiltrator" later in this chapter.
 11. As this term is used in Chatman pp. 138–41, "The place and collection of objects 'against which' the character's actions and passions appropriately emerge" — including human "walk-ons."
 12. In the sense used in Wright, p. 126, as the minimal requirement for a narrative.
 13. Another female hero is the title character of *Giarettiera Colt*, among the most anonymous of spaghetti Westerns, except for dismissive notes by Lhassa (1987) p. 57 and Weisser p. 127.
 14. See chapter 8.
 15. See chapter 3.
 16. Wright p. 137.
 17. The "theme story" concept is close to Frank Gruber's foundational "stories" of the (American) Western — "Gunfighter story," "Western Union story," etc.
 18. Cawelti (1971) p. 48. Of course, within the vast corpus of the American Western, one will find sisters in spirit to those characters.
 19. However, unlike other such situations in Westerns like *Johnny Oro* and *Gringo* her performance is discretely interleaved in the action during the funeral (!) dinner.

Chapter 3

1. See chapter 5, note 6.
 2. See "The Manipulation Sequence" in chapter 2.
 3. Courtesy of *A Man Called Horse*, though the treatment is administered by whites this time.
 4. The "stacked-deck" phrase is in fact taken from the American Western *Shane*, which also contains a prime example, when the gunfighter Wilson insults the South to make the farmer Torrey draw first.
 5. See chapter 8.
 6. See chapter 5.

Chapter 4

1. Dave Kehr. "On Anthony Mann." *They Went Thataway*. Originally published in the *Chicago Tribune*, July 5, 1992.
2. See chapter 7.
3. *Catalogo Bolaffi del cinema italiano* p. 268. Poppi-Pecorari gives a considerably lower box office figure for this film.
4. See chapter 2, table 2A.
5. Cf. chapter 6.
6. Wright p. 74.
7. Aficionados of Morricone music will even find an instance of the violin chords that were to be used as the main theme of the TV series *La Piovra* many years later. Less exciting is the movie's insipidly sweet main theme.
8. *Le pistole non discutono* also has the same kind of silhouetted title graphics as *Fistful of Dollars*. Possibly inspired by the James Bond titles, they would be widely used the next couple of years in Italian Westerns.
9. Hustlers being caught up with and/or using the revolution would later reappear as ironic variants, especially with Tessari's *Viva la muerte ... tua!* (see chapter 7, "...and the comedies").
10. In the same scene he shoots off the ear of one of the gang, pointing forward to the renowned *Django* by the same director, where Hugo cuts off an ear of the preacher who spies for Jackson (see chapter 5).

Chapter 5

1. Frayling (1998) pp. 87–88.
2. Umberto Eco. "The Myth of Superman," *Diacritics*, Spring 1972. Ithaca, New York: Cornell University, discussed in Frayling (1998) pp. 75–79.
3. The character was introduced already in the classic *Cabiria* (1914).
4. Among Italowesterns, there are a few (unnoticed) stories built around historical Westerners—*Buffalo Bill, l'eroe del far west*; *Sette ore di fuoco*; and *Sfida a Rio Bravo*. We will also encounter occasional cases of fictional characters biographically bonded between films.
5. Both were made in 1965 or 1966, which is before or in the same year as *Django*. Frayling notes that in the first of them Django is more like "a stock figure of the Hollywood 'B' Western." For the second film, the hero is listed as "Peter Lambrok," not Django. Frayling (1998) p. 84.
6. In his work on Lévi-Strauss, Leach uses some ancient Greek myths to illustrate his analysis of myth transformations. His Agamemnon variation — "Paramour kills father and invites vengeance of the son" — is the inspiration for *Il pistolero dell'Ave Maria*, and by way of Hamlet, also for *Dans la poussière du soleil* and *Quella sporca storia nel west/Johnny Hamlet*. Storywise, there are also striking similarities between *Il ritorno di Ringo* and the last song of the Odyssey. *Fedra West* (also *Io non perdono ... uccido*) should be expected to conform to the Hippolytos variation. Edmund Leach. Lévi-Strauss. London: Fontana/Collins, 1970 p.80.
7. The effect is enhanced by the "flow" of the title song during the sequence. Belonging to the breed of "driving theme song" that appeared in some early spaghetti Westerns (See "Visuals and Soundtrack in chapter 4), this composition (by Lallo Gori) might be the one that functions most satisfyingly in its context.
8. See chapter 6.
9. The proper/false/hidden/involuntary distinction is an adaptation of Greimas (1973) pp. 165–66.
10. There is a short model of a prodigal daughter constellation/plot told in flashbacks in the mixed-gender partnership film *The Belle Starr Story* (see chapter 7).
11. See "Supervised Duel" in chapter 3.
12. This story has affinities with other stories of women who are tortured and ravaged and then exert a violent revenge, the most notorious being *I Spit on Your Grave*.
13. Wright pp. 59–74.
14. See also "Sleeping Partnerships Together with Other Plots" in chapter 7 about *Django spara per primo*.

Chapter 6

1. Up to the pyramidal success of Enzo Barboni's *Trinity Is Still My Name* (1971), *Few Dollars More* was the most commercially successful Italian Western, with only Leone's next — *The Good, the Bad and the Ugly* (1966) coming close.
2. See chapter 5, p. 111.
3. See "A Plethora of Duels" in chapter 3.
4. Leone's assertion that "the protagonist was the same"— quoted in Frayling (1998) p. 146 — is open to different interpretations.
5. In *The Good, the Bad and the Ugly* the Marisol figure appears again briefly as the victimized Mexican prostitute whom "the bad" Angel Eyes slaps around the room to get information.
6. See "Infiltrator Variations" in chapter 2.
7. Cumbow points out that rationally Mortimer is wrong, as Indio assaults the bank because he has learned where in the bank the money *really* is kept (p. 28). Still, as Cumbow also says, "Things happen the way they do in Leone's films because they cannot happen otherwise" (p. 57).
8. See Lhassa (1987) p. 191 and Frayling (1998) p. 169 for two (divergent) recounts of the pieces in this armory.
9. See "The Position of the Woman in the Infiltrator Film" in chapter 2.
10. Brice played Winnetou in all films of the series. When his partner instead was played by Stewart Granger or Rod Cameron, the coupling between Barker and the Shatterhand character was respected by giving their characters other, though similar, names (Old Surehand and Old Firehand, respectively).
11. Frayling (1998) p. 87.
12. Similarly, in *Johnny Oro*, also released in 1966, the hero goes only for bad guys with a bounty. See "The Devious Hero and the Straight Sheriff (Retake): *Johnny Oro*" in chapter 4.
13. See chapter 8.
14. See " Involuntary Infiltrators in Other Spaghetti Westerns" in chapter 2.
15. See "Django as a Trans-Story Hero" in chapter 5.

Chapter 7

1. See "Men in Black" in chapter 4.
2. As in *Black Killer* from the same year, see later in this chapter.
3. See "Enter the Bounty Killer" in chapter 6.
4. See chapter 5.
5. See "Unsophisticated" in chapter 9.
6. See "The Sociocultural Code" in chapter 2.
7. Though it seems to be a sound idea to search for a treasure in burial grounds— Cisco for example temporarily hides the loot in a grave — both *Acquasanta Joe* and *Sette winchester per un massacro* indicate that it is self-destructive to look for it in Indian burial grounds!
8. See "Prodigal Sons— Pretended or Real" in chapter 5.
9. It is notable that the geographical settings of these stories are similar to *Few Dollars More*, a story roaming through several localities, while the "sleeping partner" stories discussed earlier are more like *Fistful of Dollars*, which revolves around one or two localities.
10. As another low-end characteristic, the scenes with the O'Haras were cannibalized into another story in *Un bounty killer a Trinità*.
11. See "The Position of the Woman in the Infiltrator Film" in chapter 2.
12. Frayling (1998) p. 202.
13. I believe there is some connection (conscious or not) between this hero style with its "flea market" ambience and the contemporary "hippie" subculture with its liking for odd, outstanding dress (among other things ponchos and furs).
14. See "Massacro al Grande Canyon," in chapter 4.
15. Both films were box office hits, with an intake of more than 1 billion lire, according to AGIS.
16. See chapter 5.
17. In the early Italowestern *Le pistole non discutono* (see chapter 4), George is a

tainted youth who is put on the right track due to the characteristically strong character and superior competence of the hero, while Billy is the bad young contender who is constantly bested by the older hero and eventually perishes.

18. See chapter 5.
19. Frayling (2000) pp. 361–62.
20. Frayling (1998) pp. 247–55. Cumbow pp. 100–06 presents a very similar line of reasoning.
21. In fact, the (main) director Valerii and the scriptwriter Ernesto Gastaldi both worked with *I giorni dell'ira*.
22. Both Frayling (1998) and Cumbow suggest that a veiled egoistic motive from Nobody would be to enhance a fame that he himself will inherit, as the one who (in appearance) does away with Beauregard. However, this is not put forward as any significant motivation in the story.
23. Frayling (1998) p. 51.
24. Story was by Salvatore Laurani.
25. This name is an obvious reference to Leone's film. In fact, you find a lot of villages called San Miguel in spaghetti Westerns after 1964.
26. To paraphrase a keen observation by Cumbow, "Leone's bad guys are always destroyers of the innocent," p. 24.
27. To enhance the overlap, in both movies Franco Nero plays the Anglo money-oriented specialist (Sergei/Yod) and Jack Palance his evil Anglo money-oriented double (Curly/John), while Eduardo Fajardo is Garcia in the first movie and an army colonel in the second.
28. The term "social bandit" has been culled from Eric Hobsbawm. *Bandits*. London: Weidenfeld and Nicolson, 1969 p. 13, though I use it for fictional characters instead of the historical phenomena that he studies, even though the bandits' imprints in fiction and folklore are included in his material.
29. Cawelti (1971) p. 51.
30. See chapter 9.
31. In the seminal American *Viva Villa*, a rape plays a similar dramatical role and, according to Slotkin, it is similarly shown in a benevolent perspective (Slotkin p. 414).

32. Frayling (1998) pp. 232–33, also 238 and 242.
33. Slotkin considers the Villa character a variant of the Western bandit hero that became popular during the Depression (e.g., in *Jesse James*), only depicted according to ethnic "south of the border" stereotypes, pp. 411–418.
34. Slotkin p. 402.
35. Slotkin pp. 433–40 and pp. 474–86. *Vera Cruz* might be a source of inspiration for Italowesterns. Its story might easily be mapped to an "unstable partnership" plot involving the consistently money-oriented mercenary Joe Errin, while his partner Ben Trane gets a second non-monetary motive. For *The Magnificent Seven* see also "A Professional Plot?" in chapter 8. "Counter-insurgency" refers to the military and political stratagems employed by the United States, e.g., in Vietnam.
36. Frayling (1998) p. 217, and Slotkin p. 413. Wallace Beery's performance might be the mother load to the long suite of garrulous Latin characters brought to the Italowestern genre by Fernando Sancho—from *I tre implacabile* and onwards.
37. Frayling (1998) pp. 185 and 228.
38. Quoted in Frayling (1998) p. 225.
39. See "The Bounty Killer Adversary" in chapter 6.
40. Possibly to spare Catholic sensibility, this scene is cut from my Spanish video print.
41. Or even more relevant, the social and historical moment of Cawelti, who more than Wright stresses the opposition wilderness/civilization as the basic one, with outlaws and Indians representing the former, Cawelti; (1971) pp. 51–2.
42. For the latter, see the classical exposé in Jeffrey Richards. *Visions of Yesterday*. London: Routledge & Kegan Paul, 197 pp. 2–270.
43. See "The Female Double" in chapter 5.
44. This epilogue is often cut from video editions, as it goes against audience expectations about Terence Hill characters. However, in his early career, as Mario Girotti, he met with a villain's death in *Duell vor Sonnenuntergang*.

45. See "Variants of the Motivation" in chapter 5.
46. See chapter 5.
47. See "Carrarcho's Return" in chapter 4.
48. See chapter 4.
49. See chapter 9.

Chapter 8

1. He is thus designated by a side character in a later scene.
2. However, regarding his catchwords for Leone's first Westerns, I would argue that *Fistful of Dollars* is just as much about infiltration and manipulation as about "avarice" and that *Few Dollars More* is about expertise — and also betrayal — as much as about "obsession." Cumbow pp. 38, 42, 58 and 73.
3. Blondie to Tuco when sharing the reward: "There are two kinds of people in the world, my friend, those with a rope around their neck, and those who have the job of doing the cutting." Tuco to Blondie in the hotel room (after Blondie has killed Tuco's men, alerted by the sound of their spurs): "There are two kinds of spurs, my friend, those that come in by the door and those that come in by the window." Blondie to Tuco after the final gunfight: "There are two kinds of people, my friend, those with loaded guns and those who dig."
4. Cumbow discusses at length the many ways that the war influences the story pp. 52ff.
5. See "The Bounty Hunter Gets His Men" in chapter 6.
6. See chapter 3.
7. As it is not included in Wright's list of Westerns, it did not meet his $4 million requirement for "Top-Grossing Westerns"— though it certainly has shown more historical staying power and influence than most of the Westerns that made his list (Wright p. 30ff).
8. Another inverse infiltration of this kind is executed by Pembroke in *Una ragione per vivere ... una per morire* (see chapter 2).
9. See "Involuntary Infiltrators in Other Spaghetti Westerns" in chapter 2.

10. See "Vestiges of the Non-Monetary Motive" in this chapter.
11. The Sartana character played by the same actor — John (Gianni) Garko — earlier in Alberto Cardone's *Mille dollari sul nero* has only the name in common. Carmineo also directed *Il momento di uccidere*, discussed earlier.
12. See *Killer Kid* in chapter 7.
13. See "The Unsophisticated" in chapter 9.
14. See chapter 9.
15. See chapter 5.
16. Frayling (1998) pp. 83–87.
17. In *Arriva Sabata!* the rivalry among the three leading characters might be open to a homosexual interpretation, but the syuzhet contains nothing to substantially support this interpretation, even if the Mexican protagonist Mangosta does pursue the hobby of knitting!

Chapter 9

1. There is an indisputable biographical bonding between the stories, with some inconsistencies. In the first film Trinity is a renowned gunfighter —called the right hand of the devil. In the second, he is described as someone without any established status who needs to learn how to become an outlaw. In *Trinity 1* their mother has a whorehouse in New Orleans, and the brothers have different fathers; in the second film she is a (former?) saloon girl living in a shack with their (common) father.
2. The thematic role of a small, choleric Latin character is not totally unknown among stereotypes in American films. For quite a different genre, note the parts played by Eric Rhodes in the Astaire-Rogers musicals *The Gay Divorcee* and (especially) *Top Hat*.
3. See "Mystery and Surprise" in chapter 8.
4. The mother also says grace to a female Lady in heaven — "You had a son that gave you quite a few words too."
5. See "The Physical Pair of Colizzi" in chapter 7.
6. See chapter 8.

7. See "The Gemma Icon" in chapter 5.
8. See chapter 3.
9. Meaning "Providence," like "Trinity" a religious concept with a very loose connection to the character wearing the name.
10. William J Hynes, William G Doty ed. *Mythical Trickster Figures*. Tuscaloosa and London: University of Alabama Press, 1993 pp. 33–45.
11. See chapter 6.

Chapter 10

1. See "A Professional Plot?" in chapter 8.
2. See "...and the comedies" in chapter 7.
3. Sandro Graziani. "Western Italiano Western Americano." Rome: Bianco e Nero 9/10/1970.
4. See chapter 2.
5. Inspired by a comic is the late-late "spaghetti Western" *Tex e il signore degli abissi* from 1985 by the old faithfuls Tessari and Gemma.

Bibliography

Altman, Rick. *Film/Genre*. London: British Film Institute, 1999.
Associazione Generalo Italiana dello Spettacolo. *Catalogo generale dei film italiani dal 1965 al 1978*. 5th ed. Rome: AGIS, 1978.
Bädekerl, Klaus. "Western und Italowestern." *Filmkritik* 10 (1969).
Baldelli, Pio. "Western à l'italienne." *Image et Son* 206 (1967).
Baudry, Pierre. "L'idéologie du western italien." *Cahiers du Cinéma* 233 (1971).
Bengtsson, Åke. "Spaghetti-Westerns." *Filmrutan* 1 (1968).
Bordwell, David. *Narration in the Fiction Film*. Madison: University of Wisconsin Press, 1985.
Borek, Gilbert. "Sergio Leone och anti-hjälten." *Chaplin* 102 (1970).
_____. "Spagettivästerns." *Filmrutan* 2 (1971).
Bützov, Poul. "Sergio Leones film." Paper presented at the Institut for Filmvidenskabe. Københavns Universitet, 1973.
Catalogo Bolaffi del cinema italiano. Turin: Giulio Bolaffi Editore, 1967.
Cawelti, John G. "Reflections on the new western films." In Jack Nachbar, ed. *Focus on the Western*. Englewood Cliffs NJ: Prentice Hall, 1974.
_____. *The Six-Gun Mystique*. Bowling Green OH: Bowling Green University Popular Press, 1971.
Chatman, Seymour. *Story and Discourse*. Ithaca NY: Cornell University Press, 1978.
Cumbow, Robert C. *Once Upon a Time: The Films of Sergio Leone*. Metuchen NJ: Scarecrow, 1987.
Daney, Serge. "Once Upon a Time in the West." *Cahiers du Cinéma* 216 (1969).
della Fornace, Luciana. *Il labirinto cinematografico*. Rome: Bulzoni Editore, 1983.
Dumont, Etienne. "Anthony Ascott." *Travelling* 42 (1974).
Fahdel, Abbas. "Un genre métis: le western italien." *CinémAction*, July 1990.
Faldini, Franca, and Goffredo Fofi, eds. *L'Avventurosa storia del Cinema Italiano. Raccontata dai suoi protagonisti 1960–69*. Milan: Feltrinelli, 1981. Pp. 285–315.
Ferrini, Franco. "Sergio Leone e il Western." *Bianco e Nero* 9/10 (1971).
Fox, William Price. "Wild West Italian Style." *Saturday Evening Post*, 6 April 1968.
Frayling, Christopher. "Italian Western: Sergio Leone." *Cinema* 6&7 (1970).
_____. *Sergio Leone: Something to Do with Death*. London: Faber, 2000.
_____. *Spaghetti Westerns: Cowboys and Europeans from Karl May to Sergio Leone*. Revised edition. London: I. B. Taurus, 1998.
_____. "The Wretched of the Earth." *Sight and Sound*, June 1993.
Fridlund, Bert. "Classical American Western and Spaghetti Western: A Comparison of

Shane and *A Fistful of Dollars.*" In *2003 Film & History CD-ROM Annual.* Cleveland OH: Film & History, 2005.
_____. *Död åt Johnny Gringo.* Stockholm: Department for Film Studies, University of Stockholm, 1975.
_____. "Sergio Leone en västernregissör." *Filmrutan* 3 (1972).
Gili, Jean A. "...un univers fabrique de toutes pièces...." *Cinéma* 140 (1969).
Graziani, Sandro. "Western Italiano Western Americano." *Bianco e Nero* 9/10 (1970).
Greimas, A.J. *In Semiotique narrative et textuelle.* Paris: Larousse, 1973.
Haustrate, Gaston. "Faut-il brûler les westerns italiens?" *Cinéma* 154 (1971).
Hembus, Joe. *Western-Lexikon.* Munich: Hanser Verlag, 1976; Rev. ed., 1995.
J.S. "Der Rächer von Cinecittà." *Illustrierte Film-Kurier* 279.
Jameson, R.T., ed. *They Went Thataway: Redefining Film Genres.* San Francisco: Mercury House, 1994.
Jameson, Richard. "Something to Do with Death." *Film Comment*, March/April 1973.
Joyeux, François. "Django." *Vampirella* 19 (1975).
_____. "Sartana Gianni Garko Anthony Ascott." *Vampirella* 13 (1974).
_____. "Sergio Corbucci: Le western Italien." *Vampirella* 9 (1973).
_____. "Sergio Corbucci bis." *Vampirella* 11 (1973).
Joyeux, François, and Alain Petit. "Fantastique et Western." *Vampirella* 11 (1973).
Kaarsholm, Preben. "Oprørets dialektik." In Michael Bruun Andersen, ed., *Filmanalyser*. Copenhagen: Røde Hane, 1974.
Kaminsky, Stuart. "The Grotesque West of Sergio Leone." *Take One* 3:9 (1973).
Kezich, Tullio. "Western all'Italia." *Cataloga Bolaffi del cinema italiano I.* Turin: Giulio Bolaffi Editore, 1967.
Kliess, Werner. "Kino dass Frei Macht." *Film* 1969 (yearbook).
Königstein, Horst. "Es war einmal ein Western." In Hermann K. Ehmer, ed., *Visuelle Kommunikation.* Schauberg: Verlag M. DuMont, 1971.
Kwiatkowski, Alexander. "Italienska western i Sverige." *Film & Bio* 7 (1968).
Lambert, Gilles. *Les Bons, les sales, les méchants es les propres de Sergio Leone.* Paris: Solar, 1976.
Leone, Sergio. Interview. *Chaplin* 146 (1976).
_____. Interview. *Bianco e Nero* 9/10 (1971).
_____. "...j'ai aborde le western avec un grand amour...." *Cinéma* 140 (1969).
_____. "Sergio Leone Talks" (interview). *Take One* 3:9 (1973).
Lepenis, Wolf. "Der Italowestern — Romantik und Gewalt." In Karsten Witte, ed., *Theorie des Kinos: Ideologikritik der Traumfabrik* Frankfurt am Main: Suhrkamp, 1972.
Lévi-Strauss, Claude. *From Honey to Ashes: Introduction to a Science of Mythology 2*, London: Jonathan Cape, 1973. (Originally published in French, 1966).
_____. *The Raw and the Cooked: Introduction to a Science of Mythology I.* New York: Octagon, 1979. (Originally published in French, 1964).
Lhassa, Gian, with the collaboration of Michel Lequeux. *Seul au monde dans le Western italien. Vol. 1: Une poignée de thèmes.* Mariembourge: Editions Grand Angle, 1982.
_____, with the collaboration of _____. *Seul au monde dans le Western italien. Vol. 2: Des hommes seuls.* Mariembourge: Editions Grand Angle, 1987.
_____, with the collaboration of _____. *Seul au monde dans le Western italien. Vol. 3: Dictionnaire du western italien.* Mariembourge: Editions Grand Angle, 1983.
Liholm, Bent. "Westerns — et genreselvmord." *Spotlight* 1 (1973).
Mendez-Leite, Fernando. "Las Muertes tienen su Precio o algunas palabras sobre el 'Spanish Western.'" *Film Ideal* 201–204 (1967).
Mengershausen, Joachim von. "Der Italienische Western." *Film* 1 (1967).
Molinari, Mario. "Prima che arrivassero gli 'spaghetti.'" *Segnocinema*, March 22, 1986.
Moscati, Massimo. *Western all'italiana.* Milan: Pan Editrice, 1978.

Newman, Kim. "Thirty Years in Another Town: The History of Italian Exploitation." *Monthly Film Bulletin* 624, pp. 20–4; 625, pp. 51–5; and 626, pp. 88–91 (1986).
Petit, Alain. "Sergio Sollima." *Vampirella* 12 (1974).
Pierre, Sylvie. "Clio veille." *Cahiers du Cinéma* 218 (1970).
_____. "Coups de feu dans la Sierra Leone." *Cahiers du Cinéma* 200–201 (1968).
Pintus, Pietro. *Storia e film: trent'anni di cinema italiano, 1945–75*. Rome: Bulzoni Editore, 1980. Pp. 61–66.
Poppi, Roberto, and Mario Pecorari. *Dizionario del Cinema Italiano: I Film del 1960 al 1969*. Rome: Gremese Editore, 1992.
_____, and _____. *Dizionario del Cinema Italiano: I Film del 1970 al 1979*. Rome: Gremese Editore, 1996.
Propp, Vladimir. *Morphology of the Folktale*. Austin: University of Texas Press, 1968.
Ramonet, Ignacio. "Italian Westerns as Political Parables." *Young Cinema* 2–3 (1988). Published with the same title in *Cineaste* 15:1 (1986). Originally from Ramonet, Ignacio, *Le Chewing-gum des yeux*. Paris: Alain Moreau, 1980.
Rønning, Helge. "Krutrøyk og kapitalisme — revolvere och revolusjon." *Kontrast* 1 (1980).
Sabatier, Jean-Marie "Le cinema 'bis' et le concept d'auteur." *Image et Son* 302 (1976).
_____. "Profile exemplaire d'un genre 'bis': le 'spaghetti western.'" *Image et Son* 305 (1976).
_____. "Le titre, une arme pour l'exploitation." *Image et Son* 302 (1976).
Salomonsen, Steen. "Westerngenrens ekstase." *Kosmorama* 192 (summer 1990).
Sarris, Andrew. "The Spaghetti Westerns." In *Confessions of a Cultist*. New York: Simon & Schuster, 1970.
Scarrone, Carlo. "Frenologi di una spaghetto story I–II." *Segnocinema* 22 and 23 (1986).
Schöler, Franz. "Django." *Film* 2 (1967).
Seesslen, Georg. "Western." In Bernt Kling and Georg Seesslen, eds., *Das Grosse Unterhaltungslexikon*. Bayreuth: Bernhard Roloff Verlag, 1973.
Simsolo, Noel. "Notes sur les westerns de Sergio Leone." *Image et Son* 275 (1973).
Slotkin, Richard. *Gunfighter Nation: The Myth of the Frontier in Twentieth-Century America*. New York: HarperPerennial, 1993.
Staig, Laurence, and Tony Williams. *Italian Western: The Opera of Violence*. London: Lorrimer, 1975.
Vergara, Vicente. "10.000 dólares por una massacre un estudo sobre el spagheti-western." In *Cine Español Cine de Subgeneros*. Valencia: Fernando Torres, 1974. Pp. 77–128.
Wagstaff, Christopher. "A Forkful of Westerns: Industry, Audiences and the Italian Western." In Tichard Dyer and Ginette Vincendeau, eds., *Popular European Cinema*. London and New York: Routledge, 1992. Pp. 245–61.
Wallington, Mike. "Italian Western: A Concordance." *Cinema* 6 and 7 (1970).
Weisser, Thomas. *Spaghetti Westerns: The Good, the Bad and the Violent*. Jefferson NC: McFarland, 1992.
Wörsel, Troels "Spaghetti-Westerns," Copenhagen: *Kosmorama* 96, 1970
Wright, Will. *Sixguns and Society: A Structural Study of the Western*. Berkeley: University of California Press, 1975.
Zimmer, Jacques. "Notes sur la production et l'exploitation." *Image et Son* 302 (1976).

Index

Numbers in **bold italics** indicate illustrations.

Abbot, Alan (Ezio Marano) 240
Acquasanta Joe 133, 139
Adios gringo 114, 115, 117, 146
Al di là della legge 28, 31, 32, 34, 39, 42, 43, 49, 149, 150
Alleluja e Sartana figli di ... Dio 35, 226, 235, 239, 240
All'Ombra di una colt 61
All'ultimo sangue 156, 158, 165
Altman, Rick 3, 6, 9, 11, 12
Los amigos 151, *152*, 153, 154, 161
Ammazzali tutti e torna solo 65, 209–11, 229
Anda muchacho spara! 142, 162, 165
Un animale chiamato uomo 39, 235, 240, 243
Anthony, Tony 13
Aristocrats 41–44, 82, 95, 124, 182, 188, 230
Arizona Colt 49, 50, 55, 62, 63, 118, 119, 132
Arriva Sabata! 226, 227
Arrivano Django e Sartana ... è la fine! 226
Avenger 27, 69, 79, 97, 101, 107, 109, 110, 112–14, 118, 119, 131, 140–42, 144, 146, 158, 161, 166, 179, 201, 226, 228, 258
Avenger constellation/plot 1, 101, 110, 113, 120, 133, 163, 226
Avenger stories 107, 109, 118–21, 133, 135, 143, 145

Baird, Harry 237
La Banda J & S. Cronaca criminale del far west 196
Bandidos 57, 110, 113, 167
Barboni, Enzo 5, 199, 231, 238, 246, 251
Barker, Lex 5, 131
Barnes, Walter *214*, 215
Barrato, Luisa *27*
Baseheart, Richard 4
The Belle Starr Story 33, 39, 42, *45*, 160, *172*

Berger, William 67, 221
Bergonzelli, Sergio 86
Betrayal constellation/plot 2, 34, 144, 208, 213, 216–17, 226–30, 240–41, 245, 248, 259
Il bianco, il giallo, il nero 258
Big boss stories/villains 41–43, 60, 105–6, 108, 113, 140, 148, 161, 201, 221, 223–24, 233, 238–39, 242, 257
Black Killer 62, 159, 163
Blindman 12
Bordwell, David 16
The Bounty Killer 9, 67, 132, 188
Bounty killer/bounty hunter 19, 27, 29, 33, 38, 41, 61, 63, 82, 83, 97, 100, 101, 107, 108, 110, 122–24, 128, 129, 131–34, 136–39, 142, 145, 148–51, 153, 158, 165, 168, 181, 188, 200, 205, 206, 217, 219, 221, 226, 233, 239, 240, 241, 243, 245, 248, 250
Brice, Pierre 5, 131
Buddy Goes West 35, 232, 235, 237, 257
Buon funerale amigos ... paga Sartana 219, 223
Byrnes, Edd *27*, *64*

California 28, 30, 34, 35, 39, 42, 43, 58
Calvo, Pepe 4
Camasco, Claudio 100, 101
Campa Carogna ... la taglia cresce 153, 154, *157*, 162
Camus, Mario 13
O cangaceiro 13
I cannoni di San Sebastian 193
Carambola 233, 237
Carey, Harry, Jr. 5
Carmineo, Giuliano (alias Anthony Ascott) 218, 219, 225, 226, 227, 237, 248, 253
Carreras, Michael 4
Casas, Antonio 44–46

Castelnuovo, Nino *106*
Casual ethnicity 41, 70, 138, 159
Cawelti, John G 9, 150, 162, 183
C'è Sartana ... vendi la pistola e comprati la bara! 219, 221, 222, 228
Che botte, ragazzi! 153, 258
Che c'entriamo noi con la rivoluzione? 138, 192
Chiari, Walter 7
Ci risiamo, vero Provvidenza? 248–50, 255, 258
Ciak Mull, l'uomo della vendetta 102, 104–5
I cinque della vendetta 209, 210
5000 dollari sull'asso 71, 72, 75, 77, 78, 107, 131
El Cisco 145–47, 162
Cjamango 140–42, 144, 162, 164
Classical plot (of Will Wright) 15–16, 32, 41, 66, 68, 71, 74–76, 82, 84–86, 89, 92, 148, 159, 194, 246, 266
Codes 1, 15, 16, 35, 57, 104, 160, 241, 259; age 85, 258; of cunning 57, 119, 243; dress 164, 208, 247; ethnic 40, 51, 68, 72, 76, 82, 113, 173, 230; gender 102, 160; metacode 38, 57, 105, 107, 259; physical 201, 246; political 174, 179; rhetorical 36, 105; socio-cultural 38, 42–43, 105, 113; sophisticated/unsophisticated 223, 241; spatial 51, 121; of violence 243
Colizzi, Giuseppe 199, 201, 246
La collera del vento 13, 197
La collina degli stivali 201, 246
La colt era il suo Dio 139
Constellation, definition 16
Corbucci, Sergio 1, 9, 62, 74, 75, 82, 87, 92, 93, 134, 137, 175, 178, 179, 184, 192, 251
Cord, Alex *137*
Corri, uomo, corri 9, 60, 175, 176, 178, 179, 181, 189
I corvi ti scaveranno la fossa 156, 158, 183
Così Sia 232, 235, 240, *244*, 245
Cressoy, Pierre 73, *116*
I crudeli 28, 31, 32, 36, 38, 39, 40, 49, 107, 213
Cut-Throats Nine 12

Da uomo a uomo 112, 165, 166, 167, 168, 169, 170
...dai nemici mi guardo io! 32, 34, 39, 146–47, 161–62. 191
D'Amato, Joe 6
Damiani, Damiano 9, 78, 173, 179, 186
Damon, Mark 118
Dans la poussière de Soleil 102
DeAngelis, Guido and Maurizio 245

El Desperado 60, 62, 101, 108, 133, 135, 155, 257
Di Leo, Fernando 43
Di Tresette c'è ne uno ... tutti gli altri son nessuno 225
Diecimila dollari per un massacro 100, 132, 133, 134, 135
Dio li crea ... io li ammazzo! 258
Dio perdona ... io no! 199, 201
The Dirty Dozen 258
Django 1, 9, 52, 59, 62, 67, 69, 80, 93–98, 100, 105, 110, 112, 118, 124, 130, 134, 135, 161, 162, 164–65, 191–92, 194, 198, 206, 218, 221, 226, 229, 231, 251, 259
Django il bastardo 63, 98, 112, 258
Django kill! 9, 11, 12, 63, 96, 118, 133, 134, 135, 147
Django non perdona 100
Django sfida Sartana 226
Django spara per primo 143, 144, 163, 164
Django 2 – Il grande ritorno 7
Un dollaro bucato 27, 28, 33, 34, 35, 36, 39, 40, 43, 61, 62, *73*, 114, 116, 119, 124
Un dollaro tra i denti 30, 31, 38, 39, 40
Dor, Karin 4
Double (position) 1–2, 48, 50, 96, 110, 122, 125, 131, 133, 135, 144, 156, 158, 178, 182, 184, 190, 212
Drums Along the Mohawk 12
Duck You Sucker 9, 125, 186, 190, 191, 192
Le due facce del dollaro 65
Duels 58, 61, 205; ceremonial 127, 129; make-believe 60, 248; special 18, 60, 62, 90, 106, 133, 148, 202–3, 218, 236; "stacked deck" 59–60, 104, 113, 168; substitute/ersatz/mock 42, 77, 87, 123–24, 126; supervised 59–61, 108, 122, 126, 129, 141, 181, 206
Dupe/dupes 30, 141–42, 147, 151, 153, 158, 160, 179, 215, 227

...e per tetto un cielo di stelle 158, 247
È tornato Sabata ... hai chiuso un'altra volta! 219, 221, 224, 230, 253
Easterners 41, 123–24, 182–83, 230, 241
Eastwood, Clint 4, 13, *18*, 90, 118, 123, *130*, 144, 204, 206
Ehi amico c'è Sabata ... hai chiuso! 61, 62, 65, 218, 221, 228
Un esercito di cinque uomini 65, 186, 210

Fabula, definition 16
Faccia a faccia 9, 28, 29, 30, 31, 38, 39, 41, 42, 43, 58, 124, 138, 181, 182, 184, 197, 257
False (position) 29, 49, 96–97, 102, 104, 107–8, 134, 153, 155, 160, 172

Index

Fernandel 7
Fidani, Demofilo 226
Il figlio di Django 113, 124
A Fistful of Dollars 1, 4, 5, 6, 7, 9, 16–20, 28–32, 34–36, 38–40, 42–43, 46–49, 51–52, 54–55, 58, 60, 62, 66, 68, 69, 71–72, 74–77, 79–83, 85, 87–90, 92, 95–96, 114–15, 119–25, 127, 135, 140, 142, 161, 164–65, 173, 180, 201, 206, 213, 218, 231, 233, 259
Un fiume di dollari **78**, 140, 142, **145**, 162, 183
Flashbacks (use of) 32, 107, 111, 112, 122, 136
For a Few Dollars More 1, 9, 19, 28, 31, 32, 36, 38, 39, 40, 41, 42, 43, 50, 58, 59, 62, 63, 71, 77, 95, 110, 112, 113, 122, 123, 124, 125, 127, 128, 129, **130**, 131, 133, 135, 140, 141, 158, 161, 164, 165, 166, 169, 173, 185, 200, 204, 206, 207, 218, 230, 231, 257, 259
Ford, John 11, 12, 124
Franchi, Franco 13
Frayling, Christopher 1, 97, 98, 100, 109, 131, 161, 169, 171, 188, 190, 226, 243
Fregonese, Hugo 13
Fun in Acapulco 12

Garko, John (Gianni) 100, 218, 221, 222
Garrone, Sergio 158
Gazzolo, Nando **145**
Gemma, Giuliano 44, 49, **53**, **73**, 114, **116**, 118, 119, 144, 165, 166, 194, 247
Un genio, due compari, un pollo 65
Gentleman Jo ... uccidi! 165
I giorni della violenza 36, 39, 42, 43, 49
I giorni dell'ira 132, 165, 166, 168, 170, 171
Il giorno del giudizio 112
Girolami, Enzo 206–9, 211
Giubbe rosse 6
Gli fumavano le colt ... lo chiamavano Camposanto 221, 222, 228, 253
The Good, the Bad and the Ugly 1, 9, 35, 59, 77, 124, 186, 192, 204, 205, 206, 207, 208, 211, 224, 230, 248
Il grande duello 60, 168
La grande notte di Ringo 141–43
Il grande silenzio 11, 137, 138, 193
Gringo 70, 76, 79, 102, 106, 108, 118, 121, 199, 251
Gunfighters of Casa Grande 66, 67, 68, 70, 72, 78, 79
Guns of the Magnificent Seven 5, 190

Hammond, Hally (Lorella De Luca) 44
Hardy, Oliver 236
Harrison, Richard 70
Heflin, Van 216

Hidden (position) 107–8
High Noon 84
Hill, Terence (Mario Girotti) 5, 7, 14, 98, **99**, 199, **234**, 237, 243, 246, **254**, 255
Hilton, George 212, **214**, 215, 216, 218, 225, 247
Huerta, Chris 224, **225**, 226, 237
Huston, John 216
Hybridization of plots 106–7, 149, 154–55, 168, 188, 196, 198, 228, 256

Indio Black, sai che ti dico ... sei un gran figlio di ... 62, 124, 218, 221, 222, 224, 227, 230
Infiltrator 28, 30, 33, 35, 42, 43, 47, 48, 49, 56, 57, 86, 87, 88, 89, 92, 94, 97, 108, 119, 124, 134, 140, 142, 149, 150, 179, 185, 194, 212, 256
Infiltrator constellation/plot 1, 19, 27–29, 34, 43, 52, 76, 80, 86, 90, 110, 155
Infiltrator stories 31–34, 35–38, 40–41, 43, 54, 89–90, 105, 121, 151, 174, 245
Ingrassa, Ciccio 13
Interleaving of plots 72, 75, 89, 106–7, 119, 144, 148–49, 197, 221–22, 256
Involuntary (position) 28, 43, 47–49, 107–8, 124, 134, 142, 149–51

Jesse e Lester, due fratelli in una posto chiamato Trinità 235, 238, 243, 245
Jim il primo 27–28, 30, 36, 39, 42–43, 257
Johnny Oro 82–90, 92, 118, 212

Kehr, Dave 66
Keoma 102, 104–5
Killer Kid 135
Kinski, Klaus 67, 216, 221
Kitses, Jim 9
Koch, Marianne 4

Là dove non batte il sole 258, **260**
Leone, Sergio 1, 4, 7, 9, 14, 16, 32, 35, 55, 59, 61, 67, 74, 75, 76, 77, 79, 80, 87, 88, 94, 122, 124, 125, 130, 161, 169, 186, 190, 191, 192, 204, 205, 206, 228, 248, 251, 259
Lévi-Strauss, Claude 1, 15, 16, 19, 259, 260
Lieh, Lo **260**
Lo chiamavano King 110, 135
Lo chiamavano Tresette ... giocava siempre col morto 225
Lo credevano uno stinco di Santo 146, 147
Lo irritarono e Sartana fece piazza pulita 226, 227
Lukschy, Wolfgang 4
Lulli, Piero 221
Una lunga fila di croci 124, 158, 162, 165
I lunghi giorni dell'odio 135

Macchiavelli, Nicoletta 145, *163*
El Macho 30, 31, 33, 39, 40, 41, 42, 43
Maciste 98
The Magnificent Seven 189, 209, 258
Il magnifico texano 13, 258
Le maledette pistole di Dallas 77
"Malignant partner" relationship/variant 146–50, 159, 166, 169, 181, 191, 199, 200
The Man from Laramie 66
Man of the East 183, 237, 239
The Man Who Shot Liberty Valance 11
Mann, Anthony 66
Mannaja 30, 39, 49, 63, 134, 135
Marisol woman (thematic role) 28, 47, 82, 124, 138, 161–62, 179, 196, 198, 240
Martin, Eugenio 9
Martin, George *53*
Martin, José Manuel *10*, 76
Martinelli, Elsa *45*, *172*
El más fabuloso golpe del far west 65
Massacro al Grande Canyon 74, 75, 76, 77, 107, 251
Mateos, Julian *37*
May, Karl 5, 6, 7, 131
Il mercenario 9, 60, 175, 176, *177*, 178, 179, 188, *195*
Metaphoric 30, 86, 107, 207
Metonymic 18, 30, 40, 57, 89, 105, 196
Mi chiamavano Requiescat ... ma avevo sbagliato 111, 114
Milian, Tomas 67, 182, *187*, 248
Mille dollari sul nero 33, 103
Minnesota Clay *10*, 63, 87–89, 92, 196
Un minuto per pregare, un istante per morire 136, *137*, 136, *163*
Il mio nome è Shanghai Joe 136, 258
Mitry, Jean 6
Il momento di uccidere 215
La morte non conta i dollari 36, 39, 118, 151, 153, 257
I morti non si contano 108, 151, 153, 154
Musante, Tony *177*
My Darling Clementine 11, 124, 183
My Name Is Nobody 9, 169, 170

Navajo Joe 74, 111, 165
Navarro, Augustin 69
Navarro, Nieves (alias Susan Scott) 44, 46
Nero, Franco 7, 97, 98, 100, *106*, 118, 165, *177*, *187*, 191
Nicol, Alex 4, 66–67
Nusciak, Loredana 80, 97
Una nuvola di polvere ... un grido di morte ... arriva Sartana 219–21

Odio per odio 196
Oggi a me ... domani a te 63, 113, 210

Ognuno per sé 216, 227
Oklahoma John 68
Once Upon a Time in the West 9, 112, 161

Pajarito 44, 47
Palance, Jack *195*
Pampa salvaje 13
Parolini, Gianfranco (alias Frank Kramer) 217, 218, 219, 224, 226, 227
Passa Sartana ... è la ombra della tua morte 226
Per centomila dollari t'ammazzo 101, 107, 131, 133, 135
Per il gusto di uccidere 138, 139
Per mille dollari al giorno 39, 111, 112, 113, 257
Per pochi dollari ancora 114, 115, 117, 119, 121
Pesce, Franco 223
"Phony sheriff" variant 149–50
Una pistola per Ringo 9, 16, 17, 18, 19, 20, 29, 30, 31, 33, 34, 35, 36, 38, 39, 42, 43, 44, 46, 48, 49, 50, 51, 52, 54, 55, 56, 59, 63, 67, 68, 69, 71, 74, 76, 79, 80, 82, 83, 84, 86, 87, 88, 90, 92, 95, 118, 120, 163
Le pistole non discutono 75–76, 78–79
Il pistolero dell'Ave Maria 105
La più grande rapina del west 65, 212–13, *214*, 215–16, 247
Pochi dollari per Django *91*, 149, 150, 165
Un poker di pistole 159, 164
Posate le pistole ... reverendo 235
Post-Trinity stories 35, 37, 231–33, 236–40, 243, 247–48
Powers, Hunt *214*
Prega per il morto e ammazza il vivo 27, 35, 39, 111
Preparati la bara! 62, 98, *99*, 111, 118, 164, 198, 243
Il prezzo del potere 194
Prima ti perdono ... poi t'ammazzo 226
"Prodigal son" constellation/plot 64, 101–3, 108–9, 120–21, 143, 162, 168, 172, 193, 215
"Prodigal son" stories 104–7, 113, 119, 121, 143, 148, 198
"Prodigal son" hero 104–5, 108–9, 120, 131, 165, 172, 212, 228
Professional plot (of Will Wright) 32, 209–10, 259
Professionals 41, 43, 79, 132, 136, 149, 189, 197, 205–6, 217, 236, 241, 248
Professionals/bandits stories 42–43, 148, 151
Professionisti per un massacro 193, 213, 215, 227
Propp, Vladimir 1, 15
El proscrito del Rio Colorado 100

I quattro dell'Ave Maria 64, 111, 114, 200, 201, 202, 203, 246, **254**
I quattro inesorabile 136
Quei disperati che puzzano di sudore e di morte 110, 112
Quel maledetto giorno d'inverno ... Django e Sartana all'ultimo sangue 226
Quella sporca storia nel west 58
Questi, Giulio 9
Quién sabe? 9, 78, 173–74, 178–81, 183, 185–86, 188, 198
Quinn, Anthony **152**
Quintanó, Gene 13
Quinto: non ammazzare 28, 32, 39

Una ragione per vivere ... una per morire 28, 30, 31, 32, 34, 35, 36, 39, 43, 258
Reed, Dean 221
Reinl, Harald 4
Requiescant 35, 193
La resa dei conti 9, 60, 124, 181, 188–89, 191, 196
Reverendo Colt 124
Rey, Fernando 4
Ringo del Nebraska 89, 92
Il ritorno di Ringo 9, 36, 42, 43, 44, 47, 48, 49, 51, 52, **53**, 54, 55, 58, 63, 102, 103, 105, 106, 118, 121, 251, 257
El Rojo 155, 164
Roland, Gilbert **64**, 216

Sanbrell, Aldo 68
Sancho, Fernando 9, **10**, 44, 46, 49, 67, 71, 72, 79, 240
Sangster, Jimmy 4
Sansone e il tesoro degli Incas 256
Sartana 8, 60, 63, 217, 220–21, 223, 228
Sartana nella valle degli avvoltoi 28, 30, 31, 33, 36, 38, 39, 40, 226
Sartana non perdona 226
The Savage Guns 4, 5, 7, 13, 66, 67, 70, 72, 76, 77, 78, 79
Scalps! 60, 108, 109
La Sceriffa 7
Der Schatz im Silbersee 7
Schöne, Reiner 221
Se t'incontro t'ammazzo 27, 30, 31, 38, 39, 110
Se vuoi vivere ... spara! 148, 161, 162, 164
Sella d'argento 111
I senza Dio 132, 142, 143, 162, 163, 165
Sette winchester per un massacro 27, 28, 31, 32, 38, 39, 41, 57, 151, 153
Shane 66, 79, 84, 89, 118, 121, 172, 216, 221, 246
Si può fare ... amigo! 237, 239
Siegel, Don 13

Silva, Henry **78, 145**
Singin' in the Rain 12
"Sleeping partner" hero/variant 140, 142–44, 147, 149–51, 153, 156, 158–60, 174, 180, 194, 200
Slotkin, Richard 188–90
Solinas, Franco 173, 188
Sollima, Sergio 9, 175, 181
Sono Sartana, il vostro becchino 124, 136, 218, 221
Southwood, Charles **37**, 221
"Specialist betrayal" constellation/plot 2, 220–21, 223, 225–26, 230, 248
Spencer, Bud (Carlo Pedersoli) 5, 7, 14, 199, **202**, 236–37, 255
La spina dorsale del diavolo 210, 258
Spirito Santo e le cinque magnifiche canaglie 226
Stagecoach 124, 183
Starr, Ringo 12
Steele, Anthony 5
Steffen, Anthony 118
Storia di karatè, pugni e fagioli 232, 235, 237, 243, 245, 258
Uno straniero a Sacramento 14, 86, 88, 90, 92, 212
Sugar colt 258
Il suo nome gridava vendetta 148
Syuzhet, definition 16

Taylor, Don 4
Tedeum 232, 235, 239, 240, 245
Il tempo degli avvoltoi 170, 171
Tempo di massacro 27, 63, 80, 100, 101, 102, 103, 104, 105, 106, 121, 131, 165, 212, 247, 251
Tepepa 185, 186, 188, 190, 191
Tequila! 27, 29, 31, 35, 37, 39, 62, 136, 153, 163
Tessari, Duccio 4, 9, 17, 43–44, 46, 51, 80, 84, 87, 191–92, 247
Testa t'ammazzo ... croce sei morto ... mi chiamano Allelujah! 61, 225
Texas addio 61, 63, 100, 101, 102, 104, 105, 106, 118, 136, 165, 198
Thematic role 44, 47–48, 98, 104, 119, 138, 162, 166, 179, 186
Theme-story 43, 148, 221, 226
They Call Me Trinity 5, 231, 232, 233, 235, 236, 239, 240, 241, 242, 243, 245, 246, 247, 252
Tognazzi, Ugo 7
"Tragic mercenary" hero/constellation/plot 101, 107, 133–35, 137, 155–56, 171, 217, 227–28, 252
Transition theme (of Will Wright) 32, 84

Trans-story hero 98, 164, 226, 231
I tre che sconvolsero il west 207, 208, 209
Tre colpi di winchester per Ringo 106, 107
I tre del Colorado 68, 70, 79
Tre dollari di piombo 79
I tre implacabile 68–69, 71, 77–78
Tre pistole contro Cesare 256
I tre spietati 68, 69, 70, 71, 78, 79
The Treasure of the Sierra Madre 216
Un treno per Durango 215, 227
Trinità e Sartana figli di... 226, 235, 237, 240
Trinity hero/constellation/plot 183, 224–25, 231, 243, 247, 255
Trinity Is Still My Name 5, 7, 231, 232, 233, **234**, 236, 238, 239, 240, 241, 242, 243, 245, 246, 252
The Troublemakers/The Fight Before Christmas 7

Uccidete Johnny Ringo 98, 139
Uccidi o muori 90, 92
Uomo avvisato mezzo ammazzato ... parola di Spirito Santo 222–25, 228, 237, 253
L'uomo che viene de Canyon City 71–72, 76–79, 131, 199
L'uomo dalla pistola d'oro 149–50

Vado, l'ammazzo e torno **64**, 132, 206, 207, 209, 211, 212, 217, 253
Vamos a matar, companeros! 9, 62, 175, 176, 178, 179, **187**, 189, 190, 192, 197, 241
Van Cleef, Lee **130**, 165, 168, 294, 218, 258

Vendetta 60, 61, 102, 104, 105, 114, 115, 117, 119, 120, 121, 168, 199
La vendetta è il mio perdono 112–13
La vendetta è un piatto che si serve freddo 28–29, 31, 33, 35, 38–39, 43
Il vendicatore di Kansas City 69, 77
Il venditore di morte 258
Vengeance ceremonial 112–13, 127, 129–30, 144, 155
Vengeance variation (of Will Wright) 69, 74, 76, 81, 86, 113
Vera Cruz 70, 189, 192
Vianello, Raimondo 7
Vindication hero/constellation/plot 114, 121, 144, 147, 169, 181, 259
La vita a volte, è molto dura, vero Provvidenza? 248, 250
Viva la muerte ... tua! 191, 258
Viva Villa 188
Vivi, o preferibilimente morti 61, 247
Volontè, Gian Maria 4, 67, 79, 122, **130**, 173, 182, 204

W Django! 60, 145–47, 164
Wallace, Eli 192, 204
Wanted 56, 64, 114–15, 119, 120, 136
Il west ti va stretto amico ... è arrivato Allelujah! 225, 230, 253
Winnetou II 4, 5, 7
Woods, Robert **172**
Wright, Will 1, 11, 15, 16, 32, 40–41, 51, 66, 69, 71, 74, 76, 80, 82, 84–86, 89, 90, 113, 133, 150, 162, 194, 209

www.ingramcontent.com/pod-product-compliance
Ingram Content Group UK Ltd.
Pitfield, Milton Keynes, MK11 3LW, UK
UKHW041926140426
5217IPUK00014B/334